Justice before the Law

Michael Huemer

Justice before the Law

palgrave
macmillan

Michael Huemer
Philosophy Department
Univ of Colorado at Boulder
Boulder, CO, USA

ISBN 978-3-030-67542-4   ISBN 978-3-030-67543-1 (eBook)
https://doi.org/10.1007/978-3-030-67543-1

© The Editor(s) (if applicable) and The Author(s), under exclusive licence to Springer Nature Switzerland AG 2021
This work is subject to copyright. All rights are solely and exclusively licensed by the Publisher, whether the whole or part of the material is concerned, specifically the rights of translation, reprinting, reuse of illustrations, recitation, broadcasting, reproduction on microfilms or in any other physical way, and transmission or information storage and retrieval, electronic adaptation, computer software, or by similar or dissimilar methodology now known or hereafter developed.
The use of general descriptive names, registered names, trademarks, service marks, etc. in this publication does not imply, even in the absence of a specific statement, that such names are exempt from the relevant protective laws and regulations and therefore free for general use.
The publisher, the authors and the editors are safe to assume that the advice and information in this book are believed to be true and accurate at the date of publication. Neither the publisher nor the authors or the editors give a warranty, expressed or implied, with respect to the material contained herein or for any errors or omissions that may have been made. The publisher remains neutral with regard to jurisdictional claims in published maps and institutional affiliations.

Cover illustration: © hundreddays, United States Supreme Court, Washington D.C., Image ID: 157188161

This Palgrave Macmillan imprint is published by the registered company Springer Nature Switzerland AG.
The registered company address is: Gewerbestrasse 11, 6330 Cham, Switzerland

Preface

I wrote this book for two reasons. The first is that the U.S. legal system, which has a powerful influence on the rest of society, appears to me to be among the most dysfunctional aspects of American society. The nation traditionally known as "the land of the free" has become the world leader in incarceration. Many are sent to prison for nonviolent offenses, including many victimless crimes. Convicts often serve draconian sentences in overcrowded prisons rife with abuse. Almost all prisoners were convicted and sentenced without a trial, because prosecutors threaten defendants with drastically higher sentences in the event that the defendant requests a trial. Both the criminal and the civil courts are widely feared by Americans, who know that being involved in legal difficulties can threaten to bankrupt one, regardless of who is in the right. My first goal in these pages has thus been to describe the largest problems with the American legal system, along with some proposed remedies.

My second reason for writing this book is that the field of jurisprudence has long seemed to me to be burdened with philosophical assumptions, of central import to the field, that are indefensible. Such assumptions are more common among legal professionals than among scholars. For instance, one may hear judges and prosecutors declare that the proper function of juries is solely to evaluate the factual evidence in a trial, never to exercise moral judgment. Similarly, many believe that the proper role of judges is only to faithfully interpret and apply the law, not to exercise independent moral judgment. And nearly all legal professionals will tell you that a lawyer is ethically bound to do his best to serve his clients' interests, regardless of the interests of justice; hence, it is thought appropriate for a defense attorney to attempt to set dangerous criminals free, or for a litigator to attempt to extract exorbitant compensation in a civil case. These assumptions are often held with extreme confidence, as if they were proven facts rather than debatable philosophical stances. When arguments are offered, they tend to be among the least plausible arguments to be found in any branch of philosophy or political discourse. Thus, my second goal in this book is to address the largest errors in conventional jurisprudence. These errors, by my read, have one main thing in common: they direct agents in the justice system to disregard considerations of justice and morality.

The practical problems in the American justice system are related to the intellectual problems in American jurisprudence. In accordance with conventional legal philosophy, most participants in the justice system do not directly pursue justice in individual cases. They seek to carry out their social role as they understand it, regardless of whether the result be good or evil, just or unjust. It is unsurprising that injustice often results. In this book, I argue for prioritizing justice. It is not only, in my view, that the system should be reformed to reduce the most egregious injustices; individual agents within the system should explicitly aim at achieving justice and should carry out their assigned roles under that constraint.

I wrote most of this book while on sabbatical from the University of Colorado and serving as a Visiting Research Professor at the Murphy Institute at Tulane University, in 2018–2019. I wish to thank the Institute as well as my home institution for their support. In addition, I want to thank Chris Surprenant, Brian Talbot, Stuart Rachels, Matt Skene, and two anonymous referees for their valuable comments on the manuscript, which helped to correct numerous mistakes and shortcomings. Of course, none of these other scholars are responsible for any errors that remain. All mistakes and shortcomings of the book are most likely the fault of the government. Undoubtedly, a much better book could be written by a philosopher at a private school.

Boulder, CO, USA   Michael Huemer

Contents

Part I Foundations for a Defense of Justice 1
1 Introduction 3
2 Law and Morality 13

Part II Legal Injustices 43
3 Unjust Laws 45
4 The Price of Justice 75
5 Extorted Pleas 111
6 Unjust Punishments 143
7 Abuse of Power 169

Part III In Defense of Justice 227
8 The Primacy of Justice 229
9 The Authority of Law 255
10 Role Playing 271
11 The Rule of Law 313
12 Conclusion 345

Index 369

List of Figures

Fig. 2.1 Taxonomy of appearances 36
Fig. 4.1 Length of the Code of Federal Regulations 86
Fig. 4.2 Prevalence of lawyers and lawsuits 102

Part I
Foundations for a Defense of Justice

1

Introduction

1.1 The Problem of Legal Injustice

If there is any institution in our society that should embody the pursuit of justice, it is the legal system. The division of the system concerned with criminal law is commonly referred to as "the justice system". Many courthouse grounds are decorated with statues of Lady Justice. The motto engraved in stone on the West side of the U.S. Supreme Court building reads, in capital letters, "EQUAL JUSTICE UNDER LAW", while the East side bears the inscription, "JUSTICE THE GUARDIAN OF LIBERTY". So one might assume that the system focuses mainly, if not entirely, on justice, and that the details of legal procedures, doctrines, and decisions will be explicable in terms of that concern for justice. And that, indeed, is often true.

But not always. Frequently, there are clear, serious injustices built into legal rules and practices. Some laws unjustly penalize behavior that is morally blameless. Some legal norms encourage or expressly direct actors within the system to place other concerns ahead of justice. Some practices violate individuals' rights or create unreasonable risks of unjust outcomes. In the following chapters, I will have much to say about these problems. But for now, it will help to describe one simple example. This is an actual case from early America, when New York was a British colony.

The Zenger Trial: In 1735, John Peter Zenger, then publisher of the *New York Weekly Journal*, was put on trial for seditious libel. Zenger had published a series of articles in his newspaper attacking the governor of New York, and the governor had directed the prosecutor to prosecute Zenger for printing these articles. During the trial, Zenger's attorney freely admitted that Zenger had published the material in question. His defense was that the material was all *true*, and he offered to present evidence that this was so. The prosecutor, however, argued that the accuracy of Zenger's articles was irrelevant to the charges; indeed, it was *worse* to publish *accurate* criticisms of public officials than false ones, because accurate criticisms were more likely to undermine public confidence in the government. The judge agreed with the prosecutor and therefore prohibited the defense from offering any evidence of the truth of the published material. The judge instructed the jury that British law did not recognize truthfulness as a defense against a charge of libel, and he all but ordered the jury to find the defendant guilty. The jury, however, defied the judge and the law and returned a verdict of *not guilty*.[1]

This was among history's most famous instances of *jury nullification*, the practice wherein a jury votes to acquit a defendant on the grounds that it would be unjust or otherwise wrong to punish the defendant, regardless of whether the defendant violated the law. This case played a role in establishing the American tradition of freedom of the press.

Though the case had, to my mind, a happy ending, the case nevertheless illustrates two kinds of problem that appear in the legal system. The

[1] Zenger (1736), Linder (2001).

first is an unjust law. It is obviously unjust, as well as socially harmful, to prohibit citizens from truthfully criticizing government officials. The second type of problem is the failure of agents in the legal system to prioritize justice. In the Zenger trial, the judge placed the value of deference to authority, or deference to existing legal rules, ahead of the value of doing justice to the defendant in the particular case before the court. Accordingly, he considered the jury duty-bound to convict. It was the jury of ordinary citizens not steeped in legal tradition who decided to place the dictates of justice ahead of the dictates of government officials, including the judge and the original lawmakers.

Many cases have less happy endings. When the law clashes with justice, the law usually wins. That is because individuals acting within the system—judges, juries, lawyers, and so on—wrongly choose to place fidelity to law, convention, or authority ahead of fidelity to justice. I have two central theses in this book: (i) The current legal system contains frequent, serious injustices in its rules and practices. (ii) When the rules and practices of the legal system conflict with justice, we should place justice first.

1.2 Injustice in the Legal System

There are a great variety of legal systems across the world and across history, and it would not be possible to survey legal systems generally.[2] Hereinafter, I shall focus on the practices and doctrines of the current U.S. legal system, which is very similar to that of the U.K. and other British-influenced nations. In the following chapters, I shall review some of the most widespread, clear, and serious failures in this system.

The injustices are of several kinds. First and most obvious are the unjust laws. There will naturally be controversy surrounding any attempt to identify unjust laws. However, a particularly strong case can be made, for example, that the laws prohibiting recreational drug use are unjust. These laws presently account for about 450,000 prisoners in the U.S., so if these laws are unjust, they cause an enormous amount of unjust

---

[2] But see Friedman et al. (2019) for an interesting survey of thirteen very different legal systems.

punishment.[3] A strong case can also be made that current immigration law is unjustly restrictive. The number of people seriously harmed by these laws is unknown, but it includes millions of individuals who could effect enormous, permanent improvements in their lives, if they were permitted to migrate out of poor, oppressive states. There are many other unjust laws, but these are two of the most salient and consequential ones. My contention will be not merely that these are suboptimal policies, but that they constitute serious violations of the rights of many individuals. It is for this reason that they become an issue of justice.

The second category of injustice is that of unjust conditions for using the legal system. In particular, to pursue justice within the legal system, in a large range of cases, one is forced to expend very large amounts of time and money. Legal cases can cost individuals thousands to hundreds of thousands of dollars, which means that often, only the rich can afford justice, and even they must suffer unreasonable burdens to pursue it. As I shall argue, this constitutes an *injustice on the part of the state*, both because the state is largely to blame for exorbitant prices and because the costs must frequently be incurred to avoid other unjust treatment by the state.

Third, there are objectionable legal practices which create excessive risks of generating unjust legal outcomes. In the U.S. and other common-law countries, criminal defendants *in theory* have the legal right to have their cases tried before an impartial jury and their guilt proved beyond a reasonable doubt before they may be punished. In reality, despite the amount of attention paid to trials by theorists and popular media, very few cases ever see a trial. The overwhelming majority are resolved through plea bargains, which are usually described as cases in which prosecutors offer to reduce charges or punishments for a defendant in return for the defendant's guilty plea.[4] An alternate description would be that prosecutors coerce defendants into giving up their right to a trial by threatening to charge the defendant with more crimes, or more serious crimes, if the defendant insists on asserting that right.

Fourth, there are unjust punishments. Incarceration is particularly overused in the U.S., which has by far the highest incarceration rate in

---

[3] Wagner and Sawyer (2020).
[4] The Week (2017).

the world. Multi-year prison sentences are often assigned for nonviolent offenses. While serving these sentences, prisoners are vulnerable to abuse by guards and other inmates. Given that such abuse would clearly be unconscionable as an official punishment, sentences that have such abuse as a known likely consequence are extremely dubious from the standpoint of justice.

Fifth, there are unjust legal decisions, most notably false convictions. False convictions are probably much more common than judges or prosecutors are prepared to admit and are often caused by police and court practices that are obviously untrustworthy, including high-pressure interrogation techniques used against underage or mentally disabled suspects, threats issued against suspects to extract confessions, the offering of bribes to criminals for testimony against suspects, and leading methods of questioning witnesses.

Finally, there is abuse of power and other misconduct by government officials. This includes especially cases of police brutality, malicious prosecutions by the state, and illegal actions ordered by political leaders. Serious official misconduct typically receives at most minor penalties in comparison with the punishments handed down for similar wrongs committed by private parties. Often, it receives no punishment at all.

The reader may wonder why some of these injustices, especially those of the last category, call for philosophical treatment. In any large institution, some unjust actions can naturally be anticipated as a result of the general flaws in human nature and the impracticality of excluding all individuals with impure motives from the institution. If the injustices occurring in our legal system were merely the inevitable and circumscribed result of the moral flaws of a few individuals, then I should indeed have little to say about them. What interests me here is the justice of *the system*. What makes abuse of power a systemic injustice, rather than merely an individual-level moral vice, is the way in which widespread attitudes, doctrines, and practices contribute to abuse or culpably fail to address it. I have in mind, for example, the extreme difficulty of successfully suing or prosecuting government officials, the extreme differences in punishments received by government officials and private individuals, and the excessive deference shown by courts to government officials.

1.3 The Primacy of Authority and the Primacy of Justice

How should one react to injustice in the legal system? There are at least two broad views we might take. The first can be labeled the *Primacy of Authority*. On this view, the most important value in the legal system is respect for authority, that is, for the conventionally recognized authorities, including the accepted laws and procedures. In case of a conflict between our intuitive sense of justice and the existing laws, legal procedures, or decisions of authority figures, we should generally obey the existing laws, procedures, or authority figures. For a stronger doctrine of the Primacy of Authority, one might add that we should maintain traditions and institutions that give wide discretion to authority figures so that they may do what they see to be best. In cases of uncertainty, we should give the benefit of the doubt to the state and assume that its actions are well-motivated and well-considered unless proven otherwise.

The Primacy of Authority dictates that one must follow the law or the orders of authority figures (provided that these are legally proper), even if they appear unjust or immoral. And not only should one obey the law oneself; one should help to enforce the law against others if one is in a position to do so. Thus, the police should arrest those who violate the law, juries should convict them, and judges should sentence them in accordance with any applicable sentencing guidelines. None of these people, it is thought, have any right to allow their own sense of justice or morality to interfere with their performance of these duties.

I stress that this is not an unusual view in the legal world—it is not just, for example, the view of far-right judges, or far-left judges. The Primacy of Authority (though not under that name) is the *orthodoxy* in legal circles; it is often taken for granted by mainstream judges and legal scholars, whether liberal or conservative, and, when stated at all, the view is advanced as a self-evident axiom, like 1+1=2. Thus, for example, many legal scholars and most judges would say that the jury in the Zenger trial (§1.1) obviously decided wrongly. When the judge in that case gave his instructions to the jury, he did not offer them an *argument* that they should defer to the existing legal rules, however unjust they might seem; he simply *presupposed* this.

We should find this striking. The legal system is ostensibly designed to achieve justice. Is it really obvious that we should set aside what appear to be the demands of justice in individual cases, in deference to the demands of authority?

I think this not only is not obvious; it is obviously false. My second central thesis in this book is that of the *Primacy of Justice:* the primary, guiding concern of the legal system, and of all who are involved in it, should be *justice to the individual.* Not respect for authority, or the rule of law, or the state's broader policy objectives, but what justice demands for the individuals in the case at hand. Citizens have no obligation to obey unjust laws or other commands, and those involved with the system should not assist in the implementation or enforcement of such laws. When individuals violate unjust laws, it is morally wrong for the police to arrest them, for prosecutors to charge them, for juries to convict them, or for judges to sentence them. On the other hand, when individuals violate *just* laws, it is morally wrong for anyone, including defense attorneys, to attempt to prevent their being justly punished. Nor should any special deference be given to the state or its officials; they should receive no special leeway and should be punished in the same way as anyone else when they wrong others.

What is justice, and how should we decide what it demands? Roughly, justice, in the present context, requires respecting the rights of individuals and giving each what they deserve. In criminal cases, for example, individuals should be punished if and only if they have committed wrongs serious enough to *deserve* punishment, and then they should be punished proportionately to the seriousness of those wrongs and their culpability for them. In civil cases, defendants should pay damages proportionate to the harm they have wrongly caused and their culpability for it. There are many philosophical questions about the specification and application of these broad norms. Our concern, however, is not to provide a comprehensive theory of justice. It is enough that some rules and procedures can be argued to be unjust based upon weak and widely-shared ethical judgments, as I hope will emerge in later chapters. This suffices to raise the question of how one should react to legal injustices.

Those who embrace orthodox legal doctrine might object to being described as opponents of justice. They might argue that what I consider as the improper privileging of respect for authority over justice is really driven by a more subtle, more far-sighted concern for justice. Perhaps it is necessary to uphold respect for authority in order to prevent a kind of social chaos which would ultimately create more injustice overall. Or perhaps authority figures actually have the power to alter the moral status of actions, to convert a normally unjust action into a just one, simply by commanding it. Thus, it is perhaps a mistake to portray authority and justice as two separate, competing values.

I don't mean to prejudge that sort of defense here. When I describe conventional legal doctrine as privileging *deference to authority* over *justice*, I am not assuming that there could not ultimately be some justice-based argument for deferring to authority figures. What I mean is that conventional legal doctrine privileges deference to authority figures over *non-authority-based* considerations of justice in the individual case. By "non-authority-based considerations of justice", I mean justice considerations other than those pertaining to deference to authority—for instance, the principle that *individuals should be punished proportionately to the wrongs they have committed* is a non-authority-based justice norm.

Note also that I speak of justice in the individual case: if, for example, a defendant has been brought to trial for a crime, justice in the individual case would be for *that individual*, on *that occasion*, to have his rights respected and to receive the treatment he deserves. There may be justice-related effects on other people and other cases (perhaps the treatment of this individual will affect whether others receive their due or have their rights respected), but that is another matter. The *primary* concern of the courts, in each case, should be to do justice to the parties in that case—or so I shall maintain.

To clarify, I am no absolutist. I do not say "Let justice be done though the heavens fall". If punishing one innocent person would stop the deaths of a million others, one must punish the innocent person. (What if it was only a thousand others? Or a hundred? Or ten? I have no formula for answering that sort of question. *Some* injustices may be accepted to prevent *some* much greater harms, but I don't know exactly which ones, or how much greater the harms must be.) My claim is that this is not our situation—nothing like that is realistically at stake in any of the cases I am concerned with. In the cases in which orthodox legal doctrine allows seemingly unjust harming of individuals, doing so does not save a million others, or a thousand, or even—in most cases—anyone at all from unjust harm. It is normally a gratuitous harming, accomplishing nothing other than to satisfy a passing preference of the powerful.

Why should justice take precedence over respect for authority? My core reasoning is simple: justice is the purpose of the legal system. We have laws and authority figures so that they may provide justice—so that they may protect our rights, hold wrongdoers to account, and vindicate the innocent. It is irrational to value a means to an end over the end itself. Therefore, it is prima facie irrational to value deference to law or authority figures over justice.

I say here "prima facie". Perhaps there could be other moral considerations that override the importance of doing justice in the individual case. We will consider proposals of that kind in due course. But the natural presumption must surely be that one ought to strive to bring about justice in the individual case. One should do this *unless* there is some powerful reason not to. I take it, therefore, that my task in what follows is not to argue positively in favor of seeking to do justice in the individual case, but merely to rebut reasons that could be given against doing so. I shall contend that, in realistic cases in which the demands of justice seem to conflict with the dictates of authority figures, there simply are no good arguments for setting aside one's sense of justice.

1.4 A Brief Preview

In the next chapter, I lay the philosophical foundations for my conception of justice. I explain the notion of moral rights, why one should believe in such things, and why one should take at least some truths about rights and justice to exist independent of the law. This discussion will unavoidably be abstract and theoretical.

Readers who are mainly interested in the defects in the American legal system may wish to proceed directly to chapter 3. It is in chapters 3, 4, 5, 6, and 7 (part II of the book) that I describe those flaws at length. Then, in chapters 8, 9, 10, and 11, I explain and defend the Primacy of Justice. Chapter 12 summarizes the book, adds some speculations concerning why American jurisprudence has often gone wrong, and ends with remarks in appreciation for some of the things that the justice system has fortunately gotten right.

References

Friedman, David, Peter Leeson, and David Skarbek. 2019. *Legal Systems Very Different from Ours*. Independently published.

Linder, Douglas. 2001. The Trial of John Peter Zenger: An Account. http://law2.umkc.edu/faculty/projects/ftrials/zenger/zengeraccount.html. Accessed 5 Apr 2012.

The Week. 2017. Plea Bargaining: A Threat to Basic Human Rights? *The Week*, September 21. https://www.theweek.co.uk/88453/plea-bargaining-a-threat-to-basic-human-rights. Accessed 24 June 2020.

Wagner, Peter, and Wendy Sawyer. 2020, March 24. *Mass Incarceration: The Whole Pie 2020*. Prison Policy Initiative. https://www.prisonpolicy.org/reports/pie2020.html. Accessed 24 June 2020.

Zenger, John Peter. 1736. *A Brief Narrative of the Case and Trial of John Peter Zenger*. Available at http://law2.umkc.edu/faculty/projects/ftrials/zenger/zengerrecord.html. Accessed 5 Apr 2012.

2

Law and Morality

2.1 The Autonomy of Ethics

In this chapter, I discuss foundational philosophical questions about the nature of justice, our knowledge thereof, and the relationship between law and morality.

To begin with, since I aim to indict the legal system for insufficient commitment to justice, it is essential to my project that it be possible in general to identify moral facts, especially facts of justice, independent of legal rules. We must be able to know that a person is morally entitled to x, is obligated to do y, or has a right to z, independent of the existing rules of the legal system. I refer to this assumption as the Autonomy of Ethics. (Herein, I use "ethics" and "morality" interchangeably.) Of course this does not rule out that legal facts may *influence* the moral facts or vice versa in certain cases.

There are two philosophical views that may pose challenges to the Autonomy of Ethics:[1]

---

[1] I assume herein that there are moral facts and that it is possible to know them. For defense of these assumptions, see Huemer (2005, 2013, 2016).

(i) *Natural law theory* holds that morality partly determines what the law *is*, such that an unjust law is not a genuine law at all.
(ii) The view I shall call *legal relativism* holds that the law determines the moral facts, or some large class of moral facts, such as the facts about justice. Because laws vary from one society to another, justice varies from one society to another on this view.

If either of these views is correct, then my critique of the injustice of the legal system fails.

2.2 The Challenge of Natural Law

2.2.1 "Unjust Law Is Not Law"

Traditional natural law theory holds (1) that there are objective moral facts, and (2) that these moral facts determine or constrain what the law actually is. The second thesis is expressed by Saint Augustine's famous maxim, "unjust law is not law".[2] Saint Thomas Aquinas quotes Augustine approvingly, adding that laws that are contrary to human good "are acts of violence rather than laws".[3]

Taken literally, Augustine's maxim entails that there are no unjust laws, since such a thing would have to have the contradictory property of being a law that is not a law. Natural law theorists intend this idea, not to constrain our evaluation of what is *just*, but to constrain our assessment of what is *the law*. On finding some socially sanctioned rule that appears to be an unjust law, we are meant to deny that it is a genuine law.

---

[2] Augustine (1993, I.5 (originally written circa 387 A.D.)). The context is a philosophical dialogue in which one character suggests that to commit violence, even in self-defense, is to exhibit "inordinate desire". Augustine responds: "Then the law is unjust that permits a traveler to kill a highway robber in order to keep from being killed himself, or that permits anyone who can, man or woman, to kill a sexual assailant, before he or she is harmed. The law also commands a soldier to kill the enemy; and if he refuses, he is subject to penalties from his commander. Surely we will not dare to say that these laws are unjust, or rather, that they are not laws at all. For it seems to me that an unjust law is no law at all."
[3] Aquinas (1920, I-II, Q. 96, Art. 4 (originally written circa 1270 A.D.)).

But Augustine's thesis appears obviously false on its face. In pre-Civil War America, there were laws such as the Fugitive Slave Laws, which required escaped slaves to be returned to their masters. Since this is unjust, Augustine's maxim dictates that the "Fugitive Slave Laws" were not laws. In modern times, one could argue on similar grounds that the "drug laws" are not laws (see §3.2 below)—and hence, that recreational drug use is actually legal everywhere. This is not how the words "law" and "legal" are used in English.

2.2.2 Normative Reading

The most obvious defense of Augustine's remark is to deny that the statement was intended literally. Compare Martin Luther King's words, penned in explanation for his civil disobedience to protest racial segregation:

> [T]here are two types of laws: just and unjust. I would be the first to advocate obeying just laws. One has not only a legal but a moral responsibility to obey just laws. Conversely, one has a moral responsibility to disobey unjust laws. I would agree with St. Augustine that "an unjust law is no law at all".[4]

The last sentence seemingly contradicts the first: if an unjust law is literally no law at all, then there cannot be any unjust laws. Presumably, Dr. King did not intend such an obvious contradiction. What he meant was presumably something along the lines of: an unjust law is not binding, is not legitimate, does not provide reasons for obedience.

This interpretation of natural law theory is confirmed by at least one contemporary natural law theorist, who writes that "The meaning of 'an unjust law is not a law' is essentially identical to Hart's 'This is law but too iniquitous to be applied or obeyed.'"[5]

If this is what natural law theorists intend, then there is no objection to be found here to the theses of this book; indeed, despite the infelicitous manner in which the point is sometimes communicated, I would insist on this point: When a law is unjust, there is no duty to obey.

---

[4] King (1963).
[5] Finnis (2020, section 4).

2.2.3 Weak Descriptive Readings

There are weaker views on which moral facts affect what the law *is*, and not merely what it should be or how we should react to it, that are coherent and plausible.[6] It may be, for example, that in case of ambiguity in the law, the correct interpretation is at least partly determined by which interpretation makes the law more just, fair, or rational.

Views of this kind may be divided into two categories, depending on the extent to which they permit law to diverge from morality: views that allow us to recognize some laws with seriously unjust content, and views that do not allow this. On an extreme version of the thesis, morality's influence on law is so profound that, for example, the Fugitive Slave Laws are correctly interpreted as *not* requiring escaped slaves to be returned to their masters, despite that the text of the statutes explicitly call for escaped slaves to be returned. The issue here, again, concerns what the law *in fact is*, not what it should be, or what a judge *ought to say* that the law is. After the passage of the Fugitive Slave Law of 1850, was it in fact illegal to aid slaves in escaping their masters?

If a version of natural law theory answers "no" to this question, the theory is semantically absurd; given the standard use of the word "illegal" in English, and given the undisputed descriptive facts of the case, aiding escaped slaves after 1850 is a perfectly clear case of an illegal action.

If, on the other hand, a version of natural law theory answers "yes" to this question, then there is no conflict between the natural law theory and my theses in this book. None of my arguments require me to deny that moral facts *influence* the correct interpretation of laws, as long as we agree that they do not so overpower plain meaning (and author's intent, and every other interpretive criterion) that no statute can be correctly interpreted as imposing unjust demands. For example, the correct interpretation of the Fourth Amendment's prohibition on "unreasonable searches and seizures" plausibly depends upon normative facts in a way that guarantees the amendment, in its proper reading, a certain degree of justness. Surely, at least when the text of a law explicitly uses a normative term such as "reasonable", then normative truths may influence the

---

[6] See, e.g., Dworkin (1986).

correct interpretation of that law. And this need not be the only circumstance in which moral facts influence the legal facts. Nevertheless, no correct interpretive principle prevents, say, the Controlled Substances Act from being a legal prohibition on certain recreational drugs, however unjust such a prohibition may be.

2.2.4 Semantic Disputes

For the reasons explained, I doubt that many natural law theorists would disagree with my claim that there are unjust laws. But suppose a natural law theorist disagreed, perhaps because the theorist took Augustine's slogan literally and without exception.

Even so, there would be no *interesting* disagreement between the extreme natural law theorist and myself. There would be only a semantic disagreement: does the word "law", in English, have a normative meaning that rules out the possibility of an unjust law? I believe it does not. If I am mistaken about this, the result would be that some of my central claims in the following chapters are *misstated* rather than substantively mistaken. Rather than saying that there are many unjust laws, I should say that there are many unjust commands of the state that *purport* to be laws.

2.3 The Challenge of Legal Relativism

The only interesting remaining challenge, then, would be the challenge deriving from legal relativism, the view that legal facts determine the facts about justice, and perhaps the facts about right and wrong in general. On such a view, my central theses would be incoherent. There would be no legal injustices, nor could one make sense of the notion of prioritizing justice over fidelity to law.[7]

---

[7] This sort of view was held by Thomas Hobbes (1996, chs. XIV, XV; originally published 1651) and Jeremy Bentham (1987, p. 73; originally published 1795). As Bentham put it, "Right is with me the child of law; from different operations of the law result different sorts of rights. A natural right is a son that never had a father."

One problem for legal relativism is what the view implies for interactions with individuals outside the jurisdiction of the law. Consider the following hypothetical case:

Island Hermit: You meet a single hermit living on a remote island previously unknown to your society. The island and its single inhabitant are outside the jurisdiction of any government, and the hermit has not created any laws of his own. Would it be morally wrong for you to kill the hermit purely for enjoyment?

It seems undeniably wrong to kill the hermit. Yet this wrongness could not be explained by any law; therefore, there are at least some moral obligations that are independent of the law. Indeed, it seems that killing the hermit would be both *unjust* and a violation of the hermit's *rights*; hence, justice and rights are not solely created by law.

Suppose the legal relativist denies that killing the hermit is wrong at all, claiming that murder is wrong only when it violates a law. This might be a consistent view, but one that lacks any plausible motivation. The legal relativist, on the present view, would have to maintain that there is a general moral obligation *to obey the law*, yet deny that there is a general moral obligation *to abstain from killing people for fun*. But there is no plausible way in which we could be justified in holding that combination of views.

Suppose, to begin with, that we simply take the duty to obey the law as an unargued moral starting point. After all, we must start from *some* moral premises for which we give no arguments; we cannot have an infinite series of moral arguments. And perhaps the assumption of a duty to obey law is sufficiently intuitively plausible to be such a starting point; at least it seems that most laws should be obeyed on most occasions. But the assumption that killing people for fun is wrong is much *more* intuitively plausible than the assumption that one is generally obligated to obey laws. Hence, it would be very odd to admit "We ought to obey laws" as a starting premise yet refuse to admit "We ought not to kill people for fun."

Next, suppose we have some deeper argument for the wrongness of breaking laws that would not apply to killing hermits on remote islands. There are, indeed, arguments of this kind. However, all such arguments contain *some* normative premise as a starting point. For example, the social contract theory takes as a normative starting point that one ought to keep one's agreements, argues that we have an implicit agreement to obey the laws, and concludes that we ought to obey the laws.[8] But the premise that one ought to keep one's agreements is no more obvious than the premise that one ought not to murder; it would thus be arbitrary to accept as a starting premise "We must keep agreements" yet reject "We must not murder." Similar points apply to all arguments for an obligation to obey the law. According to a well-known principle sometimes called "Hume's Law", it is not possible to validly derive a conclusion stating what *ought* to be solely from premises describing what *is*.[9] All non-fallacious moral arguments will contain at least one moral premise. But there is no moral premise that is more plausible on its face than the premise that murder is wrong, including in the Island Hermit case above. So it would be unreasonable to reject that murder is wrong in the Island Hermit case, if one accepts any moral premises at all.

Perhaps there is an exception to this: one might claim that normative terms such as "ought" are simply *defined* in terms of legal requirements, that is, that to say something ought to be done just *means* that it is required by law. Theories that attempt to define "ought" in non-normative, non-evaluative terms, as this theory does, have been refuted in general by

---

[8] This is true at least of Locke's social contract theory. Hobbes' theory, however, rests on the alleged obligation to serve one's own self-interest. This view is subject to the same objection, *mutatis mutandis*, to the view discussed in the text.
[9] Hume (1992, p. 469 (originally published 1739)), Karmo (1988), Huemer (2005, section 4.3).

G.E. Moore and others.[10] I will not rehearse those arguments here. Here I will simply observe that *if* one thinks that "ought" can be defined in non-normative terms, it is *nevertheless* highly implausible to define it simply in terms of law. The examples I have given above show that ordinary English speakers do not use "ought to be done" to mean "is required by law", since we think one *ought not* to kill the hermit in the above example. If one is going to define moral terms using non-normative, non-evaluative terms, one ought at least to attempt to capture how moral terms are used.

Now suppose that the legal relativist grants that killing the hermit would be wrong, yet denies that it would be *unjust* or a *rights-violation*, because the notions of *justice* and *rights* (but not the more general notion of wrongness) are dependent on the law. Jeremy Bentham, for example, would say that killing the hermit would be wrong, not because it would violate the hermit's rights, but merely because it would decrease the sum total of pleasure in the world, assuming the hermit's life was overall enjoyable.

This view remains ill-motivated. Bentham claimed to have no understanding of what was meant by a natural right, nor of how natural rights are created; it was thus that he motivated his rejection of natural rights. But once we have accepted law-independent moral facts in principle—in particular, that there are facts about moral permissibility and impermissibility, independent of the actual laws of any society—there is no further difficulty with law-independent *rights* or law-independent principles of *justice*. These notions can be defined in terms of the general notion of moral permissibility, and the needed principles of rights and justice can be justified in the same manner that moral principles in general are justified. I will explain this in §2.4 below. Assuming that I can make good on this promise, there would be no reason for claiming that moral principles about rights and justice must depend on law while allowing that moral principles in general need not so depend.

---

[10] Moore (1960), Huemer (2005, section 4.2).

2.4 In Defense of Moral Rights

2.4.1 Intuitive Support for Rights

What are moral rights, and why should we believe in them? Moral rights (hereafter, "rights") are *agent-centered, enforceable moral constraints against harm or interference*.[11]

The central reason for believing in moral constraints derives from widely shared ethical intuitions concerning cases in which it seems morally wrong to harm or interfere with individuals, even though doing so in that situation would prevent a larger harm. The following are two famous examples from the ethics literature.

Organ Harvesting: A doctor in a hospital has five patients who need organ transplants, without which they will die. One needs a heart, another needs a lung, another needs a liver, and two need kidneys. He also has one healthy patient, in for a routine checkup, who happens to be compatible with the five. Should the doctor kill the healthy patient and distribute his organs to the other five?[12]

Framing: A crime has been committed that has caused great public outrage in a certain town. The sheriff knows that unless someone is punished for the crime, there will be riots, during which multiple innocent people will be unjustly injured and possibly killed. The sheriff cannot find the actual perpetrator; he can,

---

[11] On the notion of agent-centered constraints, see Nozick (1974, pp. 28–33), Scheffler (1994). The sort of rights I am concerned with herein are claim rights, rather than mere liberty rights. A claim right is a right that imposes a corresponding obligation on other parties, whereas a liberty right is a mere absence of obligation on the part of the right-holder to refrain from some action (see Hohfeld 1913). Note that this distinction should not be confused with the distinction between positive and negative rights; a claim right may impose on others either positive obligations (to take some type of action) or negative obligations (to refrain from some type of action).

[12] This example derives originally from James Rachels in informal conversations in the 1960s.

however, frame an innocent person, which will cause that person to be seriously and unjustly punished but will forestall the riots. Should the sheriff frame the innocent?[13]

In both of these cases, nearly everyone judges that the proposed action would be ethically wrong, despite that it would avert a greater harm than the harm directly inflicted on the action's victim.

The first example, Organ Harvesting, shows that it is morally worse to murder one person than to fail to save five lives. If the doctor refrains from harvesting the organs, then, although the five sick patients will die, none of them will be *murdered*; they will die of natural causes. We might therefore be tempted to conclude simply that murder is worse than death from natural causes—or more generally, that it is worse for an individual to be harmed unjustly than to suffer non-unjust harm. This interpretation, however, would not account for the second example, the Framing case, in which the harm to be averted by the unjust action would also be unjust: the rioters are expected to *unjustly* harm many innocent people (for example, by attacking them without provocation); nevertheless, the sheriff may not unjustly frame the innocent person to prevent this.

To account for the intuitive judgments in both cases, we must postulate *agent-centered constraints*. Agents have a stringent duty to avoid harming others in certain ways—for instance, killing them or causing them to be punished for crimes they did not commit—even if doing so would prevent other agents from perpetrating a larger number of harms of comparable seriousness. This moral constraint is agent-centered in the sense that it requires each individual agent to be concerned in the first instance with avoiding violations *by the agent's own hand*, rather than simply with reducing the total number of violations that occur in the world.[14]

---

[13] This example derives from McCloskey (1957, pp. 468–9).

[14] The moral constraint is also time-centered and action-centered: it is also impermissible to harm others in these ways, even if doing so would prevent oneself from committing a larger number of similar violations at another time, or committing a larger number of violations through distinct acts.

Why should we accept agent-centered moral constraints, rather than adopting the utilitarian view that we should maximize the sum of benefits minus harms in the universe? Briefly, the answer is that utilitarianism occupies an epistemically unstable position between amoralism and common sense morality. If we attach some weight to intuitive ethical judgments, then we must take seriously the intuitions about Organ Harvesting, Framing, and other cases that appear to provide counterexamples to utilitarianism. We need not hold to these intuitions *dogmatically*; we might take them merely to provide a kind of presumption. But the intuitive judgments that stand against utilitarianism include ones that are very firm and widely-shared, as in the Organ Harvesting and Framing cases. There are numerous additional cases in the literature that illustrate a variety of non-utilitarian moral considerations.[15] So the utilitarian would have a very difficult task showing that the intuitive judgments in all these cases are incorrect—something that, in my judgment, no utilitarian has done.[16]

It might seem that utilitarianism would fare better if the utilitarian starts by denying that any initial weight should be attached to intuitive ethical judgments. Indeed, some utilitarians have appeared to take this approach.[17] In this case, however, the utilitarian will have trouble fending off nihilists (who hold that nothing is right or wrong), egoists (who hold that it is always right to serve one's own interests, regardless of the consequences for others), and moral skeptics (who hold that we cannot know what is right or wrong). The only reason we have for thinking that we should promote benefits rather than harms, or that we should take account of other people's interests, is intuitive. It *seems* morally wrong to harm others without a good reason. There is no *demonstration* of this, nor is it supported by any scientific theory. If we attach no weight to intuitive

---

[15] See, e.g., Ross (1988, ch. II), Williams (1973), Nozick (1974, pp. 41–5), Thomson (1985, p. 1409), Wolf (1982), Scanlon (1998, p. 235).
[16] The task is not, however, in principle impossible. In Huemer (2008), I discuss how utilitarianism might be defended, consistent with an ethical intuitionist epistemology.
[17] Singer (2004), Greene (2014).

ethical judgments, then we cannot assume that there is anything wrong with harming others for no reason.[18]

My task here is not to address egoists, skeptics, or nihilists. My question here is, given that we accept some non-egoistic form of morality, why should we adopt a deontological rather than a utilitarian moral view? Given that we accept morality at all, we have already attached weight to ethical intuition. But utilitarianism on its face fares very poorly at accommodating intuitive ethical judgments. A deontological ethics that incorporates the notion of rights does better at this task. Hence, barring strong arguments to the contrary, we should accept the notion of rights, understood as a kind of agent-centered moral constraint.

There was one other element in my definition of rights that I have not yet discussed. This is that rights are *enforceable*. Here, I mean "enforceable" in a normative sense: rights are *apt* for enforcement. It is ethically appropriate to use force against potential rights-violators to prevent their violation of rights, or against actual rights-violators to punish or remedy their violation of rights, even when this use of force would otherwise have been a violation of the rights of the person against whom it is used. For instance, shooting a person is normally a violation of that person's rights; nevertheless, it is permissible to shoot a person if doing so is necessary to prevent that same person from unjustifiably violating someone else's rights in a serious manner. (Of course, one may not shoot a person merely to prevent a *minor* rights violation.) This provides a qualification to rights principles: individuals have the right not to be treated in certain ways, *unless* doing so is necessary to prevent or remedy their own treatment of others in those ways. This principle of enforceability is crucial to explaining why a criminal justice system is permissible in general and not inevitably unjust.

On my view, the noun "right" does not refer to some special kind of object; rather, talk about rights is a kind of shorthand for talk about ways in which one is ethically permitted or required to treat others. There is a set of ways of treating other persons such that (i) under normal

---

[18] For discussion of the argument that ethical beliefs must rest on ethical intuition, see my 2005, chs. 4–5.

circumstances, one ethically may not treat others in those ways, even if doing so prevents a greater harm or prevents a larger number of occurrences of someone treating someone in those ways, *except* that (ii) one normally *may* treat a person in those ways if doing so is a necessary and proportionate means to either prevent or remedy that same person's own wrongful treatment of others in those ways.

All that is what I take to be communicated when one says that persons "have the right" not to be treated in certain ways. Clause (i) expresses the deontological aspect of rights, the fact that rights impose agent-centered restraints. Clause (ii) is the principle of the enforceability of rights. The "under normal conditions" clause is intended to allow for the possibility of additional exceptions and qualifications, including the possibility that treating others in the normally-proscribed ways might be justified when necessary to produce vastly more benefit or prevent vastly more harm. It is not, however, meant to allow for the consequentialist view that any form of ill treatment of others may be justified by the production of even slightly greater benefits; that is, I take the consequentialist view to be ruled out by the ordinary notion of rights.

Why must the enforceability condition be included in the definition of rights? The reason is that there may be moral constraints that are not apt for enforcement, and for these constraints, talk of "rights" would be out of place. Perhaps, for example, malicious gossip is ethically wrong, and perhaps there is an agent-centered constraint against it, such that it is wrong to engage in malicious gossip even if doing so would prevent five other people from engaging in malicious gossip. Nevertheless, it would sound out of place to speak of a *right* against malicious gossip. This is because the anti-gossip constraint is not apt for enforcement: one may not deploy force against others to prevent or remedy malicious gossip. By contrast, one may deploy force, or call upon the state to deploy force on one's behalf, to prevent or remedy physical violence, destruction of property, or breaches of contract. Hence, individuals can be said to *have the right* not to be subjected to violence, destruction of their property, or contract violations.

My account takes as primary the notion of a right against being treated in a particular way. Other rights attributions are to be understood in terms of rights against certain kinds of ill-treatment. For instance, the "right to life" is a right *against being killed*; the right of free speech is a right against certain kinds of interference with one's speech; property rights are rights against others' interference with certain external objects to which one bears a special relationship. Positive rights, usually understood as rights to receive benefits, can be accommodated within this framework, provided that we recognize negative forms of "treatment"; thus, the right to health care would be a right against certain others' (presumably the state or society) *failing* to make health care available to one.

There is controversy concerning exactly what rights individuals possess. There are some who reject positive rights, and even among those who accept positive rights in general, there is disagreement about to which goods individuals have positive rights. Some reject property rights in general, or reject certain classes of property rights. And so on. There is, however, widespread agreement (leaving aside consequentialists) that there are *some* rights in my sense, because this follows from the common sense moral judgments about cases such as Organ Harvesting and Framing. The Organ Harvesting case establishes a right not to be killed (or something in that neighborhood, such as a right against being *intentionally* killed, or against having one's body damaged), and the Framing case establishes a right not to be punished for crimes one did not commit (or something in that neighborhood).

2.4.2 The Trolley Objection

I have argued that common sense ethical intuitions support a view of rights as agent-centered constraints. But not all widely shared ethical intuitions are friendly to rights theories. Some cases elicit consequentialist intuitions, intuitions that favor the action that produces the best consequences even when this action would seem to violate the rights of the individual. Thus, consider the famous Trolley case:

Trolley: A runaway trolley is headed for a group of five people who are unable to move out of the way. If no one intervenes, the trolley will kill all five. You have the option to flip a switch that will send the trolley down a side track, which will save the five people; however, there is one person on the side track who would be killed instead. Should you flip the switch?[19]

Most who consider this case intuitively think it both permissible and desirable to turn the trolley from the five toward the one. This poses a puzzle: in cases such as Organ Harvesting and Framing, it seems wrong to sacrifice one person to save several others, yet in the Trolley case, it seems permissible to do so. Why? There must be some difference between the Trolley case and the Organ Harvesting case, but it is difficult to say what that difference is. (I assume that whatever feature makes the action wrong in Organ Harvesting applies also to Framing, so that we need not separately discuss the Framing case. This assumption is consistent with the theories discussed in §2.4.4 below.)

This creates two potential challenges for my above defense of rights. First, some would argue that the Trolley case undermines the intuitions I have appealed to about such cases as Organ Harvesting. The argument would be that it is permissible to turn the trolley, that this situation is relevantly similar to the Organ Harvesting case, and therefore that it is *permissible* to kill the healthy patient in the latter case. This would be the view of the utilitarians.[20]

Second, even if I am correct about cases like Organ Harvesting, there is reason to doubt that such cases are correctly understood in terms of *rights*. For if individuals have rights, then it would seem that these should include the right to life. If so, it is hard to see how turning the trolley could fail to be a violation of the right to life of the person on the side track. (Note that if there were no one on the main track and you turned

---

[19] This case (with slight modification) is derived from Foot (1967). A similar case occurred in reality in 2003, when a collection of runaway train cars heading toward downtown Los Angeles was diverted toward a less populated area in Commerce City (CNN 2003). The cars predictably derailed and damaged some houses but luckily did not kill anyone.
[20] See Unger (1996).

the trolley to the side track anyway, killing the one person, you would be guilty of murder.) If this is correct, then it is hard to see how turning the trolley could be morally permissible. If we are persuaded that turning the trolley *is* permissible, then perhaps we should give up on rights theories.

In what follows, I will address these objections, arguing that consequentialism is not a plausible response to the Trolley problem and that we can accommodate the Trolley intuition within a rights theory.

2.4.3 Against Consequentialism

Consequentialists hold that there are no morally relevant differences between the Trolley and Organ Harvesting cases, and moreover that in both cases the action is permissible: harvesting the organs and turning the trolley are both permissible, because both acts are for the greater good.

My reason for rejecting consequentialism was given above (§2.4.1): Either we accept ethical intuition as a source of justification for ethical beliefs, or we do not. If we accept ethical intuition, then we should reject consequentialism since it conflicts with many firm, widely-shared ethical intuitions. If we reject ethical intuition, then we should still give up consequentialism since we would have no reason to believe any ethical claims at all.

The Trolley case does not alter the basic argument. The intuition about Organ Harvesting is stronger and more widespread than the intuition about the Trolley case. Almost everyone, on hearing about Organ Harvesting, judges the action wrong, with very high confidence. It is not as obvious that turning the trolley is permissible (there is, after all, a case to be made that turning the trolley is an act of murder).[21] Therefore, it would be unjustified to reject the intuition

---

[21] This reflects my experience in surveying students informally, as well as the results of psychological studies. Gleichgerrcht and Young (2013), for example, found that 62% of subjects supported turning the trolley, while 83% rejected organ harvesting. In the PhilPapers survey, 62% of philosophers favored switching the trolley, 9% opposed switching, and 29% gave some other answer (PhilPapers 2009; population: all respondents; AOS: all respondents). The organ harvesting case was not

about Organ Harvesting based on the intuition about Trolley. If we should be convinced that the cases are relevantly similar, it is more plausible to conclude that sacrificing the one person is *impermissible* in all cases, rather than permissible in all cases. This is the view most recently taken by Judith Thomson, the best-known writer about the Trolley and related cases.[22]

But of course, we need not hold that the cases are relevantly similar. Some difference or differences between the cases must explain our differing intuitions. Our failure to identify the difference is not surprising, since it is often very difficult to identify the sources of our intuitive judgments, and this problem affects all areas of philosophy. Even consequentialists do not claim that there is *no difference at all* between the cases; they claim that whatever the difference is, it is *not morally significant*, that is, it is something that does not matter morally. There is, however, no good reason to assume this. Before we have determined what the difference is, it is more reasonable to assume that it is morally significant. This is because ethical reasoning in general depends on treating our intuitive ethical judgments as correct unless and until we have specific grounds for doubt. Observers who have never before encountered any of these hypothetical cases regularly share the intuitive reactions I have cited above. The fact that our intuitions differ between the Organ Harvesting case and the Trolley case is thus an argument that those cases are in fact morally different.

2.4.4 Differences Between Trolley and Organ Harvesting

Most audiences, on being introduced to the Organ Harvesting and Trolley cases, are unable to identify any defensible candidates for the relevant difference between them. Nevertheless, philosophers have proposed a number of accounts of this difference.

---

included in the PhilPapers survey; anecdotally, however, it appears to this author that almost all philosophers have the very strong intuition that organ harvesting is wrong.
[22] Thomson (2008).

Some ethicists hold that there is a moral constraint against *intending* harm to others, such that it is much more difficult to justify an action that *aims* at harming a person, either as an end or as a means to an end, than it is to justify an action that merely harms a person as a foreseeable side effect. This principle, the "Doctrine of Double Effect", was advanced by Aquinas and has been widely held since long before the Trolley problem was first discussed.[23] In my view, the principle is more plausible with two modifications, which I think most supporters of the Doctrine of Double Effect would accept. The first modification is to say that what matters is not whether a harmful ultimate outcome is intended, but whether some interference with or use of something that another person has rights over, such as their own body, is intended, where this use or interference is in fact highly likely to be harmful.[24] Second, what matters is not the agent's *actual* intentions, but what the intentions would have to be for the action to be part of a rational plan to bring about the benefit at issue, given the circumstances.

In the Trolley case, the rational plan for saving the five people would not *aim* at harming the one person on the side track; indeed, the agent should hope for the one person to somehow escape. If the person on the side track should escape, the plan to save the five would be in no way frustrated. By contrast, in the Organ Harvesting case, the doctor aims to take the healthy patient's organs and could not coherently hope for the healthy patient to escape. The doctor's plan to save the transplant patients could not be satisfied without the use of the one victim.

A related observation is that in the Trolley case, if the agent *refuses* to divert the Trolley out of concern for the individual on the side track, then this one person will be serving as an impediment to the saving of the others and will thus be (unintentionally, of course) *harming* them by his presence. To convince yourself of this, imagine that I foresaw that the runaway trolley would endanger the five on the main track, and that there was initially no one on the side track. I knew that you would come along and switch the trolley to save the five as long as no one was on the

---

[23] See Aquinas (1920, 2a2ae, Q. 64, art. 7), Anscombe (2001), Nagel (1986, pp. 179–85).

[24] This blocks the defense of organ harvesting wherein the doctor would claim not to have intended to kill the healthy patient, since his plans would have succeeded just as well if, after removal of his organs, the healthy patient had miraculously survived.

side track, but that you would *not* switch it if there was anyone on the side track, since you would consider this murder. And now suppose that, knowing all this, I decided to jump onto the side track myself, solely to prevent you from switching the trolley. When the five on the main track die from a trolley collision, I will then be guilty of their murder. If this is correct, then it must be correct to say that, in this case, I intentionally *cause* the deaths of the five through my presence on the side track. And if that is so, then in the case where I *accidentally* fall onto the side track and this prevents you from switching the trolley, I also cause the deaths of the five by my presence, albeit of course unintentionally.

But in the Organ Harvesting case, it could not be said in any case that the one potential victim would be harming anyone or serving as an impediment by his presence. If the doctor fails to kill the healthy patient, it will be false that the healthy patient, by his presence, prevented the doctor from saving the others. In this case, the healthy patient serves only as a potential *means* to helping others, whereas in Trolley, the individual on the side track is a potential *impediment* to helping others.

Another account holds that there is a moral constraint against *originating* threats, such that it is much more difficult to justify creating a new threat against a person than to justify diverting an existing threat from one target to another. This view derives from remarks of Judith Thomson's (before Thomson revised her view to hold that turning the trolley is impermissible).[25] The motivation for the view derives from its ability to account for the difference between Trolley-like and Organ-Harvesting-like cases.

In the Trolley case, one diverts an existing threat, a runaway trolley, away from five victims toward a single victim. The result is that the one person on the side track dies from the same thing that was originally threatening the five. In the Organ Harvesting case, the proposed action would not divert the existing threat, since the healthy patient would not die from the diseases originally threatening the transplant patients. The doctor would instead create a new threat, the threat of being killed by one's doctor.

---

[25] Thomson (1985, pp. 1407–8); for her revised view, see Thomson (2008).

There is a large literature on the Trolley Problem, in which many other proposals have been made to account for the differing intuitions.[26] Every proposal thus far made is open to reasonable objections, and there is no consensus among ethicists on a correct account. The distinctions I have discussed here—intended vs. merely foreseen harms, potential impediment vs. potential means to benefit, and originated vs. diverted threats—are the ones I take to be the most plausibly relevant.

2.4.5 Accommodating Rights to the Trolley Exception

Even if we accept the Trolley intuition—that it is permissible to turn the trolley away from the five and toward the one—we may continue to speak in terms of rights, though this may require revisions to standard descriptions of our rights. Rather than ascribing a right not to be killed, for example, we might ascribe to individuals a right not to be the target of an *intention* to kill, or not to have a deadly threat *originated* against one. Alternately, we might retain familiar descriptions of what individuals have rights *to*, but revise our account of what it means to ascribe a right to something. Perhaps to say that a person "has the right" not to be treated in a particular way only means that there is an agent-centered moral constraint against *intending* to treat the person in the specified way, or against *originating* a threat of treating the person in the specified way—or in general, a constraint against treating the person in the specified way in cases that have whatever feature is present in the Organ Harvesting case but absent from the Trolley case.

These different descriptions reflect semantic, not substantive, differences. Because the vocabulary of "rights" is only a shorthand for communicating facts about permissible and impermissible ways of treating others, it does not matter how we characterize the situation with regard to rights, as long as we retain the same judgments about how agents may and may not treat others. Thus, if we agree that Trolley-like situations pose an exception to the usual moral constraints against harming others,

---

[26] For a survey, see Bruers and Braeckman (2014).

it does not matter whether we incorporate this exception into the description of what one has a right to, or into our account of what it takes to violate a right to *x*.

Because it would be tedious to amend every rights claim with a modifier referring to intentions, or the origination of threats, or whatever feature differentiates Organ Harvesting from Trolley, I will assume that whatever qualification is needed to accommodate the Trolley case is to be incorporated into our account of what it is to violate a right. Thus, for example, to violate the right to life is to kill a person in a situation that has whatever feature is present in Organ Harvesting but absent from Trolley.

2.4.6 Why Speak of Rights?

Some thinkers employ much stronger conceptions of rights, conceptions that would make it impossible for a right to be outweighed and would allow fewer qualifications or exceptions to rights claims.[27] The common notion of a *right* to life, for example, might be thought to rule out the possibility that one may kill an innocent person to save vastly more people, as well as the possibility that one may kill an innocent person to avert a slightly larger harm as long as the killing is carried out through the *diversion* of a threat rather than the *origination* of a threat. One may think that the incorporation of qualifications permitting such killings defeats the point of speaking in terms of "rights".

Why do I continue to use the vocabulary of rights? First, though my interpretation of the term "right" may be semantically revisionary, I have avoided revisionary *moral* views. In ordinary parlance, it is commonly said that we have a right to life, a right to free speech, rights to property, and so on. Yet it is also widely accepted that it would be

---

[27] See Dworkin's (1978, p. xi) characterization of rights as "trumps" and Nozick's (1974, pp. 28–33) notion of rights as "side constraints". But note that even these authors seem to leave open that a rights violation *might* be justifiable if necessary to prevent a catastrophe (Dworkin 1978, p. 191; Nozick 1974, p. 30n).

permissible to kill a person, restrict a person's speech, or use a person's property without consent, if this would be necessary to prevent some vastly worse outcome. If we insist that "rights", as a matter of the meaning of the word, must be absolute, then we should have to convict common sense morality of obvious inconsistency. Similarly, most who consider the Trolley case find it acceptable to turn the trolley. Yet it remains counterintuitive to say, "There is no right to life." We can reconcile this by interpreting the notion of a right, for example, as implying a constraint against originating threats but not necessarily against diverting threats. So my first reason for reinterpreting "rights", if that is indeed what I have done, is that this avoids a larger and less palatable kind of revision.

Second, the vocabulary of rights simplifies moral discussion. Were I to abandon this vocabulary, I would have to tediously reiterate phrases referring to agent-centered, enforceable constraints against origination of threats.

Third, I want to insist that the qualifications I have accepted to the notion of rights are not in fact large qualifications. More precisely, they are theoretically interesting but *practically* of little import, because the qualifications I have introduced—in particular, the vastly-greater-harm exception and the Trolley Exception—almost never apply in reality. In nearly all cases in which a person seriously, coercively harms another, the agent does so by originating a threat. And in almost no cases does the agent produce vastly greater benefits by so doing. Usually, the possibility that the agent merely diverted a threat or produced vastly greater benefits does not need to be discussed. (That is why in homicide trials, defendants almost never raise trolley-like defenses or defenses based on their having prevented vastly greater harms.) For this reason, in normal conditions, a rights claim settles a question of permissibility for practical purposes. That is to say, in normal conditions in the actual world, rights claims function in more or less the way that absolutists about rights want them to function.

2.5 Intuition and Moral Knowledge

2.5.1 The Concept of Ethical Intuition

I have appealed to common sense ethical intuitions about a number of cases above to draw important ethical conclusions, and I continue to do so in the following chapters. It is worth saying a few words about this methodology. First, let us clarify the notion of ethical intuition.

The term "intuition" is a technical term in contemporary philosophy. This philosophical use is not to be confused with the ordinary English use of the word. "Intuition" in philosophy does not refer to a non-rational, supernatural revelation; nor does it mean "unreflective guess"; nor does the term suggest that a judgment occurs easily, immediately, or with no need for background experience or thinking.[28] Those are all potential misunderstandings that arise from lack of awareness of the term's technical use. An intuition, in the contemporary philosophical sense, is a non-inferential, intellectual appearance.

Now to explain what I mean by that. When we reflect on an intellectual question, there is often an answer that seems to us correct. For instance, when we think about what is the shortest path between two points, it seems that the answer is a straight line. When we think about whether a green object can also be entirely blue, it seems that the answer is no. When we think about the Organ Harvesting case, it seems that killing the healthy patient would be wrong. In all of these cases, one has a mental state of something's seeming to one to be the case; I refer to such states as "appearances". In each of the examples just given, the appearance is *intellectual* in the sense that it results from intellectual reflection. This is contrasted with sensory appearances, which result from looking, listening, tasting, touching, or smelling; memory appearances, which result from the operation of memory; and introspective appearances, which result from our capacity of self-awareness. The examples just given are also non-inferential, in the sense that the appearance does not require the

---

[28] On these points, see Ross (1988, pp. 29–30, 32–33), Audi (2004, pp. 45–54).

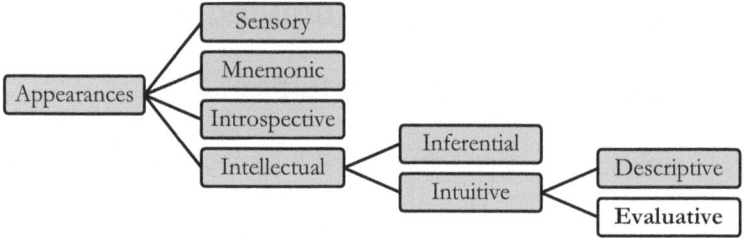

Fig. 2.1 Taxonomy of appearances

subject to entertain an argument leading to the proposition in question. This is contrasted with inferential appearances, in which a proposition seems correct *in the light of* a particular chain of reasoning leading to it. Note that, for present purposes, non-conscious cognitive processing does not affect the classification of appearances; thus, the existence of unconscious or sub-personal information processing leading to the formation of an appearance does not prevent the appearance from counting as non-inferential or intuitive.

There are intuitions about any number of subjects, perhaps every subject. For instance, there are intuitions about geometry ("the shortest path between two points is a straight line"), about colors ("nothing can be entirely green and entirely blue"), and about ethics ("It would be wrong to kill the healthy patient in the Organ Harvesting case"). The subject of ethics concerns *evaluative* questions, that is, questions of what is good, bad, right, and wrong; all other questions are by stipulation referred to as "descriptive". Thus, *ethical intuitions* are non-inferential, intellectual appearances about evaluative questions (see Fig. 2.1).

There are debates in the philosophical literature about the nature of intuition and its role in moral knowledge. Some philosophers, for example, view intuitions as a kind of belief or disposition to form beliefs, while others (myself included) view intuitions as a *sui generis* kind of experience. Most questions about intuitions, however, are not important for our purposes. For our purposes, it is important that there are ethical intuitions, that they are states of something's seeming correct to us, and that they include such examples as the appearance that killing the healthy patient in Organ Harvesting is morally wrong, that it is wrong to cause harm to others without good reason, and so on.

2.5.2 Intuitionist Methodology

My methodology in addressing normative questions relies on ethical intuitions as dialectical starting points. Intuitions are not, however, to be employed *dogmatically*; nearly all beliefs, including intuitive judgments, are open to revision in the light of countervailing evidence. The role of intuitions is rather to establish a kind of *presumption*: it is reasonable to assume that what is good, bad, right, or wrong is what *seems* good, bad, right, or wrong, until we have specific reasons for doubting this.[29]

Why adopt this methodological approach? If we do not accept ethical intuitions even as establishing a presumption—that is, we do not accept what seems ethically correct even when we have no specific reasons for doubting it—then we should never accept any ethical propositions. There is no other situation in which we will be better positioned with respect to an ethical proposition.

One might suppose that there is the alternative possibility of accepting ethical propositions only once they have been supported through reasoning. But this is not in fact an alternative possibility. No actual chain of reasoning is infinitely long; furthermore, though authors occasionally produce circular arguments, this is generally agreed to be fallacious. Therefore, all actual, non-fallacious reasoning begins from some premises accepted without argument. Now, it is widely known that it is not possible to correctly reason from purely descriptive premises to an ethical conclusion. For example, one can argue that individuals ought to obey the laws of their society because this is required by the social contract, to

---

[29] The function of the word "specific" here is to rule out general skeptical arguments, which object to all appearances or all ethical intuitions. Thus, we may assume that something that seems wrong is wrong, until we have grounds for doubting that that specific thing is wrong.

which all members of society are party. But this argument requires the implicit assumption that *individuals must keep to their contracts*, which is an ethical premise. Similarly, one can argue that property rights should be respected because societies in which property rights are consistently respected are more prosperous and happy than those in which those rights are not consistently respected. But this requires some implicit ethical premises in the neighborhood of *prosperity and happiness are good* and *we should follow the rules whose adoption produces the most good*.[30]

All correct reasoning for an ethical conclusion, then, will rest on one or more ultimate ethical premises, often assumed implicitly. By hypothesis, no reasons are given for these premises. What explains why one begins with certain ethical premises without providing reasons for them? The answer, in general, will be that one begins with the ethical premises that seem correct when we think about them and that we have no particular reason for doubting. Those things are ethical intuitions. For example, we may take it as a premise that murder is wrong, since murder seems wrong and we have no reason to think otherwise.

Some confusion on this matter has unfortunately been caused by the existence of ethicists who purport to reject the use of ethical intuitions.[31] These thinkers do not in fact reject intuitions in general. Rather, they (i) reject certain *kinds* of intuitions which conflict with their favored theo-

---

[30] In the metaethical literature, there have been a number of efforts to show that one can derive an "ought" from an "is", that is, deduce an ethical conclusion from purely descriptive premises (Searle 1964; Rand 1964; Gewirth 1973; Prior 1976; Geach 1977). I will not discuss these attempts in detail here. All are widely and correctly viewed as fallacious. Karmo (1988) has proved in general that an "ought" statement cannot be soundly derived from an "is" statement. I discuss these issues in Huemer (2005, section 4.3).

[31] See, e.g., Singer (2004), Greene (2014). But note that these authors may have intended only to criticize intuitions about concrete cases, as opposed to intuitions regarding abstract principles. Later, Singer and de Lazari-Radek (2012) defend a kind of intuitionist approach to ethics, relying on an intuitive "principle of universal benevolence". In a different context, LaFollette (2018, pp. 83, 86) has criticized my use of intuitions, claiming that no other contemporary rights theorist uses intuitions. As I argue in the text, *all* non-skeptical normative theorists use intuitions, with the possible exception of the thinkers mentioned in footnote 30 who fallaciously attempt to bridge the is-ought gap.

ries, (ii) embrace the intuitions that support their favored theories, and (iii) refuse to use the word "intuition" to describe the latter intuitions. Thus, for example, utilitarians sometimes claim to reject intuitions. The truth is that they reject intuitions that conflict with utilitarianism, such as the standard intuitions about Organ Harvesting or Framing, but they accept intuitions that support utilitarianism, such as the intuition that pleasure is intrinsically good or that one ought to take account of the interests of others, and they simply decline to call the latter sorts of premises "intuitions". The putative intuition skeptics are mainly philosophers who want to restrict acceptable intuitions to those that support their own favored theories.

What alternative methodology might one advance? There are only the following logical possibilities: One may (a) reason from ultimate ethical premises that seem true, (b) reason from ultimate ethical premises that do *not* seem true, (c) avoid ethical reasoning entirely, (d) produce an infinite chain of reasoning, (e) reason in a circle, or (f) bridge the is-ought gap (reason from purely descriptive premises to evaluative conclusions). Option (a) is the option of "using ethical intuitions". Options (b)-(f) are the only logically possible alternatives to "using ethical intuitions". But the putative intuition skeptics do not as a rule claim to be doing any of those things. Most likely, then, these thinkers simply react negatively to the word "intuition" without attending to its technical meaning in the philosophical context.

2.6 Moral Realism

A final metaethical question: do my arguments in this book presuppose *moral realism*, the belief that there are objective moral facts? If so, this might be a cause for concern, since there are many philosophers, as well as thinkers in other fields, who reject moral realism.

The answer is that my arguments in this book presuppose moral realism *if and only if* anyone who thinks that murder is wrong is presupposing moral realism. In that case, however, to object to my arguments on this account would be obviously unreasonable.

To explain: Most anti-realist philosophers, while denying the objectivity of values, attempt to accommodate common sense claims. Thus, they seek to explain why, despite the absence of objective values, one may nevertheless perfectly aptly say such things as "Murder is wrong", "Needless suffering is bad", and "Hitler was evil." (This of course is not true of *nihilists*, who claim that all those moral statements are false. But very few anti-realists have been nihilists.) This is because most philosophers aim to articulate positions that are at least minimally plausible on their face. Some would say, for example, that "Murder is wrong" is true, or aptly affirmed, when the speaker has a certain negative emotional attitude, one of moral disapproval, toward murder, or perhaps when society in general disapproves of murder. The lack of *objectivity* should not prevent us from sincerely affirming "Murder is wrong", any more than the non-objectivity of funniness prevents us from sincerely affirming "Stephen Colbert is funny", or the non-objectivity of sexiness prevents us from sincerely affirming "Scarlett Johannsen is sexy." Or so these philosophers would argue.

Whether these arguments succeed is open to debate. But *if* they succeed, then anti-realists have no reason to object to the contentions of this book. If the non-objectivity of wrongness poses no obstacle to sincerely affirming "Murder is wrong", then the non-objectivity of "unjust" should pose no obstacle to sincerely affirming "The legal system in the United States is unjust."[32] On the other hand, if the usual anti-realist arguments fail, so that anti-realists must *reject* "Murder is wrong", then anti-realism is extremely implausible. It would be unreasonable to object to my arguments in this book by relying on a theory that also requires rejecting "Murder is wrong."

References

Anscombe, G.E.M. 2001. Medalist's Address: Action, Intention and "Double Effect". In *The Doctrine of Double Effect: Philosophers Debate a Controversial Moral Principle*, ed. P.A. Woodward, 50–66. Notre Dame: University of Notre Dame Press.

---

[32] This is assuming that we reject legal relativism, as discussed above (§2.3).

Aquinas, Thomas. 1920. *The Summa Theologica of St. Thomas Aquinas*. Second and revised edition. Translated by Fathers of the English Dominican Province. London.

Audi, Robert. 2004. *The Good in the Right: A Theory of Intuition and Intrinsic Value*. Princeton: Princeton University Press.

Augustine of Hippo. 1993. *On Free Choice of the Will*. Trans. Thomas Williams. Indianapolis: Hackett.

Bentham, Jeremy. 1987. Supply Without Burthen or Escheat Vice Taxation. In *Nonsense upon Stilts: Bentham, Burke and Marx on the Rights of Man*, ed. Jeremy Waldron, 70–76. London: Methuen.

Bruers, Stijn, and Johan Braeckman. 2014. A Review and Systematization of the Trolley Problem. *Philosophia* 42: 251–269.

CNN. 2003. Runaway Freight Train Derails Near Los Angeles. *CNN News*, June 20. https://www.cnn.com/2003/US/West/06/20/train.derails/index.html. Accessed 24 June 2020.

Dworkin, Ronald. 1978. *Taking Rights Seriously*. Cambridge, MA: Harvard University Press.

———. 1986. *Law's Empire*. Cambridge, MA: Harvard University Press.

Finnis, John. 2020. Natural Law Theories. *Stanford Encyclopedia of Philosophy*. https://plato.stanford.edu/entries/natural-law-theories/. Accessed 24 June 2020.

Foot, Philippa. 1967. The Problem of Abortion and the Doctrine of Double Effect. *Oxford Review* 5: 5–15.

Geach, Peter T. 1977. Again the Logic of 'Ought'. *Philosophy* 52: 473–476.

Gewirth, Alan. 1973. The 'Is-Ought' Problem Resolved. *Proceedings and Addresses of the American Philosophical Association* 47: 34–61.

Gleichgerrcht, Ezequiel, and Liane Young. 2013. Low Levels of Empathic Concern Predict Utilitarian Moral Judgment. *PLoS One* 8: e60418. https://doi.org/10.1371/journal.pone.0060418.

Greene, Joshua D. 2014. Beyond Point-and-Shoot Morality: Why Cognitive (Neuro)Science Matters for Ethics. *Ethics* 124: 695–726.

Hobbes, Thomas. 1996. *Leviathan*, ed. Richard Tuck. Cambridge: Cambridge University Press.

Hohfeld, Wesley Newcomb. 1913. Some Fundamental Legal Conceptions as Applied in Judicial Reasoning. *Yale Law Journal* 23: 16–59.

Huemer, Michael. 2005. *Ethical Intuitionism*. New York: Palgrave Macmillan.

———. 2008. Revisionary Intuitionism. *Social Philosophy & Policy* 25: 368–392.

———. 2013. An Ontological Proof of Moral Realism. *Social Philosophy & Policy* 30: 259–279.

———. 2016. A Liberal Realist Answer to Debunking Skeptics: The Empirical Case for Realism. *Philosophical Studies* 173: 1983–2010.
Hume, David. 1992. *Treatise of Human Nature*. Buffalo: Prometheus.
Karmo, Toomas. 1988. Some Valid (But No Sound) Arguments Trivially Span the 'Is'-'Ought' Gap. *Mind* 97: 252–257.
King, Martin Luther, Jr. 1963, April 16. Letter From a Birmingham Jail. Available at https://www.africa.upenn.edu/Articles_Gen/Letter_Birmingham.html. Accessed 24 June 2020.
LaFollette, Hugh. 2018. *In Defense of Gun Control*. New York: Oxford University Press.
McCloskey, H.J. 1957. An Examination of Restricted Utilitarianism. *Philosophical Review* 66: 466–485.
Moore, George Edward. 1960. *Principia Ethica*. Cambridge: Cambridge University Press.
Nagel, Thomas. 1986. *The View from Nowhere*. Oxford: Oxford University Press.
Nozick, Robert. 1974. *Anarchy, State, and Utopia*. New York: Basic Books.
PhilPapers. 2009. Preliminary Survey Results. https://philpapers.org/surveys/results.pl. Accessed 25 June 2020.
Prior, A.N. 1976. The Autonomy of Ethics. In *Papers in Logic and Ethics*, ed. P.T. Geach and A.J.P. Kenny, 88–96. London: Duckworth.
Rand, Ayn. 1964. The Objectivist Ethics. In *The Virtue of Selfishness*, 13–35. New York: Signet.
Ross, W.D. 1988. *The Right and the Good*. Indianapolis: Hackett.
Scanlon, T.M. 1998. *What We Owe to Each Other*. Cambridge, MA: Harvard University Press.
Scheffler, Samuel. 1994. *The Rejection of Consequentialism*. Oxford: Clarendon.
Searle, John R. 1964. How to Derive 'Ought' from 'Is'. *Philosophical Review* 73: 43–58.
Singer, Peter. 2004. Ethics and Intuitions. *The Journal of Ethics* 9: 331–352.
Singer, Peter, and Katarzyna de Lazari-Radek. 2012. The Objectivity of Ethics and the Unity of Practical Reason. *Ethics* 123: 9–31.
Thomson, Judith Jarvis. 1985. The Trolley Problem. *Yale Law Journal* 94: 1395–1415.
———. 2008. Turning the Trolley. *Philosophy and Public Affairs* 36: 359–374.
Unger, Peter. 1996. *Living High and Letting Die: Our Illusion of Innocence*. Oxford: Oxford University Press.
Williams, Bernard. 1973. A Critique of Utilitarianism. In *Utilitarianism: For and Against*, ed. J.J.C. Smart and Bernard Williams, 75–100. Cambridge: Cambridge University Press.
Wolf, Susan. 1982. Moral Saints. *Journal of Philosophy* 79: 419–439.

Part II

Legal Injustices

3

Unjust Laws

In this part of the book, I argue that the American legal system is unjust in a number of respects. It does not merely suffer from minor or occasional injustices. It suffers from *serious, pervasive* injustices. Many of these injustices are so obvious as to call into question whether the state is even aiming at justice at all. We begin, in this chapter, with the problem of unjust criminal laws.

3.1 The Presumption Against Law

3.1.1 An Argument that Laws Are Presumptively Unjust

Criminal laws—that is, laws to which the state attaches criminal punishments for their violation—are presumptively unjust. (Hereinafter in this chapter, by "laws" I refer to criminal laws.) This may sound like an odd view, so let me first explain what I mean by this. I do not mean that most laws are unjust, or that the initial probability of a randomly chosen law being unjust is over one-half. What I mean is that those who support a law have a burden of citing moral reasons that justify the law, and that if sufficient justifying reasons do not exist then the law is unjust.

To explain this notion of presumption, compare the presumption of innocence in a criminal trial: the doctrine of the presumption of innocence does not mean that most defendants should be acquitted, nor does it mean that one's initial credence that a defendant is guilty should be less than 50%. If it did, the doctrine would be readily refuted by simple knowledge of base rates: the overwhelming majority of defendants are factually guilty,[1] so one's initial credence that a defendant is guilty, before knowing any facts of the case, should be high. Rather, the presumption of innocence simply means that it is the prosecution's responsibility to bring forward sufficient evidence of guilt, and that *if* the prosecution fails to do so, the defendant is to be acquitted. It happens that in the overwhelming majority of cases, sufficient evidence is indeed brought forward, so that defendants are rightly convicted; this is perfectly compatible with the claim of a "presumption" of innocence.

Similarly, I claim that unless sufficient reasons in favor of a law can be adduced, we should reject the law. This is compatible with the possibility that in the overwhelming majority of cases, sufficient reasons can indeed be found. But note one difference: in the case of a criminal trial, it is not the case that, in the absence of sufficient evidence of guilt, the defendant *is* factually innocent; it is merely the case that the probability of guilt is not high enough to justify punishment. But in the case of the presumption against law, I am not merely claiming that in the absence of sufficient moral reasons for a law, there is not a sufficiently high probability that the law is just; I am claiming that in the absence of sufficient moral reasons for a law, the law *is unjust*.[2]

My claim is not merely that laws are presumptively unwise, immoral, or generally bad, but specifically that they are presumptively *unjust*. Why unjust? First, individuals have a prima facie right against harmful

---

[1] U.S. Department of Justice statistics show a 94% conviction rate in federal trials in the U.S. (ABC News 2010). Earlier data show a conviction rate of between 85 and 90% for state courts (Ramseyer et al. 2008, p. 17).

[2] To elaborate, the presumption of innocence demands epistemic reasons (evidence) for believing that a defendant is guilty, whereas the presumption against law demands moral reasons for enacting a law. Thus, the failure to satisfy the presumption results in an epistemic failure in the former case (insufficient probability of guilt) and a moral failure in the latter case (injustice of the law).

coercion. This right is not violated by all instances of harmful coercion, but it is violated by instances of harmful coercion that do not have the right kind of moral justification. Second, harmful coercion is essential to criminal laws. Thus, *if* these laws lack the right kind of justification, then they violate individual rights. Finally, justice, in the sense at issue in the present context, requires respecting the rights of individuals. Hence, laws that lack the right kind of justification are unjust.

In the remainder of §3.1, I elaborate on this argument.

3.1.2 The Right Against Harmful Coercion

We have defined moral rights as agent-centered, enforceable moral constraints against certain kinds of ill-treatment of others. That is, to say that a person "has a right" not to be subject to certain treatment is to say that it would normally be ethically impermissible to treat the person in that way, even if doing so would prevent a larger (but comparable) amount of bad consequences for others, and it is morally appropriate to enforce this ethical prohibition through coercion. The existence of rights is supported by widely-shared intuitions about such cases as the Organ Harvesting and Framing cases, in which it is ethically wrong to sacrifice an individual for the sake of preventing harm to several others (§2.4.1).

There is one right that plays an especially large role in identifying unjust laws: the right against harmful coercion. This is a right not to be subjected to use or threats of physical force of a kind that set back one's interests.[3]

Why believe in such a right? The kind of intuitions that lead us to posit rights in the first place can be elicited for cases of harmful coercion in general. For instance, the Organ Harvesting case leads us to posit a right to life, since it is intuitively wrong to kill the healthy patient, even to prevent five deaths. Killing is only one, particularly extreme form of harmful coercion; we could devise examples involving lesser harms. As

---

[3] Some use the term "coercion" more restrictively, to cover only *wrongful* exercises of force (see Edmundson 1998, ch. 4), or more broadly, to include forms of coercion that do not involve physical force. I stipulate that "coercion" in my sense applies to the use or threat of physical force, whether justified or not.

long as the element of harmful coercion is retained, with roughly the same ratio of benefits to harms, and other features of the case are similar, common sense morality will continue to judge the action wrong. Thus, if one is faced with the option of beating up one innocent person to prevent five other innocent people from being beaten up, one should refuse to beat up the innocent person. If given the chance to falsely imprison one person for a year to prevent five other people from being falsely imprisoned for a year, one should refuse to imprison the innocent person. And so on. Among those who accept rights in general, the intuitions I have just cited are orthodox. It would be odd to hold that it is wrong to kill one person even to prevent five other deaths, yet permissible to engage in other forms of harmful coercion to prevent five times as many harms of a comparable kind. Thus, those who accept the right not to be killed should accept the broader right not to be harmfully coerced.

Why endorse a general right not to be harmfully coerced, rather than merely endorsing rights against each specific form of harmful coercion— a right not to be killed, a right not to be beaten, a right not to be falsely imprisoned, and so on? The answer is that, given my understanding of rights discourse, endorsing a right against each form of harmful coercion is semantically equivalent to endorsing a right against harmful coercion. To endorse a right against certain treatment is to say that it is wrong to engage in that treatment of others (except in certain conditions). If each specific form of harmful coercion is wrong (in certain conditions), then ipso facto, harmful coercion is wrong (in those conditions). Hence, if there is a right against each form of harmful coercion, then there is a right against harmful coercion.

Why posit a right specifically against *harmful* coercion, rather than against coercion in general? The reason is that, though rare, cases of harmless or even beneficial coercion exist, and it is preferable not to take a stand on whether such cases constitute rights violations. Consider the following case:

Suicide Prevention: A friend of yours plans to commit suicide by jumping off a bridge. Arriving at the bridge shortly before the friend is to jump, you physically restrain him from jumping. Afterwards, as you reasonably expected, your friend is treated for depression and goes on to live a happy and valuable life. Was your action wrong?

In this case, you *coerced* your friend, forcefully interfering with his plan of action, but this was beneficial rather than harmful to the "victim" of the coercion. Some would deny that this action violates a right. Others would hold that the action is a rights violation but nevertheless justified, perhaps because it produced vastly greater benefits than harms. But it is not necessary to enter into that debate, as it does not bear on the cases of injustice I aim to discuss below. To avoid needless debate concerning such cases as Suicide Prevention, we can stipulate that we are considering only cases of harmful coercion, that is, cases in which the person who is coerced is also thereby made worse off. In doing so, we are not denying that beneficial coercion violates rights; we are merely failing to take a stand on whether harmless or beneficial coercion violates rights. We are limiting ourselves to the uncontroversial stand against harmful coercion.

Now, why posit a right specifically against harmful *coercion*, rather than a right against harm in general? The reason is that there are many cases of non-coercive harms that do not violate rights. Consider:

Market Competition: You own a restaurant in Boulder. I open a restaurant across the street from yours and, through my delicious and ethically superior vegan options, manage to lure away most of your customers, ultimately driving you out of business.[4] Is this permissible?

In this case, my action is clearly permissible and not a rights violation, even though it harms you. To avoid classifying this case as a rights violation, we restrict ourselves to positing a right against being *coercively* harmed. In doing so, we are not denying that there are non-coercive harms that violate rights; we are merely failing to take a stand on which non-coercive harms, if any, violate rights.

---

[4] This would happen in the far away possible world in which the majority of diners were minimally ethical (see Huemer 2019).

3.1.3 In Defense of Prima Facie Rights

The right against harmful coercion is a prima facie right, not an absolute right. That is, despite the general right against harmful coercion, *some* cases of harmful coercion are nevertheless morally permissible. There are two kinds of reasons for this.

The first sort of reason is that the right is of finite weight and therefore can be *outweighed* by sufficiently important moral considerations. Thus, if violating one individual's rights were somehow necessary in order to prevent World War III, then one should violate that individual's rights. Most people find this judgment intuitive. In addition, this judgment is supported by the argument from risk:[5] suppose we hold that there is a right against harmful coercion that can never be outweighed. On this view, if an action definitely coercively harms a person, then the act cannot be justified regardless of the benefits. Now consider an action that is similar to one that definitely coercively harms a person, except that the *probability* of harming another person is less than one. A strong case can be made that, *if* we posit an absolute prohibition against coercive harms, then we must also posit an absolute prohibition against taking *any risk* of coercively harming. (Note that, if we are sometimes permitted to take some nonzero risk of harming individuals in a certain way, then with a sufficient number of such permissible actions, we can be practically assured of harming someone in that way.) But the view that one may never take any nonzero risk of coercively harming other persons would render normal human life impossible.

Of particular interest for our purposes, absolutism about rights would rule out any practicable criminal justice system. Presumably, punishing an innocent person is a violation of that person's rights. Suppose we hold that rights are absolute, such that it is always impermissible to knowingly punish an innocent person, regardless of any benefits to be obtained or harms to be avoided by doing so.[6] If we hold this view, what should we think about punishing individuals who have some nonzero *probability* of being innocent? If we hold that it is impermissible to punish anyone who

---

[5] Jackson and Smith (2006), Huemer (2010b).
[6] This view is taken, for example, by Anscombe (1981, pp. 39–40).

has any nonzero probability of being innocent, then we must dismantle the criminal justice system, since every person has *some* chance of being innocent. If, on the other hand, we hold that it is permissible to punish a defendant as long as the defendant's probability of guilt exceeds some threshold (where the threshold is one that can be met in some real cases), then we can be for all practical purposes assured that, over the course of many cases, the justice system will in fact punish some innocent individuals. Therefore, by operating a justice system, the state knowingly punishes some innocent individuals, as the cost of its ability to punish the guilty and deter crime in general.

For this reason, if we were to adopt an absolutist conception of rights, the case against the criminal justice system would be too easy. My aim is not to indict all realistically possible criminal justice systems. My aim is to identify specific, reasonably remediable flaws in the system of the present day United States. Thus, I adopt a non-absolutist notion of rights, on which rights can be outweighed by sufficiently large cost/benefit considerations.

The second sort of reason why harmful coercion can be justified, despite the general right against harmful coercion, is that there are qualifications or exceptions to the right, cases in which an act of harmful coercion does not count as a rights violation at all. One such exception is the case where harmful coercion is necessary to prevent or remedy the coercee's own wrongful, harmful coercion. Another exception applies when the coercee (with full information, and being mentally competent) *consents* to the harmful coercion. In these cases, the right against harmful coercion is not outweighed; rather, the right is suspended, such that the action need not produce much greater benefits than harms to be permissible.

None of these concessions weaken the case for a general right against harmful coercion, because the conditions for justifying harmful coercion are just the usual conditions for justifying forms of harsh treatment that we commonly say individuals possess rights against. Thus, we say that persons possess a right not to be killed, yet killing a person can be justified if necessary to prevent that person from wrongfully killing others, or perhaps if the person consents to be killed, or if the killing is necessary to prevent some vastly greater evil. The existence of these justifying conditions does not refute the claim of a right to life. Similarly, the existence of the analogous conditions for justifying harmful coercion is consistent with the existence of a general right against harmful coercion.

3.1.4 Laws Are Harmfully Coercive

All criminal laws are harmfully coercive to some individuals.[7] My claim here is of course not that all relevant laws are *overall* harmful, that is, harmful to society in general. My claim is that they are harmful to *some individuals*. If there were a law that was never broken, or if, when broken, the law was not enforced through legal punishment, then perhaps that law might fail to harm anyone. In fact, however, all laws restricting the behavior of individuals are sometimes broken, and these laws generally specify legal punishments to be imposed on violators. These punishments are predictably harmful to those who are punished; indeed, this is the *point* of punishment. That harm is also coercive. Prison sentences are imposed by physically compelling the convict to enter the prison and then forcibly confining him there for an extended period. Fines and other penalties are typically imposed by threatening to forcibly imprison the convict should the convict fail to pay the fine or otherwise fail to comply with the specified punishment.

Since all criminal laws call for such punishments, they are harmfully coercive to all who are punished for violating the laws. They may in addition be harmfully coercive to those who would have benefitted by engaging in the behavior that the law prohibits but are deterred from doing so by the law. Given the general right against harmful coercion, all laws are, presumptively, unjust. That is, they are unjust *unless* there exist adequate justifying conditions.

This conclusion allows for the possibility that most laws are nevertheless perfectly just, for perhaps the state regularly *has* sufficient justifying reasons for the harmful coercion entailed by its laws. The effect of the

---

[7] Are there any laws at all that fail to be harmfully coercive? The constitution, peace treaties, laws renaming government buildings, and laws specifying internal government procedures (where no punishment is specified for government officials' failure to follow the procedures) might be cases of laws that are not harmfully coercive. But these are not the sort of law we are concerned with here.

reasoning thus far is to shift the burden of justification: it is not necessary for the critic of a law to identify reasons why the law should not exist, apart from the general fact that some individuals are punished under that law. Given the existence of such punishment, it is the burden of the defender of a law to cite positive reasons to justify the law.

3.2 Drug Prohibition

3.2.1 Prohibition Violates Prima Facie Rights

There are many laws that fail to meet this burden of justification. Drug prohibition is perhaps the most important contemporary example. Not all recreational drugs are prohibited in the U.S.—most obviously, alcohol, tobacco, and caffeine are all legal for recreational use under state, federal, and local laws. But most other drugs that individuals use for recreational purposes (marijuana, cocaine, heroin, and so on) are legally prohibited. In recent years, many states have legalized marijuana for recreational or medical use, but marijuana remains illegal for any use under federal law, and other drugs remain illegal under both federal and state laws.[8] As of this writing, the drug laws account for nearly half a million inmates, or about 20% of the inmates in prisons and jails in the United States.[9] These individuals are directly suffering from extremely harmful coercion at the hands of the state.

In addition to the right against harmful coercion, there is a plausible argument that the drug laws violate individuals' rights to control their own bodies. If individuals have rights in general, then it is extremely plausible that these include rights over one's own body; indeed, one's body is the most plausible candidate for a thing that one has the right to control. If this is correct, it is hard to see how ingesting drugs would fail

---

[8] As of this writing, recreational marijuana is legal in eleven states plus the District of Columbia, and medical marijuana in an additional twenty-eight. Eleven states still prohibit all marijuana use (DISA Global Solutions 2020).

[9] Aggregating federal, state, and local jails and prisons, about 450,000 of the nation's 2.3 million prisoners have a drug charge as the most serious charge for which they are incarcerated (Wagner and Sawyer 2020).

to count as an exercise of those rights; the salient effects of drug use occur literally inside the user's body.

In light of the right against harmful coercion and the right to control one's own body, the drug laws are unjust *unless* there is a justification for them sufficient to outweigh or suspend these rights. To assess this, it is not necessary to identify every possible justification. It suffices to identify the reasons actually offered for prohibiting drugs and to examine whether any of these reasons is of a kind that plausibly either outweighs the rights of drug users or identifies an exception to these rights. If not, then it is reasonable to conclude that the presumption against law is undefeated and the drug laws are thus unjust.

3.2.2 Harm to Users

The most obvious reason for prohibition is harm to the user. Recreational drug users are in danger of becoming addicted. Overuse of drugs, especially addiction, can damage users' relationships with others, prevent them from maintaining steady employment, and generally interfere with non-drug-involving life activities. Some drugs have serious health harms, and in some cases overdose even leads to death. Serious problems do not occur in all cases, but drug prohibitionists argue that they happen often enough that it is best if no one is permitted to use certain drugs.

Do these reasons provide a justification for the law sufficient to overcome the prima facie right against harmful coercion? This question raises at least two important theoretical issues. First is the issue of *paternalism*: is it permissible to coerce individuals for their own good, restraining them, not from harming others, but from harming themselves? In the Suicide Prevention example (§3.1.2), you use force to restrain a friend from jumping off a bridge. Many would regard this use of force as justifiable, despite that the friend posed no threat to *others*. But note two differences between this case and that of the state's use of force against recreational drug users. One difference is that in Suicide Prevention, the friend's death is imminent and highly likely, whereas the state's coercion against drug users is designed to prevent harms in the further future that are, in any given case, speculative, with the most serious harm (death) being very rare.[10] Another difference is that in Suicide Prevention, your coercion is brief and only minimally harmful if at all. In the case of drug prohibition, the state's coercion is prolonged and extremely harmful, with drug convicts frequently spending years in prison. The drug prohibition case also raises questions about the proper function of government—what tasks government exists to perform—that do not arise in the Suicide Prevention case.

Above, I have emphasized the right of individuals against harmful coercion. Given the paternalistic rationale for drug prohibition, one might wonder whether the law qualifies as *harmful* coercion. Perhaps prohibition is beneficial to those who are coerced, because potential drug users are better off overall if they are forcibly restrained from using drugs. This claim has some prima facie plausibility in the case of individuals who are actually prevented from using recreational drugs by the laws. But those are not the chief targets of coercion with whom I am concerned. My chief concern is with those who *break* the law and are punished by the state for doing so, especially those who are sentenced to jail time. These individuals are forced to spend months or years of their lives in cages, surrounded by criminals. The prison environment is extremely unpleasant and dangerous, and it often hardens criminals and makes it more difficult for them to rejoin mainstream society. Being sent to prison does not even reliably stop individuals from using drugs *while in prison*, to say nothing of their lives after prison, and virtually no one thinks that prison rehabilitates criminals.[11] It is thus extremely implausible to claim that those punished by the state are rendered better off by the drug laws.

This brings us to the second theoretical issue raised by the "harm to users" justification for drug prohibition: to what extent is it permissible to coercively harm some individuals for the sake of benefitting *others*? The drug laws coercively impose serious harms on a large number of individuals who are caught possessing illegal drugs. This allegedly produces a

---

[10] The Centers for Disease Control (2019) estimates, for example, that 5 million Americans are current cocaine users, while in 2017, about 14,000 (0.3%) of users died from cocaine overdoses. Ritchie and Roser (2019) estimate that 71 million people worldwide have a "drug use disorder", while about 750,000 deaths per year are directly or indirectly caused by drug use (1% of the number of addicts).

[11] On the problems with incarceration, see Chap. 6 below.

greater benefit for others by deterring them from using those drugs. Even if true, this represents an extremely dubious ethical justification. As we saw in §2.4, it typically is not permissible to coercively harm a person to produce greater benefits, or prevent greater harms, for others. That is the point of positing a *right* against harmful coercion. In the case of drug prohibition, there are two further conditions that make the state's behavior even more problematic: (a) In the drug prohibition case, the people allegedly saved (those who would use recreational drugs if not for the laws against them) would only be in danger in the first place through their own voluntary, imprudent choices. (b) In the drug prohibition case, the people allegedly benefitted do not want the benefit—that is, the individuals who would use drugs if not for prohibition do not generally want the state to prohibit drugs.

A rough analogy would be if, in the Organ Harvesting case, the five transplant patients only needed transplants due to their own foolish and voluntary choice to damage their own organs, and if these transplant patients also did not want the doctor to take the healthy patient's organs. The Organ Harvesting case was already an example of an extremely immoral action. But these modifications would make it even more outrageous.

That is by way of explaining on a theoretical level why the "harm to users" argument for drug prohibition fails. Principles of individual rights do not contain an exception for the case where otherwise unjust harms can be deployed to deter third parties from making foolish life choices.

An easier way to see the failure of the "harm to users" rationale is to consider other cases in which individuals, without using drugs, harm themselves in ways qualitatively similar to how drug users sometimes harm themselves. If drug prohibition is justified because drug use sometimes harms users in certain ways, then presumably the state would also be justified in prohibiting citizens from *directly and intentionally* harming themselves in those same ways.

Thus, it is said that overuse of recreational drugs makes it difficult for individuals to maintain steady employment. On the other hand, it is possible for an individual to directly and intentionally fail to maintain steady employment—by, say, quitting one's job and refusing to seek another.

Would it be appropriate for the state to prohibit citizens from quitting their jobs and intentionally remaining unemployed?

It is said that drug use can damage users' relationships with their family and friends. It is also possible for an individual to directly and intentionally damage his or her relationships with others—for example, by divorcing one's spouse, refusing to speak to one's family, and so on. Would it be appropriate for the state to prohibit these actions?

It is said, finally, that drug use harms users' health. Suppose a person expressly decides to become unhealthy. He refuses to exercise, eats junk food all day, shares food with sick people, and never visits the doctor. The health risks of such behavior are comparable to or worse than the risks incurred by most illegal drug use; many thousands of Americans die prematurely due to such poor habits every year. Would it be appropriate to prohibit this behavior and send this person to prison?

In all of these cases, it seems that the proposed laws would not only fail to be expedient; they would go beyond the legitimate functions of the state and violate individuals' rights to control their own lives. If so, then drug laws surely cannot be justified on the grounds that drug use *might* cause the same results that citizens can permissibly pursue directly and intentionally.

3.2.3 Harm to Others

It is also said that drug use causes harm to others around the user, including the user's family, friends, employer, and neighbors, due to the tendency of drug users to become unreliable, unproductive, and unsympathetic people.[12]

As noted earlier (§3.1.2), not all harms that a person may cause render that person subject to just preventative or remedial coercion. For example, if I threaten to harm your business interests by setting up a competing business, I am not thereby legitimately open to defensive or retaliatory force by you. Therefore, it is not enough to ask whether drug users *harm* others by their use of drugs. It is necessary to ask whether users harm

---

[12] Wilson (1990), ONDCP (2002).

others *in relevant ways*, that is, ways that render them liable to defensive or retaliatory force.

Here we can employ a similar pattern of reasoning to that used above. It is possible for persons to *directly and intentionally* bring about the harms to others that often occur as side effects of drug use. One could directly choose to be an unproductive worker, an improvident and uncaring family member, and an apathetic neighbor disengaged from the good of the community. Almost no one believes that such choices should be criminalized, nor would they render one a just target of coercion. One may not, for example, justly beat one's spouse for being a poor provider. One may not hold employees prisoner in cages as punishment for insufficient productivity. One may not threaten one's neighbors with violence to compel them to be more engaged in the life of the community. This suggests that the harms in question are not the kind of harms that open one up to defensive or retaliatory force.

Why not? The theoretical explanation is that individuals only have rights against being harmed *in certain ways*. These ways include coercion and fraud but do not include, for example, general improvidence, laziness, or apathy. The principle of enforceability for rights dictates that harmful coercion is justified to prevent or remedy rights violations. It is not, however, justified to prevent or remedy non-rights-violating harms. Because an individual's failure to be a productive worker is not a rights violation, harmful coercion is not justified to prevent or remedy such lack of productivity. Similar points apply to being an improvident family member or apathetic citizen.

Sometimes, indeed, drug users and sellers violate others' rights. A great deal of theft and violence is associated with the drug trade. However, these harms cannot justify prohibition, for two reasons. First, because drug prohibition itself is the cause of most of this crime. The prohibition regime causes the product to be supplied by criminal organizations rather than by ordinary businesses. It drastically increases drug prices, which has the twin effects of driving users to crime to support their habits, and greatly enriching criminal organizations. It prevents those involved in drug transactions from relying on the state for protection and enforcement of agreements, thus inducing them to rely instead on private violence. These effects are so well-known that even staunch advocates for prohibition will on occasion admit that the prohibition regime increases crime.[13] In general, one is not justified in deploying harmful coercion in response to a particular threat if one's use of harmful coercion drastically worsens that very threat.

Second, it is not in general permissible to punish a person merely on the grounds that that person *might* have violated someone's rights, or might do so in the future if not punished. The present suggested justification for drug prohibition proposes that individual drug users are legitimate targets for coercive punishment by the state because drug users as a class are at increased risk of committing non-drug crimes. But defensive or remedial coercion generally requires strong evidence, specific to the individual target of coercion, that that individual in fact committed or will commit a rights violation. If, for example, the state determines that there is a 50% chance that I will become a thief at some future date, say, because I am poor but have expensive tastes, I am not thereby a legitimate target for coercive punishment by the state now. Only when I actually commit a theft, or attempt to do so, or at least plan to do so, do I become a valid target of defensive or retaliatory force. Similarly, merely possessing drugs, though this may mark one as being at increased risk for committing property crimes, does not render one justly subject to harmful coercion.

3.2.4 Other Problems of Prohibition

The largest harm of drug prohibition, as I have suggested, is the harm it directly imposes on those who are punished for drug crimes. There are, however, a number of other serious problems with the prohibition regime. Laws of this kind are difficult to enforce because a very large number of people want to engage in the behavior in question and do not believe it to be wrong, and because there is generally no victim willing to come forward to report the crime. As a result, the laws tend to be ineffectual, which tempts the state to take increasingly extreme measures. One measure is increasingly draconian penalties. On average, drug criminals are

---

[13] Wilson (1990).

sentenced to about 60 months in federal prisons, but sentences can be much longer.[14] It is possible to serve decades in prison for drug possession.[15] Another increasingly popular enforcement measure is known as "civil asset forfeiture", a process whereby law enforcement officials seize citizens' property (for example, a car, a pile of cash, or even a house), accuse *the property* of being involved in a crime, and then auction off the property to fill government coffers. This process only requires the government to show by a preponderance of the evidence, rather than beyond a reasonable doubt, that the property was involved in a crime, and this process may be used if the government loses the criminal case, or does not even bring a criminal case, against the property's owner.[16] Civil asset forfeiture is thus a mechanism for circumventing traditional protections of the rights of defendants. This has become more popular in the U.S. in recent years as a tool in the drug war. The drug laws have thus led to undermining long-standing norms of the justice system.

On a more speculative level, the prohibition of activities that large numbers of people have engaged in and do not consider wrong may breed general disrespect for the law. By recent estimates, 134 million Americans over the age of 11 have used some illegal drug at least once in their lifetimes (in most cases, marijuana).[17] This includes, by their own admission, at least three former Presidents, one former Vice President, one former Speaker of the House, and one Supreme Court justice.[18] All this makes it more difficult to take seriously the moral censure supposed to be attached to violations of the law.[19]

The drug laws make drug use itself more dangerous, since they cause drugs to be supplied by criminals rather than ordinary businesses, and they prevent effective regulation of the industry. For these reasons, drug users cannot be sure of the purity and concentration of the products they

---

[14] U.S. Department of Justice (2019, table 7).

[15] Louisiana law, for example, provides a sentence of up to twenty years in prison for a third conviction of drug possession (LA Rev. Stat. § 40:966(E)).

[16] Cassella (2007).

[17] Substance Abuse and Mental Health Services Administration (2019, table 1.1A).

[18] I refer to Barack Obama, George W. Bush, Bill Clinton, Al Gore, Newt Gingrich, and Clarence Thomas. Sources: Obama (2004, p. 93), Zeese (2002), Taipei Times (2005), Labaton (1991).

[19] This point, regarding overcriminalization in general, is advanced by Husak (2008, p. 12).

buy. The drug trade is pervaded by crime and violence due to prohibition. Drug prohibition drives up the prices of drugs, which tempts users to commit crimes to obtain drugs. The high prices at the same time make criminal organizations rich and increase the temptations for corruption by government officials interacting with the drug trade. All of this costs the government around $47 billion per year.[20] Despite all of these costs, the government's war on drugs has fared very poorly at actually stopping recreational drug use. Recent estimates suggest that about 28 million Americans have used some illegal drug (usually marijuana) in the last month. There is no way of knowing how much drug use would occur without prohibition, but the current situation hardly inspires confidence in the effectiveness of the laws.

It would take us too far afield to explore all of these problems with drug prohibition. They are nevertheless worth keeping in mind because they bear on the question of whether the drug war has sufficiently large benefits to justify overriding the prima facie rights of individual drug users against being harmfully coerced. Given the nature of rights as moral constraints, in order for prohibition to be justified, the policy would have to produce vastly greater benefits than the harms that the policy inflicts on drug users. This does not appear to be the case; rather, the prohibition policy has costs that are probably many times greater than its benefits.

3.2.5 Why Drug Laws Exist

I do not believe that the drug laws are the result of a reasonable mistake by government officials sincerely concerned with justice. The drug laws are the result of a failure to take justice seriously on the part of both voters and government officials. This is not a problem unique to the drug issue, of course; it is a widespread problem with democracy.

On the rare occasions when government officials attempt to justify the government's drug policy—including remarks made by politicians about the drug war, as well as official reports by the U.S. Office of National Drug Control Policy (ONDCP)—nearly all of the remarks given in

---

[20] Drug Policy Alliance (2020).

explanation for the policy consist of lists of harms of illicit drug use (including harms that are chiefly the result of prohibition itself) and hopeful speculation about how the government's efforts to stop drug use will shortly become much more effectual than they have been hitherto.[21] The rights of those incarcerated for drug offenses are virtually never considered. Almost never do officials mention, for example, the question of whether individuals have the right to control their own bodies and whether that right is violated by prohibition. Never or almost never do they mention the general right not to be harmfully coerced. Often, they misrepresent legalization advocates as chiefly driven by pessimism about the efficacy of prohibition.[22]

My complaint is not that government officials *reject* the right not to be harmfully coerced or the right to control one's body. Rather, the problem is that government officials fail to even *consider* the rights of those they are coercing, in a case in which such rights are obviously and centrally implicated. The same is true of most public discourse on the subject, aside from that of some legalization advocates. Having a genuine concern for justice is compatible with *disagreeing* with the idea of a general right against harmful coercion, or that of a right to control one's body. But it is not compatible with *indifference* to those ideas. One who is concerned for justice but disagrees with those rights claims might be expected to explain how he or she arrived at the conclusion that there are no such rights. (I assume that these rights claims are well-known and prima facie plausible.) Indifference is shown by the failure to consider the rights claims, even when one is ostensibly addressing opponents of one's favored policy and when the rights claims are obviously of central import to the disagreement.

If not concern for justice, what motivates drug prohibition? We can only speculate on this score, since politicians' statements cannot be taken at face value and public opinion surveys do not probe average citizens' *reasons* for their opinions. What seems likely is that politicians fear that

---

[21] ONDCP (2002, 2010).
[22] ONDCP (2002, p. 3).

support for legalization would tarnish their public image by associating them with drug users, thus causing them to lose conservative voters. Since most politicians are indifferent to the plight of drug users and others harmed by the drug laws, they are unwilling to risk a loss of popularity for the sake of helping drug users. These politicians may be right in their political calculations: some significant class of voters would indeed vote against any candidate who supported legalization, while a much smaller number would support a candidate solely for that reason. The likely reasons for this are extremely superficial. Most voters have next to no knowledge about drug policy issues and have never seriously considered such questions as whether prohibition violates individual rights. Surveys repeatedly show in general that most voters have almost no political knowledge. Their votes are largely based on vague emotional associations, including such factors as whether a given candidate is vaguely perceived as "on the side of" drug users.[23]

Thus, the ultimate reason why 450,000 Americans are behind bars is that some significant portion of ordinary Americans have negative feelings about them, and most voters and politicians are indifferent to the rights or interests of these prisoners. No part of this process was sensitive to justice. At no point in the process whereby those 450,000 people came to be imprisoned was there anyone taking up the question of the rights of the individual or the moral limits of the law. The judgment that locking these people up was *just* did not enter into the causal chain.

This point is a central aspect of my critique of the legal system. It is not merely that the legal system sometimes accidentally misses its target. It is that the system often goes badly wrong because it is not even *aiming* at justice. Those who make and enforce laws have placed many other pursuits ahead of justice, and often forgotten about justice entirely, when justice ought to be the foremost concern.

---

[23] There is extensive literature confirming the ignorance and irrationality of voters. See especially Achen and Bartels (2017), Huemer (2015), Caplan (2007), Somin (2013), Brennan (2016).

3.3 Immigration Restrictions

I have spent some time on the drug laws since they are the most salient example of unjust laws, the one for which the largest number of people are presently imprisoned, and the one that average citizens are most likely to be called upon to enforce as members of a jury. In this section, I will mention one other unjust law that is particularly important.[24]

Perhaps the most harmful class of contemporary unjust law is immigration restrictions, which prevent millions of individuals from effecting dramatic, permanent improvements to their lives by leaving impoverished, oppressive states. These laws are coercive: they direct government agents to physically bar migrants from entering the country and physically, forcefully remove immigrants who have already entered illegally. The laws are also extremely harmful to potential immigrants. Compare the following case:

> *Starving Marvin*: Marvin is in desperate need of food, without which he will soon starve. He plans to walk to a nearby marketplace to buy food. In the absence of outside interference, this plan would succeed. Sam, however, accosts Marvin on the road and physically bars Marvin from reaching the marketplace, knowing that this will result in Marvin's starvation. Does Sam thereby harm Marvin?

In this case, Sam's action obviously harms Marvin; it does not, for example, merely fail to benefit Marvin. This illustrates the principle that coercive interventions that *prevent* a person from *remedying* a problem that they would otherwise be able to remedy count as a kind of harm. Since it is also coercive, Sam's action is a prima facie rights violation.

Government restrictions on immigration are analogous to Sam's behavior in the Starving Marvin case (though usually less serious, since they rarely lead to death). The government coercively prevents would-be immigrants from bettering their situations, which is a kind of harm.

---

[24] For extended discussion, see Huemer (2010a).

3 Unjust Laws

Since the government's policy is also coercive, it is a prima facie rights violation. As such, the policy is unjust in the absence of some satisfactory justification.

Several justifications are offered by proponents of restriction. The most common arguments for immigration restrictions, however, do not cite any reasons that could plausibly be thought to either outweigh or create exceptions to the right against harmful coercion; rather, most arguments ignore the rights of potential immigrants. Thus, by far the most common argument is that immigrants compete with native-born workers for employment opportunities. Another common argument is that immigrants may change a nation's culture in ways the native population prefers not to occur. Both of these arguments fail for the same reason: it is not permissible to deploy harmful coercion against others, solely to secure something that one does not have a right to. One does not have a right to hold a particular job if the employer would prefer to employ someone else. Nor does one have a right to have the society around one practice the culture one prefers, or to have the culture of one's society not change. Because one has no right to these things, one may not deploy harmful force against others to secure them. It is not permissible, for example, to use physical force to stop someone from competing with oneself for a job, or to stop others from converting to a religion one disprefers. And if one may not do these things, third parties also may not thus deploy force on one's behalf for these kinds of reasons.

Another popular argument is that immigrants cost taxpayers money by consuming government services. However, *if* consuming government services is ethically permissible and not a rights violation, then it is difficult to see why immigrants would become just targets of harmful coercion merely because of their consumption of government services. Perhaps, therefore, the argument assumes that consumption of at least some government services (most likely, redistributive social welfare programs) is a violation of the rights of those who are forced to pay for those services. If so, however, the primary rights violation would be attributable to the government itself, and the government thus could not justly use it as a rationale for harmfully coercing would-be immigrants. The government would be morally obligated to end the rights-violating social programs *and* cease restricting the free movement of potential immigrants. Its failure to satisfy the first obligation would not give it any justification or excuse for failing to satisfy the second obligation. In general, one may not harmfully coerce a person solely because one has unjustly decided that if one does not do so, then one will instead violate someone else's rights.

Some argue that unrestricted immigration would alter the political institutions and culture of host nations in ways that would make the host nations more similar to the nations from which the immigrants came.[25] The consequences of this could be very serious, essentially converting prosperous, well-ordered societies into impoverished, corrupt, and even tyrannical states.

However, even if this concern is well-founded, it could not justify the majority of immigration restrictions. Even when one is justified in deploying harmful force against others to prevent some much worse outcome, one is obligated to adopt only the least harmful, least coercive means available. The government thus would be obligated to enact only the minimal restrictions thought to be necessary to avert the threatened corruption of social institutions. It is difficult to view the current regime as such a minimal intervention, since current policies place major barriers in the way of nearly all migrants from anywhere in the world. There is no effort on the part of the state to tailor its restrictions to those who pose a significant threat of undermining social institutions.

What would such an effort look like? The government could, for example, require immigrants (and even native-born citizens, for similar reasons) to demonstrate knowledge of American institutions and values. It could admit larger numbers of *legal residents* while strictly limiting those who are granted *citizenship*, where only citizens have voting rights. It could adopt guest worker programs for those from nearby nations whose primary reason for seeking entry is to earn wages. It could restrict migration from countries judged to be at high-risk for negatively influencing domestic institutions, while allowing open immigration from low-risk nations. All of these would be much less harmful than the current regime. If the government adopted any of these approaches, it would thereby display some concern for the rights of those on whom the burden of its coercion falls.

---

[25] Jones (2016).

3.4 Other Unjust Laws

The drug laws and immigration laws are only two of the largest examples of contemporary unjust laws. Many other cases could be cited, but it would take us too far afield to discuss other unjust laws in detail. Here, I will briefly review the most important criteria for unjust laws as well as the reasons why many unjust laws exist.

Justice requires that one respect the rights of others and give others their due. Unjust laws are generally laws that violate the rights of individuals or punish those who do not deserve to be punished. The right most commonly violated by the state is the right against harmful coercion. Cases such as Organ Harvesting and Framing (§2.4.1) show that it is very difficult to justify harmful coercion, and that it cannot be justified merely by citing larger but comparable benefits for others. However, harmful coercion may be justified when it produces *vastly* greater benefits. In addition, there is an exception for the case in which harmful coercion is required to prevent or remedy rights violations by the person who is to be harmed—in such cases, harmful coercion is typically permissible, even without vastly greater benefits.

Thus, for the most part, the just laws will be those under which the state punishes only those who would violate or have violated the rights of others. Laws prohibiting non-rights-violating behavior are normally unjust. In order to be permissible, such laws would have to at least produce vastly greater expected benefits than the expected harms they coercively impose. This condition, I believe, is virtually never satisfied.

Some prima facie plausible candidates for unjust laws, on this account, include laws against prostitution, laws against euthanasia or assisted suicide, laws against practicing a given profession without a license, minimum wage laws, and laws against buying or selling drugs without a prescription. It is plausible, though I shall not argue the point here, that none of these prohibited activities are rights violations. Hence, deploying harmful coercion against those who undertake those activities would incur a very high burden of justification, one which is unlikely to be met.

Why are there so many unjust laws? I have hinted at the major explanation above. The reason is that the process by which laws come about is by and large insensitive to justice considerations. Political leaders mainly attend to what sorts of positions will make them look vaguely good or bad to voters. Most voters, for their part, have almost no knowledge of, and have spent almost no time reflecting on, any given political issue. Thus, their political attitudes by and large consist only of the most superficial and unprincipled emotional responses. In many cases, voters are either indifferent or hostile to the plight of particular groups—for example, drug users, foreigners, prostitutes, or wealthy business owners—so that they feel no emotional discomfort at the prospect of coercively harming people of those types. Reflection on principles about rights and justice play almost no role in the formation of political positions, either for voters or for legislators.

Granted, lawmakers are sometimes moved by their own beliefs about what is good for society, rather than by the reactions of average voters. But even in these cases, there is little evidence of serious reflection on their part about rights and justice. Lawmakers virtually never spare a word for the rights of those who will be punished under a contemplated law.

The reason for this is a matter of speculation. Perhaps ideologies that defend the rights of unpopular groups are less emotionally satisfying than those that seek to restrict and hurt unpopular people. Perhaps the emotional rewards of exerting power over others crowd out concern for the rights of other persons. Or perhaps those with a strong commitment to respect for others' rights are simply less likely to seek political power to begin with. Whatever the reason, politicians' reasons for passing laws are largely indifferent to the requirements of justice.

3.5 The Trolley Exception

Earlier (§2.4), we introduced what might be called the Trolley Exception, the moral principle that permits agents to coercively harm others in situations like the following:

Trolley: A runaway trolley is headed for a group of five people, who will be killed unless the trolley is switched onto a side track, where it would instead kill only one. Is it permissible to turn the trolley away from the five toward the one?

Notwithstanding the general right against harmful coercion, it is plausible that turning the trolley is permissible. We cited three accounts of what differentiates this case from impermissible cases of harming one to benefit several others: (i) that in this case the harm would be a foreseen side effect rather than something *aimed* at, (ii) that the action would *divert* a threat rather than originating a threat, (iii) that the victim serves only as a potential impediment to benefitting the others, rather than a potential means to benefitting the others.

I have not discussed the Trolley Exception in connection with unjust laws until now because it does not plausibly make a difference to the evaluation of which laws are unjust. Consider, for example, the case of drug prohibition, whereby the state coercively imprisons individuals who are caught ingesting certain drugs, in the hope that this will deter others from using those same drugs. This is not a case in which the state merely diverts the harms of drug abuse from a larger group to a smaller group; rather, the state creates a new threat, the threat of being imprisoned by the state. In addition, the imprisonment of drug users is obviously something the state *aims* at, and the state's plan to deter others from using drugs could not be carried out if the drug offenders were all to escape. Hence, the people punished under the drug laws are a means to the state's goal of deterrence, not a potential impediment.

More generally, very few laws could plausibly be justified by the Trolley Exception. When the state passes a law, it creates a threat of punishment for those who disobey that law. As a rule, there will be no relevant persons who were under threat of punishment independent of the law, so the law will qualify as creating a new threat rather than diverting an existing threat. In enforcing the law, the state will expressly aim at punishing violators—for example, imprisoning or fining them; it is not the case that violators will merely wind up fined or imprisoned as a side effect of something else the state is doing. In general, imprisoning people for breaking a law simply does not on its face resemble turning the trolley in the Trolley case.

3.6 Just Laws

Despite what I have said, there are many laws that are perfectly just, including the vast majority of laws that people are convicted for violating—laws against theft, murder, assault, and so on. It is important to the credibility of my critique of unjust law that this critique *not* apply to these paradigmatically just laws. So it is worth taking a moment to discuss this.

I have claimed that all criminal laws are presumptively unjust. The murder law, for example, is "presumptively unjust" since it deploys harmful coercion against those convicted of murder—they are forcibly confined in prisons for long periods of time, often the rest of their lives. Furthermore, the threat of being imprisoned for murder is an original threat created by the state, not a diverted threat, and the state clearly *aims* at thus imprisoning murderers. The imprisonment of murderers prevents greater harms but not, in most cases, *vastly* greater harms, since most murderers, if set free, would not murder vast numbers of people.

All this sounds reminiscent of what I have said above about the drug laws and the immigration laws. So it might sound as though my views would, absurdly, make it difficult to defend laws against murder.

Of course this is not the case. It is trivial to defend murder laws on my view, since they fall under the enforceability-of-rights principle. Murder violates rights and thus subjects one to retaliatory coercion. The same is true of theft, assault, and other obvious rights violations.

This illustrates a point about the structure of my earlier arguments. The initial presumption is that one should not harmfully coerce. This simply means that one needs an adequate reason for engaging in harmful coercion. If one's reason is that the harmful coercion is a necessary and proportionate response to a rights violation, this suffices to justify one's action. One does not then need to consider whether the action diverts or originates a threat, whether the harm is aimed at or merely foreseen, or whether the benefits are vastly greater than the harm. One only needs the one adequate reason.

The problem with the unjust laws, such as drug prohibition and immigration restrictions, is that they do not serve to enforce rights. Drug users do not violate any rights by ingesting drugs recreationally, nor do immigrants violate any rights by entering the country and doing work for hire. This sets off the search for other justifications for harmfully coercing these people. The requirements for such justifications are rightly taken to be very demanding. We should not use harmful force against others lightly.

3.7 Ideological Controversy

One might be tempted to object that my critique of allegedly unjust laws presupposes a controversial, libertarian political ideology. For I have seemingly assumed that the only legitimate function of law is to protect individual rights, an assumption rejected by other ideologies. Other ideologies may claim, for instance, that law legitimately serves to promote moral virtue, to promote the good of society, or to reduce economic inequality. Therefore, one might think, those who do not subscribe to libertarian ideology need not be troubled by my allegations against the legal system.

This objection is not correct. Libertarianism *is* controversial, but I have *not* assumed libertarianism. My premises are non-ideological intuitions shared by nearly all members of our society, whether liberal, conservative, libertarian, or other. For example, I assume that it is wrong to kill the healthy patient in the Organ Harvesting case (§2.4.1). This is not a libertarian political premise; this is a moral judgment that seems obvious to nearly everyone. I argue that intuitions of this kind support the ascription of rights, including a general right against harmful coercion. I assume also that it is wrong to kill the hermit in the Island Hermit case, and I argue that this shows moral rights to be independent of law (§2.3). Again, this is not a libertarian ideological assumption.

In discussing particular laws, I deploy intuitions about analogous cases—for instance, the intuition that Sam wrongs Starving Marvin by preventing Marvin from reaching the marketplace (§3.3). These, too, are non-ideological intuitions widely shared by those of varying political orientations. I have also argued that one ought to accept ethical intuitions as a source of justification for moral beliefs, provided that one accepts morality at all. Of course, my *conclusions* are congenial to libertarianism. But this cannot be a principled reason to set them aside.

As noted, there are a number of alternative political ideologies that conflict with my central *conclusions*. This does not, however, show my conclusions in this chapter to be weakly supported. None of these alternative ideologies comes close to being as obvious or as widely accepted as the sort of *premises* from which I have argued. In the great majority of cases, those who support a more extensive role for law—for instance, those who find drug and immigration laws proper—have simply failed to confront the issues I have raised. They have not, for example, developed an alternative theory that explains why we have no right against harmful coercion or why these laws fail to violate that right if we have it; they simply have not considered the right against harmful coercion. They do not reject the underlying ethical intuitions I have appealed to; they simply have not considered how those intuitions bear on the justification of their favored laws. For this reason, the existence of large numbers of people who are ideologically in conflict with my conclusions in this chapter is not a strong reason for doubting those conclusions. Almost certainly, our current legal system contains a number of laws that unjustly constrain and harm large numbers of individuals, in violation of their moral rights.

References

ABC News. 2010, August 4. Feds' Conviction Rate Bad Sign for Blago. http://abclocal.go.com/wls/story?section=news/local&id=7593302. Accessed 3 Oct 2012.

Achen, Christopher H., and Larry M. Bartels. 2017. *Democracy for Realists: Why Elections Do Not Produce Responsive Government*. Princeton: Princeton University Press.

Anscombe, G.E.M. 1981. *Ethics, Religion, and Politics: The Collected Philosophical Papers of G. E. M. Anscombe*. Vol. 3. Minneapolis: University of Minnesota Press.

Brennan, Jason. 2016. *Against Democracy*. Princeton: Princeton University Press.

Caplan, Bryan. 2007. *The Myth of the Rational Voter*. Princeton: Princeton University Press.

Cassella, Stefan D. 2007. Overview of Asset Forfeiture Law in the United States. *United States Attorneys' Bulletin* 55: 8–21.

Centers for Disease Control. 2019. Other Drugs. https://www.cdc.gov/drugoverdose/data/otherdrugs.html. Accessed 25 June 2020.

DISA Global Solutions. 2020. Map of Marijuana Legality by State. https://disa.com/map-of-marijuana-legality-by-state. Accessed 25 June 2020.

Drug Policy Alliance. 2020. Drug War Statistics. https://www.drugpolicy.org/issues/drug-war-statistics. Accessed 26 June 2020.

Edmundson, William A. 1998. *Three Anarchical Fallacies: An Essay on Political Authority*. Princeton: Princeton University Press.

Huemer, Michael. 2010a. Is There a Right to Immigrate? *Social Theory and Practice* 36: 429–461.

———. 2010b. Lexical Priority and the Problem of Risk. *Pacific Philosophical Quarterly* 91: 332–351.

———. 2015. Why People Are Irrational About Politics. In *Philosophy, Politics, and Economics*, ed. Jonathan Anomaly, Geoffrey Brennan, Michael Munger, and Geoffrey Sayre-McCord, 456–467. Oxford: Oxford University Press.

———. 2019. *Dialogues on Ethical Vegetarianism*. New York: Routledge.

Husak, Douglas. 2008. *Overcriminalization: The Limits of the Criminal Law*. Oxford: Oxford University Press.

Jackson, Frank, and Michael Smith. 2006. Absolutist Moral Theories and Uncertainty. *Journal of Philosophy* 103: 267–283.

Jones, Garett. 2016. Do Immigrants Import Their Economic Destiny? *Economics*, September 17. https://evonomics.com/do-immigrants-import-their-economic-destiny-garrett-jones/. Accessed 26 June 2020.

Labaton, Stephen. 1991. Thomas Smoked Marijuana But Retains Bush Support. *New York Times*, July 11, p. A17. https://www.nytimes.com/1991/07/11/us/thomas-smoked-marijuana-but-retains-bush-support.html. Accessed 26 June 2020.

Obama, Barack. 2004. *Dreams from My Father*. New York: Random House.

ONDCP (White House Office of National Drug Control Policy). 2002. *National Drug Control Strategy 2002*. Washington, DC: Government Printing Office. https://www.ncjrs.gov/pdffiles1/ondcp/192260.pdf. Accessed 26 June 2020.

———. 2010. *National Drug Control Strategy 2010*. Washington, DC: Government Printing Office. https://obamawhitehouse.archives.gov/sites/default/files/ondcp/policy-and-research/ndcs2010.pdf. Accessed 26 June 2020.

Ramseyer, J. Mark, Eric B. Rasmusen, and Manu Raghav. 2008. Convictions Versus Conviction Rates: The Prosecutor's Choice. Harvard Law and Economics Discussion Paper No. 611. http://papers.ssrn.com/sol3/papers.cfm?abstract_id=1108813. Accessed 3 Oct 2012.

Ritchie, Hannah, and Max Roser. 2019. Opioids, Cocaine, Cannabis and Illicit Drugs. Our World in Data. https://ourworldindata.org/illicit-drug-use. Accessed 25 June 2020.

Somin, Ilya. 2013. *Democracy and Political Ignorance*. Stanford: Stanford University Press.

Substance Abuse and Mental Health Services Administration. 2019. *Results from the 2018 National Survey on Drug Use and Health: Detailed Tables*. Rockville: Center for Behavioral Health Statistics and Quality, Substance Abuse and Mental Health Services Administration. Retrieved from https://www.samhsa.gov/data/. Accessed 26 June 2020.

Taipei Times. 2005. Bush Admits to Smoking Pot in Taped Discussion. *Taipei Times*, February 21, p. 7. http://www.taipeitimes.com/News/world/archives/2005/02/21/2003224003. Accessed 26 June 2020.

U.S. Department of Justice, Bureau of Justice Statistics. 2019. *Federal Justice Statistics, 2015–2016*. https://www.bjs.gov/content/pub/pdf/fjs1516.pdf. Accessed 25 June 2020.

Wagner, Peter, and Wendy Sawyer. 2020, March 24. *Mass Incarceration: The Whole Pie 2020*. Prison Policy Initiative, https://www.prisonpolicy.org/reports/ie2020.html. Accessed 24 June 2020.

Wilson, James Q. 1990. Against the Legalization of Drugs. *Commentary* 89: 21–28.

Zeese, Kevin. 2002, October 31. Four that Didn't Get Caught. Journey for Justice press release. http://www.journeyforjustice.org/archive/0201autumn/07WashingtonDC/press/J4JPressRelease10-02.html. Accessed 26 June 2020.

4

The Price of Justice

4.1 The Price of Legal Services

There are few threats more frightening to Americans than the threat to embroil someone in legal trouble. An illustrative case occurred at a nursing home in California in 2013. An 87-year-old woman living at the facility had stopped breathing, and a nurse on staff called 911, the local emergency services. The 911 dispatcher pleaded with the nurse to start CPR, knowing that the resident would not survive without immediate assistance. The nurse refused, citing company policy. The dispatcher assured the nurse that she could not be sued if anything went wrong during the resuscitation attempt and that the local emergency services would assume all liability, yet the nurse remained unpersuaded. The resident died soon after.[1] The dispatcher's assurances to the nurse reflect common knowledge of American culture: Americans have come so far in our fear of our own legal system that a nurse might plausibly be deterred from trying to *save someone's life* by the fear of a lawsuit.

---

[1] Wozniacka (2013). The family supported the nurse's decision, having been informed in advance of the company's policy. In fairness, the resident would most likely have died even with CPR, as most resuscitation attempts fail (Murphy et al. 1994), and it is not clear whether fear of legal liability was behind the company's policy.

Americans do not only fear losing a legal dispute; we fear *getting involved* in a legal dispute in any manner, whether one is in the right or not. As soon as one is sued, let alone prosecuted, whether rightly or wrongly, one expects to endure months or years during which the legal threat hangs over one's head, and one is almost guaranteed to lose thousands to tens of thousands of dollars, no matter the outcome. On average, consumers who suffer the misfortune of needing legal services can expect to pay $260 per hour for their lawyer's time. The total cost for a criminal defense averages around $4000 (more if one goes to trial); for a divorce, $13,000. Lawsuits that go to trial typically cost tens of thousands of dollars.[2] The averages, however, do not tell the whole story. Part of the story behind Americans' fear of the legal system is about *risk*, since costs for legal cases can vary from thousands to *hundreds* of thousands of dollars and usually are not known in advance.[3]

Even at the "inexpensive" end of legal services, these costs are prohibitive for ordinary people. The average American earns just $34,000 per year, many have no savings, and most would have to empty their bank accounts for even a small legal case.[4]

This obviously poses a problem for potential consumers of legal services. But many products are expensive without raising an issue of justice. Air travel is expensive, yet no one deems this situation *unjust*. My claim in this chapter is that the high cost of legal services is not merely unfortunate; it represents an *injustice* attributable *to the state*. The expense of legal services differs from most other cases of expensive products in three ways: first, government policy is largely to blame for high price levels in the legal arena; second, the government has a duty to provide justice; third, the high costs of legal services make the government a tool of unjust actions by other agents.

---

[2] Cost estimates from Henderson (2017), Thumbtack (2019), Nolo (2020), Hannaford-Agor and Waters (2013, p. 7).

[3] In a survey conducted by the Federal Judicial Center in 2009, litigation costs for defendants in federal lawsuits ranged from $5000 at the 10th percentile to $300,000 at the 95th percentile (Gerety 2011, p. 16).

[4] Median personal income was $33,706 in 2018 (Federal Reserve Bank of St. Louis 2019). As of 2013, the average American bank balance was $4436, and 40% had less than $500 (Lake 2020).

4.2 The State's Responsibility for Legal Prices

There are two ways in which the government may contribute to exorbitant prices in the legal services industry: by restricting supply, and by increasing demand. Both methods are in widespread use by government in the U.S.

4.2.1 Supply Factors: Licensing

In every state within the U.S., as well as all or nearly all other countries, it is illegal to practice law, including offering legal advice in exchange for money or appearing in court on behalf of a client, without permission from the government. This is a direct restriction on the supply of legal services. Economic theory uncontroversially predicts an increase in prices due to such laws, and empirical studies consistently confirm this.[5]

When the state erects barriers to entering a profession, the higher the barriers are, the more they impact prices. For lawyers, the licensing requirements are among the most onerous of any profession. Besides passing the bar examination, most states require aspiring lawyers to obtain a bachelor's degree, followed by a law degree, for a total of seven years of higher education.[6] The financial cost of this education averages over $200,000.[7] Therefore, the prices of legal services must be high enough to make it worthwhile for prospective lawyers to spend seven years and over $200,000 obtaining permission to practice. Since these costs must be paid up front, the expected returns on this investment must compensate for the delay as well as the risk involved. This forces legal services to be extremely expensive.

---

[5] For an even-handed review of the evidence, see the report on licensing laws prepared jointly by President Obama's Treasury Department, Council of Economic Advisors, and Labor Department. The report notes that "the evidence on licensing's effects on prices is unequivocal: many studies find that more restrictive licensing laws lead to higher prices for consumers" (U.S. Department of the Treasury et al. 2015, p. 14).

[6] The government requires a law degree, and law schools require a bachelor's degree for admission; hence, the de facto requirement is for two degrees. Several states, however, allow an applicant to study under a judge or practicing attorney in lieu of obtaining a law degree.

[7] Rose (2019).

4.2.2 Demand Factors: Complexity

In addition to restricting supply, the government creates demand for legal services. In one sense, this is obvious: legal services are mainly services that assist people in interacting with the government—prevailing in government courts, complying with government rules, and so on. For this reason, any government that permits a legal industry will create some demand for legal services. But the government in the U.S. creates far more demand than necessary.

The first way in which it does this is through creating rules and procedures that are extremely difficult to learn. For one limited measure of regulatory complexity, the Code of Federal Regulations grew from 18,000 pages in 1938 (the first year it was published) to 186,000 pages in 2019.[8] The commands issued by the government are so voluminous and complicated that universities house separate libraries devoted to writings about them. Furthermore, most of the law, including statutes, regulations, as well as case law, is written in language incomprehensible to most people, popularly known as "legalese".[9] The style is illustrated by the following sentence from a letter by the Bishop of Blackburn:

> AND WHEREAS We have consented to the said period being so brought to an end and to the exercise of such right of presentation NOW WE HEREBY DECLARE that the said period shall come to an end on the date hereof and that the said vacancy in the said Benefice of Ansdell and Fairhaven Saint Paul in Our said Diocese of Blackburn may thereupon be filled.[10]

The problem is both qualitative and quantitative: individual legal doctrines are often difficult to understand in themselves, and there is too much legal doctrine for any human being to learn more than a tiny fraction of it. This creates the demand for an industry of experts to help people navigate these bewildering rules.

---

[8] U.S. Office of the Federal Register (2020).

[9] A popular joke asks, "What do you get when you cross a lawyer with the Godfather?" The answer: "I'm gonna make you an offer you can't understand."

[10] Quoted in Plain English Campaign (2011).

Most of the mass of contemporary law consists of regulations affecting businesses. One might therefore assume that this affects mainly the prices of corporate lawyers, rather than personal lawyers. But the prices of corporate legal services affect the prices of all legal services, because labor in one area of law is to some degree substitutable for labor in another. The high price of corporate legal services draws people who might otherwise practice personal law to practice corporate law. This diminishes the supply of personal lawyers and increases prices for personal legal services, which must remain high enough to keep a sufficient number of people working as personal lawyers.

4.2.3 Demand Factors: Overcriminalization

Whenever the state makes a law, assuming that the law will be enforced, the state thereby increases the demand for legal services. There will be prosecutions under that law, which will require additional labor by prosecutors, defense attorneys, and judges. If it is an unnecessary law, then it causes a needless increase in the prices of legal services. For reasons explained above (§4.2.2), increased demand in one area of law tends to raise prices for legal services generally.

If this were to occur only occasionally, the effect would be minor. In fact, as we have seen in chapter 3, the government has created unjust laws that result in a great many prosecutions. At the federal level, the most common type of prosecution is for immigration offenses, followed by drug offenses and firearms offenses.[11]

4.2.4 Demand Factors: The Threat of Legal Harm

Most legal cases incur thousands to tens of thousands of dollars in legal fees. The most expensive cases cost millions. Wealthy customers hire expensive attorneys, sometimes paying over a thousand dollars an hour. When Clarence Darrow, widely considered America's greatest criminal

---

[11] TRAC reports (2020a, b, c, d, e).

defense lawyer in the early twentieth century, was accused of a crime, even *he* hired an attorney rather than defend himself.[12]

Why would anyone pay so much money for legal assistance? Part of the answer is that very large interests are often at stake in legal cases. That is, people face very *serious threats* from the legal system. Criminal defendants fear being imprisoned by the government and are thus induced to expend a great deal of money to avoid or reduce jail time. Civil defendants fear being forced to pay large sums of money to plaintiffs. Plaintiffs, for their part, seek to convince the state to transfer large amounts of money from defendants to themselves.

By itself, however, this would not explain the willingness to pay large legal fees. To explain that, we must assume in addition that clients expect that hiring a lawyer *affects the outcome* of a legal proceeding—in particular, that it significantly increases one's odds of obtaining a favorable result from the legal system, or avoiding an unfavorable result, with better odds for more expensive lawyers.

Social scientists have conducted many empirical studies of the impact of legal representation on legal outcomes. Though quantitative estimates of the impact vary widely, most studies agree with the common understanding that legal representation dramatically improves one's chances of prevailing in legal proceedings.[13] This effect appears to be mainly due to lawyers' knowledge of legal procedures.[14]

4.3 From Causation to Culpability

4.3.1 When Costs Are Unjust

Some ways of imposing costs on others are unjust, while others are perfectly acceptable. For instance, if I impose a cost on you by fairly competing with you in business, there is no injustice in this, for you have no

---

[12] Cowan (1994).

[13] In Sandefur's (2015) review of seventeen studies, the effect of legal representation varies from rendering one 100% less likely to prevail (in one study, some people without lawyers won their cases, while all the lawyers lost), to rendering one 2300% more likely to prevail.

[14] Lederman and Hrung (2006), Sandefur (2015).

right against fair business competition. If, however, an action is a violation of someone's rights, then any additional costs predictably imposed by that action are unjust harms attributable to the agent. My case for injustice in the legal system therefore remains incomplete. I have argued that government is causally responsible for high costs sustained by consumers of legal services. It remains to argue that these costs are predictable results of rights-violating behavior by the state.

This obviously is not true of all policies that contribute to high legal service prices. Plausibly, the state is not only permitted but obligated both to prosecute suspected criminals and to allow accused criminals the benefit of legal counsel. This inevitably contributes to demand for legal services, but there is no injustice in this. Similarly, the state is justified in preventing at least some individuals from practicing law, such as practitioners who have used their law practice to commit crimes or who have otherwise committed serious breaches of legal ethics. Excluding these practitioners raises prices in the industry, yet there is again nothing unjust in this.

4.3.2 Licensing

Other ways that the state contributes to legal service prices are less innocent. On the face of it, the idea that it should be illegal for me to inform others about the law, and to be paid for doing so, seems absurd. Granted, if I provide *false* information, which my customers rely on to their detriment, then I may reasonably be held to account. But surely I violate no one's rights by providing *accurate* information about the law as it applies to a particular case. Surely this action is not converted into a rights violation if the recipients of this information, reasonably enough, pay me for my time. And surely it is not the case that, to avoid violating someone's rights, I must first obtain two degrees which will cost seven years and over $200,000. But if I am violating no one's rights by offering paid legal advice, then it would be prima facie unjust to punish me for engaging in this occupation. As discussed earlier (§3.1), laws are presumptively unjust; thus, if there is no adequate justification for licensing requirements, they are unjust laws.

How might licensing laws be justified? To begin with, it is plausible to hold that one who plans to offer advice to others on any matter of great import is ethically obligated to make reasonable efforts to ensure that that advice is well-founded. I should not advise others on legal, medical, career, or parenting decisions, without having some minimum level of knowledge and understanding in these areas. One might think that licensing laws only enforce this preexisting moral requirement.

As an aside, it is interesting that few people support licensing laws for the offering of career advice, parenting advice, romantic advice, or any other kind of advice for which there is not a well-established industry devoted to that kind of advice, despite the fact that low-quality advice in these other areas can cause serious, long-term harm. The licensing schemes that are actually in place strike us as natural and intuitive; those that differ widely from the status quo strike us as risible. In fact, the reason why there are no licensing laws for the dispensing of career, parenting, or romantic advice is that there are not large and politically influential industries devoted to these things; there was therefore no one to lobby for such laws.

To return to the moral obligation to ensure that one's advice is well-founded: one might argue that the government is justified in enforcing (some of) our moral obligations to each other, and that this is what licensing laws do in this case. Prospective lawyers must take the bar exam to prove to the state that they are sufficiently knowledgeable to responsibly practice law. But note that in most cases, moral obligations are enforced by either punishing individuals or allowing them to be sued, if and when they are found to have actually violated the obligation in question; we do not in general enforce moral obligations by requiring individuals to prove in advance that they are unlikely to violate their duties. For example, it is morally wrong to steal from other people, and the duty not to steal is enforced by punishing people who are found to have actually stolen. It is not enforced, nor should it be enforced, by requiring everyone to prove to the government that they have not stolen, or that they are not likely to steal. It is unclear, then, why legal practitioners must prove to the government that they are not going to give incompetent legal advice; why would it not be sufficient to allow legal practitioners to be punished or sued if and when they are proven to have actually given incompetent legal advice?

Most defenders of licensing requirements claim that the laws are needed to ensure quality and protect consumers. There are two problems with this argument. First, empirical studies of the effects of licensing regimes generally do not find this effect. A report prepared by President Obama's economic advisors in 2015 concluded, "most research does not find that licensing improves quality or public health and safety."[15] A survey of nineteen studies of licensing requirements reported that just three studies found overall positive effects on quality, four found overall negative effects, and the rest found unclear, mixed, or neutral effects.[16] This may at first seem surprising, since licensing requirements presumably at least eliminate some very low-quality practitioners. However, they also reduce competition, and competition tends to improve quality; hence, licensing regimes can actually worsen quality.

The second problem is that even if licensing requirements only eliminated low-quality providers, this still would not benefit consumers. The result of eliminating all low-quality lawyers is not that all who need legal services then receive high-quality services. The result is that the total supply of legal services is reduced by about the amount that the low-quality lawyers would have provided. If the low-quality lawyers would have provided services to one million customers, the result of excluding these providers is that about one million people have no legal services.[17] Prices will rise until this result is achieved. The people who are priced out of the legal services market must then either represent themselves, forego whatever action they would have taken that would have required legal services, or proceed with the action without the benefit of legal advice. In recent years, courts have seen increasing numbers of litigants representing themselves, though most of these *pro se* litigants report being unable to understand what is said in court.[18] It is difficult to argue that these people are well served by laws designed to protect them from hiring low-quality lawyers.

---

[15] U.S. Department of the Treasury et al. (2015, p. 13; cf. p. 58, table 1).
[16] McLaughlin et al. (2014).
[17] David Friedman (1989, ch. 7) makes this point regarding doctors and medical licensing. However, there are two complications. First, some customers will merely consume less legal services than they otherwise would have, rather than no services. Second, the increase in prices may cause other, high-quality providers to enter the market who otherwise would not have done so. Thus, fewer than one million customers will go entirely without legal services.
[18] Dugan (2017).

There are alternatives to the status quo that would have much smaller adverse impacts on competition and prices in the legal industry. For instance, the state could simply punish practitioners if and when they are found to have actually given incompetent legal advice. Or, to avoid contributing to the problem of overcriminalization, we could simply rely on the existing tort system, whereby lawyers guilty of malpractice may be required to compensate the clients whom they harm. Alternately, if licensing is for some reason necessary, the requirement to obtain a law degree could be eliminated in favor of an exam-only method of certifying expertise. These alternatives would drastically reduce the barriers to entry into the legal profession. They would thus increase competition and reduce prices in the industry. If the government's chief concern is for the benefit of consumers, why has it not adopted some such alternative?

The most obvious explanation is that the purpose of the licensing regime is to make entering the legal profession burdensome, so as to reduce competition and raise prices. Lawyers not only control the judicial branch of government; they have dominated the U.S. legislature since the founding of the nation and have usually headed the executive branch as well.[19] Moreover, lawyers make up the state bar associations and licensing boards that determine who should be allowed to practice law in their state. It is not surprising, therefore, that the existing regime is extremely profitable for lawyers.

It is not my view, however, that legislators or bar associations, in crafting the requirements to practice law, explicitly asked themselves, "What set of rules would maximize profits for existing lawyers?" My view is that lawyers, like people in every profession, are cognitively biased toward their own self-interest. They are aware of basic facts about how possible systems of rules affect their own financial interests. This awareness influences how they evaluate arguments about those rules, making it easier for them to appreciate any arguments in favor of those rules that benefit themselves, and harder to appreciate arguments against those rules. As

---

[19] Lawyers have made up a majority of the Senate in every year for the past two centuries and in most years a majority of the House as well (Bonica 2017, p. 3). Lawyers are less well-represented in state legislatures, where only about 17% have a law degree, though even there, legal services remains the most well-represented single industry (Kurtz 2015). As of this writing, 26 of America's 45 Presidents have been lawyers (Wikipedia 2020).

Upton Sinclair wrote, "It is difficult to get a man to understand something, when his salary depends on his not understanding it."[20] This self-interested bias, together with the political power of lawyers, is the central explanation for why the legal profession has the onerous licensing requirements that it does. This makes it fair to say that the purpose of these requirements is to drive up prices, even if few legislators have consciously adopted that goal.

4.3.3 Complexity

There are understandable reasons for much of the complexity of modern law. Some of the growth of modern legal doctrine simply results from necessary clarifications to what the law requires in an increasing range of circumstances. Furthermore, laws are written in complicated, unnatural language because they are designed to cover a wide range of contingencies and to exclude loopholes. Ordinary individuals are not accustomed to this type of language and therefore have difficulty following it, because the norms of ordinary conversation are designed for cooperative communication rather than communication involving ingenious and litigious parties bent on exploiting any ambiguity. For these reasons, some need for legal expertise is to be expected even under an optimally designed state.

Having acknowledged this, it remains difficult to view the status quo as anything close to the optimal level of legal complexity. Figure 4.1 shows the growth of the Code of Federal Regulations over the history of its publication, from 18,000 pages in 1938 to 186,000 pages today.[21] To put this in perspective for philosophically-minded readers, I have included a bar at the end representing the length of the collected works of Aristotle, which come in at 3300 pages. It is on its face implausible that over 186,000 pages of commands issued by the federal government are genuinely necessary, or that in most years, the government discovers new, dangerously underregulated matters that call for thousands of additional pages of regulations.

---

[20] Sinclair (1994, p. 109).
[21] U.S. Office of the Federal Register (2020).

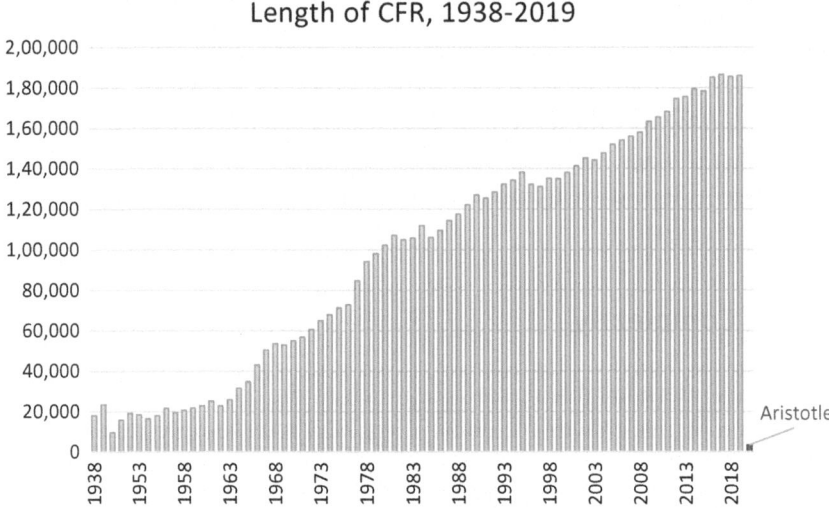

Fig. 4.1 Length of the Code of Federal Regulations

Government agencies regularly project large net benefits from their regulations.[22] However, retrospective studies of regulations by academic economists usually find overall net costs. Ronald Coase, Nobel laureate economist and editor of the *Journal of Law and Economics* for 18 years, reported in an interview that his journal had published many studies of the effects of regulations during his time as editor. According to Coase, the results were uniformly negative: the regulations studied made products more expensive and less adapted to consumers' needs. Asked for an example of a bad regulation, Coase replied:

> I can't remember one that's good. Regulation of transport, regulation of agriculture—agriculture is a, zoning is z. You know, you go from a to z, they are all bad. There were so many studies, and the result was quite universal: The effects were bad.[23]

In fairness, the regulations selected for study by economists were not a random sample from all regulations; economists writing for Coase's

---

[22] U.S. Office of Management and Budget (2017).
[23] Hazlett (1997).

journal may have selected relatively controversial regulations for study, rather than regulations whose benefits were widely accepted. Thus, we should not conclude (nor does Coase claim) that *all* regulations are harmful. Nevertheless, it is likely that many are.

Most academic studies concern particular regulations, rather than the effect of regulation in general. Among the very few general studies of regulation was a 1991 study that estimated the overall effect of federal economic and social regulations in the United States as a net cost of $44 billion per year.[24] A 2013 study estimated that regulations added since 1949 had caused a decrease in the economic growth rate of about two percentage points per year. Compounded over many years, this decrease in the growth rate has an enormous impact. The authors concluded, "GDP at the end of 2011 would have been $53.9 trillion instead of $15.1 trillion if regulation had remained at its 1949 level."[25] Bearing in mind that a law that is not adequately justified is unjust, it seems likely that a large number of regulations are unjust, as are the costs that they predictably impose.

Turning now to the difficulty of understanding legal language, the state needs to strike some balance between excluding loopholes and producing legal doctrines understandable to non-lawyers. Lawyers may appreciate legal language, but it acts as a barrier to understanding for the rest of the population. The incomprehensibility of the law to ordinary citizens is not merely unfortunate. It is an issue of justice, because the government that writes the law also holds individuals accountable for following that law, whether they understand the law or not, under the doctrine that "ignorance of the law is no excuse".

In some cases, understanding of the law is irrelevant to culpability, since what the law prohibits is something that all mentally competent adults should know to be wrong. For example, it does not matter if the statutes prohibiting murder are written in incomprehensible language, since one should know not to murder others irrespective of what the law says.

---

[24] Hahn and Hird (1991, p. 253).
[25] Dawson and Seater (2013, p. 168).

But there are many criminal laws that do not correspond to anything in common sense morality. In Florida, for example, it is illegal to ride a manatee.[26] In Alabama, it is illegal to play cards on Sunday.[27] In Boulder, Colorado, it is illegal to put a couch on your porch.[28] Citizens could not be expected to know these things to be wrong solely on the basis of a normal grasp of morality. If the behavior in question is wrong at all, it could only be wrong because it has been prohibited by law—in legal terminology, these behaviors are "*mala prohibita*".

In the case of these *mala prohibita* offenses, individuals can be justly held responsible only in a regime in which knowledge of the law is reasonably accessible. If the law is incomprehensible to the average person, and legal advice that would clarify its implications is prohibitively expensive, then it is unjust to blame an individual for failing to know the law. Given, therefore, that the state intends to continue to prosecute individuals who unknowingly violate the law, the state has an obligation of justice to make the content of the law reasonably simple and accessible.

4.3.4 The Threat of Legal Harm

Almost anyone familiar with the legal system would advise a friend, when facing any serious legal case, to hire a good lawyer. Almost no one would advise a friend, for example, to simply present her case herself and trust in the system to arrive at the right outcome. This is despite the fact that hiring a lawyer commonly costs thousands to tens of thousands of dollars.

Such advice is an unintentional indictment of the legal system. If the legal system operated perfectly justly, then expending large amounts of money on legal representation would be wasteful, since one would end up with the just outcome regardless of how much one spent. Notice that to make this argument, we need not agree on what the principles of justice are, nor need we assume that the just outcome of a case is known in advance. On *any* reasonable account of justice, the requirements of justice in a given case do not depend upon whom the parties to the case have

---

[26] Murray (2012).
[27] Alabama Code, section 13A-12-1.
[28] Boulder Municipal Code, section 5-4-16.

hired to represent them or how much money the parties each spend on attorneys. Therefore, on any reasonable account of justice, *if* legal cases are reliably resolved according to justice alone, then hiring an expensive attorney will not affect the outcome.

An analogous argument applies to any supposition on which the outcomes of legal cases are predictable based on the law and the facts of the case. If the outcome is predictable based on the law and the facts of the case, then hiring a good lawyer cannot help one, since the lawyer cannot change either the law or the underlying facts of the case. Since lawyers do in fact significantly affect the resolution of cases (§4.2.4), legal outcomes are not determined solely by the law and the facts of the case.

This does not tell us whether the impact of lawyers is overall good or bad from the standpoint of justice, compared to the possible situation in which individuals represent themselves in all legal matters. It is possible that the presence of an attorney, or a highly skilled attorney, enables individuals to secure unjust outcomes, such as being acquitted of crimes that one actually committed, winning lawsuits that lack merit, or successfully defending against meritorious lawsuits. It is also possible that the presence of an attorney, or a highly skilled attorney, prevents *miscarriages* of justice that would otherwise occur. Most likely, the truth is some combination of these possibilities.

But our aim here is not to evaluate lawyers as a profession, but to evaluate the *legal system*. The legal system looks seriously deficient in any case: It is obviously troubling if skilled lawyers enable one to secure unjust outcomes. But even if skilled lawyers somehow only enable one to secure justice, the implication remains that the state creates demand for legal services by imposing a significant risk of unjust legal outcomes for those who do not hire lawyers.

The legal services industry takes in revenues of more than $300 billion per year.[29] In most cases, the revenues collected by an industry are an indicator of the value produced by that industry. The large revenues of the cellular telephone industry, for example, indicate the high value that consumers place on the functions provided by cellular phones. But the situation is different in the case of legal services. A large part of the

---

[29] Huhn (2019).

function of legal services is either to defend oneself from threats of harm intentionally created by other agents (whether the state or private plaintiffs), or to actually create such threats against others. The threats in question are implemented through the medium of the legal system. If the legal system were fully just, just threats would always succeed and unjust threats would always fail, regardless of the amount of money spent trying to influence the system. The revenues of the legal industry are therefore a symptom of (*i*) the magnitude of the harms that people are threatening each other with through the legal system, as well as (*ii*) the corruptibility of that system, in the sense of its susceptibility to manipulation by expenditure of money. The nearly $300 billion spent on legal services is a measure, not of the value produced by the legal services industry, but of the failure of the legal system.

My point here is not that the legal profession has no value, given our current system. It is entirely compatible with my argument to say that high-quality lawyers enable courts to achieve justice by helping judges and juries to figure out what justice requires. But even if this is the only thing that lawyers do, this implies that the *legal system* operated by the state is morally defective, since it implies that those defendants who either hire low-quality lawyers or represent themselves do not reliably receive justice.

To summarize the argument of §§4.2 and 4.3:

1. If an action is unjust, then harms predictably caused by that action are unjust harms attributable to the agent.
2. The state has adopted policies that
    (a) are unjust, and
    (b) predictably raise the prices of legal services, placing a burden on all who require legal services.
3. So the high prices of legal services are an injustice attributable to the state.

4.4 The Duty to Provide Justice

4.4.1 The Function of Government

All agents have a *negative* duty of justice, that is, a duty to avoid committing injustices. But the state, in addition, has a *positive* duty of justice, a duty to *provide* justice to its citizens. The state must, for instance, enforce the rights of its citizens and fairly adjudicate their disputes. This is obvious when a legal case is before the courts, since the failure to provide a just resolution will generally entail providing an unjust resolution.

One might nevertheless question whether the state has a positive duty to *take up* cases in the first place, so that it may enforce the demands of justice. If an individual claims to have been wronged, must the state address that person's case to ensure that justice is done, or may government officials stand back and merely refrain from adding to the alleged injustice?

The answer is that government has a positive obligation to make reasonable efforts to address injustices—for example, to investigate crimes and award compensation for torts. There are two main reasons for this. The first reason is that the state's performance of these duties is central to the justification for having a state at all. Government requires a justification because the government, by its nature, seizes money from individuals and coercively imposes rules on them. These sorts of behaviors are not typically permissible for most agents. Thus, there must be some special justification for them in the case of the government.[30] That justification, according to standard theories, appeals to some crucial functions that government is needed to serve, and essentially all theories include the protection of rights and the just resolution of disputes as among those functions.[31]

---

[30] For discussion, see Huemer (2013).
[31] See, for example, Locke (1980 (originally published 1690)), Hobbes ([1651] 1996), Hume ([1777] 1987). Some disagree that government has any ultimate justification (Huemer 2013, part II). But even if government is ultimately unjustified, it remains plausible that, *given* that a government exists, that government is obligated to perform those duties for the sake of which citizens are paying it.

The second reason why the government is obligated to provide justice is that the government forcibly prevents its citizens from securing justice from non-governmental sources. The government, for example, prohibits crime victims from meting out punishment themselves, it prohibits citizens from setting up their own private police forces and prisons to provide justice for crimes not addressed by the state, and so on. Because the state forcibly prevents anyone else from providing justice, it becomes incumbent on the state itself to provide justice.[32]

In describing this obligation, I have said that the state must make *reasonable efforts* to address injustices. No organization could reasonably be expected to prevent or remedy *all* injustice. Therefore, if we claimed that government is obligated to successfully protect all our rights, we might be charged with setting an unreasonably high bar. But one could not object to the requirement of *making a reasonable effort* at protecting rights, remedying injustice, and the like. For example, if a citizen informs the police of a crime in progress, and the police have available resources to respond, yet they fail to respond through incompetence or lack of concern, this would constitute a breach of the state's duty to make reasonable efforts to protect the rights of its citizens.

4.4.2 Duties to Society Vs. Individuals

The U.S. government disagrees with the foregoing assessment of its duties. The government considers itself exempt from essentially any obligation to individuals. This has emerged in a number of court cases in which the government has been sued for failing to protect its citizens. In one case, three women sued the District of Columbia Police Department for failing to protect them, after they called to report a break-in at their house. In response, the police drove by the house, looked at the front door, then left, without checking the back door where the criminals had in fact broken in. The women called a second time to request urgent police aid; the dispatcher assured them that help was on the way but never sent anyone. As a result, the women were beaten, robbed, and

---

[32] Cf. Nozick's (1974, pp. 110–13) argument that a dominant protective agency, upon prohibiting individuals from enforcing their own rights, must provide protection to those individuals.

raped by the two criminals who had broken into the house. The women sued the police department, but the court dismissed the women's lawsuit without a trial, citing "the fundamental principle that a government and its agents are under no general duty to provide public services, such as police protection, to any particular individual citizen".[33] Other cases involving similar degrees of negligence by the government have occurred, and in each case the courts have summarily dismissed the complaint.[34]

The government's theory, articulated in the court decision, is that its duty is only to provide a deterrent to crime for the benefit of society in general, not to protect any particular individual. The court's argument for this theory consisted entirely of citing *other* decisions in which courts refused to hold the government accountable for failure to protect individuals. The theory is on its face surprising, since the government also holds that each particular individual, and not merely society in general, owes obligations of obedience to the state. Individuals, not merely society in general, are required to pay taxes. The justification for requiring individuals to pay taxes is unclear if these individuals are not then entitled to some form of public services.

4.4.3 Prohibitive Pricing Violates the Duty to Provide Justice

The state is obligated to provide justice for all persons under its jurisdiction, not only the wealthy. This is because the arguments establishing the obligation to provide justice apply generally: (i) Any individual involved in a legal case, regardless of the individual's wealth, is treated unjustly by the government if the government resolves the case wrongly. (ii) Nearly all individuals in the government's jurisdiction pay taxes to the government. (iii) All individuals in the government's jurisdiction are coercively prevented, by the government, from receiving justice-protecting services from other sources.

---

[33] *Warren v. District of Columbia*, 444 A.2d 1 (1981). The Appeals Court approvingly quoted this phrase from the trial court's opinion.
[34] *Riss v. New York*, 22 N.Y.2d 579 (N.Y. 1968); *Hartzler v. City of San Jose*, 46 Cal.App. 3d 6 (1975); *DeShaney v. Winnebago County Department of Social Services*, 489 U.S. 189 (1989).

Given very broad features of the legal system—in particular, that it is an adversarial system with complex rules in which outcomes are strongly dependent on the skill of lawyers—individuals can expect to reliably receive justice only if those who face legal issues have adequate legal representation. Prohibitively high prices for legal services put adequate legal representation out of the reach of the poor. Indeed, none but the rich can afford to obtain justice from the state in the current system. Therefore, these high prices prevent the government from satisfying its duty to provide justice. The government has an obligation of justice to remedy the problem, either by eliminating the need for legal representation or by rendering legal representation accessible for non-wealthy citizens.

4.4.4 Indigent Defense in the Status Quo

The state's obligation to make legal representation accessible is recognized to some degree in current legal doctrine in the U.S., which requires the government to provide legal representation without charge in certain cases.[35] This doctrine is largely creditable to the famous case of *Gideon v. Wainwright*. Clarence Gideon was accused of burglarizing a pool hall on the basis of weak evidence that a good defense attorney would have dismantled. Gideon, however, was too poor to hire a lawyer; as a result, he was convicted and sentenced to five years in prison. Through his appeal to the Supreme Court, Gideon won the right to a new trial represented by a court-appointed defense attorney, at which he was acquitted.

Defendants in similar circumstances are today represented by public defenders paid by the state. Nevertheless, the status quo falls short in several respects:

(a) The right to legal representation is not merely a right to *some* legal representation, but the right to *adequate* representation, since this is what is necessary to ensure a fair trial. Yet the legal assistance provided to indigent defendants by the government is minimal. It is widely recognized that public defenders' offices are drastically over-

---

[35] *Powell v. Alabama*, 287 U.S. 45 (1932); *Gideon v. Wainwright*, 372 U.S. 335 (1963).

worked and underfunded, with each attorney handling hundreds to thousands of cases per year.[36]

(b) The right to a court-appointed attorney is currently recognized only for defendants whom the government considers "indigent". For most cases, this amounts to having an income under 125% of the federal poverty level (currently $12,140 for individuals, so anyone with an income over $15,175 per year does not qualify).[37]

This fails as an attempt to protect those who cannot afford attorneys: a person with an income of, for example, $20,000 a year cannot afford to hire a lawyer—such individuals do not in general have thousands of unneeded dollars in their bank accounts. The 125% threshold reflects more concern for the fiscal convenience of state governments than for justice to defendants.

Moreover, the principle behind setting such a threshold is wrong. The right to counsel rests on the fact that it is nearly impossible to receive a fair trial in the current system without legal counsel. Now, the government does not owe a fair trial only to indigent defendants. The government owes a fair trial to every defendant. In general, as a matter of morality as well as of law, I cannot justly require that you do x in order to receive y, if I already owe you y independently. Thus, the state may not justly require that a defendant pay thousands of dollars in legal fees in order to receive a fair trial, even if the defendant *could* pay those fees, since the state already owes the defendant a fair trial.

(c) Courts consider the right to court-appointed counsel to apply only in sufficiently serious cases, particularly felony cases and cases in which the defendant is sentenced to a term in prison.[38] Yet individuals are entitled to a fair trial in all cases. There is no rational principle

---

[36] Eckholm (2008), Lee et al. (2013), Peng (2015). Eckholm reports that as of 2008, public defenders in Miami-Dade County handled an average of 500 felony and 2200 misdemeanor cases per year. Peng reports that the public defender in New Orleans has nine investigators to investigate 18,000 cases a year.

[37] There is a more complicated set of conditions for determining indigency; see, e.g., North Dakota Commission on Legal Counsel for Indigents (2014).

[38] See North Dakota Commission on Legal Counsel for Indigents (2014) for a fuller description of the conditions for qualifying for indigent defense. For the spurious legal justification for this practice, see *Scott v. Illinois*, 440 U.S. 367 (1979).

whereby it is permissible to give unfair trials for misdemeanors or for crimes with non-prison penalties.

Granted, providing public defenders for minor criminal cases would be expensive. If the government cannot afford to provide legal counsel for defendants in such cases, then, rather than prosecuting them in unfair trials, the government has the alternative of not prosecuting these defendants at all. Granted, the harm of convicting the innocent is diminished in the case of minor offences—but so is the importance of punishing the guilty in the first place. Furthermore, prosecutors are generally paid more than public defenders.[39] A reasonable rule of thumb, therefore, is that if it is not cost effective to pay a public defender to defend a case, then it is also not cost effective to pay a prosecutor to prosecute the case.

(d) Finally, the right to court-appointed counsel is not currently recognized for lawsuits, either for the plaintiff or for the defendant. Thus, if you are sued or you want to sue someone else, you must hire a private attorney or represent yourself.

The rationale for the right to counsel in criminal cases is that a fair trial requires legal representation. But the fairness of a civil trial in our system is no less dependent on adequate legal representation of both sides. And the government is obligated to ensure fair trials in tort cases, just as in criminal cases. It is obvious that, *given* that the state conducts a trial, the trial must be fair. Perhaps less obviously, the state also has an obligation, to plaintiffs who have reasonable complaints, to resolve their complaints through the legal system. The reason is that the government coercively prohibits individuals from obtaining relief by non-governmental means. If A owes B money, A refuses to pay, and B attempts to take the money on his own without using the legal system, the state will intervene on A's behalf, enforcing A's continued unjust possession of the disputed money. The state's prohibition on private enforcement of tort claims creates an obligation for the state to make its own tort system accessible.

---

[39] An average of $65,237 per year for prosecutors, compared to $61,790 for public defenders, according to PayScale.com (2020a, b). Prosecutors' offices in general are also better funded than public defenders' offices (Lee et al. 2013).

In summary, the government has an obligation to provide adequate legal services without charge in all categories of cases—for minor as well as major offenses, for wealthy as well as poor citizens, for civil as well as criminal cases. This duty is conditional on certain broad features of the legal system—the fact that the government prohibits the private provision of justice, that the government operates an adversarial legal system, that the rules of the legal system are very difficult for non-professionals to competently navigate, and that legal services have a non-trivial cost.

These broad features are not likely to change in the foreseeable future. It is nevertheless worth noting theoretically that the government could avoid the obligation to provide legal services by more radically altering the legal system. A shift from an adversarial to an inquisitorial system, for example, might obviate the need for professional legal representatives for plaintiffs and defendants. In inquisitorial systems, as used in France and Germany, the court or its agents actively investigate the facts of a case. This contrasts with the adversarial system, used in the U.K., U.S., and other British-influenced nations, in which the court acts as a neutral referee between opposing parties, who each deliberately present one-sided evidence and arguments. The proper functioning of the adversarial system requires that both sides be represented by skilled experts.

Another radical alteration would be one that allowed private parties who are wronged to seek justice through private exercise of force (vigilantism). (This is compatible with prohibiting substantively *wrongful* vigilantism; that is, vigilantes could still be subject to penalties in the event that they harmed innocent parties or punished guilty parties excessively.) One might reason that, in the absence of government, individuals would be morally entitled to seek private justice for wrongs suffered at the hands of other individuals. The state may prohibit this only if it provides a reasonable and accessible alternative means of resolving disputes.

In the present system, individuals very often cannot obtain a just resolution of a case at all because they cannot afford to pay the legal fees. They may then be subjected to an unfair trial, be forced to plea bargain, be forced to settle a lawsuit that should have been tried, or be forced to drop a complaint that should have been pursued. Current legal prices are so high as to prevent the legal system from even operating to resolve cases as it is intended to do. Even for those who manage to pay the legal fees to get their disputes fully resolved through the government's court system, the legal fees frequently create a major hardship that must be endured regardless of who is in the right. In criminal cases, innocent defendants are in effect subjected to enormous financial penalties for which they are never compensated. This is approximately as just as a system that fines every defendant thousands of dollars regardless of their guilt or innocence.

If prices were much lower, with no changes in who pays for legal services, these serious injustices would be replaced by comparatively minor injustices—individuals would have to pay a small amount of money that they should not in principle have to pay, but they would for the most part get their disputes resolved through a fair mechanism. For this reason, the main injustice of legal service prices could be addressed if the state were to alter the price-inflating policies mentioned above (§4.2).

4.5 Facilitation of Injustice

I turn to the final way in which the high prices of legal services amount to an injustice on the part of the state: The exorbitant prices of legal services turn the state into a tool of injustice in the hands of other agents. Private parties use the cost of the legal system to intimidate, cheat, and coerce one another.

One sort of example received public attention a few years ago: a real estate developer hires contractors to do work in a building, then refuses to pay his contractors. The state prohibits the contractors from seeking justice through any means other than the state's own legal system, but use of the state's legal system is prohibitively expensive. The developer is aware of these facts, which is precisely why he refuses to pay. In this case, the legal system does not merely fail to provide justice; the legal system functions as a tool in the hands of the unscrupulous developer for cheating other people. If legal services were much less expensive, or if the legal system were accessible without professional legal assistance, the developer would be unable to execute this type of scam.[40]

---

[40] During the Presidential debate on September 26, 2016, Hilary Clinton accused Donald Trump of cheating contractors in the manner described in the text. Trump responded: "I take advantage of

Another type of example is one in which unjustified legal action or threats of legal action are used to intimidate and coerce others. A wealthy organization, for example, may file lawsuits against those who publicly criticize the organization, knowing that these lawsuits lack legal merit. The organization loses money to legal fees for their failed lawsuits. However, the defendants also lose large amounts of time and money and are generally subjected to prolonged emotional stress; these are predictable results of being sued, regardless of the merits of the suit. In the current legal system, even a suit with no legal merit can take months or years to resolve, depending in part on how much money each side can spend on lawyers. This, in turn, frightens both the original defendant and other potential critics of the organization into remaining silent. In effect, a wealthy organization can use the legal system to silence critics, even if these critics have violated no law and would be fully within their rights in criticizing the organization. L. Ron Hubbard, the founder of Scientology, has been quoted as stating:

> The purpose of the suit is to harass and discourage rather than win. The law can be used very easily to harass, and enough harassment on somebody who is simply on the thin edge anyway … will generally be sufficient to cause professional decease. If possible, of course, ruin him utterly.[41]

The legal system is meant to be a system of justice. If it were a genuine system of justice, the threat to involve a person in legal matters would be a toothless threat, to be laughed off by the virtuous, for the virtuous have no fear of being treated justly. In our actual society, the law is a weapon aimed at the virtuous and vicious alike. Any credible threat to initiate legal proceedings involving another person is a serious threat against that person, and widely recognized as such, regardless of the other party's factual situation, regardless of what they have or have not done. Americans'

---

the laws of the nation because I'm running a company. My obligation right now is to do well for myself, my family, my employees, for my companies. And that's what I do" (Blake 2016).

[41] The quotation comes from secret Scientology materials introduced into court during one of the lawsuits the Church has been involved in (Fishman 1993). Members of the Scientology movement have frequently been accused of using this kind of tactic. See Behar (1991), Urban (2010), Morgan (1998).

widespread, blanket fear of any sort of involvement in any legal matter is a testament to how little faith we have in our system. In any legal proceeding, no matter what their role is, no matter what the facts of the case are, virtually no American expects simply to be treated justly.

4.6 Objections

4.6.1 Burdens to Taxpayers

I have argued that, given certain broad features of the legal system, the government is obligated to provide legal services to citizens without charge. This would create a significant burden for taxpayers. There is no alternative by which legal services are costless; there are only the alternatives in which legal services are paid for by those who use them (those who have legal cases), and in which legal services are paid for by someone else. Since either alternative is unfair, we are forced to ask which alternative is *less* unfair. Arguably, it is less unfair to be forced to pay for one's own legal services than it is to be forced to pay for someone else's legal services. Taxpayer-funded legal services amount to the latter alternative: innocent taxpayers are forced to pay for public defenders and, in my proposal, public plaintiff's attorneys as well, whether or not those taxpayers actually use any legal services.

There is a third alternative: the loser in any legal case could be required to pay both sides' legal fees. This is the practice in civil cases in England and most of the world, by contrast with the U.S., where each side generally must pay their own legal fees. The English ("loser pays") rule could be extended to criminal cases as well, such that defendants pay legal fees to the state if convicted, and the state pays legal fees to defendants who are acquitted. However, I shall focus on the less controversial application to tort cases.

There is an intuitive, justice-based rationale for the English rule in tort cases: the party who is in the wrong, as indicated by their loss of the legal case, is morally responsible for the costs of litigation. If the plaintiff wins a lawsuit, this indicates that the defendant wrongfully caused whatever harm the plaintiff was suing for; in doing so, the defendant also caused there to be a lawsuit, with the attendant legal costs. Of course, the plaintiff also caused these legal costs to exist by filing the lawsuit. But only one of the two parties—the defendant—caused the legal fees to occur *through wrongful behavior*. If, on the other hand, the *defendant* wins the lawsuit, this indicates that the plaintiff was at least misguided in filing the lawsuit and is thus more to blame for the legal costs than the defendant is.

All of this reasoning is plausible on its face. It overlooks, however, the responsibility of the state. For reasons explained earlier (§§4.2 and 4.3), *the state* is to blame for the majority of legal costs in any case. Therefore, the state should pay for at least the majority of legal costs for both sides, until such time as the state reforms its price-inflating policies.

Even granting the state's responsibility for high legal costs, one might wonder how just it is to require the state to pay the majority of legal fees in all cases. All of the state's funds are derived from taxation; thus, requiring the state to pay amounts to requiring *taxpayers* to pay. But taxpayers are not in general responsible for high legal costs. Therefore, why should taxpayers in general be required to pay anyone's legal costs?

In reply, note that we would not apply this logic in general to costs that the state imposes on others. Nearly everyone accepts that, when the government wrongs an individual, that individual should be able to sue the government and collect damages. This is true despite that the government's payment of these damages must come through taxation. We do not reason that, since the *taxpayers* are not to blame for torts by the state, no recovery should be possible. Granted, the taxpayers suffer undeserved financial costs whenever the state is successfully sued, but this result seems *less* unjust than the situation in which the victim of a tort by the state must suffer without remedy.

The case of legal fees is similar. Legal service prices are exorbitant mainly due to wrongful behavior by the government. It is unjust that the taxpayers should bear these costs, but only in the sense that it is unjust whenever the state wrongfully harms someone and then must pay for the harm. It would be more unjust if the burden were to fall entirely on that subclass of citizens with the misfortune to have disputes that must be resolved through the government's legal system.

4.6.2 The Problem of Frivolous Lawsuits

There is a widespread perception that America has an excess of lawsuits. This impression is supported to some degree by statistics showing the U.S. to have a high rate of lawsuits filed per unit of population, as well as a high number of lawyers per unit of population, compared to other liberal democratic nations (see Fig. 4.2).[42] In addition, a small number of infamous cases have created the impression of a court system that rewards frivolous lawsuits. The most famous of these was a 1994 case in which a woman successfully sued McDonald's for selling excessively hot coffee and was initially awarded $2.86 million by a jury.[43]

Some disagree with the popular image. Perhaps the high number of lawyers and lawsuits simply indicates that the U.S. is unusually active in promoting justice; perhaps Americans address injustices through the courts, which protect the public from wrongful and dangerous behavior that in other countries would simply go unaddressed. It is easy to ridicule jury decisions in cases in which one has not heard all the evidence, but one's initial impression of what is a meritorious case, on hearing a one-paragraph summary, is not necessarily reliable. The American legal

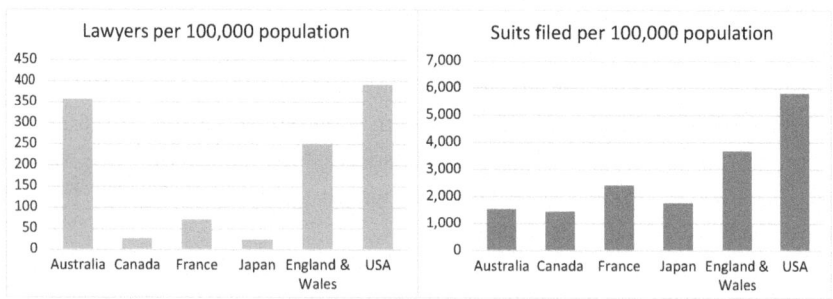

Fig. 4.2 Prevalence of lawyers and lawsuits

---

[42] Ramseyer and Rasmusen (2010, pp. 5–10). Data are from 2006–2009.
[43] *Liebeck v. McDonald's Restaurants*, P.T.S., Inc., No. D-202 CV-93-02419, 1995 WL 360309 (Bernalillo County, N.M. Dist. Ct. August 18, 1994). This was not in fact a frivolous suit, though the initial award was excessive. The judge reduced the award to $640,000, then the parties settled out of court for a confidential amount before an appeal was to be decided.

system may have acquired an unfairly derogatory image due to a few high-profile cases with counterintuitive results.[44]

Be that as it may, some would object to the proposal of state-funded legal services on the ground that this policy would add to the presumed problem of excessive litigation. If all or most legal fees are paid by the state, what is to prevent people from filing every lawsuit they can imagine that has even a small chance of success?

In reply, the state's obligation to provide legal services rests on its more fundamental obligation to provide justice. The latter obligation does not imply an obligation to provide assistance in filing frivolous lawsuits; indeed, the obligation to provide justice conflicts with the filing of frivolous lawsuits. Therefore, even in a regime in which government pays for legal services, government-funded attorneys would have no obligation to represent clients with prima facie frivolous claims; indeed, they would be obliged to refuse such cases. The government should only provide assistance in filing claims that on their face appear (to the lawyers asked to represent the case) to have a good chance of being valid. Given government budget and time constraints, it is likely that the government lawyers would tend to underestimate rather than overestimate the cases that were worth pursuing.

Nevertheless, one may worry that even a policy of providing government assistance for seemingly valid lawsuits would contribute to the presumed problem of excessive litigation. Decreasing the cost of any activity can be expected to increase the quantity of that activity. If pursuing lawsuits becomes less expensive to the litigants, there will surely be more lawsuits.

This objection is an example of the tendency to place other concerns ahead of doing justice to the individual. The primary concern of the legal system should be to achieve justice for individuals. If an individual has a seemingly valid complaint, that complaint should be pursued; we should not hope for the complaint to be dropped merely because of a general feeling that there are too many suits in the society as a whole. If an individual does not have a seemingly valid complaint, then the complaint should not be pursued—again, regardless of the number of suits that

---

[44] For this perspective, see Conlin (1993), Walter Clark Legal Group (2019).

occur in the society as a whole. If a valid legal case is not pursued because the potential plaintiff cannot afford legal representation, this is not an improvement in justice. If it is uncertain whether a complaint is valid, but each side has a good chance of being correct, then the case should in general be adjudicated to determine where justice lies.

A central reason why the quantity of litigation in the U.S. appears to be a problem is that legal fees are exorbitant. (In addition, many jury awards are excessive, but that is a separate issue.) Litigation thus represents an enormous transfer, not just from defendants to plaintiffs, but from the rest of society to the legal profession. But this problem cannot justly be addressed through preventing individuals with prima facie valid claims from seeking relief; the only just way to address the problem is to reduce the price of having legal cases resolved.

4.7 Reforms

My central aim has been to identify an injustice in the legal system. Describing the best alternative system is a distinct and more difficult task. Here, I will only briefly remark upon how the problem of the excessive price of justice could be addressed.

The main reforms are obvious. First, licensing laws for lawyers should be repealed. In place of licensing restrictions, lawyers should simply be held liable for harms caused to clients through legal malpractice. Lawyers guilty of sufficiently serious ethical breaches might be prohibited from future practice of law. If this is deemed insufficient to ensure quality, another measure would be a certification program whereby a government or private agency tests lawyers and certifies them as knowledgeable and competent. Lawyers who did not take the test or failed the test would not be prohibited from practicing but would be unable to assure potential clients that they had been certified. If the test were a genuine indicator of competence to practice law, then we would expect the market to reward those who obtained the certification. If, however, the test were *not* a strong indicator of competence (if, for example, the test were simply a method for established lawyers to attempt to exclude qualified competitors), then the certification program would do little harm, as consumers could simply ignore it.

The second obvious proposal is that nearly all regulations should be repealed. Again, empirical studies of regulations almost always find that they are overall harmful to consumers. The mass of regulations added in the last seventy years may in fact have had enormous costs, on the order of multiple times the current total GDP.

Third (though this proposal may be infeasible to implement), the laws and regulations that exist, including court decisions, should be written in more simple, direct language. Readability should be given priority over excluding loopholes. Courts can then be charged with making decisions, in individual cases, in accordance with the intent of the law.

Fourth, the legal system could be altered from the purely adversarial model to a more inquisitorial model. A significant part of the expense of legal cases derives from the efforts of zealous advocates to frustrate each other through manipulations of the system unrelated to justice. In civil litigation, intentionally wasting one another's time and money through vexatious motions or excessive discovery requests is an accepted strategy for extracting concessions from the other side. In the inquisitorial system, the judge directs the investigation, deciding what evidence to examine, which witnesses to interview, and what questions to ask. This minimizes the manipulation of the legal system for purposes of wasting time and money.

The inquisitorial system, however, requires greater trust in the competence and good faith of judges than the adversarial system requires.[45] This may pose a problem in the United States, where there is widespread (perhaps justified) distrust of government, including of government courts. This problem might be addressed by an additional cost-reducing reform: the privatization of judicial functions. More specifically, the government could refer most cases to arbitration.[46]

At present, binding arbitration, conducted by private arbitrators, is the method of dispute resolution for many business disputes. Many companies include clauses in their contracts specifying that any disputes arising out of the contract should be resolved by a private arbitrator, because such arbitration is generally much less expensive and much less time-consuming than the use of government courts. Government courts honor these clauses in almost all cases, precluding the parties from suing one

---

[45] This problem is discussed by Luban (1988, ch. 5).
[46] For further discussion, see Huemer (2013, ch. 11).

another in a government court.[47] There in addition are a few cases (particularly automobile insurance disputes in certain states) in which government courts will order disputants to seek arbitration.[48] The use of arbitration could be expanded so as to include nearly all cases presently heard by government courts.

References

Batten, Donna, ed. 2011. Arbitration. In *Gale Encyclopedia of American Law*, vol. 1, 3rd ed., 344–348. Detroit: Gale Cengage Learning.
Behar, Richard. 1991. The Thriving Cult of Greed and Power. *Time*, May 6. http://content.time.com/time/magazine/article/0,9171,972865,00.html. Accessed 12 Jan 2019.
Blake, Aaron. 2016. The First Trump-Clinton Presidential Debate Transcript, Annotated. *Washington Post*, September 26. https://www.washingtonpost.com/news/the-fix/wp/2016/09/26/the-first-trump-clinton-presidential-debate-transcript-annotated/?utm_term=.483a7874c5ee. Accessed 13 Jan 2019.
Bonica, Adam. 2017. Why Are There so Many Lawyers in Congress? SSRN. https://papers.ssrn.com/sol3/papers.cfm?abstract_id=2898140. Accessed 26 June 2020.
Conlin, Roxanne Barton. 1993. Too Many Lawsuits in America? No – There Probably Are Too Few. *Deseret News*, February 16. https://www.deseretnews.com/article/275653/TOO-MANY-LAWSUITS-IN-AMERICA-NO%2D%2D-THERE-PROBABLY-ARE-TOO-FEW.html. Accessed 15 Jan 2019.
Cowan, Geoffrey. 1994. *The People v. Clarence Darrow: The Bribery Trial of America's Greatest Lawyer*. New York: Three Rivers Press.
Dawson, John W., and John J. Seater. 2013. Federal Regulation and Aggregate Economic Growth. *Journal of Economic Growth* 18: 137–177. https://doi.org/10.1007/s10887-013-9088-y.

---

[47] Batten (2011, p. 346). Exceptions include cases of fraud or corruption on the part of arbitrators and some cases in which arbitration decisions are contrary to specific public policies. On the public policy exception, see *United Paperworkers v. Misco, Inc.*, 484 U.S. 29 (1987) and *Eastern Associated Coal Corp. v. Mine Workers*, 531 U.S. 57 (2000).
[48] Batten (2011, p. 345).

Dugan, Emily. 2017. A Record Number of People Are Representing Themselves in Court – This Is What It's Like. *BuzzFeed News*, October 1. https://www.buzzfeed.com/emilydugan/a-record-number-of-people-are-representing-themselves-in. Accessed 4 Jan 2019.

Eckholm, Erik. 2008. Citing Workload, Public Lawyers Reject New Cases. *New York Times*, November 8. https://www.nytimes.com/2008/11/09/us/09defender.html. Accessed 10 Jan 2019.

Federal Reserve Bank of St. Louis. 2019, September 19. Real Median Personal Income in the United States. FRED Economic Data. https://fred.stlouisfed.org/series/MEPAINUSA672N. Accessed 26 June 2020.

Fishman, Steven. 1993. Documents submitted in case of *Church of Scientology International v. Fishman and Geertz*, Case no. CV 91-6426 HLH (Tx), U.S. District Court, Central District of California. Excerpts available at http://www.cs.cmu.edu/~dst/Fishman/Declaration/exhibg.html. Accessed 13 Jan 2019.

Friedman, David. 1989. *The Machinery of Freedom*. 2nd ed. LaSalle: Open Court.

Gerety, Corina. 2011. *Excess & Access: Consensus on the American Civil Justice Landscape*. Denver: Institute for the Advancement of the American Legal System. https://iaals.du.edu/sites/default/files/documents/publications/excess_access2011-2.pdf. Accessed 26 June 2020.

Hahn, Robert W., and John A. Hird. 1991. The Costs and Benefits of Regulation: Review and Synthesis. *Yale Journal on Regulation* 8: 233–278.

Hannaford-Agor, Paula, and Nicole L. Waters. 2013. *Estimating the Cost of Civil Litigation*. National Center for State Courts: Court Statistics Project. http://www.courtstatistics.org/__data/assets/pdf_file/0020/25337/csph_online2.pdf. Accessed 26 June 2020.

Hazlett, Thomas Winslow. 1997. Looking for Results: An Interview with Ronald Coase. *Reason*, January 1. https://reason.com/archives/1997/01/01/looking-for-results/print. Accessed 7 Jan 2019.

Henderson, Bill. 2017. The Decline of the PeopleLaw Sector (037). *Legal Evolution*, November 19. https://www.legalevolution.org/2017/11/decline-peoplelaw-sector-037/. Accessed 1 Jan 2019.

Hobbes, Thomas. 1996. *Leviathan*, ed. Richard Tuck. Cambridge: Cambridge University Press.

Huemer, Michael. 2013. *The Problem of Political Authority*. New York: Palgrave Macmillan.

Huhn, Philipp. 2019. Industry Revenue of Legal Services in the U.S. 2011–2023. Statista. https://www.statista.com/forecasts/311177/legal-services-revenue-in-the-us. Accessed 26 June 2020.

Hume, David. 1987. Of the Original Contract. In *Essays, Moral, Political, and Literary*, 465–487. Indianapolis: Liberty Fund.

Kurtz, Karl. 2015. Who We Elect: The Demographics of State Legislatures. *State Legislatures Magazine*, December 1. http://www.ncsl.org/research/about-state-legislatures/who-we-elect.aspx. Accessed 6 Jan 2019.

Lake, Rebecca. 2020. 23 Dizzying Average American Savings Statistics. *Credit Donkey*, February 26. https://www.creditdonkey.com/average-american-savings-statistics.html. Accessed 26 June 2020.

Lederman, Leandra, and Warren B. Hrung. 2006. Do Attorneys Do Their Clients Justice? An Empirical Study of Lawyers' Effects on Tax Court Litigation Outcomes. *Wake Forest Law Review* 41: 1235–1295.

Lee, Jaeah, Hannah Levintova, and Brett Brownell. 2013. Charts: Why You're in Deep Trouble if You Can't Afford a Lawyer. *Mother Jones*, May 6. https://www.motherjones.com/politics/2013/05/public-defenders-gideon-supreme-court-charts/. Accessed 26 June 2020.

Locke, John. 1980. *Second Treatise of Government*, ed. C.B. Macpherson. Indianapolis: Hackett.

Luban, David. 1988. *Lawyers and Justice: An Ethical Study*. Princeton: Princeton University Press.

McLaughlin, Patrick A., Jerry Ellig, and Dima Yazji Shamoun. 2014. Regulatory Reform in Florida: An Opportunity for Greater Competitiveness and Economic Efficiency. *Florida State University Business Review* 13: 95–130.

Morgan, Lucy. 1998. Hardball: When Scientology Goes to Court, It Likes to Play Rough—Very Rough. *St. Petersburg Times*, January 28. https://www.scientology-lies.com/press/st-petersburg-times/hardball-scientology-plays-rough-in-court.html. Accessed 13 Jan 2019.

Murphy, Donald J., David Burrows, Sara Santilli, Anne W. Kemp, Scott Tenner, Barbara Kreling, and Joan Teno. 1994. The Influence of the Probability of Survival on Patients' Preferences Regarding Cardiopulmonary Resuscitation. *New England Journal of Medicine* 330: 545–549. https://www.nejm.org/doi/full/10.1056/NEJM199402243300807. Accessed 1 Jan 2019.

Murray, Rheana. 2012. Woman Busted for Riding a Manatee in Florida, Violating State Law. *New York Daily News*, October 3. https://www.nydailynews.com/news/national/woman-busted-riding-manatee-article-1.1173507. Accessed 26 June 2020.

Nolo. 2020. How Much Will My Divorce Cost and How Long Will It Take? https://www.nolo.com/legal-encyclopedia/ctp/cost-of-divorce.html. Accessed 26 June 2020.

North Dakota Commission on Legal Counsel for Indigents. 2014, March 20. Guidelines to Determine Eligibility for Indigent Defense Services. http://www.nd.gov/indigents/docs/guidelines.pdf. Accessed 10 Jan 2019.

Nozick, Robert. 1974. *Anarchy, State, and Utopia*. New York: Basic Books.

Payscale.com. 2020a. Average Prosecutor Salary. https://www.payscale.com/research/US/Job=Prosecutor/Salary. Accessed 26 June 2020.

———. 2020b. Average Public Defender Salary. https://www.payscale.com/

Peng, Tina. 2015. I'm a Public Defender. It's Impossible for Me to Do a Good Job Representing My Clients. *Washington Post*, September 3. https://www.washingtonpost.com/opinions/our-public-defender-system-isnt-just-broken%2D%2Dits-unconstitutional/2015/09/03/aadf2b6c-519b-11e5-9812-92d5948a40f8_story.html. Accessed 9 Jan 2019.

Plain English Campaign. 2011. Golden Bull Awards. http://www.plainenglish.co.uk/campaigning/awards/2011-awards/golden-bull-awards.html. Accessed 26 June 2020.

Ramseyer, J. Mark, and Eric B. Rasmusen. 2010. Comparative Litigation Rates. Harvard John M. Olin Discussion Paper Series, Discussion Paper No. 681. http://www.law.harvard.edu/programs/olin_center/papers/681_Ramseyer.php. Accessed 26 June 2020.

Rose, Jeff. 2019. Average Cost of Law School Tuition—Is It Really Worth It? *Good Financial Cents*, April 1. https://www.goodfinancialcents.com/average-cost-law-school-tuition-is-it-worth-becoming-lawyer/. Accessed 26 June 2020.

Sandefur, Rebecca L. 2015. Elements of Professional Expertise: Understanding Relational and Substantive Expertise through Lawyers' Impact. *American Sociological Review* 80: 909–933.

Sinclair, Upton. 1994. *I, Candidate for Governor: And How I Got Licked*. Berkeley: University of California Press.

Thumbtack. 2019, September 11. How Much Does a Defense Attorney Cost? https://www.thumbtack.com/p/criminal-defense-attorney-cost. Accessed 26 June 2020.

TRAC Reports. 2020a. Prosecutions for January 2020. https://trac.syr.edu/tracreports/bulletins/overall/monthlyjan20/fil/. Accessed 26 June 2020.

———. 2020b. Prosecutions for February 2020. https://trac.syr.edu/tracreports/bulletins/overall/monthlyfeb20/fil/. Accessed 26 June 2020.

———. 2020c. Prosecutions for March 2020. https://trac.syr.edu/tracreports/bulletins/overall/monthlymar20/fil/. Accessed 26 June 2020.

———. 2020d. Prosecutions for April 2020. https://trac.syr.edu/tracreports/bulletins/overall/monthlyapr20/fil/. Accessed 26 June 2020.

———. 2020e. Prosecutions for May 2020. https://trac.syr.edu/tracreports/bulletins/overall/monthlymay20/fil/. Accessed 26 June 2020.

U.S. Department of the Treasury Office of Economic Policy, Council of Economic Advisers, and Department of Labor. 2015. Occupational Licensing: A Framework for Policymakers. https://obamawhitehouse.archives.gov/sites/default/files/docs/licensing_report_final_nonembargo.pdf. Accessed 26 June 2020.

U.S. Office of Management and Budget. 2017. 2017 Draft Report to Congress on the Benefits and Costs of Federal Regulations and Agency Compliance with the Unfunded Mandates Reform Act. https://www.whitehouse.gov/wp-content/uploads/2017/12/draft_2017_cost_benefit_report.pdf. Accessed 26 June 2020.

U.S. Office of the Federal Register. 2020. Code of Federal Regulations Total Pages 1938–1949, and Total Volumes and Pages 1950–2019. https://s3.amazonaws.com/production.uploads.wordpress.federalregister.gov/uploads/2020/04/01123111/cfrTotalPages2019.pdf. Accessed 26 June 2020.

Urban, Hugh B. 2010. The Rundown Truth: Scientology Changes Strategy in War with Media. *Religion Dispatches*, March 18. http://religiondispatches.org/the-rundown-truth-scientology-changes-strategy-in-war-with-media/. Accessed 13 Jan 2019.

Walter Clark Legal Group. 2019. Are There Too Many Frivolous Lawsuits in the U.S.? (blog post), January 4. https://www.walterclark.com/blog/many-frivolous-lawsuits-u-s/. Accessed 15 Jan 2019.

Wikipedia. 2020. List of Presidents of the United States by Previous Experience. https://en.wikipedia.org/wiki/List_of_presidents_of_the_United_States_by_previous_experience. Accessed 26 June 2020.

Wozniacka, Gosia. 2013. Family Backs Decision Not to Do CPR. *Boston Globe*, March 6. https://www.bostonglobe.com/news/nation/2013/03/05/calif-woman-dies-after-nurse-refuses-cpr/xn9P8De8ruF0WME9RgvREI/story.html. Accessed 1 Jan 2019.

5

Extorted Pleas

5.1 The Practice of Plea Bargaining

Almost all criminal convictions in the United States are obtained by plea bargains. This is a type of deal in which the defendant agrees to plead guilty and forego a trial, in return for the prosecutor's agreement to dismiss some charges against the defendant, or reduce one or more charges from a more to a less serious crime, or recommend a lighter sentence than the prosecutor would otherwise recommend. From the standpoint of self-interest, the defendant must weigh the chance of being acquitted at trial against the harsher expected punishment if he insists on a trial and is convicted.

When the defense and prosecution arrive at a plea agreement, they present the deal to a judge. The defendant is required at this time to promise that he is freely and knowingly confessing to his crime and foregoing a trial.[1] The judge has the power to reject the plea bargain and require the parties to go to trial. This, however, virtually never happens; as long as the defendant says that the plea is voluntary, the judge will almost certainly accept it.

---

[1] *Federal Rules of Criminal Procedure*, Title IV, Rule 11, https://www.law.cornell.edu/rules/frcrmp/rule_11

The effect of accepting a plea deal is generally to greatly reduce one's punishment; equivalently, the effect of insisting on a trial is to greatly *increase* one's punishment. The increase in sentence resulting from going to trial is sometimes called "the trial penalty". In the U.S. at present, the trial penalty is more than twice as large as the typical punishment for a crime—defendants who go to trial and are convicted receive, on average, 3.3 times the punishment that they would have gotten from taking a plea bargain.[2]

Plea bargaining was not always an accepted practice. Guilty pleas were judicially discouraged in common law countries before the nineteenth century, and plea bargaining was virtually nonexistent in pre-civil war America.[3] Early judicial opinions are extremely unfavorable to the prospect of plea bargaining. For instance, a Mississippi court wrote in 1900:

> As the plea of guilty is often made because the defendant supposes that he will thereby receive some favor of the court in the sentence, it is the English practice not to receive such plea unless it is persisted in by the defendant after being informed that *such plea will make no alteration in the punishment.*[4]

An earlier Michigan court wrote, "No sort of pressure can be permitted to bring the party to forego any right or advantage however slight."[5]

Nevertheless, the practice began to rise in the twentieth century, particularly during the Prohibition era, due in part to widespread corruption and in part to the increasing power given to prosecutors by an expanding criminal code.[6] Finally, in the 1970 case of *Brady v. United States*, the Supreme Court explicitly accepted plea bargaining as inherent in the

---

[2] NACDL (2018, p. 20).
[3] The present summary is derived from Alschuler (1979).
[4] *Deloach v. State*, 77 Miss. 691, 692, 27 So. 618, 619 (1900); emphasis added. For additional examples, see Alschuler (1979, pp. 19–24).
[5] *O'Hara v. People*, 41 Mich. 623, 624, 3 N.W. 161, 162 (1879), quoted in Alschuler (1979, p. 20).
[6] Alschuler (1979, pp. 24–9), Dervan (2012, pp. 61–4).

American system of justice.[7] The practice of plea bargaining has expanded since then, so that today, of state and federal criminal cases that are not dismissed, under 3% receive a trial; the other 97% are disposed of by bargaining.[8]

5.2 The Injustice of Plea Bargaining

Despite its routine use in the modern legal system, scholarly opinion tends to be sharply against plea bargaining, for obvious reasons.[9] The practice seems to involve coercing confessions from defendants by threats of increased punishment (a guilty plea being, among other things, a kind of confession delivered in court). Such coerced confessions are hardly proof of guilt. In the status quo, prosecutors are in a position to exert so much pressure as to extract confessions from the guilty and the innocent alike. In the case of those few defendants who refuse to plead guilty, the system delivers extremely harsh punishments simply for choosing to exercise their legal rights. This violates the principle that a just punishment must be proportionate to the wrong committed. We examine these problems more closely in what follows.

5.2.1 Plea Bargaining as Coerced Confession

It is universally agreed in legal theory that coerced confessions are unacceptable. The main reason is that to accept coerced confessions would conflict with the central purpose of the court system. The purpose of the court system is not to maximize convictions or to speed defendants through as quickly as possible. The purpose of the system is to determine the truth and administer justice. Coerced confessions do not establish the truth, nor do they promote justice, since the innocent can be coerced to confess as well as the guilty.

---

[7] *Brady v. United States*, 397 U.S. 742 (1970).
[8] NACDL (2018, p. 5), United States Sentencing Commission (2019, table 11).
[9] Langbein (1978), Alschuler (1983), Lippke (2008), Dervan (2012), Gertner et al. (2015).

This is a lesson brought home by the history of judicial torture in continental Europe in the middle ages.[10] After acquiring enough evidence to suspect someone of a crime, interrogators would question the suspect under torture. As it turns out, under torture, nearly anyone will confess to nearly anything. Medieval law, however, dictated that only *voluntary* confessions could be used. Therefore, once the suspect confessed, the torture would stop. The next day, the suspect would be questioned again, without torture. If he repeated his confession, this second confession would be deemed voluntary. If he recanted, the entire process could be repeated. Most suspects quickly realize that they must make a persuasive "voluntary" confession if they are to avoid future torture.

To modern eyes, that process is a paradigmatic and uncontroversial example of coerced confession. The suspect's second confession, made the day after being tortured, is obviously not rendered voluntary in any relevant sense merely because the suspect is not being tortured *at the moment*. Consider two interpretations of the notion of "voluntariness" in the context of a proscription against non-voluntary confessions:

(a) *Voluntariness as Rational Choice:* A choice to confess is voluntary, provided that the confessor is well informed about his situation, able to rationally weigh the advantages and disadvantages of confessing, and he consciously chooses to confess in the light of such a weighing.
(b) *Voluntariness as Lack of Pressure:* A choice to confess is voluntary only if the confessor is not subject to any pressure to confess of a sort that might plausibly cause an innocent person to confess.

The medieval courts appear to have adopted something like the Rational Choice interpretation. While one is being tortured, the intense pain and terror may render one unable to rationally deliberate. But the day after one's torture, one's rational faculties should again be online. Then, one's act of confessing is consciously chosen, from a rational and well-informed weighing of costs and benefits.

---

[10] Langbein (1978), from whom my account of medieval practice is derived, explicitly draws the parallel between the medieval law of torture and the modern law of plea bargaining.

But that obviously is not the relevant sense of "voluntariness". The relevant sense of "voluntariness" must be Voluntariness as Lack of Pressure. The Rational Choice interpretation is irrelevant, since it does not answer to the central reason why we care about voluntariness, which is that only a suitably voluntary confession provides genuine evidence of guilt. That a suspect deliberately chose to confess to a crime, in view of his accurate and fully rational assessment that failure to do so would result in his own extreme suffering in the future, does not provide satisfactory evidence of his factual guilt. For the confession to serve as evidence, the accused must confess without having any such motivation.

This point, I take it, will be uncontroversial. Yet the U.S. Supreme Court has taken up essentially the position of the medieval courts when it comes to assessing the "voluntariness" of plea bargains.[11] In *Brady v. United States*, Robert Brady claimed that he had pled guilty to a kidnapping charge because he was afraid that he might receive the death penalty if he went to trial. According to the law at the time of his original trial (a provision of law subsequently struck down by the Supreme Court), Brady could have been sentenced to death, if and only if he had been found guilty after a jury trial. Brady argued that this rendered his guilty plea non-voluntary, and he thus requested a jury trial at which he could plead not guilty with no risk of execution. The Supreme Court unanimously rejected Brady's argument. Among other things, the Court decided that, even if Brady's plea had been motivated by the fear of death, this did *not* render it coerced or non-voluntary. Brady's guilty plea was voluntary, according to the court, because Brady had been represented by counsel, who had competently and correctly informed him about his situation, and Brady had chosen a guilty plea as a result of a rational and intelligent weighing of costs and benefits. He was not, for example, mentally incompetent, nor was he misinformed, nor was he so overcome by emotion as to be unable to deliberate rationally.[12]

---

[11] But note that in other cases, the same Court has held it impermissible to impose any cost for the exercise of a Constitutional right: *Griffin v. California*, 380 U.S. 609 (1965), 614; *Spevack v. Klein*, 387 U.S. 511 (1967), 515.

[12] *Brady v. United States*, 397 U.S. 742 (1970). This is my best rational reconstruction of the intrinsically unclear opinion written by Justice Byron White; this is what the opinion must mean if it is to serve, as it is usually taken, as a validation of current plea bargaining practice. See, for example,

This is essentially the Rational Choice reading of "voluntary". Accordingly, the *Brady* decision is flawed for the same reason that the medieval law of torture was flawed: it ignores the purpose of the voluntariness condition. That purpose dictates that voluntariness must be understood as lack of undue pressure.

5.2.2 When the Innocent Plead Guilty

It is not obvious that all plea bargain offers apply undue pressure. Suppose that a murder suspect is offered three years off his expected thirty-year sentence if he agrees to plead guilty and forego a trial. It is not plausible that an innocent person would be driven to confess to murder by such an incentive; therefore, such a deal arguably does not impugn the voluntariness of the defendant's plea of guilt.

But that is not the sort of plea deal commonly seen in the American justice system. In the actual status quo, defendants, in return for pleading guilty, are commonly offered sentences *one third* as severe as they could expect if they were convicted at trial. Standard rational choice theory dictates that in such a situation, a rational defendant accepts the plea bargain as long as his probability of being convicted at trial is greater than one third.[13] Imagine, then, the spectacle of a defense attorney advising his client that, since he is "only" 60% likely to be acquitted at trial, it is in his interests to plead guilty. Or imagine a prosecutor deciding that, since the evidence he has gives him about a 35% chance of convicting a suspect at trial, it is worth going ahead and filing charges. Something has gone very

---

p. 750: "… nor is there evidence that Brady was so gripped by fear of the death penalty or hope of leniency that he did not or could not, with the help of counsel, rationally weigh the advantages of going to trial against the advantages of pleading guilty." However, the opinion also contains statements that seem to entail a rejection of plea bargaining, as where White agrees that a guilty plea may not be induced by threats or promises (pp. 753–5) and that plea bargains would be problematic "if the encouragement of guilty pleas by offers of leniency substantially increased the likelihood that defendants, advised by competent counsel, would falsely condemn themselves" (p. 758).

[13] I assume for simplicity that the defendant is risk neutral and that the disvalue of a prison sentence increases linearly with duration. But any reasonable assumptions here will preserve the central point: the current incentive structure makes it rational for many innocent defendants to plead guilty. Risk averse defendants would plead guilty given even lower probabilities of conviction at trial.

wrong in a justice system in which those would be correct calculations. Surely a defendant who would probably be acquitted should not be given incentives sufficient to make it rational to plead guilty.

Note that 3.3 is only the *average* factor by which sentences produced by trials exceed those offered in plea bargains. Prosecutors have enormous control over this factor and can and do adjust it in individual cases to take account of the strength of the case against the defendant. A prosecutor thus has a good chance of extracting a confession from a rational defendant given almost any nonzero probability of obtaining a conviction at trial. For instance, if there is just a 10% chance of convicting the defendant at trial (more precisely, if the defense believes there is a 10% chance), the prosecutor need only adjust his offer to ensure that the expected punishment if the defendant goes to trial and is convicted is more than ten times greater than the punishment offered in the plea agreement.

How do prosecutors have so much control over expected punishments? One reason is the multiplication of overlapping criminal statutes. Today, the criminal law is so extensive that most actions that intuitively seem to constitute a single crime in fact violate multiple statutes. A person who burglarizes a safe might be charged with three crimes: breaking and entering, safe robbery, and possession of burglary tools.[14] An action also might be interpreted as a more or less serious crime, depending on debatable characteristics of the act. For instance, the same attack might be charged as battery, aggravated battery, or attempted murder. In some cases a defendant can be charged with violating a single statute many times in the same way. Finally, there are now a number of laws with mandatory minimum sentences, which enable a prosecutor to demand a certain minimum sentence irrespective of what the judge may consider reasonable or just. In this legal environment, prosecutors can exercise enormous control over the punishment faced by defendants, through the prosecutor's discretion as to how many and what sort of charges to file.

One dramatic illustration of charge stacking was the case of Khalid Berny, a California goat farmer who in 2004 was charged with having goats at large, after his goats accidentally wandered off his property. The

---

[14] As in the case of Gary Allison; see *Blackledge v. Allison*, 431 U.S. 63 (1977), one of the key precedents establishing plea bargaining as an accepted practice.

district attorney charged Berny with a separate count for *each goat* on each occasion, making a total of 170 charges and subjecting Berny to a total fine of $17,340 ($102 per goat) and *60 years* in prison. (In this case, the district attorney ultimately dismissed the charges, once it became clear that the judge would not look favorably on the case.)[15]

Another illustration is the case of Paul Lewis Hayes, who was indicted for forging an $88 check, an offense that carried a possible prison sentence of two to ten years.[16] The prosecutor offered to recommend a sentence of 5 years if Hayes would plead guilty and "save the court the inconvenience and necessity of a trial". Otherwise, the prosecutor threatened to secure a new indictment against Hayes under an habitual offender statute, which provided for a mandatory minimum sentence of life in prison for a third felony conviction (Hayes had two prior felony convictions at the time). Hayes rejected the plea deal. The prosecutor, true to his word, charged Hayes as an habitual offender, and Hayes was sentenced to life in prison. Hayes appealed to the Supreme Court, which upheld his conviction along with the life sentence.

In the two cases just mentioned, there is no reason to doubt that the defendants were indeed guilty. Regardless, the cases serve to illustrate the amount of pressure prosecutors can bring to bear. Under current U.S. law, prosecutors are empowered to credibly threaten defendants with wildly disproportionate, outrageously unjust punishments in the event that the defendants should lose at trial. This effectively forces defendants who are uncertain of a trial outcome to plead guilty.

Experimental evidence confirms that innocent people can be induced to admit to wrongdoing. In one study, students were accused of cheating and were encouraged, through offers analogous to plea bargains, to admit their guilt. The study created conditions in which some students actually cheated, while others were innocent. The researchers found that actually guilty students were *more* willing to admit their guilt in exchange for leniency (89%), but that the majority of innocent students (56%) would

---

[15] Greenwald (2007).
[16] *Bordenkircher v. Hayes*, 434 U.S. 357 (1978).

falsely condemn themselves in conditions analogous to those of defendants in the criminal justice system.[17]

There are many known cases in the actual criminal justice system in which prosecutors have induced innocent people to plead guilty. In 1986, a young woman named Lori Roscetti was kidnaped, raped, and murdered in Chicago. Police accused four teenagers of the crime: Larry and Calvin Ollins, Omar Saunders, and Marcellius Bradford. After applying high pressure interrogation techniques for hours, the police convinced 14-year-old Calvin Ollins to sign a confession by telling him that he could go home if he signed. Instead of letting him go home, they arrested him as soon as they had the confession. Marcellius Bradford accepted a plea deal with the prosecutor, whereby Bradford agreed to plead guilty to kidnapping and testify against the other three teenagers, in exchange for the prosecutor's dropping the rape and murder charges against him. Finally, a police crime lab expert falsely testified that the DNA from the crime scene was consistent with three of the defendants. All four were convicted. Bradford spent six and a half years in prison, and the other three each spent over fourteen years in prison, before new DNA analysis proved that none of the men was Lori Roscetti's assailant. In 2001, the convictions against all four were vacated and the charges dropped.[18]

This case illustrates several of the things that often go wrong in false conviction cases: police interrogation techniques that bully or trick individuals into signing confessions written by the police (often used against underage or mentally disabled suspects), false testimony by prosecution witnesses, and—of particular interest here—deals offered by prosecutors for pleading guilty or testifying against other defendants. The point that a person can be induced to lie if offered incentives to do so seems to be lost on officials of the American justice system, who continue to rely on testimony that has in effect been purchased or extorted by the prosecutor's office.

Many similar cases have been documented. The Innocence Project provides descriptions of 361 DNA exonerations on its website, of which 41 were of people who had pled guilty.[19] The National Registry of

---

[17] Dervan and Edkins (2013).
[18] Innocence Project (2020b). This case was the subject of the *This American Life* podcast episode "Perfect Evidence" (Glass and DuBow 2002).
[19] Innocence Project (2020a).

Exonerations reports 2154 exonerations between 1989 and 2019, of which 412 were of defendants who had confessed to crimes they did not commit.[20] This must represent only a fraction of the innocent people who have been coerced into pleading guilty, since once one has pled guilty, it is extremely difficult to get anyone interested in investigating one's case—we must therefore assume that most people who falsely condemn themselves are never exonerated.

5.2.3 Disproportionate Punishment

Plea bargaining as currently practiced creates unjust sentences even for guilty defendants. The case of Paul Lewis Hayes described above illustrates the problem: Hayes was offered a five year sentence for forgery, provided that he pled guilty. Since he chose to exercise his right to a trial, he instead received life imprisonment.

In the theory of punishment, the Proportionality Requirement dictates that a just punishment must be proportionate to the crime—the severity of the sentence should match the degree of wrongness of the crime (for discussion, see §6.1.3 below). Certainly, it is wrong to forge a check for $88. Perhaps it is also wrong, after forging such a check, to refuse to admit that one has done so and thus to waste the time and money of the state in conducting a trial. But surely the latter wrong is not so serious as to call for spending the rest of one's life (after the first five years) in prison. There is no plausible way that five years in prison could be a proportionate punishment for a crime, *and* that life imprisonment could also be a proportionate punishment for that same crime when one refuses to plead guilty to it.

That is an extreme case. Nevertheless, as we have noted, very large differences between sentences produced by trials and those produced by plea bargains are the norm. There is no plausible way of maintaining that a crime is rendered three times as bad if, after being caught for it, one insists on a trial. Therefore, the enormous trial penalty represents an abandonment of proportionality. Either plea bargain sentences are much

---

[20] National Registry of Exonerations (2014, 2015, 2016, 2017, 2018, 2019, 2020).

too short, or trial sentences are much too long. (As the Hayes case illustrates, the situation is typically that both are too long.)

One might deny that there is a particular sentence length that is proportionate to a given crime. "Proportionality" may be vague, so that for a given crime, there is some range of sentences that could reasonably be considered proportionate. In that case, if punishments produced by plea bargaining were at least *close* to those produced by trials, both might be within the permissible range of punishments. But again, this could not plausibly be the case if the two differ by a factor of three, as in the actual world.

5.3 Plea Bargaining Is Unconstitutional

The Fifth and Sixth Amendments to the U.S. Constitution bear directly on plea bargaining:

Amendment V: No person shall be held to answer for a capital, or otherwise infamous crime, unless on a presentment or indictment of a Grand Jury, except in cases arising in the land or naval forces, or in the Militia, when in actual service in time of War or public danger; nor shall any person be subject for the same offence to be twice put in jeopardy of life or limb; *nor shall be compelled in any criminal case to be a witness against himself*, nor be deprived of life, liberty, or property, without due process of law; nor shall private property be taken for public use, without just compensation. [emphasis added]

Amendment VI: In all criminal prosecutions, *the accused shall enjoy the right to a speedy and public trial*, by an impartial jury of the State and district wherein the crime shall have been committed, which district shall have been previously ascertained by law, and to be informed of the nature and cause of the accusation; to be confronted with the witnesses against him; to have compulsory process for obtaining witnesses in his favor, and to have the Assistance of Counsel for his defence. [emphasis added]

Each of these amendments is incompatible with the practice of plea bargaining. In current practice, as discussed in §5.2.1, prosecutors coerce defendants into pleading guilty. By pleading guilty, the defendant simultaneously serves as a witness against himself and gives up his right to a trial. But the idea of a legal right is centrally bound up with that of a legal protection against coercion. To hold that one may permissibly be coerced to give up x is precisely to deny that there is any right to x.

If the case were one of a prosecutor beating a confession out of a defendant, the point would be readily conceded by all parties in the justice system. Similarly if the prosecutor merely *threatened* to beat the suspect, without ever actually touching him. Yet somehow, the threat to drastically increase a defendant's prison term is not considered as coercive. Even the threat of execution is not deemed coercive by the courts.

Perhaps one might argue that the threat of an increased prison term is permissible, since the threatened harm would be applied only if and when the defendant is actually convicted at trial—acquitted defendants suffer no added punishments for exercising their right to a trial. This differs from the imagined case of a prosecutor who threatens to beat a recalcitrant defendant—there, we anticipate the beating being carried out in the absence of a criminal conviction. One might think this matters, because perhaps legally authorized harms either do not count as coercive, or else count as a special, permissible kind of coercion.

But that argument is ruled out by the Supreme Court's decision in *United States v. Jackson*.[21] That case concerned a federal kidnapping statute, which provided a possible death penalty for kidnapping, if and only if such penalty was recommended by the jury.[22] This provision implied that defendants who were convicted *without* a jury trial were immune from execution, whereas those who elected a jury trial were at risk of death. The Court deemed this provision a violation of the Fifth and Sixth Amendments:

---

[21] 390 U.S. 570 (1968).
[22] Federal Kidnapping Act, 18 U.S.C. § 1201(a) (as written in 1968): "Whoever knowingly transports in interstate … commerce, any person who has been unlawfully … kidnaped … shall be punished (1) by death if the kidnaped person has not been liberated unharmed, and if the verdict of the jury shall so recommend, or (2) by imprisonment for any term of years or for life, if the death penalty is not imposed."

The inevitable effect of any such provision is, of course, to discourage assertion of the Fifth Amendment right not to plead guilty and to deter exercise of the Sixth Amendment right to demand a jury trial. [...]

It is no answer to urge, as does the Government, that federal trial judges may be relied upon to reject coerced pleas of guilty and involuntary waivers of jury trial. For the evil in the federal statute is not that it necessarily coerces guilty pleas and jury waivers, but simply that it needlessly *encourages* them.[23]

Notice that, per the Supreme Court, it did not matter that the death penalty was legally authorized, nor that it would only be imposed if a defendant was convicted. The prospective *risk* of receiving the death penalty as a result of exercising one's right to a trial was deemed sufficient to render the law unconstitutional. Notice also that the Court took an even stronger position than the one I have taken: I claim that the government may not coerce a person to surrender a Constitutional right. The Supreme Court in *Jackson* took the stronger position that the government may not even *encourage* a person to waive a Constitutional right.

Two years later, Robert Brady brought a case, claiming that he himself had succumbed to exactly the pressure that the *Jackson* court had worried about—he'd been charged under the very law that *Jackson* ruled unconstitutional, and he'd surrendered his right to a jury trial due to the very incentive that made that law unconstitutional. Yet the Court unanimously declared that, even if that was true, Brady's rights had *not* been violated. Despite citing the *Jackson* decision several times, the *Brady* opinion does not address the obvious inconsistency. The opinion argues that Brady was not *coerced*, but it never denies that Brady was *encouraged* to plead guilty in precisely the manner that the *Jackson* decision held to be unconstitutional. Nor did the Court explain why *prosecutors* might have the power to discourage the exercise of Constitutional rights if the *legislature* does not.

---

[23] 390 U.S. 570, at pp. 581, 583; emphasis in original.

5.4 Plea Bargaining Defeats Due Process Protections

Over the course of their history, American courts have developed a body of sophisticated legal doctrine concerned with the rights of criminal defendants. This body of law addresses threats to justice that the courts have identified over the years. It protects the innocent from wrongful conviction; it protects the guilty against abuses to which none should be subject; it protects ordinary citizens against privacy invasions and other abuses by the police. The legal doctrines serving these functions include, for example, the doctrines that suspects must be apprised of their rights, that they have the right to have an attorney present during questioning, and that illegally obtained evidence may not be introduced at trial.[24] These protections are far from perfect, and perhaps even far from the best that human beings can design; nevertheless, they answer to serious justice concerns and cannot reasonably be abandoned in the absence of some superior way of addressing the same concerns.

Most of these protections are implemented through the mechanism of the criminal trial, especially through the decisions judges are to make in the course of a trial. The modern fashion of plea bargaining circumvents due process protections by almost entirely eliminating criminal trials. Conviction and punishment are now almost entirely decided by prosecutors, with minimal input from judges and even less from juries. Thus have prosecutors managed to sideline modern jurisprudence and overthrow judges as the centers of power in the judicial system.

Granted, traditional due process protections continue to play *some role* in a plea-bargain-based justice system: as long as there remains the *possibility* of going to trial, the outcomes that could reasonably be expected from a trial will influence the offers that prosecutors are willing to make and that defendants are willing to accept.[25] But the influence of due process protections is diluted. Lawyers rely on past cases to guess what a judge would say about a particular case; they now rarely put their assump-

---

[24] *Miranda v. Arizona*, 384 U.S. 436 (1966); *Escobedo v. Illinois*, 378 U.S. 478 (1964); *Mapp v. Ohio*, 367 U.S. 643 (1961).
[25] This point is emphasized by Church (1979, pp. 514–15).

tions about what judges would say to the test. Furthermore, the legal doctrines that judges would embrace might evolve over time, *if* judges were given the chance to rule on certain disputed questions—but this evolution is forestalled if questions that would be disputed are never adjudicated in court because the lawyers plea bargain the cases. This limits the ability of judges to control the system. This is worrisome because, in the adversarial system of justice, it is the judges and juries who are meant to serve as objective referees, with an eye toward justice. An adversarial system requires such referees, in addition to the partisan advocates, if it is to remain oriented toward justice.

Equally worrisome is how easily misconduct by police and prosecutors can be concealed in a plea-bargaining system and the offending officials protected from censure. If a prosecutor knows some particular aspect of how a case was handled by police or prosecutors to be legally questionable, the prosecutor can include in the plea bargain agreement a clause stipulating that the defendant must never challenge that particular aspect. A prosecutor can even demand that a defendant waive his right to receive exculpatory evidence that the prosecutor may have in his possession.[26] Defendants can be coerced to accept such unjust demands, since, again, the prosecutor has the power to threaten outrageously disproportionate punishments if the defendant is convicted. Society has an interest in uncovering questionable behavior by police or prosecutors, but few defendants are willing to risk an outrageously harsh punishment in order to bring to light such official misconduct, nor will their lawyers advise them to do so. In some cases, when evidence is uncovered exonerating individuals who have been wrongfully imprisoned, prosecutors use their power to delay the exonerees' release as a bargaining chip—offering, for instance, to let the prisoner be released immediately if the prisoner agrees not to sue the government.[27]

This system effectively turns what are meant to be prohibitions on official misconduct into mere *bargaining disadvantages*—it is not that the government can't violate your rights; it is that after doing so, they may have to offer you less time in prison than they otherwise would. Given

---

[26] NACDL (2018, p. 28).
[27] Armstrong and Possley (1999).

the extremely wide discretionary power prosecutors start out with, this may be of little comfort. Misconduct by the police or prosecutor's office may merely mean that the prosecutor has to step up his threats against the defendant in order to coerce the defendant into giving up the right to challenge that misconduct.

5.5 Defenses of Plea Bargaining

Despite what I have said, plea bargaining has its defenders. In this section, we consider philosophical and practical defenses that have been offered for the practice.

5.5.1 "Plea Bargaining Is Not Coercive"

Some believe that plea bargain offers do not count as coercive, because coercion is a partly moral concept.[28] On this view, A coerces B, roughly, when A threatens to render B worse off than B *had a right to be*, in order to induce B to perform some action desired by A. In a normal plea bargaining case, a prosecutor first files some serious charges against a defendant. Assuming these charges are legally justified (which requires that the prosecutor has probable cause to believe that the defendant committed the crimes for which he is to be charged), one might argue, the defendant has no right against being subject to those charges, nor has the defendant any right to leniency in sentencing. Therefore, the threat to let those charges stand does not count as coercive, nor does the threat to recommend the full legal punishment attached thereto.

We might question this as an analysis of the meaning of "coercion" in English. Perhaps, for example, physically forcing a person to perform some action counts as coercive *even if* one has the right to so force them; perhaps also, threatening to violate someone's rights in a minor way *fails* to coerce. But it is not necessary to resolve this semantic question. The key claim in defense of plea bargaining is that plea bargain offers only

---

[28] Wertheimer (1979, pp. 215–23), Sandefur (2003, p. 30).

offer to render defendants better off than they have a right to expect, where rejection of the offer results in the defendant's being treated no more harshly than the government already has the right to treat him—and that this implies that such offers cannot be impermissible.

The core problem with this argument lies in the assumption that typical plea bargain offers involve no threat of unjust treatment. Recall the case of Paul Hayes, the defendant who, having two prior felony convictions, was arrested for trying to pass a forged check for $88. What would be a proportionate punishment for such a crime? In a proportionate punishment, the criminal suffers a harm roughly as great as, or at least not *vastly* greater than, the harm the defendant imposed (or tried to impose, or threatened to impose) on others. We could make refinements to this, depending on the defendant's degree of responsibility, his motives, and so on; nevertheless, in a normal case, we would expect something like this rule to obtain.

In the Hayes case, the harm the defendant tried to impose on others was a loss of $88. This harm is perhaps as serious as a night in jail, or perhaps several nights in jail, depending on the person, his financial situation, and so on. The prosecutor offered to recommend a sentence of *five years* in prison. This appears to be literally hundreds of times greater than the harm the defendant tried to impose on others. But the defendant rejected the plea, as a result of which the prosecutor instead had Hayes sentenced to *life in prison*. It could not seriously be claimed that this was a just sentence. Therefore, on the moralized conception of coercion, the prosecutor's plea bargain offer *was* coercive.

That was an extreme case. Nevertheless, grossly disproportionate sentences are regularly threatened in the U.S. criminal justice system. When an individual is alleged to have engaged in behavior that intuitively seems to constitute a single crime, the accused is often subject to multiple charges, *each* of which is of comparable seriousness to what one would intuitively think was the single crime. Furthermore, prison sentences in the U.S. are much more common, and much longer—sometimes several times longer—than would be the norm in other advanced, Western nations.[29] That is to speak of the average sentences in the status quo, in

---

[29] Whitman (2003, p. 57), Petteruti and Fenster (2011, pp. 21–2).

which almost all sentences are the results of plea bargaining; the sentences defendants were *threatened* with are, on average, about three times longer. America's incarceration rate is by far the highest in the world, due largely to the long prison terms handed out by American prosecutors and courts.[30]

For another example, in 2010, a group of six men engaged in a string of armed robberies. Five of the men accepted plea bargains and received sentences between 9 and 20 years in prison for their deeds. One defendant, Quartavious Davis, requested a trial. At the trial, he was sentenced to 162 years in prison.[31]

The point, again, is that prosecutors in reality are clearly threatening defendants with excessive sentences. The notion that the punishment sought by prosecutors at trial is simply justice, so that any downward deviation is a matter of supererogatory mercy on the part of the government, defies belief.

One might be tempted to argue that these excessive sentences are a problem with the particular statutes involved, or perhaps with particular prosecutors who misuse their discretion, rather than a problem with the practice of plea bargaining as such.[32] The proper remedy, one might think, is to adjust the laws, or perhaps to hire better prosecutors, not to eliminate plea bargaining.

This argument would be misguided. The problem is indeed a problem with plea bargaining, because the excessive sentences are an entirely predictable consequence of the acceptance of plea bargaining, given robust other features of the American justice system. These other features include the adversarial nature of the system, as a result of which prosecutors strive to attain a "winning" record; the very extensive, complex, and overlapping body of presently existing law; and the political incentives for legislators and prosecutors to appear "tough on crime". Given these factors, it is almost inevitable that in most real cases, there will be a wide range of punishments that could be legally justified for a given defendant, including some excessive sentences, and that prosecutors would threaten

---

[30] Mauer (2018).
[31] NBC News (2015); *United States v. Quartavious Davis* 785 F.3d 498 (11th Cir. 2015).
[32] This view is suggested by Sandefur (2003, p. 28).

defendants with excessive sentences to induce them to plead guilty. It would be extremely surprising if this did not occur.

It is not feasible to propose altering hundreds or thousands of statutes to reduce excessive sentences, eliminate overlapping prohibitions, and generally prevent the possibility of widely disparate sentences being legally supportable for the same crime. This would be extremely difficult even if legislatures were sympathetic to the problem of unjust treatment of criminal suspects. Nor is it feasible to suggest replacing prosecutors across the nation with a class of much more virtuous people who would pursue impartial justice regardless of the incentives they personally face. The most feasible way to address the problem of coercive plea bargain offers is in fact to change the plea bargaining system. That is why the problem is properly viewed as a problem with plea bargaining, not merely with certain statutes or certain prosecutors.

Another argument in defense of the plea bargaining system is that, however things may stand with regard to *morality*, it remains the case that the prosecutor in the typical case is *legally* entitled to pursue the most serious legally supportable charges and to recommend the harshest legally prescribed punishment. Because these things are legally allowed, one might claim, the *law* cannot view the prosecutor's threat to do them as coercive. Granted, the prosecutor's conduct might be *immoral*, but at least this argument might show that the plea bargaining system is not *unconstitutional*.[33]

In reply, this notion of "legal coercion" could not be accepted for purposes of Constitutional interpretation, lest the force of nearly all Constitutional rights be undermined. The proposed test of coerciveness amounts to this: the government counts as *coercing* an individual only if the government threatens to harm the individual in a way that is not authorized by the laws made by the legislature. On this account, the legislature has available a straightforward way of circumventing all or nearly all Constitutional rights, without having to amend the Constitution: the government can induce people to waive all their Constitutional rights by issuing sufficiently dire threats against those who refuse to waive. To avoid the legal challenge arising from this apparent coercion, the

---

[33] Something like this argument is suggested by Sandefur (2003, p. 30).

legislature would need only to *authorize itself* to issue those threats and they would immediately become "legally non-coercive". Since this would defeat the purpose of recognizing individual rights within the Constitution to begin with, this interpretation of "coercion" cannot be accepted as faithful to the Constitution.

5.5.2 "Individuals Have the Right to Sell Their Rights"

Some believe that due process rights ought to be freely saleable, just as many other rights are. For example, members of the military are forbidden to verbally disrespect the President. This does not violate the First Amendment right to free speech, because the restriction is voluntarily accepted when one joins the military. More generally, market transactions regularly involve conditional transfers of rights, and these are not considered as violations of those rights. Why should the right to a fair trial or the right against self-incrimination be any different from the many other rights that we permit individuals to trade or sell?[34]

Indeed, we might find it perverse to prohibit an individual from engaging in such transactions. If a defendant is willing to accept a plea bargain offer, this is strong evidence that the plea bargain is in that defendant's interests, compared to the alternative of going to trial on the original charges. How can one, out of respect for *that defendant's* rights, argue against an option that the defendant consents to and that renders the defendant himself better off?[35]

In reply, legal rights may serve more than one function. Some legal rights function to protect important interests of the individual rights-bearer. Some legal rights, however, function to protect more general societal interests, such as the need to restrain government from becoming too powerful or abusive.

Consider the right of *freedom of the press*. Freedom of the press serves *partly* to protect the interests of news organizations, but that is a minor part of its function; it would not explain the importance of freedom of

---

[34] Sandefur (2003, pp. 29, 31).
[35] Church (1979, p. 514); Hammond (2006).

the press compared to, say, the freedom of cobblers to repair shoes. The main reason why freedom of the press is deemed a crucial right in the American political system is the role it plays in protecting the country against abusive, incompetent, or otherwise bad government: it guarantees that the government's errors, or possible errors, can be pointed out and openly discussed. When the government prohibits the *New York Times* from publishing the Pentagon Papers, the main problem is not that the *Times* is harmed by being unable to sell newspapers with a juicy story.[36] The main problem is that *the country* is under threat of being deceived by the government in ways that enable the government to carry on harmful or unjust policies—in that particular case, the Vietnam war.

That is why it would not be acceptable for the government to *buy* the right of freedom of the press. Suppose that, rather than obtaining an injunction prohibiting the *New York Times* from publishing the Pentagon Papers, the Nixon administration had instead *paid* the *Times*, and every other newspaper that had the document, to keep it secret. Assume for the sake of argument that the newspapers would have accepted these bribes. This would not have been acceptable. True, the interests of the media organizations would have been as well served or better by this arrangement than by the actual situation, in which they published the document. But to say this is to say nothing to address the societal interest that is the central point of the right to a free press. The ability to sell to the government one's right to report on government malfeasance does not protect society from government malfeasance. That is why the right of freedom of the press should not be legally saleable, and no such agreement should be enforced by any court.

Similar points apply to the freedom of speech, the right to vote, and, of particular interest here, the right to a trial. The purpose of the right to a trial is not to unconditionally serve the interests of criminal defendants. The purpose of establishing such a right is to safeguard *justice*. The

---

[36] The Pentagon Papers was a secret government report detailing the history of the U.S. involvement in Vietnam, which showed that the government had systematically lied to the public about that involvement. It was leaked by Daniel Ellsburg in 1971, during the U.S. war in Vietnam. The government obtained an injunction to prevent the *New York Times* from publishing the report. The Supreme Court ultimately struck down that injunction as a violation of the First Amendment, in *New York Times Co. v. United States*, 403 U.S. 713 (1971).

assumption behind this is that a trial is the best known, practicable method of determining the actual truth about a criminal accusation—who did what, with what degree of culpability. The court needs to know this truth, in order to ensure that justice is done—that the innocent are acquitted, and the guilty punished to that degree, and only that degree, merited by their crimes. This purpose is not served by a system that allows defendants to be paid in exchange for their agreement to substitute a less reliable mechanism for disposing of cases.

One might wonder, then, why defendants should *ever* be permitted to plead guilty and waive their right to a trial. The reason is that, in the special case where a defendant voluntarily pleads guilty, without having been subjected to any undue pressure, this fact is powerful evidence of factual guilt—perhaps more powerful even than a trial conviction. Thus, the court's need to determine the truth is satisfied. But when a defendant pleads guilty after having been threatened with much more serious charges or a much heavier sentence, this fact is *not* powerful evidence of factual guilt, nor is it strong evidence that the punishment recommended in the plea agreement is in fact just. The court is unconditionally obligated to strive for justice—this obligation cannot be removed by a release signed by the defendant, or the prosecutor, or both combined.

One further point is relevant to the claim that plea bargain offers serve the defendant's interests, as perceived by the defendant. Though this claim is plausibly true of individual cases *given* the current system, it is far from clear that defendants' interests are served by a system that makes plea bargaining possible. For the possibility of plea bargaining encourages prosecutors to file excessive charges and seek excessive penalties to start with, in order to give themselves a strong bargaining position from which to secure a guilty plea.

5.5.3 "Trials Are Too Expensive"

The legal reasoning given by the Supreme Court in defense of plea bargaining is of uncharacteristically poor quality (see §5.2.1). Usually, the Court fares better at protecting due process and Constitutional rights. Certain remarks in the Court opinions concerning plea bargaining suggest an explanation for the Court's shortcomings on this issue:

> For the State, there are also advantages [to plea bargains]—the more promptly imposed punishment after an admission of guilt may more effectively attain the objectives of punishment, and, with the avoidance of trial, scarce judicial and prosecutorial resources are conserved ... It is this mutuality of advantage that perhaps explains the fact that, at present, well over three-fourths of the criminal convictions in this country rest on pleas of guilty, a great many of them no doubt motivated at least in part by the hope or assurance of a lesser penalty ....[37]
>
> Whatever might be the situation in an ideal world, the fact is that the guilty plea and the often concomitant plea bargain are important components of this country's criminal justice system. Properly administered, they can benefit all concerned. ... Judges and prosecutors conserve vital and scarce resources. ...[38]

These remarks suggest that the Court, in devising legal justifications for plea bargaining, had one eye on questions of expediency. Had the Supreme Court struck down plea bargains as unconstitutional, it would have, by the Court's own estimate as of 1970, more than quadrupled the number of trials that had to be conducted to deal with the then-current volume of criminal cases. That is to say nothing of all the *past* plea bargain convictions that would have had to be re-litigated.

In all probability, the court was simply unwilling to impose such a large cost on the legal system. But of course, there is no provision in the Constitution for suspending defendants' Constitutional rights simply because it is too expensive to satisfy them. Therefore, the court had to do its best to devise some other rationale for permitting plea bargaining that sounded more legally valid. The best the judges could come up with was the medieval-style theory of voluntariness vaguely and inconsistently invoked by Justice White in *Brady v. United States*.

All this sounds disreputable on the part of the judges. But it is easy to sympathize with their dilemma. The dilemma would be even starker today. Trials today are more expensive than ever (see Chap. 4). They commonly take up multiple days for a judge, a prosecuting attorney, a defense attorney, and between 6 and 12 jurors, depending on the crime. American

---

[37] *Brady v. United States*, 397 U.S. 742 (1970), p. 752.
[38] *Blackledge v. Allison*, 431 U.S. 63 (1977), p. 71.

courts face large backlogs, forcing defendants to wait months or even years for a trial. In some cases, defendants spend more time in jail waiting for a trial than the actual sentence they would receive if convicted.[39] That is the situation at present, when just 3% of cases go to trial. Imagine the situation after the trial caseload is multiplied by a factor of *30*, as it would be if every case went to trial. We might evolve to a system in which defendants are simply held in "pretrial" detention for the entire sentence that they would serve if convicted, with neither trial nor plea bargaining.

Without minimizing the seriousness of this practical problem, I do not believe it can be taken to justify the abandonment of due process or the distortion of Constitutional rights represented by the acceptance of plea bargaining. The result of the Supreme Court's refusal to enforce the Fifth and Sixth Amendments back in 1970 is that by now, the right to a trial and the right against self-incrimination have been eliminated in the U.S. in all but name, and the central function of the judicial branch has been nearly eliminated. These are not minor rights; without these rights, there is little meaning in any rights accorded to defendants. We essentially have a system in which police and prosecutors decide who should be punished and how much. The ability to dispense punishment with almost no oversight is not the sort of power that should be granted to the executive branch in a liberal democracy.

The practice of plea bargaining needs to be eliminated or severely restricted, and legislatures need to provide adequate funding to handle caseloads faced by the courts. Today, when political leaders wish to be tough on crime, they call for increased funding for *police*, to make more arrests. The courts need to make clear that there must also be increased funding for courts to try those arrestees; otherwise, they will go free. Courts cannot react to being flooded with cases, without adequate resources to try them, by simply giving up the effort to do justice.

Part of the problem is that trials have grown excessively costly and time-consuming. In eighteenth-century England, out of which the American legal system was born, a court would hear between 12 and 20 cases in a day.[40] In present-day America, a single case usually stretches

---

[39] Brennan (2014).
[40] Langbein (1978, p. 10).

over multiple days. In addition to the need for the legislature to provide greater resources to the courts, there is a need for more sweeping reforms to reduce the costs of trials and of handling criminal cases generally (see Chap. 4).

5.6 Reforms

5.6.1 Limiting the Trial Penalty

Despite the arguments given above, it is not necessary to eliminate the practice of plea bargaining entirely. Courts could instead place strong *constraints* on plea bargain offers, beginning with constraints that limit the trial penalty, either to some fixed absolute amount, or to some fixed percentage of the expected sentence. Thus, perhaps prosecutors, in the event of a trial, would be barred from seeking punishments more than 20% greater than those that had been offered during plea bargaining.[41]

How could such a constrained plea bargain system be permissible, in light of all the problems with plea bargaining cited above? The most serious problem with plea bargaining as currently practiced is that it creates incentives sufficient to induce rational defendants to plead guilty *even if* they are innocent and would probably be acquitted in a trial. In such a system, a defendant's willingness to plead guilty does not provide strong evidence of his guilt; a court therefore cannot proceed to punish a defendant on that basis without violating its central duty to pursue justice in the case.

This problem is mitigated by a sufficiently tight constraint on the trial penalty. A 20% trial penalty is unlikely to induce an innocent person to plead guilty. Granted, there will always remain some chance of inducing innocent persons to plead guilty as long as any plea bargaining is allowed.

---

[41] Lippke (2011) proposes that sentence discounts might be fixed, perhaps at 10% (pp. 49, 241), or negotiable but capped, perhaps at 20% (p. 77). He argues that this type of scheme can be expected to generate a large number of guilty pleas despite the small discounts in sentences. He cites the experience of England and Wales, where sentence discounts for guilty pleas are limited to a maximum of one third of the normal sentence, depending on the timing of the plea (Sentencing Council for England and Wales n.d.). Under this scheme, upwards of 90% of defendants in Magistrate courts and 70% of defendants in Crown courts plead guilty (Lippke 2011, pp. 77–8).

But any justice system that punishes anyone at all must incur some risk of punishing the innocent. If the trial penalty is limited to 20%, then rationally self-interested defendants should plead guilty only if the probability of conviction at trial is greater than 83%.[42] Note that an 83% chance of conviction does not mean there is an 83% chance that the defendant is factually guilty; it means there is an 83% chance that, in the eyes of a jury, the evidence of guilt would count as *proof beyond a reasonable doubt*. We may plausibly consider this to be sufficient assurance of factual guilt for a court to proceed with punishment in good conscience.

In the present system, something between 85% and 95% of trials result in convictions.[43] This of course has much to do with why almost all defendants take plea bargains rather than going to trial. Therefore, the typical defendant has an 85–95% chance of being convicted at trial. Thus, under the proposed 20% cap on the trial penalty, it would remain rational for *most* defendants to accept a plea bargain. Only those defendants who are (or take themselves to be) unusually likely to be acquitted would be rational to proceed to trial. That is the result we should aim for.

The proposed cap on the trial penalty, by greatly reducing the incentives for the innocent to plead guilty, also mitigates the concern about coercing individuals to waive their Constitutional rights. Recall that the relevant notion of "coercion" in this context is that of something that exerts pressure plausibly sufficient to induce the innocent to plead guilty (§5.2.1). If the immediately preceding argument is correct, the cap on the trial penalty would plausibly render plea bargain offers non-coercive. This, in turn, would prevent them from violating the Constitutional rights to a trial and against self-incrimination.

Finally, the cap on the trial penalty addresses the problem of disproportionate punishment. This is because it can plausibly be held that a defendant who takes responsibility for his crime by pleading guilty is at

---

[42] This calculation assumes risk neutrality and that disutility of imprisonment increases linearly with duration. Given this, the defendant is indifferent between trial and plea bargain when $B = P \times T$, where B is the offered plea bargain sentence, P is the probability of conviction at trial, and T is the expected sentence at trial if convicted. When $T = B \times 120\%$, P must be $B/T = B/(B \times 120\%) = 83\%$.

[43] U.S. Department of Justice statistics show a 94% conviction rate in federal prosecutions in the U.S. (ABC News 2010). Earlier data show a conviction rate of between 85 and 90% for state courts (Ramseyer et al. 2008, p. 17).

least slightly less blameworthy than one who insists on a trial despite his factual guilt. We might even deem it morally wrong (though not extremely so) to insist on a trial when one is in fact guilty, since doing so imposes needless costs on society.

This last consideration (concerning proportionality) may suggest a fixed *absolute* maximum on the trial penalty, whereas the earlier consideration (concerning the risk of inducing the innocent to plead guilty) suggested a fixed *percentage* limit. To respect both considerations, perhaps the optimal system would impose a dual limit—for example, perhaps the trial penalty might be limited to the lesser of (a) one year in prison or (b) 20% of the penalty offered in a plea agreement.

The quantities "one year" and "20%" are chosen for illustrative purposes. A range of other values could reasonably be proposed. Nevertheless, it seems clear that some such limits are required, and limits much lower than the current typical trial penalties.

5.6.2 The Right to Sue

Plea bargaining should never be used to protect government misconduct, or alleged misconduct, from being examined. To so use the process is a form of corruption, a misuse of the powers of the prosecutor's office for the benefit of the prosecutor, rather than for the benefit of the public—no less than it would be to use the threat of criminal charges to extract bribes for the prosecutor and his friends. Therefore, judges should reject any plea agreement that seeks to constrain the ability of defendants to sue police or prosecutors, or in any other way to challenge the conduct of public officials. If such an agreement is somehow made, it should be unenforceable. To prevent prosecutors from making unethical secret agreements with defendants, courts should require that all meetings between prosecutors and defendants or defense counsel be recorded.

These constraints address to some degree the threat that current plea bargaining practice poses to Constitutional rights (see §5.4). Unfortunately, some rights, in the present system, are protected only through rules that come into play during a trial, for example, the exclusionary rule, whereby evidence that the government obtained illegally is barred from being introduced at trial. If a prosecutor convinces a defendant to plead guilty, this forestalls a trial, thus preventing a judge from ever ruling on whether a given piece of evidence was obtained illegally.

The proper remedy for cases of police or prosecutorial misconduct, however, is not to have a judge exclude evidence during a defendant's trial. The proper remedy is for the victim of the misconduct—whether or not that victim is ever himself put on trial—to file a lawsuit against the government officials responsible for the misconduct. Of this, we shall have more to say in a later chapter (§§7.3.3 and 7.6).

5.6.3 Cost Reduction

The main cause of the growth of plea bargaining appears to be the high cost of trials. Therefore, reforms that would reduce plea bargaining, as the above-suggested reforms would, must be combined with methods of reducing costs. Here, I refer the reader to the suggestions for reducing costs given in the previous chapter (see §4.7).

Perhaps the most important reform, but also the most controversial, would be a move toward privatization of court functions. I suspect that no satisfactory solution to the cost problem will be possible without such a move. This is for well-known reasons: any good or service tends to become more expensive, often drastically so, in the absence of price competition. This phenomenon is most often seen in the case of government services, but it applies to any area in which a single organization holds a monopoly on some good or service. If a single company controlled all food sales in the U.S., food prices would shortly begin to skyrocket. If one organization controlled all housing, housing prices would swell. It is impractical to imagine that government courts can avoid escalating costs over the long term while still maintaining a monopoly on the resolution of criminal cases.

The government should therefore provide an option whereby criminal defendants may have their cases resolved by private arbitrators. The government could of course regulate arbitrators to maintain certain standards of justice, though the quantity of regulation should be kept modest to avoid defeating the cost-control purpose. The prosecutor and defendant might jointly select an arbitrator by alternately crossing names off a list of available arbitrators. For reasons discussed above (§§4.4 and 4.6), the government should pay the fees for private arbitration. The prosecutor's office would thus need to take cost considerations into account during the process of selecting an arbitrator.

Why would a criminal defendant opt for private arbitration over a government court? Chiefly to save time. Recall that the court system is presently overburdened, so that many defendants (those who are denied bail or cannot afford bail) spend months in jail awaiting trial. Backlogs in government courts would likely increase once the practice of plea bargaining was properly restricted. As in other areas of the economy, however, the market would be able to meet the demand that government is unable to meet. A key difference generally observed between government provision and market provision of goods and services is that the market generally supplies as much of a good or service as people are prepared to pay for, whereas government-provided goods and services are often in chronic short supply. The service of resolving criminal cases of course differs from other goods and services in important ways, but probably not in this specific way.

Is this proposal Constitutionally acceptable? One might worry that defendants, faced with long periods in jail waiting for access to government courts, would effectively be *coerced* to accept arbitration. Because arbitrators do not in general use juries (and presumably would continue not to do so), one might worry that this violates the Sixth Amendment right to a trial by jury.

In reply, I do not know whether the foregoing proposal would be, all things considered, Constitutional. It would, however, be *superior to* the status quo with regard to respecting the Constitution. This is because the status quo coerces almost everyone into giving up, not only the right to a *jury* trial, but the right to any trial at all. In addition, the status quo already allows defendants to spend months or even years in jail awaiting trial. To give defendants an additional option, that of accepting private arbitration, cannot be more coercive than the status quo.

What of our earlier arguments to the effect that the right to a trial should not be saleable (§5.5.2)—do they also show that one ought not to be able to trade the right to a jury trial for a speedy resolution of one's case?

I believe not. The reason is that allowing individuals to select private arbitration does not defeat the purpose of the right to a jury trial, in the way that allowing individuals to plead guilty to avoid excessive charges by the prosecutor *does*. The latter option (the status quo plea bargaining option) defeats the purpose of the right to a trial by encouraging prosecutors to stack charges in order to extort guilty pleas from defendants. In the current plea bargaining system, guilty pleas cannot be trusted as genuine proof of guilt, since both guilty and innocent people may succumb to this pressure.

The private arbitration option does not do anything comparable, since it does not prejudice the *outcome* of the case—it does not require the defendant to confess guilt, nor the prosecutor to dismiss the charges. Provided that private arbitrators are of at least comparable reliability to juries, this option would not defeat the goal of determining the truth so that justice may be done.

References

ABC News. 2010, August 4. Feds' Conviction Rate Bad Sign for Blago. http://abclocal.go.com/wls/story?section=news/local&id=7593302. Accessed 3 Oct 2012.

Alschuler, Albert W. 1979. Plea Bargaining and Its History. *Columbia Law Review* 79 (1979): 1–43.

———. 1983. Implementing the Criminal Defendant's Right to Trial: Alternatives to the Plea Bargaining System. *University of Chicago Law Review* 50: 931–1050.

Armstrong, Ken, and Maurice Possley. 1999. The Verdict: Dishonor. *Chicago Tribune*, January 11. http://www.chicagotribune.com/news/watchdog/chi-020103trial1-story.html. Accessed 3 Oct 2019.

Brennan, Alice. 2014. Right to a Speedy Trial? This Innocent Teenager Waited 3 Years in Jail. *Fusion*, April 28. https://fusion.tv/story/5419/right-to-a-speedy-trial-this-innocent-teenager-waited-3-years-in-jail/. Accessed 16 Mar 2019.

Church, Thomas W. 1979. In Defense of 'Bargain Justice'. *Law and Society Review* 13: 509–525.

Dervan, Lucian E. 2012. Bargained Justice: Plea-Bargaining's Innocence Problem and the *Brady* Safety-Valve. *Utah Law Review* 51: 51–97.

Dervan, Lucian E., and Vanessa A. Edkins. 2013. The Innocent Defendant's Dilemma: An Innovative Empirical Study of Plea Bargaining's Innocence Problem. *Journal of Criminal Law & Criminology* 103: 1–48.

Gertner, Nancy, Bruce Brower, Paul Shechtman, and Jed S. Rakoff. 2015. 'Why the Innocent Plead Guilty': An Exchange. *New York Review of Books*, January 8. https://www.nybooks.com/articles/2015/01/08/why-innocent-plead-guilty-exchange/. Accessed 4 Mar 2019.

Glass, Ira, and Shane DuBow. 2002. Perfect Evidence (Podcast). *This American Life*, April 19. https://www.thisamericanlife.org/210/perfect-evidence. Accessed 3 Aug 2019.

Greenwald, David. 2007. Khalid Berny: A Case of Discriminatory Prosecution by the Yolo County District Attorney. *The Davis Vanguard*, January 3. https://www.davisvanguard.org/2007/01/khalid-berny-a-case-of-discriminatory-prosecution-by-the-yolo-county-district-attorney/. Accessed 3 June 2019.

Hammond, Scott D. 2006, October 17. The U.S. Model of Negotiated Plea Agreements: A Good Deal with Benefits For All. Address before the OECD Competition Committee Working Party No. 3. http://www.usdoj.gov/atr/public/speeches/219332.pdf. Accessed 27 June 2020.

Innocence Project. 2020a. All Cases. https://www.innocenceproject.org/all-cases/. Accessed 27 June 2020.

———. 2020b. Marcellius Bradford. https://www.innocenceproject.org/cases/marcellius-bradford/. Accessed 27 June 2020.

Langbein, John H. 1978. Torture and Plea Bargaining. *University of Chicago Law Review* 46: 3–22.

Lippke, Richard L. 2008. To Waive or Not to Waive: The Right to Trial and Plea Bargaining. *Criminal Law and Philosophy* 2: 181–199.

———. 2011. *The Ethics of Plea Bargaining*. Oxford University Press.

Mauer, Marc. 2018. Long-Term Sentences: Time to Reconsider the Scale of Punishment. *UMKC Law Review* 87: 113–131.

NACDL (National Association of Criminal Defense Lawyers). 2018. *The Trial Penalty: The Sixth Amendment Right to Trial on the Verge of Extinction and How to Save It*. Washington, DC: NACDL. http://www.nacdl.org/trialpenaltyreport. Accessed 27 June 2020.

National Registry of Exonerations. 2014. *Exonerations in 2013*. http://www.law.umich.edu/special/exoneration/Documents/Exonerations_in_2013_Report.pdf. Accessed 27 June 2020.

———. 2015. *Exonerations in 2014*. http://www.law.umich.edu/special/exoneration/Documents/Exonerations_in_2014_report.pdf. Accessed 27 June 2020.

———. 2016. *Exonerations in 2015*. http://www.law.umich.edu/special/exoneration/Documents/Exonerations_in_2015.pdf. Accessed 27 June 2020.

———. 2017. *Exonerations in 2016*. http://www.law.umich.edu/special/exoneration/Documents/Exonerations_in_2016.pdf. Accessed 27 June 2020.

———. 2018. *Exonerations in 2017*. http://www.law.umich.edu/special/exoneration/Documents/ExonerationsIn2017.pdf. Accessed 27 June 2020.

———. 2019. *Exonerations in 2018*. http://www.law.umich.edu/special/exoneration/Documents/Exonerations%20in%202018.pdf. Accessed 27 June 2020.

———. 2020. *Annual Report*. http://www.law.umich.edu/special/exoneration/Documents/Exonerations_in_2019.pdf. Accessed 27 June 2020.

NBC News. 2015. Quartavious Davis, First-Time Offender with 162-Year Prison Term, Gets Appeal. *NBC News*, February 21. https://www.nbcnews.com/news/crime-courts/quartavious-davis-first-time-offender-162-year-prison-term-gets-n305776. Accessed 27 June 2020.

Petteruti, Amanda, and Jason Fenster. 2011. *Finding Direction: Expanding Criminal Justice Options by Considering Policies of Other Nations*. Washington, DC: Justice Policy Institute. http://www.justicepolicy.org/uploads/justicepolicy/documents/finding_direction-full_report.pdf. Accessed 27 June 2020.

Ramseyer, J. Mark, Eric B. Rasmusen, and Manu Raghav. 2008. "Convictions versus Conviction Rates: The Prosecutor's Choice", Harvard Law and Economics Discussion Paper No. 611, http://papers.ssrn.com/ sol3/ papers.cfm?abstract_id=1108813. Accessed October 3, 2012.

Sandefur, Timothy. 2003, Fall. In Defense of Plea Bargaining. *Regulation*: 28–31.

Sentencing Council for England and Wales. n.d. *Reduction in Sentence for a Guilty Plea: Definitive Guideline*. https://www.sentencingcouncil.org.uk/wp-content/uploads/Reduction-in-Sentence-for-Guilty-Plea-definitive-guideline-SC-Web.pdf. Accessed 27 June 2020.

United States Sentencing Commission. 2019. *2019 Annual Report and Sourcebook of Federal Sentencing Statistics*. https://www.ussc.gov/research/sourcebook-2019. Accessed 25 June 2020.

Wertheimer, Alan. 1979. Freedom, Morality, Plea Bargaining, and the Supreme Court. *Philosophy & Public Affairs* 8: 203–234.

Whitman, James Q. 2003. *Harsh Justice: Criminal Punishment and the Widening Divide Between America and Europe*. Oxford: Oxford University Press.

6

Unjust Punishments

6.1 Principles of Just Punishment

6.1.1 Why We Punish

Punishment is, roughly, a kind of action in which an agent intentionally inflicts harm on a person in retaliation for that person's (alleged) performance of some action that is considered wrongful or otherwise undesired. The state generally enforces its laws by punishing lawbreakers, usually with monetary fines or imprisonment. I shall assume that some punishment is just.[1] Nevertheless, I shall argue, the present U.S. justice system generates an enormous amount of unjust punishment. I focus on *incarceration*, because it is this form of punishment that currently raises the most pressing issues.

To assess the justice of present policies, we must first reflect on what justifies incarceration in general. Traditionally, there are three main reasons for imprisoning criminals:

---

[1] Some philosophers deny this (see Boonin 2008), but it would take us too far afield to address the skeptical position in detail.

(i) *Incapacitation:* Imprisonment directly, physically prevents convicts from committing further crimes against the general population for the duration of their sentence.
(ii) *Deterrence:* We imprison criminals in the hope that fear of (further) imprisonment will prevent those individuals or other individuals from committing (further) crimes.
(iii) *Retributive Justice:* Many believe that those who have committed wrongs *deserve* to suffer harm in return, and that justice demands giving to each individual what that individual deserves.[2]

Philosophers and legal theorists debate which of these rationales is the most important. In particular, some think that retribution lies at the core of criminal justice, while others reject retributive notions of justice altogether.

6.1.2 The Need for Retributive Justice

In my view, the retributive rationale is essential to an adequate theory of criminal justice. I do not, however, claim that the retributive rationale alone would *suffice* to justify punishment. My claim is that the retributive rationale is *necessary* to account for just punishment. In other words, a punishment is just *only if* the individual to be punished deserves that punishment; incapacitation and deterrence are not enough to render a punishment just.

To see what I mean, consider a case in which the deterrence rationale applies yet the punishment is clearly undeserved:

Deterrence Framing: A high-profile crime has been committed in a certain town. The sheriff cannot find the actual perpetrator; he can, however, frame an innocent person, which will convince the town that the innocent person is guilty and will cause that person to be sent to prison for the crime. Since almost everyone will *believe* that the perpetrator was punished, this will deter crime just as well as

---
[2] Moore (1997); Lippke (2007).

punishing the actual perpetrator would have done.³

In this case, it would obviously be unjust and morally wrong to bring about the punishment of the innocent person. Yet the deterrence rationale would be equally well satisfied in this case as it normally is when the state punishes convicted criminals. If deterrence were sufficient to justify punishment, then punishment would be justified in Deterrence Framing. This shows that, while deterrence may play some role in justifying punishment, it alone cannot justify a punishment that is undeserved.

Next, consider a case in which the incapacitation rationale applies yet the punishment is undeserved:

Forged Check: In the 1970's, Paul Lewis Hayes was convicted of attempting to pass a forged check for $88, which was classified as a felony in his state. Because Hayes had two prior felony convictions, he was charged under an habitual offender statute, which prescribed a life sentence for a third felony conviction. Accordingly, Hayes was sentenced to life imprisonment for his crime, and this sentence was upheld on appeal.⁴

This seems to be about as clear a case of an unjust punishment as one can find. Now, assume for the sake of argument that it would have been just to sentence Hayes to *some* time in prison, and that this could be justified by the incapacitation rationale for incarceration. (If you disagree that forgery justifies imprisonment, imagine some other crime for which you think some prison time, but not life imprisonment, would be appropriate.) Assume also, as might be true, that Hayes' probability of re-offending upon release would remain constant, no matter how long he spent in prison. In that case, the incapacitation rationale would continue to apply to Hayes with equal force for the rest of his life. If imprisoning Hayes for the first month were justified simply because it physically prevented Hayes from committing further crimes during that time, then, after the first month was up, imprisoning him for a *second* month would have been

---

³ This is a variant of the Framing case discussed in §2.4.1 above.
⁴ *Bordenkircher v. Hayes*, 434 U.S. 357 (1978), discussed in §5.2.2 above.

justified because it again would have physically prevented Hayes from committing crimes during that time ... and so on. But obviously this is not correct. Incapacitation may play some role in justifying punishment, but it cannot by itself justify a punishment that is not deserved.

We can also combine deterrence and incapacitation with an undeserved punishment:

Incapacitative Framing: A high-profile crime has occurred in a certain town, and the sheriff is unable to find the perpetrator. The sheriff locates an ex-convict who has served time for similar crimes in the past. The sheriff knows that the ex-convict did not commit this particular crime; nevertheless, due to his record, the ex-convict is at risk of committing similar crimes in the future if he remains free. Therefore, the sheriff decides to frame the ex-convict for the crime, thus causing him to be sent back to prison.

The punishment in this case is again unjust, despite that it achieves incapacitation and deterrence just as effectively as normal cases of criminal punishment do.

6.1.3 The Proportionality Principle

The above cases show that desert is a *necessary* component of just punishment. Now, among those who believe in retributive justice, it is universally agreed that retributive justice is governed by a *Proportionality Principle*, namely, that the severity of a punishment should be proportional to the seriousness of the offense for which the punishment is given. Minor offenses call for light punishments; serious offenses call for severe punishments.

As stated, the Proportionality Principle does not require the cost imposed by a punishment to be *equal* to the harm caused by the crime for which one is punished; it only requires that the more serious a crime is, the more punishment the crime incurs. Suppose, for example, that a petty thief is caught stealing $50 from a local store. It seems permissible to punish the thief with a fine greater than $50, despite that the thief's crime, if successful, would only have imposed a cost of $50 on its victim. Plausibly, for example, it would not be unjust if the thief were forced to pay $500 (some such augmented punishment may also be necessary for deterrence reasons). There is no precise amount that is the uniquely just fine; a range of possible fines could be considered just. It would, however, be unjust to punish the thief by cutting off his hand, as has been done in some countries.[5] A plausible reading of the Proportionality Principle must accommodate these judgments: it should allow punishments that are somewhat more harmful to the criminal than the crime itself was (or would have been, had the crime succeeded), but it should not allow punishments that are *vastly* more harmful. This is to say that Proportionality, as I understand it, requires not only that more serious crimes receive harsher penalties than less serious crimes, but also that penalties in general not be vastly greater than the harms that the criminal caused (or tried to cause, or risked causing).

There are many more philosophical and practical questions raised by the Proportionality Principle. We may wonder how to gauge the seriousness of a crime. Presumably, one should take account of how much harm the crime caused, or could reasonably have been expected to cause, or was intended to cause, as well as the motives behind the crime. Perhaps the seriousness of a crime is affected by the degree of agency exercised by the perpetrator; thus, perhaps premeditation increases seriousness, whereas the influence of drugs or powerful emotions diminishes it. There are questions about crimes that are not harmful in themselves (or not harmful at all), such as attempts, conspiracy, prostitution, selling foods not approved by the FDA, practicing law without a license, and so on; how "serious" should these be taken to be? It can also be difficult to compare harms of different kinds. If a defendant is to be imprisoned for breaking a victim's arm, how much prison time is comparable to a broken arm?

I will not attempt to answer these questions here. It will not be necessary to do so, because current U.S. practice is unjustly punitive on *any* plausible interpretation of the Proportionality Principle.

---

[5] AP News (2014).

6.1.4 Unconscionable Punishments

There is one more principle about just and unjust punishment that ought to be discussed. This is that some punishments are too barbaric to be imposed by a civilized society. For example, I assume that no court ought to sentence a defendant to be raped or tortured, even if the defendant himself has been convicted of raping or torturing another.

Notice that such sentences would not violate Proportionality. Rape would be a perfectly proportionate response to the crime of rape; indeed, paradigmatically so. Nevertheless, it is not an acceptable judicial punishment. I am not going to *argue* for that; I simply assume this intuitive judgment.

Some cases are controversial. Many believe that the death penalty is barbaric and thus should not be assigned for any crime, even if the criminal is guilty of taking the lives of others. Others, however, consider execution a just punishment for sufficiently heinous crimes. I will not attempt to resolve any such difficult cases. Again, it will not be necessary to do so, as the argument against the current punishment regime in the U.S. can be made using central, non-controversial judgments.

6.2 Disproportionate Punishments

6.2.1 The Origins of Mass Incarceration

With well over two million prisoners—close to a quarter of the entire world's prison population—America has the dubious distinction of being the world's leader in imprisoning people. The justice system was not always so punitive. Before 1973, the nation's incarceration rate held steady for fifty years at about 160 inmates per 100,000 population. After that, incarceration grew steadily for four decades, to its current rate of close to 700 prison and jail inmates per 100,000 population.[6]

---

[6] National Research Council (2014, ch. 2). Hereinafter, I use "prison" and "imprisonment" broadly, to cover (detention in) jails, state and federal prisons, and other government detention facilities.

There are many reasons to be concerned about this. There are concerns that incarceration renders criminals more dangerous than they were before they entered prison. This occurs because convicts acquire new criminal contacts while in prison, learn new criminal skills from the other prisoners, absorb antisocial values from the prisoner community, and acquire greater resentment toward society and the state due to their experiences in prison. This has led some experts to wonder whether the practice of incarceration actually causes more crime than it prevents.[7] There is general agreement that incarceration does not rehabilitate criminals and that most will re-offend once released.[8] As the satirical newspaper *The Onion* put it, "It just doesn't seem possible that an inmate could live for a decade and a half in a completely dehumanizing environment in which violent felons were constantly on the verge of attacking or even killing him and not emerge an emotionally stable, productive member of society."[9]

Incarceration also disrupts social relationships; for example, when a man is sent to prison, his children are left fatherless, and his spouse left to attempt to provide for them on her own.[10] All of this is accomplished at a cost of 80 billion taxpayer dollars per year in the United States, or more than $30,000 per prisoner per year.[11] That is in addition to the economic costs of having more than two million people, mostly able-bodied men, removed from the labor market.

I will not explore all of these costs of mass incarceration further, however. My central concern here is with retributive justice. Retributive justice, again, requires proportionality; the demands of justice are violated equally by overly harsh sentences and by overly lenient sentences.

The stunning growth in incarceration in America from the 1970's on was not chiefly due to a rise in crime, nor to higher arrest rates, nor (as libertarians are wont to suppose) to an increase in the number of behaviors that are prohibited. The drug war has played a role in the rise of mass incarceration, but it is not the main factor either; drug offenders

---

[7] Pritikin (2008); Clear (2007).
[8] Slifer (2014); Pritikin (2008, pp. 1055, 1092–3).
[9] The Onion (2014).
[10] Clear (2007, pp. 618–21).
[11] Kyckelhahn (2015), table 1; Henrichson and Delaney (2012, p. 9).

comprise only 20% of the inmate population.[12] Rather, the main reason why America's incarceration rate more than quadrupled since the 1970's is that the justice system has become drastically more punitive. More crimes are being punished with prison terms, and prison terms have grown much longer.[13]

This was chiefly due to a conscious choice by legislators to "get tough on crime" by forcing courts to give more and longer prison sentences. A variety of laws require judges to assign some minimum prison term for a given offense, provide sentence enhancements for a variety of attributes of the offender and the offense, or restrict or eliminate the possibility of parole. As of this writing, parole has been eliminated in sixteen U.S. states and at the federal level.[14] Half the states have "three strikes" laws, which provide draconian sentences, usually life imprisonment, for a third serious criminal conviction.[15]

6.2.2 Excess Punishment

Conceivably, this could all be just; perhaps American criminals were once drastically *under*punished, and the changes over the last fifty years have merely served to bring punishments up to the appropriate level. There are, however, a number of reasons for doubting this.

(i) Sentences for a given crime in America are typically much longer than those given for the same crime in other advanced, democratic nations. American convicts typically serve sentences five to ten times longer than similarly situated convicts in France or Germany.[16] Sentences for robbery in America are more than twice as long as in England and Wales and more than five times longer than in Finland. American sentences for assault and fraud are four times longer than those in England and Wales and over five times longer than those in

---

[12] Wagner and Sawyer (2020).
[13] National Research Council (2014, pp. 50–56).
[14] Renaud (2019); Hoffman (2003).
[15] Folk (2019).
[16] Whitman (2003, pp. 57, 70–71).

Finland. Other nations rely more on fines rather than prison. American courts sentence defendants to prison terms twice as often as Canadian courts, seven times more often than courts in England and Wales, and nine times more often than those in Germany or Finland.[17] It is on its face unlikely that judges in all these other countries are for some reason extremely biased toward criminals; it is more likely that America has become overly punitive.

(ii) The increases in punishments have resulted from legislatures overruling judges—that is, legislators force judges to assign much harsher sentences than the judges would have assigned based on their own judgment. There are obvious reasons why judges would be better positioned to determine appropriate criminal sentences than legislators. The judge who has presided over a case knows the facts of that individual case. Judges on the whole also have much greater experience with criminals and the criminal justice system and have devoted much more time to considering questions about crime and punishment than legislators have. Finally, legislators are subject to political pressure of a kind that undermines their objectivity; they must answer to a base of voters who have little to no understanding of the justice system but who react emotionally to promises to "get tough on crime". There is no reason for thinking that judges would be systematically biased in favor of criminals, but it is easy to see why voters and legislators would be systematically biased towards harsher sentences. Thus, the effect of shifting sentencing decisions from judges to legislators is almost certainly to worsen those decisions.

The move toward legislative control of sentencing may have resulted in greater *uniformity* and *predictability* in criminal sentences. But there is no good reason to think that this constitutes an improvement with respect to *justice*. It is more likely that the change has been from a system of inconstant justice, dependent on individual judges' sense of justice, to a system of constant injustice.

(iii) Third, many prison sentences intuitively seem extremely disproportionate. Recall the Forged Check example from §6.1.2: Paul Hayes

---

[17] Petteruti and Fenster (2011, pp. 21–2).

was actually sentenced to life imprisonment for an $88 forged check in the 1970's. After adjusting for inflation, this was equivalent to an attempt to steal about $400 today. If one sought to assign a prison term that would be equally harmful as the theft of $400, how long would that prison term need to be? Something under one week seems plausible (most individuals, I conjecture, would pay more than $400 to avoid a week of imprisonment). Taking into account the principle that a just punishment may impose a cost somewhat greater, but not *vastly* greater, than the harm the offender tried to impose on others (§6.1.3), we could perhaps contemplate a sentence of several weeks as just. Hayes received the life sentence for a third felony conviction; note, however, that even the standard punishment for this crime, with no prior convictions, was between two and ten *years* of imprisonment.

There are many similar cases to be found more recently. In 2007, Anthony Crutcher was arrested in Mississippi for selling $40 worth of cocaine to a police informant. In view of his two prior drug convictions, Crutcher was sentenced to 60 years in prison.[18] In 2010, Larry Dayries committed "aggravated robbery" at a Whole Foods Market in Austin; that is, Dayries stole a tuna fish sandwich and threatened a guard with a three-inch pocket knife in order to get away with the sandwich. No one was hurt. Due to his prior convictions for burglary and theft, Dayries was sentenced to 70 years in prison.[19] It is difficult to believe that anyone, even the staunchest proponent of law and order, who looked at these cases would consider these to be fair sentences. Indeed, these sentences seem to be hundreds if not thousands of times harsher than "an eye for an eye".

(iv) Finally, punishments produced by the American criminal justice system must often be unjust, because circumstances that are either morally irrelevant or only slightly relevant can have an enormous impact on the punishment one receives for a given offense. As we have seen, defendants commonly receive drastically harsher sentences for a third serious conviction than they would for a first or

---

[18] *Crutcher v. State of Mississippi* et al., No. 2:2012cv00118 —Document 12 (N.D. Miss. 2012).
[19] Hannaford (2016).

second conviction. But one's third serious crime is not in general vastly worse than one's first two crimes, nor does the commission of a third offense prove one to be drastically more blameworthy or vicious. Habitual offender statutes appear to be motivated by an *incapacitation* rationale, but they are extremely difficult to justify on retributive justice grounds.

A more egregious injustice is represented by the "trial penalty". As we have noted earlier (§5.1), pleading not guilty and insisting on a trial has the effect, on average, of tripling one's sentence. Defendants who inconvenience the government by insisting on a trial do not deserve three times more punishment than those who save the government money by pleading guilty.

In view of these considerations, I conclude that the American criminal justice system regularly and seriously violates the Proportionality Principle of retributive justice by assigning punishments vastly greater than any rational assessment of what is deserved.

6.3 Unconscionable Punishment

In addition to the problem of excessive sentences, the widespread abuse that occurs in prisons, carried out by both guards and other prisoners, renders *any* term in prison a morally problematic punishment on its face. In this section, I argue that incarceration should be avoided altogether for the great majority of crimes.

6.3.1 The Problem of Prison Abuse

In 2008, Kelly Bradley was serving a six-year prison sentence in Florida for burglary and grand theft.[20] One morning in May, as Bradley (who suffers from schizophrenia) cowered in a corner of his cell, five officers in riot gear entered the cell and jumped on him. As the officers handcuffed

---

[20] Details of this case are taken from Brown (2015).

Bradley, one of them dug into Bradley's right eye socket with a finger and gouged out Bradley's eye. The officers involved in the incident and their commanding officer attempted to cover up what happened, destroying physical evidence and claiming that they had no idea how Bradley's eyeball had gotten out of its socket. The incident came to light only because another officer, John Pisciotta, reported the abuse. In the wake of the incident, exactly one officer was prosecuted. Of the six officers who participated in the abuse and coverup, including the commanding officer, four were since promoted. Pisciotta, on the other hand, was fired.

This is a particularly severe case of prison abuse, but not the most severe. In 2015, another inmate, Samuel Harrell (who suffered from bipolar disorder), died of an apparent heart attack after being severely beaten by a group of as many as 20 guards in a New York prison.[21] In that case, the information about what took place came from other inmates who witnessed the beating. The medical examiner classified Harrell's death as a homicide, but no one was punished for the beating.[22]

How common are such incidents of prison abuse? No one knows, and some of the details of the above cases explain why: in many facilities, corrections officers have a culture of collaboration, such that officers are expected to stick together, support one another's stories, and hide evidence of abuse. In the Bradley case, officer Pisciotta was subjected to severe retaliation for refusing to go along with the coverup. Inmates often fear to report abuse by guards or other prisoners, since they live their day-to-day lives at the mercy of the guards and surrounded by other prisoners.

A 2013 report issued by the U.S. government's Bureau of Justice Statistics estimated that 4% of state and federal prison inmates and 3.2% of local jail inmates experienced some form of sexual abuse during the course of a given year, for a total of about 81,000 incidents.[23] These estimates are based on anonymous surveys of prisoners; however, it is likely that incidents are dramatically underreported due to the shame felt by victims as well as the "no snitching" culture in prisons. Over half of the incidents are perpetrated by prison staff, though violent incidents are

---

[21] Winerip and Schwirtz (2015).
[22] Weiser and Schwirtz (2017).
[23] Beck et al. (2013, p. 8).

much more likely to be perpetrated by other inmates. Prison rape has often been ignored by prison officials and the legal system. In some cases, rape is even used as a form of punishment by prison staff, or intentionally permitted by prison staff as a way to reward the rapist for cooperating with prison staff.[24] Needless to say, prison rape is an extremely brutal crime, typically resulting in severe pain and injury in addition to the violation of human dignity.

Violence and nonconsensual sexual contact are, uncontroversially, forms of abuse. Some experts also consider the increasingly widespread practice of solitary confinement to constitute a form of abuse, or even—as one U.N. observer put it—torture.[25] Studies suggest that solitary confinement causes serious psychological damage to inmates, as well as higher rates of recidivism after prisoners are released.[26]

6.3.2 The Impermissibility of Imprisonment

That is a very brief indication of the situation in America's prisons. Now consider a hypothetical. Suppose that a defendant has just been convicted of a serious crime—say, grand theft. And suppose that the trial judge sentences the defendant to be beaten and raped as punishment. Or to have his eyeball gouged out. Or to be beaten to death by government agents. In any of these cases, the punishment would be unconscionable. No morally decent society would countenance such sentences, and not merely because they would be disproportionate for the crime in question—no one should receive such a sentence for *any* crime.

And indeed, no judge in a modern society ever would assign such sentences. Judges regularly do, however, sentence defendants to serve time in facilities where such abuses are known, common occurrences. Given that it would be unconscionable to sentence a defendant to suffer these sorts of abuses, it must be considered highly morally problematic, on its face, to hand out prison sentences to defendants in the knowledge that many of them will in fact suffer prison abuse as a result.

---

[24] Human Rights Watch (2001, pp. 143–58); Parenti (1999); Harris (2001).
[25] U.N. News Centre (2011), quoting U.N. Special Rapporteur Juan Méndez.
[26] Commission on Safety and Abuse in America's Prisons (2006, pp. 14–15).

Admittedly, the actual situation is less bad than the hypothetical system that directly sentences defendants to suffer abuse. In my hypothetical scenario, the judge's action is almost certain to cause the convict to suffer severe abuse, whereas in the actual world, each inmate only has a modest chance of suffering severe abuse. Surely the probabilities matter; a smaller probability of abuse makes the prison sentence less prima facie wrong, and less difficult to justify.

Nevertheless, it seems as though even a significant *risk* of severe abuse makes a prison sentence seriously morally problematic on its face. Imagine a judge who sentences a group of twenty convicts to be thrown into the lion pit: a hungry lion is to be released, whereupon it will eat one of the convicts. Assuming that death by lion attack is not in general a morally permissible punishment, presumably this sentence, which imposes on each defendant a 5% chance of death by lion attack, is also morally unacceptable. Similarly, if prisoners have even a one in twenty chance per year of being beaten or raped in prison, it seems that this should normally be enough to make it wrong to send someone to prison. To summarize the argument thus far:

1. Severe prison abuse would be morally unacceptable as an official punishment.
2. If so, then it is also prima facie wrong to sentence individuals to live in conditions with a high, ongoing risk of severe abuse.
3. Most actual prisons have a high, ongoing risk of severe abuse for inmates.
4. So it is prima facie wrong to sentence individuals to be incarcerated, in most actual prisons.

I see no *in principle* reason why long-term confinement could not sometimes be an acceptable form of punishment. But the actual conditions prevailing in the nation's prisons seem sufficiently inhumane as to render confinement in them morally impermissible in most cases. (I shall return later to the "most cases" qualifier).

6.3.3 The Duty to Prevent Crime

A defender of incarceration might argue that, in spite of the high risk of abuse, the state is nevertheless obligated to hold most criminals in custody, since the state has an obligation to ordinary citizens to protect them from crime, and if criminals are not held in custody, there is a high probability of their committing additional crimes. Indeed, one might claim that if the state knowingly releases a criminal, and the criminal commits another crime, the state itself will then be partly responsible for that crime. Granted, if the criminal suffers abuse in prison, the state might also be held partly responsible for *that*—but, one might think, since it is worse for innocent citizens to suffer from crimes than for convicted criminals to be abused, the correct tradeoff is to hold most criminals in prison.

This argument would work best if we believed that prison rehabilitates criminals. If, as is actually the case, prison either has no effect or tends to make criminals more dangerous, then the argument works only if we are prepared to imprison criminals permanently.

But to address the argument more directly, I want to explain why, perhaps surprisingly, it makes sense for the state to show greater concern about prison abuse than about ordinary crime. The reason is that the state is *more responsible* for an inmate's suffering prison abuse than it is for an ordinary citizen's suffering from a typical crime. Three important factors contribute to this responsibility. First, when an individual suffers prison abuse, the state has intentionally, coercively placed that person into an environment that was known to be extremely dangerous. Second, the state intentionally, coercively prevents prison inmates from undertaking most courses of action that individuals outside of prison may take to protect themselves—including relocating to safer areas, avoiding threatening people or situations, carrying weapons for self-defense, or installing security systems. This gives the state a specially strong obligation to provide protection itself. Third and finally, much of the abuse that prison inmates suffer is actually carried out by agents of the state—specifically, corrections officers. None of these three points applies to the case of ordinary citizens suffering from ordinary crimes. Thus, the state has a specially strong obligation to avert prison abuse.

6.3.4 The Prospects for Reform

Why curtail the practice of imprisonment? Why not simply reform the prison system to eliminate abuse?

Obviously, if we have the option of immediately eliminating abuse, we should take it. But the world is not so simple. Even if one thinks (dubiously) that maintaining imprisonment without abuse would be superior to finding alternative forms of punishment, it still makes sense to ask: taking the existence of widespread prison abuse as given, under what conditions should convicts be sentenced to prison? This is an important question to ask, for three reasons.

First, there are systemic reasons why prisoners are prone to abuse; it is not a simple matter of a few bad prison wardens, say. Prisoners are in an inherently vulnerable position (this is compatible with the fact that they are also among society's most dangerous members). In contrast to the normal situation on the outside, if a prisoner has a conflict with or feels threatened by another member of the prison community, the prisoner does not have the option of avoiding that person. He cannot at will decide to move out of his cell, or to be guarded by a different set of officers. The prisoner is completely dependent on prison staff in his day-to-day life and is open at any time to being physically coerced by them. Because of this, retaliation for reports of abuse is a particularly serious concern.

In addition, the culture of prisons is extremely opposed to the reporting of unlawful conduct, which is referred to contemptuously as "snitching". This culture is not something that the government is likely to be able to change. Even if a prisoner reports abuse, he may simply not be believed, due to the widespread (accurate) impression that convicts are untrustworthy information sources. If the prisoner is believed, prison staff are likely to feel more loyalty to each other than to the inmates or to the law, and so may decide to cover up the abuse. If a prisoner appeals to people outside the prison system for help, this too is likely to fall on deaf ears. Convicts serving time in prison are, to put it lightly, among the least popular members of society; as a result, it tends to be difficult to mobilize concern about their plight. Finally, the prison population itself is inherently dangerous, since it consists almost entirely of criminals (apart from the prison staff and falsely convicted inmates), including some of society's most violent individuals. These are all robust features of the prison system, not easily changeable. As long as these features of the system persist, it is hard to see how one can avoid high risks of prison abuse.

Second, and related to the first point: even the most optimistic reformer can hope at best to *reduce* prison abuse; it will never be *eliminated*.[27] As long as there remains a risk of abuse in prison, that risk must be taken into account when deciding whether a particular convict or class of convicts can justly be sentenced to prison.

Third and finally, the individuals who make decisions as to whether to send criminal defendants to prison generally are not in a position to decide whether to reform the prison system to reduce abuse. For example, a trial judge must decide whether to sentence the defendant before him to prison time, given the existing state of the prison system; the judge does not have open to him at that moment the option of sending the defendant to prison and simultaneously radically reforming the prison system so as to drastically reduce the rate of abuse. Likewise, a jury in a criminal trial must decide whether to convict a particular defendant, knowing whatever they know about the likelihood that the defendant will receive jail time if convicted. The jury does not have open to them the option of convicting the defendant and simultaneously drastically reforming the prison system. If the jury convicts, and the judge sentences the defendant to prison, the defendant will enter the prison system as it actually is. If prison reform is to occur, it would have to be undertaken by the legislature, but the judge and jury in a particular case have no control over the legislature, nor is it rational for them to wishfully assume that radical reform is on the horizon.

Legislators, too, must take the present, unconscionable prison system as given in certain contexts. When deciding, for example, whether a particular offense should carry a prison sentence as a penalty, lawmakers must take into account the current and likely future conditions in the

---

[27] In 2003, the U.S. Congress passed the Prison Rape Elimination Act by unanimous consent. Needless to say, the act has not eliminated prison rape. Its main effect has been to facilitate better data collection on the problem; see Bruenig (2015).

nation's prisons; they should not assume a scenario in which prisons are safe and humane. If reform eventually eliminates or drastically reduces prison abuse, it will be rational at that time to revisit the issue; until then, jurors, judges, and legislators have reason to be very reticent about sending people to prison.

6.4 Reforms

6.4.1 Advantages of a Restitution-Based System

What alternatives are there to incarceration? In most cases, the proper response to a crime would be to require the offender to pay compensation to the victim. This could be accomplished using tort law, which is to say that most actions presently classified as crimes should instead be classified only as torts.[28]

If one considers this insufficient, some offenders might in addition be required to perform community service, be placed on probation, be placed under house arrest, or be given other movement restrictions, with their movements monitored by the state through devices such as ankle monitors.[29] 62% of all state and federal prisoners in the U.S. are serving time for non-violent offenses, chiefly property crimes and drug crimes, with drug offenses being the most common reason for admission to the prison system.[30] Compulsory restitution seems particularly appropriate for property crimes, while drug offenders should receive no punishment at all (because drug prohibition should be repealed), or at most, compulsory drug treatment and monetary fines.[31]

---

[28] For strong defenses of a restitution-based system, see Barnett (1977); Boonin (2008, ch. 5).

[29] For discussion of alternatives to incarceration, see United Nations Office on Drugs and Crime (2007); Families Against Mandatory Minimums (2013).

[30] Wagner and Sawyer (2020); Rothwell (2015). Classifications of offenders are based on the most serious offense for which the offender is imprisoned.

[31] Portugal has experimented successfully with drug decriminalization; see Hollersen (2013). The best approach would be to repeal the nation's drug laws, obviating the need for any judicial response to drug users and sellers; see Chap. 3 above.

Alternatives such as these have obvious advantages over incarceration. First, since the state has proven unable or unwilling to protect convicts in its custody, these sorts of alternatives may be the only way to prevent prison abuse. Second, they tend to be much less expensive than incarceration, which costs an average of $31,000 per inmate per year.[32] Third, compulsory restitution is better and more just for crime victims, who usually receive no compensation at all in the current system. Fourth, these alternative approaches avoid placing criminals together where they can teach each other criminal skills, reinforce antisocial values, and form new criminal contacts for purposes of carrying out future crimes.

Again, compulsory restitution should be the main response to crime. However, since most criminals are poor, most will be unable to immediately pay restitution. Offenders who cannot pay restitution immediately may have their wages garnished. Those who are unemployed should be required to take employment, either working for the state or working for private companies that agree to employ convicts. (For reasons of economic efficiency, the latter alternative is preferable, as long as there are sufficiently many businesses willing to employ convicts. In this case, the state might act as an agent matching convicts with employers. To maintain competition and prevent exploitation, convicts should be allowed to switch employers, but not allowed to cease working entirely.)

What about the demands of retributive justice—will a restitution-centered system give criminals the amount of punishment they deserve? Because restitution is based on the amount of harm caused by a crime, there is a built-in sensitivity to proportionality: more harmful crimes will require greater compensation, which means greater costs are imposed on the criminal. If additional punishment is needed, the state could also require compensation for the costs incurred in apprehending the criminal. This system promises to do a better job of providing punishments that are proportionate, or at least not wildly disproportionate as in the status quo.

Would a restitution-based system provide an adequate deterrent to crime? Note that the harm caused by a crime is usually many times greater

---

[32] Henrichson and Delaney (2012), p. 9.

than the benefit the crime would produce for the criminal. This is obvious for crimes such as assault or vandalism. It is also true for most theft, since stolen goods generally sell for a fraction of their original value. In addition, again, criminals might have to pay some amount toward the costs incurred by the state in apprehending them. Thus, the costs of paying restitution for a crime will generally be much greater than the benefits one could expect to gain from the crime. Assuming the state is reasonably effective at catching criminals, this would suffice to make crime prudentially irrational in normal circumstances.

One might nevertheless worry that deterrence would be *diminished* if prison sentences were replaced with compulsory restitution, since prison is much more harmful and frightening than a monetary cost. I have two replies to this concern. The first is that, while the suffering of prison inmates might provide a deterrent to crime, especially in view of the severe abuses that prison inmates are vulnerable to, a just and civilized society cannot rely on the threat of severe overpunishment in this way. As we saw earlier (§6.1.3), deterrence alone does not suffice to justify an undeserved punishment.

Second, the empirical evidence for the deterrence advantages of imprisonment is weak. Studies have shown that for purposes of deterrence, the probability of apprehension is far more important than the severity of punishment.[33] If potential criminals believe that they are unlikely to be caught, then severe penalties have little effect; if they believe they are almost certain to get caught, then small penalties suffice. Indeed, the probability of being apprehended by the police matters much more than the probability of being convicted if apprehended. Since most crimes are repeat offenses,[34] the justice system should focus on increasing the probability of offenders being apprehended if they recidivate, rather than on maintaining the severity of sentences. For example, suppose that offenders were fitted with permanent ankle monitors and their whereabouts were tracked and recorded on an ongoing basis. This might deter criminal activity more effectively than the threat of prison.

---

[33] Nagin (2013, pp. 201–2, 230–3).
[34] Cohen and Kyckelhahn (2010, p. 2).

6.4.2 The Need for Incapacitation

There is one important function of imprisonment that cannot be achieved by alternative sentences. This is the function of incapacitation: by holding criminals captive, the state directly, physically prevents them from committing crimes against the general population for the time that the criminals are imprisoned. There are some criminals who cannot be rehabilitated or deterred, and whose crimes are too terrible for society to risk their recurrence; in these cases, incapacitation is the only realistic approach.

Consider, for example, the notorious serial murderer Ted Bundy, who killed over thirty women during the 1970's. He escaped from police custody twice in 1977 and killed at least three more victims before being recaptured for the last time in 1978. He was then held in prison until his ultimate execution in 1989. In his case, there was no alternative to incarceration or execution. That is an extreme case, but there are in fact many criminals who can never be safely allowed out of government custody, not even with a monitoring device, since their risk of killing or severely injuring others is too high.

It is for this reason that I cannot agree with those who call for a complete end to incarceration. For example, in 2015 the National Lawyers Guild passed a resolution calling for the abolition of all prisons.[35] They did not explain what would be done with serial killers such as Bundy. Without an answer to that question, abolitionism cannot be seriously considered.

Thus, my claim in this chapter is only that *most* individuals who are actually imprisoned in the United States should not be imprisoned. More specifically, all or nearly all non-violent offenders should receive some alternative, non-custodial sentence or no sentence at all. Nevertheless, the prison system must be maintained for the most dangerous, violent criminals. Here I aim to explain how this position can be squared with the argument from unconscionable punishment (§6.3).

In discussions of justice, an absolutist stance is often tempting—for example, we may be tempted to insist that it is *never* permissible to punish

---

[35] National Lawyers Guild (2015).

an innocent person, no matter the consequences. Taken literally, this doctrine demands the abolition of all punishment, since any system that punishes anyone can be expected to *sometimes* punish an innocent person. Without going into detail here, I will simply state that I view such absolutist doctrines as untenable.[36] It must be permissible, for sufficiently weighty social goals, to incur some risk of punishing the innocent. This does not mean that anything goes—the state must take reasonable measures to reduce the risk of punishing the innocent and may only punish defendants when the expected social benefits of punishment are very high in comparison to the risks of injustice. Thus, it is often said that it is better to let n guilty people go free than to punish one innocent person, for various values of n (for example, "it is better to let ten guilty men go free than to punish one innocent man")—everyone seems to agree that the appropriate value of n is greater than one but less than infinity.[37]

Similarly, though prison abuse would be unconscionable as an official punishment, we cannot maintain the absolutist position that *no level of risk* of prison abuse is acceptable for the sake of *any* social benefit. The only reasonable position is that the state must make reasonable efforts to minimize the risk, and that the social benefits of imprisonment must be large in comparison with the risks of abuse incurred in maintaining the system.

There are three reasons why imprisonment is more morally acceptable in the case of serious, violent criminals than it is for less serious offenders. First, the inmates who are most often abused in prison are those who are relatively weak, young, and unaggressive. The most dangerous, violent criminals are the least likely to be abused; there is therefore less cause for concern in sending them to prison.

Second, prison abuse is a less serious injustice the more serious the inmate's own crime is. Of course, no inmate should suffer abuse; nevertheless, it is *worse* for a minor, nonviolent criminal to be subjected to abuse than for a serious, violent criminal to suffer such abuse. Therefore, the state has stronger reasons for eliminating incarceration for minor offenders than for serious offenders.

---

[36] See §3.1.3. For detailed argument, see Huemer (2010).
[37] Volokh (1997).

Third and most importantly, the risks to society of releasing serious violent offenders are much greater than the risks of releasing nonviolent or other minor offenders. Nonviolent criminals are generally guilty of either drug crimes or property crimes. If they recidivate, they are unlikely to cause irreparable damage. A serious violent criminal, however, may easily cause irreparable damage, indeed, damage worse than the sum total of all harm that the criminal himself could expect to suffer from a lifetime in prison.

There is one other category of criminal who may be justly imprisoned: those who refuse to make required restitution, or otherwise refuse to comply with court-ordered non-prison sanctions. In this case, the state must either escalate sanctions or allow the criminal to get away with failure to comply. If the state's policy is to give up on enforcement whenever an offender is sufficiently intransigent in refusing to comply, then offenders will thumb their noses *en masse* at the law. The state must therefore be prepared to increase penalties when a criminal fails to comply with earlier assigned penalties. This escalation may start with non-prison penalties (for example, late fees), but must at some point rise to the level of imprisonment if the offender is sufficiently recalcitrant. Fortunately, this would rarely be necessary; in point of empirical fact, the threat of prison is extremely effective at inducing compliance with non-prison penalties.[38]

In sum, the reasons for incarcerating serious, violent offenders are much stronger, and the reasons against incarcerating them much weaker, than is the case for nonviolent or nonserious offenders. It is therefore reasonable to hold that incarceration is justified only for serious, violent criminals and criminals who refuse to comply with non-prison penalties.

References

AP News. 2014. Saudi Cuts off Hand of Convicted Yemeni Thief. *AP News*, December 15. https://apnews.com/66567e20b61c439e835dbe5f8b0b3ad6. Accessed 27 June 2020.

Barnett, Randy E. 1977. Restitution: A New Paradigm of Criminal Justice. *Ethics* 87: 279–301.

---

[38] Nagin (2013, pp. 227–8).

Beck, Allen J., Marcus Berzofsky, Rachel Caspar, and Christopher Krebs. 2013. Sexual Victimization in Prisons and Jails Reported by Inmates, 2011–12, U.S. Department of Justice, Bureau of Justice Statistics. http://www.bjs.gov/content/pub/pdf/svpjri1112.pdf. Accessed 17 May 2016.

Boonin, David. 2008. *The Problem of Punishment*. Cambridge: Cambridge University Press.

Brown, Julie K. 2015. Whistleblower Prison Guard Paid the Price for Reporting Abuse. *Miami Herald*, July 18, 2015. http://www.miamiherald.com/news/special-reports/florida-prisons/article27738046.html. Accessed 17 May 2016.

Bruenig, Elizabeth Stoker. 2015. Why Americans Don't Care about Prison Rape. *The Nation*, March 2, 2015. http://www.thenation.com/article/why-americans-don't-care-about-prison-rape/. Accessed 18 May 2016.

Clear, Todd R. 2007. The Impacts of Incarceration on Public Safety. *Social Research* 74: 613–630.

Cohen, Thomas, and Tracey Kyckelhahn. 2010. *Felony Defendants in Large Urban Counties, 2006*. U.S. Department of Justice, Bureau of Justice Statistics. http://www.bjs.gov/index.cfm?ty=pbse&sid=27. Accessed 20 May 2016.

Commission on Safety and Abuse in America's Prisons. 2006. *Confronting Confinement*. New York: Vera Institute of Justice. Available at http://www.vera.org/pubs/confronting-confinement. Accessed 17 May 2016.

Families Against Mandatory Minimums. 2013. Alternatives to Incarceration in a Nutshell. http://famm.org/wp-content/uploads/2013/08/FS-Alternatives-in-a-Nutshell-7.8.pdf. Accessed 22 May 2016.

Folk, Ashley. 2019, February 21. Three Strikes Laws in Different States. Legal Match. https://www.legalmatch.com/law-library/article/three-strikes-laws-in-different-states.html. Accessed 27 June 2020.

Hannaford, Alex. 2016. No Exit. *Texas Observer*, October 3. https://www.texasobserver.org/three-strikes-law-no-exit/. Accessed 27 June, 2020.

Harris, Dan. 2001. Prison Rape Widely Ignored by Authorities. *ABC News*, April 16, 2001. http://abcnews.go.com/WNT/story?id=131113. Accessed 17 May 2016.

Henrichson, Christian, and Ruth Delaney. 2012. *The Price of Prisons: What Incarceration Costs Taxpayers*. New York: Vera Institute of Justice. Available at http://www.vera.org/pubs/special/price-prisons-what-incarceration-costs-taxpayers. Accessed 19 May 2016.

Hoffman, Peter B. 2003. History of the Federal Parole System, U.S. Department of Justice, United States Parole Commission. https://www.justice.gov/sites/default/files/uspc/legacy/2009/10/07/history.pdf. Accessed 27 June 2020.

Hollersen, Wiebke. 2013. Portugal, 12 Years after Decriminalizing Drugs. *Der Spiegel*, March 27, 2013. http://www.spiegel.de/international/europe/evaluating-drug-decriminalization-in-portugal-12-years-later-a-891060.html. Accessed 22 May 2016.

Huemer, Michael. 2010. Lexical Priority and the Problem of Risk. *Pacific Philosophical Quarterly* 91: 332–351.

Human Rights Watch. 2001. *No Escape: Male Rape in U.S. Prisons*. New York: Human Rights Watch. Available at https://www.hrw.org/reports/2001/prison/. Accessed 17 May 2016.

Kyckelhahn, Tracey. 2015. Justice Expenditure and Employment Extracts, 2012—Preliminary. U.S. Department of Justice, Bureau of Justice Statistics. http://www.bjs.gov/index.cfm?ty=pbdetail&iid=5239. Accessed 22 May 2016.

Lippke, Richard L. 2007. *Rethinking Imprisonment*. Oxford: Oxford University Press.

Moore, Michael S. 1997. *Placing Blame: A Theory of the Criminal Law*. Oxford: Oxford University Press.

Nagin, Daniel S. 2013. Deterrence in the Twenty-First Century. *Crime and Justice* 42: 199–263.

National Lawyers Guild. 2015. Resolution Supporting the Abolition of Prisons. http://www.nlg.org/sites/default/files/ResolutionSupporting the Abolition of Prisons REV.pdf. Accessed 22 May 2016.

National Research Council 2014. The Growth of Incarceration in the United States: Exploring Causes and Consequences. Washington, DC: The National Academies Press. https://doi.org/10.17226/18613. Accessed 27 June 2020.

Parenti, Christian. 1999.Rape as a Disciplinary Tactic. *Salon*, August 23, 1999. http://www.salon.com/1999/08/23/prisons_3/. Accessed 17 May 2016.

Petteruti, Amanda and Jason Fenster. 2011. Finding Direction: Expanding Criminal Justice Options by Considering Policies of Other Nations. Washington, DC: Justice Policy Institute. http://www.justicepolicy.org/uploads/justicepolicy/documents/finding_direction-full_report.pdf. Accessed 27 June 2020.

Pritikin, Martin H. 2008. Is Prison Increasing Crime? *Wisconsin Law Review* 2008: 1049–1108.

Renaud, Jorge. 2019. Grading the Parole Release Systems of all 50 States. Prison Policy Initiative, February 26. https://www.prisonpolicy.org/reports/grading_parole.html. Accessed 27 June 2020.

Rothwell, Jonathan. 2015. Drug Offenders in American Prisons: The Critical Distinction between Stock and Flow. The Brookings Institution, November 25, 2015. http://www.brookings.edu/blogs/social-mobility-memos/posts/2015/11/25-drug-offenders-stock-flow-prisons-rothwell. Accessed 19 May 2016.

Slifer, Stephanie. 2014. Once a Criminal, Always a Criminal?. *CBS News*, April 23, 2014. http://www.cbsnews.com/news/once-a-criminal-always-a-criminal/. Accessed 22 May 2016.

The Onion. 2014. 15 Years In Environment Of Constant Fear Somehow Fails To Rehabilitate Prisoner, March 4. https://www.theonion.com/15-years-in-environment-of-constant-fear-somehow-fails-1819576202. Accessed 1 Sept 2020.

U.N. News Centre. 2011. Solitary Confinement Should Be Banned in Most Cases, UN Expert Says. https://www.un.org/apps/news/story.asp?NewsID=40097. Accessed 17 May 2016.

United Nations Office on Drugs and Crime. 2007. *Handbook of Basic Principles and Promising Practices on Alternatives to Imprisonment*. Vienna: UNODC. Available at http://www.unodc.org/pdf/criminal_justice/Handbook_of_Basic_Principles_and_Promising_Practices_on_Alternatives_to_Imprisonment.pdf. Accessed 20 May 2016.

Volokh, Alexander. 1997. *n* Guilty Men. *University of Pennsylvania Law Review* 146: 173–216.

Wagner, Peter and Wendy Sawyer. 2020. Mass Incarceration: The Whole Pie 2020. Prison Policy Initiative, March 24. https://www.prisonpolicy.org/reports/pie2020.html. Accessed 24 June 2020.

Weiser, Benjamin and Michael Schwirtz. 2017. Fishkill Prison Guards Will Not Face Charges in '15 Death of an Inmate. *New York Times*, August 2. https://www.nytimes.com/2017/08/02/nyregion/fishkill-prison-guards-will-not-face-charges-in-15-death-of-an-inmate.html. Accessed 19 March 2019.

Whitman, James Q. 2003. *Harsh Justice: Criminal Punishment and the Widening Divide between America and Europe*. Oxford: Oxford University Press.

Winerip, Michael and Michael Schwirtz. 2015. Prison Guard 'Beat Up Squad' Is Blamed in New York Inmate's Death. *New York Times*, August 18, 2015. http://www.nytimes.com/2015/08/19/nyregion/fishkill-prison-inmate-died-after-fight-with-officers-records-show.html. Accessed 17 May 2016.

7

Abuse of Power

7.1 The Problem of Abuse of Power

In August 1974, Richard Nixon resigned in disgrace from the Presidency, the only U.S. President ever to have done so. The impetus was the Watergate scandal, during which it emerged that Nixon had ordered underlings to engage in illegal spying and other dirty tricks against his political opponents, and had misused the powers of his office to cover up his administration's crimes.

Three years after his resignation, Nixon gave a series of interviews with journalist David Frost. One now-famous exchange occurred when Frost asked Nixon about a campaign of illegal activities that his administration had considered taking against anti-war protestors:

Frost: Would you say that there are certain situations … where the President can decide that it's in the best interests of the nation and do something illegal?
Nixon: Well, when the President does it, that means that it is not illegal.
Frost: By definition.
Nixon: Exactly, exactly.[1]

---

[1] Frost and Nixon 2007.

This exchange provides a remarkable window into how Nixon viewed his misdeeds. In brief: the President is above the law. The 2008 movie dramatization *Frost/Nixon* portrayed this moment as a jaw-dropping confession, after which Nixon quickly starts to backpedal. But the real David Frost took Nixon's assertion in stride, and the conversation continued as if nothing remarkable had happened.

Nixon was not alone. Human beings who are given positions of power over others regularly behave as though they are above the law and as though might makes right. On this subject, Nixon was unusual only for his candor; most authority figures refrain from stating their assumed entitlement so bluntly.

This is a problem for essentially all political and legal institutions. When given power and told to use it for the good of society, very few human beings can be relied upon, of their own accord, to distinguish their own convenience, political advantage, or sheer fits of pique from the good of society. Psychological studies have also shown that possessing power reduces one's capacity for empathy.[2] This is perhaps the most fundamental problem of government.

None of this should surprise us. Government officials and private individuals belong to the same species; we do not have a special class of angelic beings to put in charge of everyone else. The same motives that lead private individuals to violate the rights of others exist also in the hearts and minds of those who take up positions in government. Nor are the human beings who wind up in positions of power, as a rule, drawn from the most virtuous members of society. On the contrary, there is some reason to expect that individuals who seek positions of power will be, on average, less virtuous than ordinary members of society. Many will seek such positions because they *enjoy exerting power* over others, which is hardly a sign of moral virtue.

All of which brings us to the final category of injustice in the legal system that I will consider: the failure to provide justice for wrongs perpetrated by government officials. Here, by "government officials", I include all who have positions of authority in government, including police officers, prosecutors, judges, lawmakers, and executive officials.

---

[2] Galinsky et al. 2006.

The legal system directs its efforts almost entirely toward private criminals. The wrongs done by government officials are rarely taken seriously, rarely investigated, and barely punished when uncovered. Yet the crimes of government agents *should* be taken *more* seriously, investigated more aggressively, and punished more severely, than the crimes of private individuals.

There are two main reasons for this. First, the fact that a particular crime is committed by a government official, using his position in the government for the purpose, renders the crime worse than an otherwise similar crime by a private individual. This is in part because, in addition to the ordinary crime, there is a betrayal of the public trust and a violation of the role obligations of a public official—obligations that individual voluntarily assumed in taking whatever government position he holds.

Relatedly, the spectacle of government officials committing crimes may have an effect of encouraging general disrespect for the law, to a greater degree than the actions of private criminals. To be held in high regard among the general public, the law must appear to be implemented with integrity, by individuals who are by and large honest and committed to the rule of law. The law should not appear as merely the tool of the gang currently in power to advance their own ends. If even the people who are responsible for enforcing the law do not respect the law, citizens may wonder, why should anyone else do so when they can get away with violating it?

Of course, in addition to not *appearing* to be merely the tool of the powerful to advance their ends, the law should not in fact *be* merely the tool of the powerful to advance their ends. When government officials misuse the powers of their offices, they set a precedent that makes it more likely that government corruption will spread.

Thus, for example, when President Nixon ordered the Watergate break-in, this was worse than an ordinary criminal breaking into a hotel, say, to steal some property. As the chief executive, Nixon had voluntarily assumed the role of overseeing the enforcement of law for the purpose of protecting the rights of the people. This gave him an especially strong obligation not to illegally violate anyone's rights. By disregarding the law, Nixon, once his crimes were discovered, may have diminished the general esteem in which the law is held. He also risked establishing, or contributing to, a culture of corruption in the federal government wherein officials cynically use their power for personal gain. This risk would have existed even if Nixon had gotten away with his crimes, because Nixon placed corrupt individuals in positions within the government and, through his actions, communicated to those close to him his view, as the leader of the government, that abuse of government power for personal benefit was acceptable.

The second reason why crimes by government agents must be taken especially seriously is that stronger measures are required to deter such crimes than is the case for ordinary crimes by private individuals. Government power is inherently prone to abuse. Because government officials are given powers not held by private individuals, they have more opportunities to commit crimes, and they are often able to cause much greater harm than private individuals. For example, a government prosecutor may be able to send an innocent person to prison for 20 years, a crime no private person could commit. A President can conduct an illegal war, killing hundreds of thousands of individuals. The power given to government officials makes it especially important that only individuals of the highest moral integrity should hold offices of public trust.

That power also makes it easier for officials who commit crimes to get away with them. In some cases, officials can directly use the powers of their office to prevent themselves from being caught, as Nixon tried to do when he ordered the CIA to attempt to stop the FBI investigation of the Watergate break-in.[3] In other cases, government officials benefit from their relationships with other government officials. For example, police officers tend to feel solidarity with each other and are therefore very unlikely to investigate or report on each other. It is thus much easier for a police officer to get away with a crime than for a private individual to do so.

In brief, government officials have more opportunity to commit crimes, there is a potential for greater harm from their crimes, and it is more difficult for them to be caught. Therefore, in order for crimes by government officials to be adequately deterred, there must be a much

---

[3] Crewdson 1974.

greater effort to investigate such crimes, and/or much *higher penalties* for such crimes, than is the case for crimes by private individuals.

As we will see in the remainder of this chapter, the state has not taken these lessons to heart. Government officials regularly regard themselves and each other as above the law. Even those who do not abuse their own power seldom make any serious effort to hold accountable those officials who do. In place of the shockingly punitive approach taken by the state toward private criminals (Chap. 6), we see a fantastic leniency, a readiness to see everything from the point of view of the perpetrator and to find any reason to avoid harsh punishments, when it comes to crimes committed by those in government. It is not the mere existence of abuse that marks the American legal system as corrupt; it is the nearly uniform failure of those working for the system to take the problem seriously.

7.2 Police Abuse

7.2.1 The Problem of Police Violence

Police abuse takes many forms. Among other things, there is excessive force, as when police wrongly beat a suspect; lying or fabricating evidence; stealing drugs or other goods obtained from criminals; all the way up to murder. No one knows how often police commit such forms of abuse, because no agency collects comprehensive police abuse statistics. Most cases are undoubtedly concealed by the officers involved, and other police officers are almost never interested in investigating misdeeds by members of their own organization. But despite the shortage of data, there is some reason to think the problem is serious. I shall focus on violence by police, since this is the most serious and widely-discussed problem.

By recent estimates, approximately 1100 people are killed per year by American police, for a rate of 34 per 100,000 police officers.[4] There is no consensus on how many of these killings are justified. Studies by police

---

[4] Mapping Police Violence Dot Org (2020) provides a database of police homicides, which lists 8239 individuals killed by the police in the U.S. from 2013 to mid-2020.

sources tend to find virtually all of them justified, while activist groups consider most or all unjustified.[5] There is no doubt, however, that the rate of police violence in America vastly exceeds the rates in otherwise similar nations. The rate of police killings per unit of population in America is about three times higher than the rate in Canada, nine times higher than in France, twenty times higher than in Germany, and 170 times higher than in the U.K.[6]

It is sometimes said that American criminals are more dangerous on average than criminals in these otherwise similar nations. In particular, American criminals are more likely to carry firearms, and American police therefore have much greater justified fear of encountering criminals armed with guns. Nevertheless, it is unlikely that the enormous disparities in police violence rates can be explained by that factor alone. In 14% of cases, the victim of a police shooting in America is entirely unarmed. In many other cases, the victim is "armed" with a vehicle, a knife, or another non-gun object—these are the sorts of cases that police in other countries are generally able to resolve without deadly violence. Only about half the victims of police shootings in America are alleged to be armed with a gun.[7]

It may nevertheless be said that American police *fear* that a suspect may be armed with a gun, even when in fact the suspect is not so armed. It is not possible to establish the number of cases in which police officers truly fear for their lives, since such fear is an internal state not observable by others, and officers can be expected to claim to have feared for their lives if that is required to avoid sanctions for their use of force. However, we can objectively assess the actual risk that American police are subject to. About 30 American police officers suffer homicides per year, meaning that American police are over thirty times more likely to *kill* someone than to *be killed* by someone. The rate of death by homicide for American police officers is approximately 3 per 100,000 population—much lower than the rate of 5.6 homicide deaths per 100,000 population that applies to Americans as a whole.[8] In other words, working as a police officer is much safer than being an average American citizen.

---

[5] Selby et al. (2016) conclude that only 7% of shootings of *unarmed* citizens are unjustified. For the activist perspective, see https://www.joincampaignzero.org; https://policeviolencereport.org
[6] Statistics for Canada, France, Germany, and the U.K. are from Wikipedia 2020a.
[7] See the database from Mapping Police Violence Dot Org 2020.
[8] Fleetwood 2017.

Shooting rates also vary greatly by state within the U.S.⁹ New York state, for instance, has a rate of 0.09 police shootings per 100,000 population per year, while New Mexico has a rate of 0.98, over ten times higher. The national average is 0.3. It is unlikely that these disparities are to be explained chiefly by variations in the numbers of dangerous criminals across states. It is more likely that they reflect variations in police culture across states.

All of this does not prove, but it at least suggests, that part of the story behind America's high rate of police violence is that American police, on average, are much more aggressive and ready to resort to violence than the police in other wealthy, democratic nations. This could be partly due to their training, which includes an average of 123 hours of training in weapons and self-defense, including 60 hours of firearms training, but only 8 hours of training in conflict management.¹⁰ One result of these training priorities may be that American police are more skilled at shooting people than at de-escalating situations.

There are other indications of the aggressive attitudes of U.S. police. In recent years, police in America have become increasingly militarized.¹¹ Since the 1990's, the U.S. military has distributed a total of $6 billion worth of military equipment among over 8000 law enforcement agencies across the country.¹² The Los Angeles School District Police Department, for example, has acquired three grenade-launchers and a mine-resistant armored vehicle (presumably to keep the sophomores in line, as one journalist put it). American police departments sometimes use military terminology, such as referring to the police department as a "Forward Operating Base".¹³ Academic research finds that transfers of military equipment to civilian police departments are positively correlated with the number of civilians killed by the police.¹⁴

---

⁹ Moskos 2019.
¹⁰ Reaves 2009, p. 6.
¹¹ For extended discussion, see Balko 2014.
¹² Mosteller 2020.
¹³ The Economist 2014.
¹⁴ Delehanty et al. 2017.

7.2.2 The System's Response

Fewer than 1% of police killings result in charges being filed against any of the officers involved. Even among those 1% of cases, most police officers are acquitted. Even among those convicted, sentences are relatively brief, averaging about four years of jail time.[15]

In general, homicides in America result in criminal charges about 60% of the time,[16] so it is surprising on its face that homicides *by police officers* result in criminal charges less than 1% of the time. What could explain this disparity? There are three salient hypotheses:

(i) Perhaps almost no police killings actually involve wrongdoing by police officers; that is, over 99% of police killings are justifiable homicides. (For comparison, among homicides committed by non-police, only about 2% are considered justifiable in our system.[17])
(ii) Perhaps more than 1% of police killings are wrongful, and the government would like to hold officers accountable, but the government is usually unable to collect enough evidence to *prove* wrongdoing by officers.
(iii) Perhaps the system is extraordinarily biased in favor of the police, to the point of frequently allowing them to get away with murder.[18]

Which of these hypotheses is most likely to be closest to the truth? The first hypothesis is disconfirmed by the information mentioned above (§ 7.2.1), including the much lower rates of police killings in other nations.

Regarding the second hypothesis, we must acknowledge the high standard of proof in criminal prosecutions and the difficulty, in many cases, of proving wrongdoing beyond a reasonable doubt. Most police departments do not use body cameras; thus, only a small fraction of police shootings are captured on video.[19] If a police officer says that a suspect

---

[15] Kindy and Kelly 2015.
[16] Federal Bureau of Investigation 2019, table 25.
[17] Federal Bureau of Investigation 2019, tables 1, 15.
[18] For this view, see New York Times Editorial Board 2020.
[19] About 6% of fatal police shootings were captured by body cameras in 2015 (Kindy et al. 2015).

made a threatening movement, which caused the officer to fear for his life, this may be impossible to refute.

However, these sorts of difficulties apply to most crimes, including homicides committed by private citizens. It is not obvious why it should be drastically harder for the government to collect evidence about homicides committed by police officers on the job than to collect evidence about homicides committed by private individuals. Admittedly, police officers may be more skilled at concealing crimes, due to their knowledge of the system; on the other hand, the government ought to have much more control over and ability to monitor police officers than private citizens, due to the fact that these officers work for the government. So it is hard to see why the difficulty of collecting evidence should lead to such a dramatically lower rate of charges being filed for police homicides, unless there is some strong bias built into the system.

If hypotheses (i) and (ii) are implausible, we are left with hypothesis (iii): the government's system of justice and law enforcement is so severely biased in favor of its own employees that those employees are able to get away with murder.

Again, there are no accepted statistics on how often police shootings are justified. There is, however, interesting anecdotal evidence derived from cases of alleged police abuse that have been widely reported in the media. Among the most famous police brutality cases (but not a shooting) was that of Rodney King, who in 1991 was captured by police in Los Angeles after leading them on a high-speed car chase.[20] The chase occurred when King refused to pull over to receive a speeding ticket. After capturing him, a group of police officers surrounded King and beat him with batons. Four officers were directly involved in the beating, while fourteen others watched on the ground and two more in a helicopter. King received 56 baton blows and six kicks before finally being swarmed and placed in restraints. The police dispatcher who called for an ambulance for King stated that King "pissed us off, so I guess he needs an ambulance now",

---

[20] The following account in the text is based on the Christopher Commission Report, which was commissioned in response to the Rodney King incident (Independent Commission on the Los Angeles Police Department 1991, ch. 1).

going on to explain that suspects "should know better than [to] run, they are going to pay a price when they do that".[21]

A nearby resident filmed part of incident with a home video camera, producing what may have been history's first viral video.[22] Clips of the beating were played repeatedly on television news, sparking outrage among citizens. On its face, the videotape appears to show a clear and serious case of police brutality.

Charges were filed against four officers for assault and excessive use of force. The defendants argued in court that King had lunged at one of the officers, then repeatedly tried to get up while the officers were trying to keep him on the ground, which necessitated the use of "power strokes" against King to subdue him. When the officers claim that King lunged at one of them, the videotape in fact shows King getting up and trying to run; it is unclear from the video whether King was lunging to attack or simply to escape. The beating continues for a minute and a half after that.

A jury acquitted the officers, setting off riots in Los Angeles.[23] However, King later successfully sued the Los Angeles Police Department, winning $3.8 million in damages. In a separate case, the four officers were tried in federal court for violating Rodney King's civil rights. Two were acquitted; the other two were convicted and sentenced to 30 months in prison, although the applicable sentencing guidelines had suggested a range of 70 to 87 months.[24]

Since the Rodney King case, many other cases of alleged abuse by police have occurred, many of which involve worse harms, up to and including death.[25] The most recent of these, the murder of George Floyd, set off protests and riots across the nation and even around the world. For the sake of brevity, I will not discuss these other cases. There are, however, a number of interesting observations to be made about the King case.

---

[21] Independent Commission on the Los Angeles Police Department 1991, pp. 14–15.

[22] This video remains available on YouTube (Holliday 1991).

[23] More precisely, the jury acquitted all four officers of assault and acquitted three of the four of using excessive force. They were deadlocked on the remaining excessive force charge (Associated Press 1992).

[24] *Koon v. United States* (94–1664), 518 U.S. 81 (1996).

[25] See, for example, the killings of Eric Garner (Southall 2019), Michael Brown (Buchanan et al. 2015), and George Floyd (Hill et al. 2020).

That King was subjected to excessive force is made clear by the convictions in federal court, King's successful lawsuit, and the famous video of the incident. It is interesting nevertheless that in the first trial, a jury was prepared to acquit the officers, despite the existence of apparently damning video evidence. Such compelling evidence is rarely present in criminal trials—very few defendants are confronted with an actual videotape showing them committing the crime—yet the overwhelming majority of criminal trials, where the defendants are not police officers, result in convictions. It is hard to avoid the suspicion that juries have drastically higher standards to convict police officers than to convict almost anyone else.

Note that in the overwhelming majority of cases, *if* a police officer or group of officers commits abuse, it will not be captured on camera. It was sheer bad luck for the officers in the King case that there happened to be a local resident with a video camera on the scene. In the ordinary course of events, then, the officers would get away with their abuse. They would beat or kill the suspect, then claim that the suspect was attacking them and that they feared for their lives, and there would be nothing to refute them. The resident who filmed the Rodney King beating first tried calling the police department to report what he knew about the incident. When the police showed no interest in his information, he decided to turn the video over to the news media. It was the resulting publicity that sparked the investigation and trial of the officers. If there hadn't been a videotape, no one would have been investigated, and certainly no one put on trial, for the King beating. And if the King case hadn't attracted so much publicity, then, even if there had been one trial, there would not have been a second, federal trial; thus, the original acquittal of the officers would have been the final word.

Realizing this, we should assume that for every case of police abuse that we hear about because of a video of the incident, there are many more cases where the police get away with their abuse and we never learn of it.

Another interesting observation concerns the large number of other police officers who witnessed some or all of the beating, yet did nothing to stop it, nor to report the misconduct after the fact. This is typical of cases of abuse of power: though perhaps the majority of officials never seriously abuse their power, they also make no effort to stop or to punish those who do.[26] In that sense, government officials tend to be complicit in one another's crimes. Apropos of this, after the King incident, the city of Los Angeles created a commission to study excessive use of force in the Los Angeles Police Department. The commission found that a significant number of officers repeatedly misused force, but that these officers generally still received positive performance evaluations. The commission also reviewed computer messages sent to and from officers' patrol cars, finding hundreds of messages sent by police officers that the commission deemed improper, including messages in which officers talked about beating suspects, expressed eagerness to be involved in a shooting, or made crudely racist remarks. These messages are stored in a database and can be reviewed by the officers' supervisors. The fact that officers nevertheless felt comfortable typing such messages suggests a culture of, at minimum, tolerance for brutality and prejudice in the police department.[27]

A final noteworthy aspect of the case is the sentence received by two of the officers once they were finally convicted. Two and a half years in prison is not obviously an overly lenient sentence for participating in an unjustified beating. Perhaps the sentence, in absolute terms, was not unjustly lenient at all. There is no doubt, however, that it was far lighter than the sentence that would have been assigned for that crime if the perpetrators were not police officers. We know this because the federal sentencing guidelines called for a sentence of between 70 and 87 months in prison. Judges have the authority, however, to depart from sentencing guidelines when they find there to be special circumstances in the particular case. The judge who sentenced the police officers for the King beating claimed that there were special circumstances that justified lowering the officers' sentence to less than half of what it would ordinarily be. (These special circumstances included the fact that Rodney King had provoked the beating with his bad behavior, that the officers' careers were already ruined, and that the officers would be at unusually high risk of abuse by other prisoners while in prison.)

This is typical of cases in which officers are convicted of crimes—police officer defendants commonly receive far lighter sentences than ordinary criminals guilty of similar offenses. Again, the small number of police

---

[26] For discussion of this problem, see Zimbardo 2007, pp. 317–19.
[27] Independent Commission on the Los Angeles Police Department 1991, pp. xix–xii.

officers who are convicted for unjustified shootings receive an average of four years in prison. In one case, an officer spent 30 days in jail, followed by probation, for an unjustified shooting. That officer was fired from his job but subsequently hired on as the police chief in a neighboring town.[28] It is hard to imagine a private citizen receiving 30 days plus probation, then making an upward career move, after an unjustified shooting of another citizen.

7.2.3 The Role of Race

Many Americans view police shootings as a racial issue. It is said that the police are much more likely to shoot blacks (especially black men) than whites, due to racial bias on the part of the police. In support of this contention, blacks comprise only 13% of the nation's total population but 25% of the people killed by the police.[29]

In reply, police supporters observe that most of the people who are ultimately shot by the police are not initially selected by the police for attention; rather, in most cases a member of the community contacts the police to report suspicious or illegal behavior by someone. And the racial composition of the group of people who are ultimately shot by the police *matches* the racial composition of the group of people reported to the police by members of the community.[30] There is thus no need to posit special racial bias on the part of the police to explain the pattern of shootings, though it remains possible that society in general suffers from racial bias, with the police sharing about the same amount of bias as the rest of society.

It may be that advocates for reform tend to advance the charge of racism for purposes of drawing more attention to the issue of police violence and motivating public concern. But this way of framing the issue is flawed, since it carries the risk that society will adopt ineffectual means of addressing the problem based on a misunderstanding of its roots—for

---

[28] Kindy and Kelly 2015.
[29] Mapping Police Violence Dot Org 2020.
[30] Selby et al. 2016, pp. 71–2. Selby's analysis is based on police shootings of unarmed suspects in 2015, of which there were 153 cases.

instance, hiring more police officers from racial minorities, providing training in reducing racial bias, or teaching police officers that whites are just as dangerous as blacks. Any of those measures might be called for if the central problem were racial bias. But they do not address the problem of a general culture of aggression among American police.

Moreover, it should not be necessary to levy charges of racism in order to motivate reform. The problem of wrongful killings would be sufficient to justify reform efforts, regardless of how the deaths were distributed across racial groups.

7.3 Prosecutorial Abuse

7.3.1 Prosecuting the Innocent

Imagine that a leader of a criminal gang targets an innocent person and has that person kidnaped and held prisoner in order to obtain some minor benefit for the gang leader. Suppose the victim is held captive under armed guard for a month before the police finally uncover the gang's misdeed and liberate the victim. Once the victim was freed, what would happen to the gang leader who ordered the kidnapping?

First, the gang leader would be prosecuted. On conviction, if this was the leader's first criminal conviction, he would be sentenced to between 15 and 20 years in prison.[31] Second, if the gang leader had money, the victim could and likely would sue the leader and collect damages for his ordeal.

Now imagine a variation on the story. Imagine that things are as described above, except that (i) instead of a month, the victim is held prisoner for 25 *years* before finally being released, and (ii) instead of a criminal gang leader, the perpetrator is a government official who uses the powers of his office to have his victim kidnaped and held prisoner. Once the innocent victim is finally released, what would happen to the perpetrator?

We don't have to guess, because the latter scenario has actually happened. The answer is that the perpetrator lost his job and spent 5 days in jail.

---

[31] United States Sentencing Commission 2018, pp. 72–3, 407.

I refer to the case of Michael Morton.[32] In 1987, Michael's wife, Christine Morton, was murdered in their home after Michael had gone to work in the morning. The sheriff who investigated the case quickly assumed, on the basis of flimsy circumstantial evidence, that Michael (who made the mistake of cooperating with the police) must have committed the murder. The police conducted a careless investigation focused on finding reasons to accuse Michael, then arrested him for the crime. The prosecutor in the case conducted a prosecution based on circumstantial evidence, attacks on Michael's personality, and the testimony of a semi-competent medical examiner who falsely placed Christine's time of death before the time at which Michael left for work that morning. There was neither eyewitness testimony nor forensic evidence linking Michael Morton to the crime. Nevertheless, a jury convicted him of his wife's murder.

It was not just that the state had little evidence of Morton's guilt. Before putting him on trial, the government had strong evidence that Michael Morton was *not* the killer. Neighbors had contacted the police to report that they had seen an unknown man park a green van on the lot behind the Morton house on several occasions. A witness had seen the man on one occasion get out of the van and walk into the overgrown area that extended up to the Mortons' privacy fence. Another witness saw the van parked there on the morning Christine was killed. There were fingerprints on the house's sliding glass door that did not belong to any member of the Morton household. There was a fresh footprint in the yard. Another witness found a blue, blood-stained bandana on the ground in a construction area near the Morton house and turned it over to the police; the police, however, failed to follow up on this evidence. Christine Morton's purse was missing, and her credit card was used at a store 80 miles away, two days after the murder, but the police made no effort to find the person who had used it. Finally, unknown to the defense, the Mortons' three-year-old son told his grandmother that he saw the "monster" that had attacked his mother, and that his father had not been present.

---

[32] For a detailed account of the case, see Colloff 2012a, b.

By law, the prosecution is required to turn over to the defense any evidence in their possession that supports the defendant's innocence.[33] A judge in the Morton case ordered the prosecutor to turn over to him (the judge) all of the notes of the lead investigator in the case, so that the judge could verify that there was no such exculpatory evidence. But the prosecutor concealed most of the preceding evidence from both the defense and the judge, including the information about the man in the green van, the credit card charge, and the Morton child's statements. This information only came out many years later, after lawyers with the Innocence Project obtained the real, complete notes from the investigation.

Morton was finally exonerated twenty-five years after his conviction, when his attorneys managed to get DNA testing done, at their own expense, on the blood-stained bandana. The then-current district attorney (different from the original district attorney who had prosecuted Morton) strenuously fought against allowing DNA testing, claiming that DNA tests would "muddy the waters" and that the bandana was too far from the crime scene to be relevant. Fortunately, a judge allowed the testing, over the district attorney's objections. When the testing was done, it revealed DNA from Christine on the bandana, together with that of a man named Mark Norwood, who had a long criminal record, including arrests for breaking and entering and aggravated assault. Michael's DNA was not present. Even at this point, government prosecutors refused to admit that Michael Morton was innocent, insisting that "there could be many innocent explanations for why DNA is on that bandana". Eventually, when it became clear that Norwood had committed a second murder with the same MO seventeen months after killing Christine, and that Norwood was still living in the area, government prosecutors gave up their campaign of legal obstruction. Morton was exonerated in court and freed shortly thereafter.

Morton's prosecutor never accepted blame; in his only public statement about the Morton affair, he insisted, "In my heart, I know there was no misconduct whatsoever", before apologizing for *the system's* failure. He was nevertheless eventually disciplined for his illegal withholding of exculpatory evidence: He was disbarred and sentenced to 500 hours of

---

[33] *Brady v. Maryland*, 373 U.S. 83 (1963).

community service, a $500 fine, and 10 days in jail. He was released after only 5 days due to good behavior.[34]

To be clear, the problem is not that the prosecutor made an *error*. Mistakes are bound to occur in any justice system, and understandable errors cannot be criminally punished, lest the system's offices become impossible to staff. The problem in this case is that the prosecutor *deliberately deceived* the court, withheld evidence showing that the defendant was probably innocent, and knowingly proceeded to send this probably innocent person to prison.

This case represents one of the most egregious miscarriages of justice to be found in the annals of American law. Of course this case was not a *typical* prosecution; most importantly, in the overwhelming majority of prosecutions, the accused is factually guilty. It is unknown how often prosecutors withhold evidence or engage in other misconduct. But the aspect of the case that I want to draw attention to is not simply that an innocent man was punished, or even that a prosecutor engaged in egregious and harmful misconduct.

What concerns me most is the aftermath. What happens to prosecutors when they engage in the most blatant and harmful kinds of misconduct, stealing decades from the lives of innocent people? Morton's prosecutor ultimately served approximately one thousandth of the jail term that one could expect to receive for the most comparable crime that a private citizen could commit (kidnapping), and 0.05% of the prison term that he had unjustly imposed on Michael Morton.

Yet that was a *surprisingly harsh* punishment in our system. When the 10-day prison sentence was handed down, news sources hailed the historic decision to hold a prosecutor accountable.[35] It was reported, incredibly, as the first time ever that a prosecutor would go to jail for convicting an innocent man.[36]

There was, however, at least one earlier case in which prosecutorial misconduct earned a jail term. In the infamous Duke lacrosse case in 2006, a black woman accused three members of the Duke University

---

[34] Osborn 2018.
[35] Gonzalez 2013.
[36] Godsey 2015.

lacrosse team (all white men) of raping her at a party hosted by the team. Prosecutor Mike Nifong proceeded with a prosecution and made public statements designed to prejudice the public against the players, despite an extremely weak case. Nifong was later disbarred for withholding exculpatory DNA evidence. He served a single day in jail for his misconduct in that case.[37]

Unlike the Morton case, in the Duke lacrosse case, the prosecutor did not send anyone to prison unjustly—but it was not for lack of trying. Had Mike Nifong been successful, three innocent men would have been imprisoned for multiple years. Had Nifong attempted to kidnap and imprison these men *without* using the power of the state to do so, he would have been subject to a prison term of between 10 and 20 months for each of his victims, assuming this was his first offense.[38] Because he used the power of the state, however, he served only one day.

These cases were actually remarkable for the fact that the corrupt prosecutors suffered any punishment at all. The Center for Prosecutor Integrity reports that, out of 3625 cases of prosecutorial misconduct identified in nine studies of the problem, only 63 cases—fewer than 2%—resulted in any punishment for the prosecutors. Even in those few cases, most punishments were slaps on the wrist at best. The most common sanction was to assess the prosecutor with the costs of the disciplinary hearings.[39]

7.3.2 Skewed Trials

Prosecutors, in conventional legal ethics, are considered to be constrained by justice. For example, it is unethical for a prosecutor to prosecute someone whom the prosecutor believes to be innocent, nor may a prosecutor withhold evidence, present false evidence, or otherwise attempt to undermine the truth-seeking functions of the criminal justice system. All of this is part of the widely accepted code of ethics in the legal profession.[40]

---

[37] Dewan 2007.
[38] For the relevant kidnapping statute, see N.C. Gen. Stat. § 14–39. For the treatment of attempts, see N.C. Gen. Stat. § 14–2.5. For the applicable sentencing table, see North Carolina Judicial Branch 1995.
[39] Center for Prosecutor Integrity 2013, pp. 13–14.
[40] American Bar Association 2017.

7 Abuse of Power

The reasons for this should be self-evident. The purpose of the justice system is not to cause harm to all who come in contact with it, nor is it to provide opportunities for lawyers to display their skills in contests with other lawyers. The justice system exists to pursue justice.

In actual fact, however, many American prosecutors focus more on "winning" than on attaining justice, and they often use the powers granted to their office to undermine the intended functioning of the criminal justice system. A fascinating window into this mindset was inadvertently provided by former Philadelphia Assistant District Attorney Jack McMahon, who in 1986 made a training video for other lawyers in the Philadelphia District Attorney's office. In the video, McMahon explains the goals of a prosecutor during the jury selection process:

> [C]ase law says that the object of ... *voir dire* is to get a competent, fair, and impartial jury. Well, that's ridiculous. You're not trying to get that. ... You're there to win. ... And the only way you're going to do your best is to get jurors that are as unfair and more likely to convict than anybody else in that room.
>
> ... [T]he blacks from the low-income areas are less likely to convict. ... [A]s a result, you don't want those people on your jury. And it may appear as if you're being racist or whatnot, but again, you're just being realistic. You're just trying to win the case.
>
> I've learned, and my opinion is, you don't want smart people. You do not want smart people. I wish that you could ask everyone's IQ. If you could know their IQ, you could pick a great jury all the time. You don't want smart people. ... They take those words "reasonable doubt", and they actually try to think about them.
>
> You don't want them to analyze your case. Because generally speaking, if they analyze it too well, they're going to say, "This isn't enough to convict."[41]

---

[41] McMahon 1986 at 37:08, 39:14, 42:00, and 53:00. The video was leaked to the public many years later, when Jack McMahon happened to be running for District Attorney, challenging the incumbent D.A. It was during the campaign that the incumbent leaked the video in an effort to discredit McMahon with minority voters and win the election (Siegel 1997). The incumbent won. McMahon now works as a criminal defense lawyer.

When this video was made public (many years after it was recorded), McMahon took fire for his opposition to poor, black jurors. In American criminal courts, prosecutors and defense attorneys are each permitted to strike a certain number of potential jurors from the jury pool without stating a reason (this is known as exercising "peremptory challenges"). In Philadelphia, each side was granted seven such peremptory challenges.[42] However, attorneys are *not* permitted to reject a juror on the basis of race, even using a peremptory challenge.[43] Thus, McMahon advised fledgling prosecutors that they should (i) use peremptory challenges to remove poor black jurors anyway, but (ii) when doing so, invent some spurious alternative rationale for removing those jurors and make a note of it so that they can later report this spurious rationale, in case they are accused of excluding jurors on the basis of race. It does not matter how unreasonable the alternative rationale is, as long as it is not race-based.

For anyone seeking to understand the American justice system and the role of prosecutors therein, the McMahon training video is worth watching in its entirety. For present purposes, a number of things are worth remarking about it. For one, it seems never to have occurred to McMahon that the job of a prosecutor is anything other than "winning". He does not seriously entertain the possibility that a prosecutor might in good faith try to obtain an impartial jury in order to enable the system to function as intended. He doesn't expect anyone else in the room to take that idea seriously either, and the fact that the District Attorney at the time used his lecture as a training video suggests that McMahon was correct in his assessment of the attitudes of other prosecutors. Three judges who were interviewed after the video was released told reporters that methods like those McMahon recommends are in widespread use in American courts.[44]

In an interview many years later, McMahon made clear that he believes all prosecutors think similarly to himself. When questioned about the possibility that his recommended practices might deny defendants their Constitutional rights, McMahon replied:

---

[42] McMahon 1986 at 3:50.
[43] *Batson v. Kentucky*, 476 U.S. 79 (1986).
[44] Siegel 1997.

So you're saying that if you're the prosecutor you should say, "Oh, well, this guy'll probably be worse for me, he'd probably believe those cops are lying, but I'm going to take him because I want to uphold the [Constitution]"— you know, come on, I mean that's just not realistic. There isn't a prosecutor in the country that would do that.[45]

Noteworthy also is that the worst of the practices McMahon recommends are perfectly legal. As we have noted, it is illegal for a prosecutor to exclude jurors solely on the basis of race, though this restriction is easily circumvented by simply lying about one's motives. But excluding *intelligent* jurors, simply to prevent the jury from scrutinizing one's case, is a perfectly legal and accepted practice.

In fact, the reasons McMahon gives for excluding jurors are reasons why the jurors in question should be *included*, from the standpoint of the goals of the system. Individuals who will carefully scrutinize the prosecution's case and reflect on the meaning of "reasonable doubt" are precisely the sort of individuals who belong on a jury. In his later interview, McMahon further explained the "problem" with black jurors:

> If you're a prosecutor ... and you're trying a drug case so to speak, and the defendant is going to claim that the cops are lying ... What demographic group has had more exposure to police lying than minority communities? They have seen police lie, and will believe police lie, more than some white guy who lives in a rich area and believes that police officer, everything he said.[46]

Notice that McMahon's rationale for excluding black jurors actually implies that black jurors are *more* qualified to serve on juries. For the explanation implies that police are in fact untrustworthy but that white jurors don't realize this.

McMahon was never punished (except by losing an election) for his practices of excluding qualified jurors in an effort to skew trials. Such tactics are par for the course in American courts and never call forth serious sanctions.

---

[45] Abumrad 2016 at 30:32.
[46] Abumrad 2016 at 28:48.

7.3.3 Civil Immunity

In American law, both prosecutors and judges enjoy *absolute immunity* against lawsuits for abuses that they commit in the course of carrying out their prosecutorial or judicial functions—meaning that if you file suit against a judge or prosecutor for abusing their power, your suit will be summarily dismissed, regardless of how clear and serious the abuse may have been. (Police officers are granted a *qualified* immunity, which means that it is possible to sue them for violating your civil rights, but the standards for prevailing are much higher than in an ordinary lawsuit against a private party.) This principle is both legally and morally indefensible.

Let us begin with the legal situation. In the legal world, courts sometimes make demonstrable legal errors based on reasoning that no one today would defend, yet as soon as they make these errors, the errors immediately become accepted as authoritative, particularly if made by the Supreme Court. One such case was that of *Imbler v. Pachtman*, decided in 1976.[47] In that case, a plaintiff (Paul Imbler) who had been wrongfully convicted sued the prosecutor (Richard Pachtman) for knowingly presenting false evidence at trial and suppressing evidence tending to support Imbler's innocence. The legal basis for the suit was the following federal law:

> Every person who, under color of any statute, ordinance, regulation, custom, or usage, of any State or Territory, subjects, or causes to be subjected, any citizen of the United States or other person within the jurisdiction thereof to the deprivation of any rights, privileges, or immunities secured by the Constitution and laws, shall be liable to the party injured in an action at law, suit in equity, or other proper proceeding for redress.[48]

In brief, the law states that if someone uses the law to violate your rights, you can sue them.

---

[47] 424 U.S. 409 (1976). But note that absolute immunity does not apply to a prosecutor's investigatory actions before judicial proceedings begin; *Buckley v. Fitzsimmons*, 509 U.S. 259 (1993).

[48] Rev. Stat. §1979. The earliest version of the law was the Ku Klux Klan act of 1871 (17 Stat. 13). The provision was later reclassified as 42 U.S.C. §1983 and amended twice. It is often referred to today as "Section 1983".

Notwithstanding that statute, the U.S. Supreme Court in the *Imbler* case ruled that citizens *cannot* sue either prosecutors or judges for using the law to violate citizens' rights. In essence, the Justices thought that Congress, in passing that statute, had not really intended to end the common law tradition of judicial and prosecutorial immunity but had merely used the overly broad expression "every person" through oversight, failing to notice that it might be taken to include judges and prosecutors.

This interpretation is untenable. The original law was passed during Reconstruction after the Civil War, to address the problem of racist government officials in some states who had been denying black Americans their civil rights. During the original debate in Congress, opponents of the law explicitly pointed out that the law would end judicial immunity (absolute prosecutorial immunity did not exist at the time[49]) and subject judges to lawsuits for errors made on the bench. Congress did not amend the text in light of that objection, and proceeded to pass the statute as written without qualification. It therefore cannot be claimed that Congress did not anticipate that judges might be sued under the statute. And the Supreme Court that decided *Imbler* had reason to know this, because Justice William O. Douglass had pointed it out to his colleagues in a different case nine years earlier, a case that the *Imbler* court itself cited.[50]

Let us turn now to the moral and political case: is absolute immunity a good idea? Hereafter, I shall focus on civil liability for prosecutors, though much the same considerations apply to judges. In his opinion in the *Imbler* case, Justice Lewis Powell explained the public policy considerations that have led judges to create the doctrine of absolute immunity and that, in his view, continued to justify it.[51] In paraphrase:

1. The specter of civil liability would alter how prosecutors performed their duties, interfering with their fearless pursuit of justice.
2. If prosecutors were not immune, then responding to lawsuits might come to dominate a prosecutor's time, distracting from the performance of his duties.

---

[49] See Justice Antonin Scalia's remarks in *Kalina v. Fletcher*, 522 U.S. 118 (1997) at 132.
[50] *Pierson v. Ray*, 386 US 547 (1967). See esp. pp. 561–3 in Douglas' dissent. Douglas was no longer on the Supreme Court by the time of the *Imbler* decision, else he would doubtless have written a dissent for *Imbler* as well; as it was, the *Imbler* decision was unanimous.
[51] 424 U.S. 423–9.

3. Honest prosecutors might sometimes be unfairly held liable for understandable errors of judgment.
4. Civil liability is not needed because prosecutors can be criminally prosecuted instead.

Let us address each of these in turn.

First argument: Civil liability would interfere with prosecutors' fearless pursuit of justice.

Reply: Compare the following parallel argument that could be made about physicians: "Doctors must be able to perform their duties without fear of lawsuits, so that they can focus on patients' health. Therefore, doctors should have absolute immunity from liability for any wrong that they commit in the course of treatment. For instance, if a doctor deliberately murders a patient under his care, that doctor should face no liability."

No one would take such an argument seriously. Why not? It is true that absolute immunity would facilitate the fearless performance of a doctor's duties. It is not true that a general lack of fear on the part of doctors would uniformly promote desirable health outcomes. Liability for malpractice mainly causes doctors to fear committing malpractice. Since medical malpractice is bad, that fear is good.

Similarly, it is true that absolute immunity facilitates the fearless performance of a prosecutor's duties. It is not true that a general lack of fear on the part of prosecutors uniformly promotes justice. Liability for prosecutorial misconduct would mainly cause prosecutors to fear committing prosecutorial misconduct. Since prosecutorial misconduct is bad, that fear is good.

Admittedly, the fear of medical malpractice suits has negative consequences as well. It can motivate doctors to practice "defensive medicine"—ordering unnecessary tests, deferring too much to conventional practice, avoiding high-risk patients, and so on.[52] Yet no one believes that to avoid these problems, we should immunize doctors from all liability for malpractice of any kind. The problem would be only too obvious: immunity would increase medical malpractice and would mainly benefit the most negligent and malicious of doctors. Moreover, it would be obviously *unjust to patients who have suffered from malpractice.* The central concern of the courts is not to formulate public policy; it is to do justice to the individuals who come before the courts.

Similarly, perhaps the fear of lawsuits would lead prosecutors to practice "defensive law". Prosecutors might be overly careful about keeping the defense fully informed, about filing only legally defensible charges, and so on. But this risk does not justify adopting absolute immunity, which increases misconduct and mainly benefits negligent or malicious prosecutors. Moreover, it is obviously unjust to citizens who have suffered from prosecutorial misconduct.

Second argument: Responding to lawsuits could come to dominate a prosecutor's time, distracting from the performance of his duties.

Reply: Consider again the parallel argument for physicians. Some doctors treat large numbers of patients, many of whom can be expected to have adverse health outcomes. Therefore, if doctors are held open to civil liability, then responding to lawsuits could come to dominate a physician's time, distracting from the performance of his medical duties. This prediction is about as plausible and as troubling as the parallel prediction for prosecutors.

It is important to bear in mind that in standard tort law, individuals (whether doctors or anyone else) are not held liable for just any harm they might cause. Only harms that one causes *intentionally* or *negligently* incur legal liability. Doctors who consistently act carefully and in good

---

[52] Sekhar and Vyas 2013.

faith should not therefore be overly fearful of lawsuits. Malicious or negligent doctors face financial peril, but that is as it should be.

The same may be said of prosecutors. If prosecutors were held liable for negligent or intentional misconduct, as members of nearly all other professions are, then honest prosecutors who consistently act carefully and in good faith need not be overly fearful. Malicious or negligent prosecutors would face serious financial peril, but that is as it should be.

Perhaps Powell's concern was not that prosecutors would face a flood of valid suits, but that litigious individuals would inundate the prosecutor's office with frivolous suits.

This problem can affect other professions as well. Journalists sometimes face nuisance lawsuits from those who receive unflattering news coverage. Wealthy celebrities often face nuisance suits from individuals hoping to gain easy money from a settlement. All of this creates serious problems due to the expense, inefficiency, and unreliability of the court system (see § 4.5). Some remedy to reduce the costs of frivolous lawsuits and the incentives for filing them is surely needed. But for no other group of people, besides government officials, would anyone claim that the solution to the threat of nuisance suits is *absolute immunity*. No one says, for example, that because journalists may be harassed by individuals who receive unflattering news coverage, journalists should be immunized against suits for anything they may print, regardless of how false and malicious it may be.

Third Argument: Honest prosecutors might sometimes be unfairly held liable for understandable errors of judgment.

Reply: Again, under standard tort law, in the absence of immunity, prosecutors would not be held liable for understandable mistakes; they would only be held liable for errors resulting from malicious intent or negligence.

Granted, courts sometimes make mistakes, so prosecutors might sometimes be held liable when they should not be. But this problem applies to court cases of all kinds, both civil and criminal. No one claims that the solution to the problem of legal error is to dismiss all cases, and there is no reason to think that courts would be especially biased against prosecutors, relative to all other individuals; indeed, quite the opposite is true.

Fourth Argument: Civil liability is not needed to deter prosecutorial abuse, because it remains possible for prosecutors to be criminally prosecuted.
Reply: This could be said with far greater plausibility about members of other professions—it is far more likely that a physician, a journalist, or a member of any other profession besides prosecutor would be criminally prosecuted for wrongdoing on the job. (In fairness, Powell most likely did not intend this argument to provide independent support for prosecutorial immunity, but only to mitigate the most obvious problem with such immunity.) But in the particular case of prosecutors, it is nearly impossible that they will face justice for abuse of their office. This would generally require another prosecutor to file charges against the misbehaving prosecutor, which is unheard of. As we have seen (§ 7.3.1), prosecutorial abuse almost never receives any sanctions at all in American courts, and even the most egregious of cases resulted in no more than a few days in jail, for a crime that would have earned decades of imprisonment if the perpetrator had been a private citizen. Civil liability, therefore, most certainly is needed to deter prosecutorial abuse.

I conclude that none of the arguments for prosecutorial and judicial immunity withstand scrutiny.

7.4 Executive Abuse

Many government leaders have used their offices to commit crimes and rights violations. It may be that every U.S. President has done so at least to some degree. When they do, U.S. Presidents never face justice, because government officials never see fit to charge any President or ex-President for their crimes. Here, I will discuss just three interesting cases that could have resulted in criminal charges, if members of the U.S. government had wished to hold their leaders accountable.

7.4.1 Richard Nixon

I began this chapter with the case of Richard Nixon, the U.S. President best known for abuse of power. Nixon, of course, was never prosecuted for his actions. When Nixon resigned from office, Gerald Ford (who himself had been appointed to the Vice Presidency by Nixon) took over as President. Shortly thereafter, Ford issued an unconditional pardon for any and all crimes that Nixon might have committed in office. This preempted any criminal investigations against the former President, thus preventing the nation from learning the full extent of Nixon's crimes, ensuring that Nixon would never face justice, and vindicating Nixon's presumption that the President is above the law.

Ford, of course, did not see matters this way. In explaining his decision, Ford opined that Nixon and his family had already suffered enough due to the public humiliation to which they had been subject, and that he (Ford) ought to show mercy. Ford worried about whether Nixon could receive a fair trial. And he expressed concern that prolongation of the scandals and investigations surrounding Richard Nixon would further divide the nation.[53]

All of these considerations would almost certainly hold for *any* President who was found to have committed serious crimes in office. Any such President would be subject to public embarrassment, which his family would have to suffer with him. Any such President would face the same difficulties in obtaining a fair trial as Nixon faced (notably, the difficulty of finding a jury with no prior opinions about the defendant). And given the nature of politics, any President or former President will have both strong supporters and strong detractors; thus, any prosecution of a President or former President is almost guaranteed to be divisive.

---

[53] Ford 1974.

Since Ford's reasons would apply to any U.S. President guilty of serious crimes, they imply that no President should be punished for committing crimes in office. This is, in essence, to hold that the President is above the law.

One might say that this is not so, since President Nixon certainly suffered costs for his behavior—including both serious public opprobrium and the loss of his position. But while these are real costs, they would not be accepted as sufficient punishment if the criminal in question were anything other than a government official. If a revered, non-governmental celebrity were caught in criminal activity, and if that celebrity and his family were subjected to serious public embarrassment and loss of a cherished job, this would not suffice for punishment. The government would not drop charges against the celebrity on the ground that he had already suffered enough. The President would not issue a pardon. The virtue of mercy would not be invoked.

Therefore, the sensitivity that Ford showed to the importance of mercy and fairness in the treatment of Richard Nixon was in fact a rejection of the rule of law as applied to Presidents. Had Ford showed this solicitude toward *all* accused criminals, the message would have been different. As it was, Ford's decision carried the message that Presidents are not subject to the same rules as the rest of us.

7.4.2 George W. Bush

President George W. Bush served in office from 2001 to 2009, including the time of the infamous terrorist attack against America on September 11, 2001. America's "war on terror" thus came to dominate his Presidency. As part of its campaign against terrorism, the Bush administration ordered the use of what it termed "enhanced interrogation techniques" against prisoners suspected of terrorist ties. This included inflicting waterboarding, hypothermia, extreme stress positions, sleep deprivation, and other forms of physical and psychological abuse. The abuse was so severe that at least one hundred detainees died in U.S. custody.[54] Many observers have

---

[54] Greenwald 2009.

found that the Bush administration's methods constituted torture, including United Nations special rapporteur on torture Juan Mendez, President Barack Obama, Attorney General Eric Holder, and the European Court of Human Rights.[55] These torture techniques were approved by several senior Administration officials. President Bush approved enhanced interrogation at least in general terms in 2002; it is unclear how much he knew about the details of the techniques to be used.[56]

Torture is illegal under international law. The torture of prisoners is prohibited by the Geneva Conventions and the United Nations Convention Against Torture, both of which the United States has signed.[57] Granted, the Bush Administration had an understandable motive: they believed that torture would help to prevent further terrorist attacks on the U.S. The U.N. Convention Against Torture, however, stipulates that "No exceptional circumstances whatsoever, whether a state of war or a threat of war, internal political instability or any other public emergency, may be invoked as a justification of torture" (Article 2). The U.S. Constitution provides that treaties entered into by the United States have the force of the highest law of the land (Article VI), so this suffices to render torture illegal under U.S. law.

In addition, torture is directly prohibited by the United States Code, as follows:

> Whoever outside the United States commits or attempts to commit torture shall be fined under this title or imprisoned not more than 20 years, or both, and if death results to any person from conduct prohibited by this subsection, shall be punished by death or imprisoned for any term of years or for life. (18 U.S.C. § 2340)
>
> Whoever, whether inside or outside the United States, commits a war crime, in any of the circumstances described in subsection (b), shall be fined under this title or imprisoned for life or any term of years, or both, and if death results to the victim, shall also be subject to the penalty of death. (18 U.S.C. § 2441)[58]

---

[55] Colvin 2010; Associated Press 2009; Stout 2009; Lyman 2015.
[56] Peralta 2014.
[57] International Committee of the Red Cross 2014; United Nations 1984.
[58] The "circumstances in subsection (b)" referred to in the statutory text are "that the person committing such war crime or the victim of such war crime is a member of the Armed Forces of the United States or a national of the United States".

The code goes on to list several types of war crimes, including:

> Cruel or inhuman treatment.—The act of a person who commits, or conspires or attempts to commit, an act intended to inflict severe or serious physical or mental pain or suffering (other than pain or suffering incidental to lawful sanctions), including serious physical abuse, upon another within his custody or control.

There is no doubt, therefore, that Bush administration officials, likely including President Bush himself, were guilty of serious violations of the law. If any group of private citizens had organized a comparable program of torture, those individuals would most likely now be serving life sentences in prison, if they had not been executed. None of the laws against torture contain an exemption for government officials (if they did, this would defeat their main purpose). So the Bush officials, as well as the agents who directly carried out their orders, were justly liable to prosecution.

None were ever prosecuted, however, because when Barack Obama took over the Presidency, he decided to grant immunity to everyone involved in the torture program. Early on, Obama's Attorney General, Eric Holder, explained that "it would be unfair to prosecute dedicated men and women working to protect America for conduct that was sanctioned in advance by the Justice Department".[59]

Note, however, that the U.N. Convention Against Torture explicitly stipulates that "An order from a superior officer or a public authority may not be invoked as a justification of torture" (Article 2). Holder's statement in any case fails to explain why the Bush officials who *ordered* the torture were not to be prosecuted. The U.N. Convention requires signatory nations to prosecute torturers (Articles 6–7). This is not up to the government's discretion. Therefore, in addition to the Bush administration, the Obama administration violated the U.N. Convention Against Torture when it refused to prosecute known torturers.

---

[59] Greenwald 2012.

Obama tried to defend his decision by stating that the nation needed to "look forward, not backward".[60] But all criminal prosecutions require looking backward, since it is not possible to prosecute a crime that has not yet occurred. Therefore, if we always look forward rather than backward, no crimes will be prosecuted. The Obama administration, however, like all other administrations, had no qualms about prosecuting crimes by private citizens. It remains to be explained, therefore, why looking backward was objectionable specifically in the case of crimes by Bush administration officials. It is difficult to escape the suspicion that Obama's philosophy was to look forward when it came to crimes committed by government officials, but look backward when it came to crimes by anyone else. In other words, government officials are above the law.

7.4.3 Barack Obama

Perhaps the reason Obama chose to forgive the Bush administration was that Obama did not want to set a precedent of holding Presidents accountable, lest he himself should be prosecuted after *he* left office. If that was part of the motivation, then the decision was a prudent one. For as it happened, after ending the Bush torture program, Obama went on to commit his own crimes while in office, also in the name of the war on terror. The most serious of these offenses was first degree murder.

Attorney General Eric Holder revealed this in a letter to the Senate Judiciary Committee dated May 22, 2013.[61] Of course, the Attorney General did not use the term "murder". But he admitted that the Obama administration had planned and intentionally carried out the killing of one Anwar al-Awlaki. Al-Awlaki, a dual citizen of the United States and Yemen, was in Yemen at the time, a country that was not at war with the U.S. He was not close to any battlefield, nor was he actively committing or attempting to commit a crime at the time he was killed, nor had he been found guilty of any crime by any court. All of this is undisputed. Nevertheless, the administration targeted al-Awlaki because, it claimed, al-Awlaki was a senior member of the terrorist organization Al Qaeda in

---

[60] Greenwald 2012.
[61] Holder 2013.

the Arabian Peninsula (AQAP), al-Awlaki had recruited terrorists to the organization, and he had participated in planning terrorist attacks; he therefore posed an ongoing threat to Americans.

I say that the administration "claimed" these things, because none of this was ever proved in court, nor did the administration ever release its evidence. Thus, Obama administration officials required the world to trust their word, particularly regarding al-Awlaki's alleged role in planning specific attacks. This is problematic since the separation of powers exists to avoid this sort of dependence on blind trust. The U.S. Constitution does not assign the executive branch the authority to determine final guilt or innocence of accused criminals, pass sentence, and execute them all on its own, because the framers did not consider such trust warranted. If such trust is unwarranted in the case of ordinary crimes, it is unclear why it would become warranted when the alleged crime is one of terrorism. Even if Obama had no intention of abusing his newly-created power of extra-judicial execution, what would prevent a future President from declaring innocent people "terrorists" and executing them, purely on his own say-so?

Nevertheless, the Attorney General proclaimed his absolute commitment to the Constitution, the rule of law, and the cause of civil liberties, all of which takes on an Orwellian air in the context of a defense of extra-judicial executions by the President. Holder insisted that Obama's assassination program was perfectly legal.

How so? The administration's theory was that it is permissible for the President to order a citizen killed, provided that (i) the target is in a foreign country, (ii) the target poses an imminent threat of violence against the U.S. (more on this later), (iii) capturing the target is infeasible, and (iv) the government follows the accepted rules of war in carrying out the killing. Killing must be allowed in such circumstances, since otherwise there would be an "unacceptably high risk that our efforts would fail, and that Americans would be killed".[62] Holder later claimed that drone strikes against U.S. citizens on U.S. soil could also be legal in some unlikely circumstances.[63]

---

[62] Holder 2012.
[63] Gehrke 2013.

What is wrong with this as a legal defense? One problem is that, whether it be a good idea or not, the doctrine Eric Holder introduced is not in fact to be found in the U.S. Constitution, any statute, or any case law. It is a "law" written by the President and his Justice Department. But neither the President nor the Justice Department are lawmakers in the American system of government. Their Constitutional function is only to enforce laws made by others.

Now, there are at least two genuine laws relevant to the assassination program. The first is the murder law. In the U.S., there are statutes against murder in each state and at the federal level. The Model Penal Code provides the following definitions:

> A person is guilty of criminal homicide if he purposely, knowingly, recklessly or negligently causes the death of another human being. ... [C]riminal homicide constitutes murder when: (a) it is committed purposely or knowingly; or (b) it is committed recklessly under circumstances manifesting extreme indifference to the value of human life...[64]

President Obama purposely and knowingly caused the death of al-Awlaki, who was a human being. So, on the face of it, Obama was guilty of murder. Note that U.S. murder statutes do not contain any exception for the President; they do not, for example, contain clauses along the lines of "...except in the case where the person causing the death of another is the President or working for the President". Nor is there an exception for the case where the victim is an alleged terrorist.

There are other special circumstances, however, in which killing is legally permitted. One is the case where a killing is judicially ordered, as in death penalty cases. But that does not apply to this case, since al-Awlaki was never convicted or sentenced to death.

Another exception is for self-defense or defense of innocent third parties. Obama officials might invoke this well-accepted doctrine, arguing

---

[64] American Law Institute 1985, sections 210.1–210.2, p. 120. Section 210.3(1)(b) provides a qualification for cases of "extreme mental or emotional disturbance", not relevant here. The United States Code defines murder as "the unlawful killing of a human being with malice aforethought" (18 U.S.C. §1111); I have not deployed this definition in the text because it leaves unclear which killings are unlawful.

that they killed al-Awlaki in defense of the unknown American citizens who likely would have been killed by al-Awlaki had he remained alive. In U.S. law, however, an appeal to self-defense or defense of innocent third parties can only be used to justify a killing when the person one kills is posing an *imminent* or *immediate* threat of serious harm to others at the time one kills that person.[65] This explains Eric Holder's otherwise odd use of the word "imminent" in describing the threat posed by al-Awlaki.

Yet Holder's insertion of the word "imminent" does not make the condition actually apply. The government put al-Awlaki on its kill list in early 2010; he was finally killed in late 2011. So the threat that al-Awlaki posed was not so immediate as to preclude a delay of more than a year before the threat was addressed, yet without the threatened harm having materialized. This does not satisfy any ordinary English use of the word "imminent". Nor does it match accepted legal usage. If, for example, you shoot your neighbor, then tell the police that your neighbor posed an imminent threat because he was probably going to attack you some time in the next few years, you will end up in jail for murder.[66]

Another exception to the murder statute exists for killing in war. This explains why Holder was keen to insist that "We are a nation at war."[67] However, this is questionable for a number of reasons.

First, no war had actually been declared as of the time that Eric Holder spoke. The Constitution grants Congress the power to declare war, which would certainly suffice legally to trigger the wartime exception to the laws against murder. The power to declare war is not granted to the executive branch. In the case at hand, Congress never declared war, although it did, ten years earlier, issue a vague, open-ended Authorization for the Use of

---

[65] The Code of Federal Regulations uses the term "imminent" (10 CFR §1047.7); the Model Penal Code uses "immediately" (American Law Institute 1985, section 3.04, p. 44).

[66] In *State v. Norman*, 324 N.C. 253 (1989), a woman had killed her abusive husband because she believed, justifiably, that no one else could or would protect her, and that he would continue abusing her for as long as he lived. She was convicted of voluntary manslaughter and sentenced to six years of imprisonment. The North Carolina Supreme Court ruled that a defense of self-defense was unavailable to her, since the harm she feared from her husband was not *imminent* at the time she killed him.

[67] Holder 2012. David J. Barron of the Department of Justice's Office of Legal Counsel invoked this justification in his then-secret memo to the Attorney General defending the drone strike (Barron 2010, pp. 20–21).

Military Force against whoever was responsible for the 9/11 terrorist attacks in 2001.[68] It is therefore not clear that America was, legally, at war.

Second, if America was at war, whom or what was America at war *with*? The war in Iraq and the war in Afghanistan were genuine (albeit undeclared) wars, by most conceptions. But neither of those could be the war of which Holder spoke, for the killing of al-Awlaki could not be claimed to be part of the Iraq or Afghanistan wars. Being at war of course does not entitle the government to kill just anyone. For example, during the Vietnam War, the government could not legally have assassinated Martin Luther King on the grounds that we were at war. Rather, the government can legally commit violence in the course of a war, against the enemy with whom it is at war. Al-Awlaki was not part of any forces fighting in Iraq or Afghanistan, so it is hard to see how his killing could be part of either of those wars.

It must be, therefore, that Holder had in mind something broader—presumably the "war on terror". But it is highly questionable that such a thing can be taken as a literal war for legal purposes. Terrorism is a tactic, not a foreign state or military or paramilitary organization. One cannot literally be at war with a tactic.

The government might claim to be at war, not with the tactic itself, but with all those people who would use the tactic. This, however, is problematic, since there are many separate individuals and organizations who might employ terrorism as a tactic. To declare war on a large class of individuals and groups united only by a common tactic is to invoke a metaphorical or extended sense of "war", similar to that involved in declaring a war on crime or a war on drugs. Indeed, terrorism is just a particular class of crime. Therefore, for the government to claim to be at war with terrorists in general is much like the claim to be at war with criminals in general.

Notice how troubling this would be from a civil liberties standpoint. If a "war" declared by the executive branch suffices to justify extra-judicial executions, and if the government may claim to be at war with a large class of individuals united only by their intention to commit a particular crime, then the executive branch can in effect circumvent all the protections of the criminal justice system by simply declaring a war on crime. It

---

[68] Pub.L. 107–40.

would then apparently become legal for the executive branch to execute suspected criminals without trial.

Another possibility is that the government would claim to be at war with the particular terrorist group of which al-Awlaki was a member, AQAP. This seems more plausible on its face. If we accept this notion, how many wars is the U.S. government presently involved in?

As it happens, the U.S. State Department maintains an official list of Designated Foreign Terrorist Organizations. Since the government has claimed the authority to kill terrorists in general, not just those belonging to one or two specific groups, presumably the government would claim to be at war with all of these groups. If that is correct, then the U.S. is, as of this writing, engaged in no fewer than 69 wars.[69] (Or perhaps it is a single war against 69 opponents.) These putative wars would be very dubious from a legal standpoint. Again, none of them has been declared by Congress per se, and for most of these putative wars, none of their conduct involves actual battles. Moreover, the proliferation of "wars" with non-governmental groups, as well as the apparently permanent character of the putative state of war, points up the potential for abuse, in which the President can claim to be at war with any group of people that he wants to target.

My point is not simply that the Obama administration's idea was dangerous. My point is that the drone strike on al-Awlaki was not the sort of event that the framers of U.S. law, either statutory or Constitutional, had in mind by "war". Al-Awlaki was not killed in battle, nor was he a combatant in any war in the standard sense. He was, rather, a member of a criminal organization who was assassinated by the CIA on orders from the President. He was, no doubt, a terrible human being whom the world is better off without. But in American law, even the worst human beings have the right to have their crimes proved in court before they are executed.

This brings us to the second important law (after the murder law) that Obama violated. The Fifth Amendment to the U.S. Constitution reads:

> No person shall be held to answer for a capital, or otherwise infamous crime, unless on a presentment or indictment of a grand jury ... *nor be deprived of life, liberty, or property, without due process of law*....
> (Emphasis added.)

---

[69] U.S. Department of State 2020 (list accessed June 28, 2020).

Presidents Bush, Obama, and Trump have all killed many individuals without due process in the course of their war on terrorism. Obama is estimated to have killed 3797 people, including at least 324 (non-terrorist) civilians, by drone strikes. As he once put it, "Turns out I'm really good at killing people. Didn't know that was gonna be a strong suit of mine."[70] Each of these Presidents could therefore be charged with many homicides.

Al-Awlaki, however, attracted special attention because he was a U.S. citizen. He was therefore, in theory, protected by the U.S. Constitution. The Constitution contains no exception permitting the government to kill its citizens during wartime without due process. So it was especially clear that al-Awlaki's execution was illegal.

Eric Holder tried to head off this concern by distinguishing "due process" from "judicial process". He conceded that al-Awlaki had been deprived of life with no *judicial* process. But he maintained that al-Awlaki had nevertheless received *due* process, namely, the process by which Obama administration officials reviewed al-Awlaki's crimes and deliberated thoughtfully about whether to kill him.

The problem is that nowhere else in American law is such a process taken to constitute "due process of law". The Fifth Amendment's protection of due process is not satisfied by executive branch officials deciding, on their own, that one is guilty and then executing one. That is in fact precisely what the Fifth Amendment was meant to rule out. Surely it does not become due process of law simply because the President and his advisors followed the process that they devised for themselves.

7.4.4 Necessity Versus Imminence

Many would say that the killings carried out by Presidents Bush, Obama, and Trump have been necessary to defend America from its enemies. Above, I objected that the threat against which Obama sought to defend us was not *imminent* at the time, so his action was not a legally valid instance of defensive force. One might argue, however, that

---

[70] Zenko 2017. Unsurprisingly, President Trump accelerated the drone strike program; see Cupp 2019.

the imminence requirement is simply unreasonable. If we must wait until a harm is imminent, it may by then be too late to prevent it. Therefore, a defender should be able to use force against an antagonist before the harm is imminent, if doing so is reasonably necessary to prevent serious harm from *eventually* befalling the defender or innocent third parties.[71]

This point is well-taken as a point about the theory of self-defense in general. In the present context, however, there are two problems with pressing this point. The first is that the state has itself crafted the law of self-defense, which it imposes on all non-state actors. The state is therefore in no position to insist that the law is unreasonable and should not be applied to itself. If the government finds the imminence requirement reasonable and just for private individuals who use defensive force, then the government must impose the requirement on its own agents as well. If the government finds the rule unreasonable, then it must alter its own laws to cease imposing this unreasonable requirement on others, rather than simply violating its own law.

The second problem is that there are good reasons for defensive force by the state to be more tightly constrained than defensive force by private agents. To see why, imagine that the police believe they have identified a serious (non-terrorist) criminal. This criminal will most likely continue committing serious crimes until someone stops him. Unfortunately, the government does not yet have sufficient evidence to prosecute this individual in court, and collecting sufficient evidence will likely take a number of months, during which time he will commit additional crimes. In such a case, may the police, legally, go to the criminal's house and summarily execute him?

The argument for execution would run as follows:

> Killing the criminal is necessary to defend other citizens from him. If the police merely arrest him, then, since they lack sufficient evidence to prosecute, the criminal will shortly go free and then commit more crimes. If they wait until they have sufficient evidence and *then* arrest him, he will

---

[71] Baron (2011) makes a strong case for this view. Eric Holder (2012) raised essentially this problem about al-Awlaki.

commit more crimes in the meantime. They can only prevent him from committing more crimes by killing him. Therefore, since the killing would be necessary for the defense of innocent third parties, it is legal and not a murder.

This is the conclusion that results from eliminating the imminence requirement for defensive force by agents of the state.

The problem is that this power in the hands of the state is too open to abuse. Certainly those who designed the American system of government intended no such power to be held by agents of the executive branch. It would largely defeat the purpose of the court system, the right to a jury trial, the right to counsel for the defense, and all the other protections of the rights of defendants built into the criminal justice system.

Is there a similar risk of abuse if private parties are permitted to use defensive force for non-imminent threats? Perhaps, and *perhaps* this justifies the imminence requirement for private defensive force. But this is not obvious; it is not obvious that the problem of abuse by private agents is equally serious as the problem of abuse by the state. Nor need we answer that question here. It is enough to understand why *at least* in the case of the state, defensive force should be permitted only to address genuinely imminent threats.

There is not only a moral point but a legal point here. It is uncontroversial that the police could not legally execute the criminal in the above example. Thus, it cannot be claimed that the government is legally exempt from the imminence requirement for the use of defensive force.

7.4.5 Divisiveness

Both Nixon and Bush escaped prosecution because, according to their successors, prosecuting these former Presidents would have been *divisive*. As Obama eloquently put it, "We must resist the forces that divide us, and instead come together on behalf of our common future."[72]

There is no doubt much truth to the concern: Each President had strong supporters, as well as strong opponents. Americans would have

---

[72] Greenwald 2012.

argued fiercely over whether the prosecutions were appropriate, and many would have been angered, no matter the outcome. Does this justify the refusal to prosecute?

It does not. There have been many controversial prosecutions in the history of American law; virtually no one argues that they should have been dropped regardless of whether the defendants were guilty, simply because they were divisive. This argument appears only when the criminal to be prosecuted is a government official.

Consider, for example, the case of Bernhard Goetz, the man who in 1984 shot four young men in New York who tried to mug him on the subway.[73] Goetz was prosecuted for attempted murder, assault, and criminal gun possession. Americans were sharply divided over the case, some viewing Goetz as a dangerous vigilante and others viewing him as a hero. The case was especially divisive because Goetz was white and the four men he shot were black.

Now, leave aside your actual opinions, if any, about Goetz. Imagine that you are the District Attorney and assume that you believe that Goetz is in fact guilty of the above-mentioned crimes, for which he justly deserves to be punished. How would you react to the suggestion that you should decline to prosecute Goetz because it would be divisive?

Virtually any prosecutor would dismiss the suggestion out of hand, and rightly so. Your responsibility is to pursue justice in the case—justice to Goetz and to the men he shot—not to try to influence public discourse or reduce disagreement in society. If your evidence shows that Goetz is guilty of attempted murder, you should prosecute him for it; if not, then not. A criminal cannot be immunized from facing justice merely because he has supporters who will be angry if he is punished.

Nor would divisions be healed by a refusal to prosecute. To refuse to prosecute would merely be to take the side of Goetz' supporters. That hardly ends the controversy or cuts off all negative reactions. Those who want him prosecuted will be angry if he is let off, just as those who want him let off will be angry if he is prosecuted. Neither decision produces social harmony.

---

[73] Raab 1985.

So it was with the crimes of the former Presidents. Justice demands punishment for wrongdoing, however politically powerful the perpetrator may be. It is the job of the executive branch of government, run by the President, to see to that punishment, even if—or, we might say, *especially if*—the wrongdoer is the previous chief executive. Nixon and Bush violated the law and justly deserved punishment. That should have been the concern of Presidents Ford and Obama. The refusal to hold criminal Presidents to account did not make Americans forget their differences and move forward into a harmonious future; it outraged those who took the crimes seriously.

It also set the crucial precedents according to which Presidents are above the law. An American President, we now know, can get away with nearly any crime, from corruption to torture to murder, because other Presidents will protect them. Because of this, we can expect Presidents to abuse their powers and disregard the laws far more often than they would if they faced the same sort of deterrent to lawbreaking faced by the rest of us. American politicians pay lip service to the Rule of Law, but this is only so much empty rhetoric if they are never willing to enforce the law against their own profession.

7.5 Diagnosing Abuse

7.5.1 Ambition

Why do government officials, especially members of the executive branch, abuse their powers? One reason is the human drive to "succeed", to attain high status in one's profession and to outcompete other human beings. This drive creates terrible incentives in a legal system. In an adversarial legal system, prosecutors perceive themselves as participating in a *contest* with defense attorneys. They therefore seek to defeat the defense lawyers in order to prove themselves "good prosecutors"—"good" not in the sense of morally good but in the sense of good at prosecuting people. Since the defense lawyers are trying to protect the interests of their clients, the prosecutors adopt the goal of *harming* the interests of those same defendants. The more harm they can inflict, the more they prove their skills as lawyers.

If an innocent defendant is exonerated, the prosecutor does not breathe a sigh of relief that a miscarriage of justice was avoided. He does not congratulate the defense lawyer for her good work in uncovering the truth. Instead, the prosecutor feels disappointed that he "lost", and he may try to mitigate the sense of losing by inflicting whatever harm on the defendant he can before the defendant leaves the justice system. The prosecutor is supposed to be an agent of justice, but most human beings have difficulty identifying with such abstract, impersonal values. They find it much easier to identify with the goals of defeating other humans and promoting their own success.

In addition, in the American criminal justice system, most prosecutors are elected officials. Hence, prosecutors also aim to "win" in the sense of winning elections. They must therefore please voters, who frequently have very superficial understandings and respond instinctively to a "tough on crime" message. In the infamous Duke lacrosse case (see § 7.3.1 above), there was evidence that prosecutor Mike Nifong pursued his groundless case against the lacrosse team for political reasons: he faced a tight election and sought to shore up the minority vote by taking the side of a poor, black woman against a group of rich, white, male athletes.[74] This would explain Nifong's eagerness to make media appearances and public statements about the case. His message about being tough on "rapists" may have resonated, since Nifong in fact won the election (albeit narrowly), before his misconduct got him disbarred. Voters in general cannot be expected to be familiar with the details of various particular cases, so a prosecutor can promote a desirable tough-on-crime image by citing his record of locking up "criminals", regardless of whether the people he locks up are guilty or innocent.

The case with police officers is similar, if less extreme. Just as prosecutors seek to increase their win-loss ratio, police seek to increase their arrest statistics. Patrol officers are evaluated partly on the basis of the number of arrests they make, and detectives on the basis of their clearance rates (the proportion of cases they receive that end in arrests). This creates the incentive to look for reasons to accuse people of crimes and to arrest people.

---

[74] Sowell 2006.

Both police and prosecutors thus have incentives to assume that a person is guilty of crimes, if they can find any way of doing so. In the Michael Morton case (§ 7.3.1), the sheriff and the prosecutor both wanted to assure local residents that they had found the killer. They found it convenient to assume that Morton was the killer, since otherwise, they would have had to admit that they did not know who the killer was and that they had thus far failed in their jobs.

American Presidents also strive to appear successful and effective. Toward this end, they strive to defeat those who are, or who can be portrayed as, enemies of the nation. Like police officers and prosecutors, most Presidents have difficulty identifying with such abstract values as justice and individual rights. Thus, *defeating* accused terrorists is more important to them than *respecting the rights* of accused terrorists.

7.5.2 Confirmation Bias

Few people fully appreciate the power of *confirmation bias*. This is the psychological phenomenon whereby, once we have formed a belief, or even a suspicion, we interpret all evidence and experience in light of that belief or suspicion.[75] When information supporting the belief appears, we accept it at face value, without scrutiny. When counter-evidence appears, we fail to notice it, forget it, or devise reasons for discounting it. When ambiguous information appears, we select the interpretation that best fits with our existing belief, then strengthen that belief because of the new "supporting evidence". If a large body of mixed, ambiguous evidence is examined, therefore, there is a tendency for individuals to progressively strengthen whatever opinion they were initially inclined toward until they wind up completely convinced, regardless of whether the initial opinion was true or false. All of this happens automatically, without our even noticing what we are doing.

In criminal cases, ambiguous evidence is common. In the Michael Morton case, once the police had decided that Morton was a suspect, many bits of information could be interpreted as evidence of guilt. For

---

[75] This is an extremely pervasive and well-documented phenomenon. For a review of the evidence, see Nickerson 1998.

example, Morton had had a disagreement with his wife the night before the murder, as a result of which he left her a note explaining how he had felt hurt. This is a common sort of occurrence between married couples, rarely betokening any major problem. But in a context where Michael was assumed to be a suspect, the police and prosecutor were able to see the disagreement as a motive for murder.

The disagreement had to do with a pornographic video, *Handful of Diamonds*, that Morton had rented to watch with his wife; she fell asleep rather than watching it. The prosecutor played an excerpt from the video during the trial. Jurors found it disgusting, which may have prejudiced them against Morton. In an ordinary context, little would be made of such a video, but in a context where a man has been accused of murder, jurors might find themselves vaguely sensing that this was the sort of video that a murderer might watch.

During his trial testimony, Morton reportedly was unemotional. This could be interpreted as an indication of shock, or emotional repression, or simply a stoical disposition. But the jury, who had already heard the prosecutor aggressively insist that Morton was a murderer, was able to instead interpret it as evidence that Morton did not care about his wife's death, because he had killed her.

On the other hand, Morton broke down at another point in the trial, when the prosecutor showed a series of grisly crime scene photos. His tears could have been viewed as an outpouring of grief over the horrible fate his wife had suffered. Instead, the jury interpreted Michael's tears as showing remorse for what he had done, thus further establishing his guilt.[76]

This example encapsulates the problem of confirmation bias. Nearly all human reactions are open to interpretation. If one is looking for indications of guilt, then a suspect who is unemotional looks guilty; at the same time, a suspect who is *emotional* looks guilty.

Confirmation bias can affect everyone involved in the justice system. It helps to explain how police and prosecutors can convince themselves that a suspect is guilty on the basis of little objective evidence. What the prosecutor actually believed in the Morton case is unclear, but we cannot

---

[76] Colloff 2012a.

discount the possibility that the prosecutor actually thought Morton was guilty. Once he had formed that opinion, the prosecutor may have decided that there was no harm done by withholding seemingly exculpatory evidence, since that evidence must be misleading and could only serve to give a murderer a chance to go free.

The problem of confirmation bias applies also to political leaders and their advisors. Once Bush administration officials had decided that "enhanced interrogation" was a good idea, they doubtless were able to devise arguments to convince themselves that it was legal. The term "torture" is vague and subjective, after all. Who is to say exactly where the line is between torture and merely forceful interrogation?

The Obama justice department faced a similar situation. They knew the administration wanted to execute terrorists via drone strikes. They therefore looked for reasons why this might be legal. Because the law is frequently complicated, vague, and less than fully coherent, it is often possible to devise plausible-sounding arguments for whichever of two legal positions one wants to support. In the present case, the terms "imminent" and "war" are both vague and subject to interpretation. The administration thus selected interpretations of these terms favorable to what they wanted to do. Though I think their interpretation of "imminent" falls too far from ordinary usage to be a legitimate, sincere interpretation of the word, their interpretation of "war" is one that might be accepted by ordinary English speakers. Whether the government's actions against terrorist organizations should be classified as a kind of war or as a kind of law enforcement action is open to debate. When matters are open to debate, those with a preexisting political agenda tend to assume whichever view is most favorable to that agenda.

7.5.3 Love of Power

Those who gravitate towards positions in government are disproportionately likely to be individuals who enjoy exerting power over other human beings. This exertion of power is the core of what government does, so those who do not enjoy, or have philosophical objections to, such exercise of power are unlikely to seek government positions, particularly those in which power is most directly and forcefully exerted. Not all government agents need be power mongers, but we should expect to see a larger proportion of power mongers in government than in the general population.

Power is exerted in different ways in different government positions. In the case of police officers, their job prominently involves direct exertion of physical force against other human beings. Prosecutors exert their power less directly, by causing other agents of the government to deploy force against criminals and suspected criminals. Presidents and other chief executives (governors, mayors) also exert force indirectly, by directing the activities of prosecutors, police officers, and the military.

The targets of this force are, ideally, limited to criminals who have unjustly threatened others. Nearly everyone is in favor of the use of force against such criminals. Nevertheless, most human beings would not themselves *enjoy* exerting force, or threatening to exert force, against other human beings, even when justified. Nor, I suspect, would most human beings enjoy *arguing for* the use of force against specific individuals on a regular basis. There is thus a wide gap between what we consider morally justified and what we would like to do as a career. Only a small proportion of human beings would find the job of police officer or prosecutor fulfilling. The job of mayor, governor, or President is less aversive because the use of power is less direct and personal—chief executives almost never directly confront the individuals whom they cause to be imprisoned or killed. Nevertheless, I suspect that most human beings would find chief executive positions too stressful to be fulfilling.

The people who occupy these governmental positions therefore are not simply ordinary people. These positions select for unusual classes of people. It is no stretch to suppose that individuals with a higher than normal capacity to derive satisfaction from exerting power over others would also be at higher risk of abusing their power. For the pleasure of showing one's power over other human beings is, unfortunately, not limited to those cases in which the exercise of that power is morally just. Indeed, unjust exercises of power may be *more* enjoyable for a power-monger, provided one can get away with them, since the injustice heightens the sense that one is invulnerable, beyond the reach of the laws and norms applicable to ordinary human beings. Consider the following exchange between O'Brien and Winston in George Orwell's *1984*:

[O'Brien:] "How does one man assert his power over another, Winston?"
[Winston:] "By making him suffer."
[O'Brien:] "Exactly. By making him suffer.... Unless he is suffering, how can you be sure that he is obeying your will and not his own? Power is in inflicting pain and humiliation."[77]

There are two important points about the desire for power. The first is, as we have said, that an initial drive for power over others is a predictor of its misuse once power is granted. The other important point is that, as Lord Acton famously wrote, "Power tends to corrupt and absolute power corrupts absolutely."[78] Even those who do not initially seek power may find, once they taste it, that they enjoy the sensation. And so finding, they may seek additional opportunities to experience their power, beyond those afforded by justice. Human beings did not evolve to serve and protect others. We evolved to get ahead. So when humans gain power over others, we do not feel like humble public servants; we feel like rulers.

7.5.4 Ingroup Bias

Members of any organization or profession develop a sense of solidarity with one another, an easy capacity to sympathize with one another's plight and to side with one another against the unenlightened outsiders with whom they all have to deal. Thus, if you work in a restaurant, you probably joke and commiserate with the other restaurant workers about difficult customers. If a waiter makes a mistake with a customer's order, you probably find it easy to see the waiter's side, and easy to find ways that the mistake might be the customer's fault. Even if the error is the waiter's fault, it is an understandable error, for which the waiter certainly shouldn't be punished.

Similarly, if you work in medicine, you probably commiserate with other doctors or nurses about difficult patients and find it easy to excuse

---

[77] Orwell 1961, Part 3, Ch. 3.
[78] Dalberg-Acton 1887.

doctors' errors. (But when you go to restaurants, you probably find it much harder to understand errors by waiters.)

If you teach in a university, you will commiserate with other professors about difficult students. If there were a court in which disputes between students and professors were adjudicated, and the court were staffed by professors, then students would almost always lose, and professors would almost always win. If it were staffed by students, the reverse would occur. The analogous points hold for any other profession or organization. Fortunately, however, professors do not have the power to imprison or execute students.

Ingroup bias becomes more problematic when it comes to government officials. When *I* make a mistake in my job, a student might get a higher or lower grade than deserved. When a police officer makes a mistake, the result could be the death of an innocent person. When a prosecutor makes a mistake, it could be years or decades of imprisonment. When the President makes a mistake, it could be thousands or hundreds of thousands of deaths. But the seriousness of these consequences does not remove the sense of professional solidarity among government officials. If anything, it heightens that sense. Many observers, including police officers, have noted the "us versus them" mentality that has arisen in many police departments (where "us" refers to the police and "them" to the non-police citizens).[79] Thus, when a police officer shoots a citizen, other officers find it easy to see the officer's side, and easy to think of reasons to blame the shooting on the citizen.

And not only other officers. Prosecutors, judges, and politicians all belong to the same organization and perceive themselves as on the same side. Hence, all these government officials sympathize with each other and have an instinctive tendency to protect each other in any dispute with the unenlightened outsiders—who, in this case, are the citizens. Even Barack Obama, on assuming the Presidency, probably found himself suddenly able to sympathize with George W. Bush's plight as Bush had to decide how to deal with the threat of terrorism.

---

[79] Balko 2015; Boivin et al. 2018.

In our political system, there is no one to hold government officials accountable except other government officials. Hence, government officials are almost never held accountable.

7.5.5 Deference to Power

The bias toward government officials is felt not only by other government officials. Even ordinary citizens tend to have a powerful bias in favor of the state and its agents. Thus, juries have a great hesitation to convict police officers of wrongdoing, even when the officers have, for example, killed unarmed citizens. There is a heavy initial presumption that the police act properly, and thus the victim probably provoked his own killing. When police officers testify in trials, if their testimony conflicts with that of other witnesses, most juries will believe the police testimony.

When police and prosecutors accuse someone of a crime, most people presume that the police and prosecutors are telling the truth. For example, in the Michael Morton case (§ 7.3.1), the government suppressed evidence tending to exonerate Morton. But even the witnesses who themselves had *given* the government that evidence tended to accept the government's assertion that Morton was guilty, which may explain why they did not share their evidence with anyone but the police. In the Duke lacrosse case (§ 7.3.1), media outlets and the university community rushed to judgment about the lacrosse players, in part because the prosecutor simply *told* them that the players were guilty.

Similarly, when the President or other government officials state that a particular individual is a terrorist, or that certain aggressive measures are necessary to protect the country, citizens tend to accept these assertions at face value, because they come from the government. Nor are we outraged or horrified by government torture or assassination as we would be by any private group engaged in similar behavior. Even those who oppose government torture and assassination tend to view the government officials engaged in these practices in a much less negative light than they would view individuals who engaged in such practices privately.

Why is this? I suspect that what makes government agents so charismatic, so easy to trust and to sympathize with, is simply the government's power. Human beings instinctively tend to align themselves with whoever has the most power. This may be an adaptation—in our evolutionary history, those who aligned themselves with the powerful tended to survive and prosper more than those who aligned themselves with the weak.[80] Of course, there are exceptions to the rule, and of course human beings do not *perceive* themselves as simply siding with whoever has power. It may seem to us that we are evaluating claims objectively; it simply happens, regularly, that the claims and arguments of the powerful seem more persuasive than the claims and arguments of the weak.

This theory is speculative. But some evidence for it can be found in the phenomenon of Stockholm Syndrome. This is a phenomenon in which individuals who are kidnaped and subject to the mercy of a criminal or group of criminals begin to sympathize with and form emotional bonds with their captors. There are many known cases in which this has occurred. The phenomenon is named after the famous 1973 bank robbery in Stockholm, Sweden, in which the robbers wound up holding four bank employees hostage in the vault for six days. The hostages bonded so thoroughly with their captors that, upon their release, the hostages defended the robbers and refused to testify against them. One even started a defense fund to assist the robbers.[81]

These cases are interesting because the reaction of the hostages is counterintuitive and cannot be explained by standard moral reasoning or the emotional reactions typical of human beings in normal situations. It cannot be said, for example, that the kidnapers have legitimate authority over the hostages, that the kidnapers have an understandable point of view, or that they have legitimate reasons for their behavior. The kidnapers are generally not sympathetic or likeable by ordinary standards, and those outside the situation tend to take extremely negative views of the kidnapers. It thus becomes difficult to see what could make the kidnapers so relatable to their victims, apart from the *power* that the kidnapers hold over those victims.

If this is correct, it is plausible that the psychological tendency extends beyond the case of literal kidnapers, to cover cases of dominant

---

[80] Cantor and Price (2007) review evidence that Stockholm Syndrome is an evolutionary adaptation.
[81] Adorjan et al. 2012, p. 457.

individuals or groups holding power over others in general. If one group of people holds an unquestioned dominant position in society, other members of that society will tend to support that group, to the point of instinctively sympathizing with the point of view of group members and taking the side of the dominant group's members in any conflict. This makes it difficult to hold government employees accountable for their misdeeds. It is difficult even to bring average members of society to *perceive* those misdeeds.

7.6 Reforms

Given the above diagnosis, how could the problem of abuse of power be mitigated? The first reform needed is to eliminate immunity (whether qualified or absolute) from lawsuits for police, prosecutors, and judges: these agents of the state should be subject to lawsuits for misconduct under the same rules as practitioners of any other profession. This would likely have an enormous impact on reducing abuse, particularly by police and prosecutors.

In addition, several other, less likely reforms could further reduce abuse of power. One reform would be to change the way in which police officers are evaluated. Police officers should not be evaluated based on arrest or clearance statistics, since this creates an obvious conflict of interests. The task of a police officer is not to make as many arrests as possible; police should make only justified and necessary arrests. The practice of evaluating performance based on arrest statistics compromises this goal and prevents officers from exercising unbiased judgment. Similarly, prosecuting attorneys should not be evaluated based on conviction statistics, since the social function of a prosecutor is not to maximize convictions. These methods of evaluation should be viewed as serious ethical violations. To make raises or continued employment contingent on conviction statistics is comparable to offering bribes to prosecutors for accusing people of crimes; similarly for police officers and arrest statistics. It is, indeed, merely an indirect way of offering such bribes.

Another needed reform is to create separate organizations dedicated to holding government officials accountable. Most large police departments have internal affairs divisions devoted to investigating complaints about officers. There should, however, be organizations devoted to investigating misconduct by government officials of all kinds, including police, prosecutors, judges, legislators, chief executives, and their staff. These organizations should be as independent as possible from the rest of the government, due to the problem of organizational solidarity (§ 7.5.4). Thus, for example, the members of such an organization should not be members or former members of any other branch of government, and its leadership should be chosen directly by voters, not appointed by other government officials. In addition to investigative bodies, there is a need for separate prosecutors and courts dedicated solely to trying government agents. Again, these must be as independent as possible from the rest of the government. They should not handle any cases other than cases of government misconduct.

It is not clear how well such watchdog organizations would work. They might remain biased in favor of government, as many believe that internal affairs divisions are generally biased in favor of police.[82] As an added measure, therefore, private citizens should be legally permitted to initiate criminal prosecutions against government officials. In most jurisdictions in the U.S., private prosecution either is not permitted at all or requires approval by the government; this creates an obvious conflict of interest in the case of crimes committed by government officials.[83] It is a fundamental principle of criminal justice that *every* agent must be accountable for wrongful behavior, and that no agent should have the power to dismiss complaints against himself.

Perhaps the most effective reform would be a fundamental alteration in institutional structure, one that introduced competition among protectors and adjudicators.[84] At present, a single police agency holds a monopoly on government-sanctioned security services in each geographical area. An alternative system would have small homeowners' associa-

---

[82] Human Rights Watch 1998.

[83] In *Linda R.S. v. Richard D.*, 410 U.S. 614 (1973), the Supreme Court held that "in American jurisprudence at least, a private citizen lacks a judicially cognizable interest in the prosecution or nonprosecution of another." This decision has (wrongly) ruled out private prosecutions in federal court.

[84] For more discussion of this type of system, see Huemer 2013, part II.

tions each select a protection agency, from among several competing agencies operating in the region, to provide security for its own neighborhood, complex, or building. This would tend to avoid the "us versus them" mentality of police in the present system. The competition among agencies would force each agency to strive to satisfy residents. Agencies that beat or shot innocent residents could expect to lose their contracts.

Similarly, the service of adjudicating disputes, including both civil and criminal cases, should be subject to competition, with the parties to a dispute selecting an adjudication service (whether a traditional court or an arbitration company) from a list of competing services operating in the region (as discussed in § 4.7). Alternately, a local homeowners' association could select the adjudicator to resolve disputes arising within its area.

Admittedly, these more radical proposals are unlikely to be taken up in the near future. Assuming that society continues to rely on monopolistic protection and adjudication services, citizens should make themselves aware of the likely flaws of government agents. If one is to serve on a jury, one should be aware of the problems outlined in § 7.5. In evaluating a case, a jury member should take into account that police and prosecutors have a self-interested reason to seek conviction, and thus a motive for lying or withholding evidence; that confirmation bias can lead government officials, as well as jury members, to interpret ambiguous or barely relevant evidence as significant evidence of guilt; and that organizational solidarity tends to lead government agents to support one another. One must take these facts into account in evaluating any case in which the testimony of government agents is used, or in which the conduct of government agents is to be evaluated.

Even apart from the role of juror, private citizens should in general be aware of the potential failings of government agents. Thus, if government officials—whether police, prosecutors, or politicians—tell us that a particular individual is guilty of a particular crime, we should not accept the assertion at face value; we should withhold judgment until the evidence is presented. In addition, if one should happen to possess evidence about a criminal case, then, in addition to giving this evidence to the police, one should also inform the defense and/or the news media. Otherwise, the government may suppress the evidence in order to avoid disturbing their preferred theory of the crime.

Whenever we interact with the state, it is worth bearing in mind that government agents have an unusual amount of power; they do not, however, have an unusual amount of virtue. They are not immune from dishonesty, selfishness, and outright criminality.

References

AP News. 2014, December 15. Saudi Cuts off Hand of Convicted Yemeni Thief. *AP News*, https://apnews.com/66567e20b61c439e835dbe5f8b0b3ad6. Accessed 27 June 2020.

Barnett, Randy E. 1977. Restitution: A New Paradigm of Criminal Justice. *Ethics* 87: 279–301.

Beck, Allen J., Marcus Berzofsky, Rachel Caspar, and Christopher Krebs. 2013. *Sexual Victimization in Prisons and Jails Reported by Inmates, 2011–12*. U.S. Department of Justice, Bureau of Justice Statistics. http://www.bjs.gov/content/pub/pdf/svpjri112.pdf. Accessed 17 May 2016.

Boonin, David. 2008. *The Problem of Punishment*. Cambridge: Cambridge University Press.

Brown, Julie K. 2015. Whistleblower Prison Guard Paid the Price for Reporting Abuse. *Miami Herald*, July 18, 2015. http://www.miamiherald.com/news/special-reports/florida-prisons/article27738046.html. Accessed 17 May 2016.

Bruenig, Elizabeth Stoker. 2015. Why Americans Don't Care About Prison Rape. *The Nation*. March 2, 2015, http://www.thenation.com/article/why-americans-don't-care-about-prison-rape/. Accessed 18 May 2016.

Clear, Todd R. 2007. The Impacts of Incarceration on Public Safety. *Social Research* 74: 613–630.

Cohen, Thomas and Tracey Kyckelhahn. 2010. Felony Defendants in Large Urban Counties, 2006,. U.S. Department of Justice, Bureau of Justice Statistics. http://www.bjs.gov/index.cfm?ty=pbse&sid=27. Accessed 20 May 2016.

Commission on Safety and Abuse in America's Prisons. 2006. *Confronting Confinement*. New York: Vera Institute of Justice. Available at http://www.vera.org/pubs/confronting-confinement. Accessed 17 May 2016.

Families Against Mandatory Minimums. 2013. Alternatives to Incarceration in a Nutshell. http://famm.org/wp-content/uploads/2013/08/FS-Alternatives-in-a-Nutshell-7.8.pdf. Accessed 22 May 2016.

Folk, Ashley. 2019. Three Strikes Laws in Different States. *Legal Match*, February 21. https://www.legalmatch.com/law-library/article/three-strikes-laws-in-different-states.html. Accessed 27 June 2020.

Hannaford, Alex. 2016. No Exit. *Texas Observer*, October 3. https://www.texasobserver.org/three-strikes-law-no-exit/. Accessed 27 June 2020.

Harris, Dan. 2001. Prison Rape Widely Ignored by Authorities. *ABC News*, April 16, 2001. http://abcnews.go.com/WNT/story?id=131113, Accessed 17 May 2016.

Henrichson, Christian, and Ruth Delaney. 2012. *The Price of Prisons: What Incarceration Costs Taxpayers*. New York: Vera Institute of Justice. Available at http://www.vera.org/pubs/special/price-prisons-what-incarceration-costs-taxpayers. Accessed 19 May 2016.

Hoffman, Peter B. 2003. *History of the Federal Parole System*. U.S. Department of Justice, United States Parole Commission. https://www.justice.gov/sites/default/files/uspc/legacy/2009/10/07/history.pdf. Accessed June 27, 2020.

Hollersen, Wiebke. 2013. Portugal, 12 Years After Decriminalizing Drugs. *Der Spiegel*, March 27, 2013, http://www.spiegel.de/international/europe/evaluating-drug-decriminalization-in-portugal-12-years-later-a-891060.html. Accessed 22 May 2016.

Huemer, Michael. 2010. Lexical Priority and the Problem of Risk. *Pacific Philosophical Quarterly* 91: 332–351.

Human Rights Watch. 2001. *No Escape: Male Rape in U.S. Prisons*. New York: Human Rights Watch. Available at https://www.hrw.org/reports/2001/prison/. Accessed 17 May 2016.

Kyckelhahn, Tracey. 2015. *Justice Expenditure and Employment Extracts, 2012—Preliminary*. U.S. Department of Justice, Bureau of Justice Statistics. http://www.bjs.gov/index.cfm?ty=pbdetail&iid=5239. Accessed 22 May 2016.

Lippke, Richard L. 2007. *Rethinking Imprisonment*. Oxford: Oxford University Press.

Moore, Michael S. 1997. *Placing Blame: A Theory of the Criminal Law*. Oxford: Oxford University Press.

Nagin, Daniel S. 2013. Deterrence in the Twenty-First Century. *Crime and Justice* 42: 199–263.

National Lawyers Guild. 2015. Resolution Supporting the Abolition of Prisons. http://www.nlg.org/sites/default/files/Resolution. Supporting the Abolition of Prisons REV.pdf. Accessed 22 May 2016.

National Research Council. 2014. *The Growth of Incarceration in the United States: Exploring Causes and Consequences*. Washington, DC: The National Academies Press. https://doi.org/10.17226/18613. Accessed 27 June 2020.

Parenti, Christian. 1999. Rape as a Disciplinary Tactic. Salon, August 23, 1999. http://www.salon.com/1999/08/23/prisons_3/. Accessed 17 May 2016.

Petteruti, Amanda, and Jason Fenster. 2011. *Finding Direction: Expanding Criminal Justice Options by Considering Policies of Other Nations*. Washington, DC: Justice Policy Institute. http://www.justicepolicy.org/uploads/justicepolicy/documents/finding_direction-full_report.pdf. Accessed 27 June 2020.

Pritikin, Martin H. 2008. Is Prison Increasing Crime? *Wisconsin Law Review* 2008: 1049–1108.

Renaud, Jorge. 2019. Grading the Parole Release Systems of All 50 States. Prison Policy Initiative, February 26. https://www.prisonpolicy.org/reports/grading_parole.html. Accessed 27 June 2020.

Rothwell, Jonathan. 2015. Drug Offenders in American Prisons: The Critical Distinction Between Stock and Flow. The Brookings Institution, November 25, 2015. http://www.brookings.edu/blogs/social-mobility-memos/posts/2015/11/25-drug-offenders-stock-flow-prisons-rothwell. Accessed 19 May 2016.

Slifer, Stephanie. 2014. Once a Criminal, Always a Criminal?. *CBS News*, April 23, 2014. http://www.cbsnews.com/news/once-a-criminal-always-a-criminal/. Accessed 22 May 2016.

The Onion. 2014. 15 Years in Environment of Constant Fear Somehow Fails to Rehabilitate Prisoner, March 4. https://www.theonion.com/15-years-in-environment-of-constant-fear-somehow-fails-1819576202. Accessed 1 Sept 2020.

U.N. News Centre. 2011. Solitary Confinement Should be Banned in Most Cases, UN Expert Says. https://www.un.org/apps/news/story.asp?NewsID=40097. Accessed 17 May 2016.

United Nations Office on Drugs and Crime. 2007. *Handbook of Basic Principles and Promising Practices on Alternatives to Imprisonment*. Vienna: UNODC. Available at http://www.unodc.org/pdf/criminal_justice/Handbook_of_Basic_Principles_and_Promising_Practices_on_Alternatives_to_Imprisonment.pdf. Accessed 20 May 2016.

Volokh, Alexander. 1997. *n* Guilty Men. *University of Pennsylvania Law Review* 146: 173–216.

Wagner, Peter and Wendy Sawyer. 2020. Mass Incarceration: The Whole Pie 2020. March 24. Prison Policy Initiative, https://www.prisonpolicy.org/reports/pie2020.html. Accessed 24 June 2020.

Weiser, Benjamin and Michael Schwirtz. 2017. Fishkill Prison Guards Will Not Face Charges in '15 Death of an Inmate. *New York Times*, August 2. https://www.nytimes.com/2017/08/02/nyregion/fishkill-prison-guards-will-not-face-charges-in-15-death-of-an-inmate.html. Accessed 19 March 2019.

Whitman, James Q. 2003. *Harsh Justice: Criminal Punishment and the Widening Divide Between America and Europe*. Oxford: Oxford University Press.

Winerip, Michael and Michael Schwirtz. 2015. Prison Guard 'Beat Up Squad' Is Blamed in New York Inmate's Death. *New York Times*, August 18, 2015, http://www.nytimes.com/2015/08/19/nyregion/fishkill-prison-inmate-died-after-fight-with-officers-records-show.html. Accessed 17 May 2016.

Part III

In Defense of Justice

8

The Primacy of Justice

8.1 Questions of Individual Ethics

In part II of this book, we saw that the American legal system contains serious and pervasive injustices. In this part, we discuss how individuals who are part of the legal system ought to behave. My central thesis is that agents involved in the legal system are morally obligated to prioritize justice—to place *justice in the individual case* above the law, above the desires of their employers, and above other non-justice considerations.

Before saying more about this, it is useful to distinguish three sorts of question one might raise about the legal system:

(a) *Legal questions:* These are questions concerning what behavior is required by, authorized by, or otherwise consonant with the law.
(b) *Political questions:* These concern how social institutions ought to be designed or what general policies the state should pursue.
(c) *Questions of individual ethics (hereafter, "ethical questions"):* These concern how an individual morally ought to behave in particular circumstances.

For example, suppose that a jury trial is held for a defendant who is accused of drug possession. Assume that drug prohibition is unjust (as discussed in § 3.2 above). Assume, nevertheless, that there is compelling evidence that the defendant did in fact possess some amount of a legally prohibited drug. The jury then has a choice to either convict or acquit the defendant (or cause a mistrial, in the event that the jurors cannot agree with one another). Now, here are three kinds of questions one might ask about this decision:

Legal questions: Is the jury *legally required* to convict? If the jury acquits, will that decision be legally valid? If conviction is not legally required, is it still in some sense legally appropriate?

Political questions: Should we have jury trials in the first place? If we do, should the jury be *allowed* (by the state) to acquit based on their assessment of the justice of the law? Should the law encourage or discourage juries from exercising their own sense of justice? If juries frequently relied on their judgments about justice, would this be good or bad for society in general?

Ethical questions: If you are an individual jury member, what is the morally right thing for you to do? Should you vote to acquit or convict? If you are the judge, would it be morally right for you to encourage or discourage the jury from judging the justice of the law?

These are all interesting questions. But my central interest here is in the third type of question, questions of *individual ethics*. Legal and political questions may be relevant to ethical questions, but they should not be confused with the ethical questions. For example, the question of what a jury member morally ought to decide is distinct from the question of what the law requires or recommends. The legal requirements may be *relevant* to what a juror ought to decide, since perhaps the juror has an ethical reason to follow the law. But even so, there are ethical reasons other than the ethical reason (if any) to follow the law; thus, it is open to debate whether, all things considered, one ought to follow the law. And thus, one must distinguish the question of what the law requires from the question of what one morally ought to do (see Chap. 2).

Similarly, the question of what government policy ought to be, or what practices would be best for society in general, may be relevant to the ethical question, but policy questions should not be confused with ethical questions. Very few individuals can significantly influence public policy; thus, the question of what public policy is best is, in most cases, quite separate from the question of what the individual ought to do.

I have taken the time to emphasize these points, because it is common in discussions of legal philosophy to substitute legal or political questions for ethical questions. Critics sometimes respond to my ethical theses by asserting some legal or political claims of dubious relevance.

8.2 The Meaning of the Primacy of Justice

What does it mean to prioritize justice? I do not claim that justice to the individual is *all that matters* to ethical decisions involving the legal system. But justice to the individual is the first and most important consideration that ought to drive such decisions. How one's choices affect the rest of society, how they relate to the requirements of one's job or the wishes of one's employer, and how they relate to the demands of law or tradition can be at most secondary considerations, which should rarely alter the outcome.

I will defend this thesis later. In the remainder of § 8.2, however, I aim simply to clarify the meaning of the thesis by explaining what it implies for three kinds of figure who play key roles in the legal system: jurors, lawyers, and judges.

8.2.1 The Ethical Juror

Jury members are given the task of deciding guilt or innocence in criminal cases, or adjudicating between plaintiff and defendant in civil cases. In my view, the primary consideration by reference to which they should make these decisions is that of individual justice: what is the just treatment of the particular defendant and/or plaintiff presently before the court, in the case presently at hand? If a criminal defendant has committed culpable wrongs, and if the punishment likely to result from a conviction is a just punishment, then that defendant must be convicted. If the defendant has committed no moral wrong, or if the defendant for any other reason does not deserve the punishment likely to result from a conviction, then the jury is morally obligated to acquit that defendant. This includes the case where the law the defendant is accused of violating is an unjust law, as well as the case where the punishment attached to the violation of the law is grossly disproportionate, barbaric, or otherwise unjust. More precisely, if the jury judges that the injustice of the punishment that would result from conviction is *greater* than the injustice inherent in allowing a guilty party to go free, then they are ethically required to acquit the defendant.

In some cases, the jury will have the option to convict the defendant of a lesser offense than the one with which the defendant was charged. For example, a defendant charged with first-degree murder can instead be convicted of manslaughter. (The jury cannot, however, convict of an unrelated offense or of a more serious offense than the one charged—that is, U.S. courts will not recognize such a verdict.) If this option results in a more just punishment, then it is ethically appropriate, even if the factual evidence supports the stronger charge.

In a civil case, if the defendant has wronged the plaintiff in a manner that justly incurs a debt on the part of the defendant to the plaintiff, then the jury should find for the plaintiff. Otherwise, the jury should find for the defendant. What matters is not whether the defendant violated a *legal* duty per se, but whether the defendant violated a moral duty to the plaintiff (but note that legal duties may well *affect* moral duties). Likewise, it matters little what effect the case will have on other potential defendants or plaintiffs; what matters is whether the defendant in fact owes compensation to the plaintiff for a wrong that the defendant committed.

The practice of voting to acquit because one finds the law or the associated punishment unjust is known as "jury nullification". Jury nullification is almost uniformly condemned by judges and prosecutors, though opinion among scholars is much more mixed.[1] Judges often write of the

---

[1] Many scholars have defended jury nullification; see, e.g., Pound (1910, p. 18); Greenawalt (1987, pp. 364–6); Brooks (2004); Butler (2004); Huemer (2018).

practice with unconcealed outrage, expressing near-absolute certainty that the practice is wrong,[2] though this confidence, as we shall later see, has no rational basis. Due to the hostility of judges and prosecutors, citizens who endorse jury nullification will regularly be excluded during the jury selection process. Thus, in order to be in a position to practice jury nullification, a citizen must first lie during the jury selection process, pretending that he (the citizen) does *not* believe in jury nullification and promising to apply the law as explained to him by the judge regardless of justice. The citizen, I shall argue, is fully justified in making this false promise, then breaking it without hesitation.

To clarify, I am not claiming that jury nullification is ethically appropriate in *all* trials, or all trials in which it actually happens, or even most trials in which it happens. I am claiming that jury nullification is *sometimes* ethically appropriate. In particular, it is appropriate when the law is unjust, or the likely punishment is sufficiently unjust to outweigh the injustice of acquitting the guilty. Of course, jury nullification to prevent *just* punishment is ethically *wrong*.

This position is analogous to the view most of us take toward, for example, lying: lying is wrong in most circumstances, but it is justified in some cases. Lying for the purpose of exploiting or harming others is wrong, but lying for the purpose of preventing a much greater harm is permissible and often obligatory.

8.2.2 The Ethical Lawyer

Turning now to the role of lawyers, lawyers in the adversarial legal system play the role of advocates for a particular side of a dispute. In a civil case, one lawyer advocates for the interests of the plaintiff, the other for the interests of the defendant. In a criminal case, one lawyer serves the interests of the defendant, while the other supposedly serves the interests of the government or "the people", but in reality mainly just opposes the interests of the defendant.

---

[2] See, e.g., Bork (1999, p. 20); Steigmann (1998); Biskupic (1999) (quoting Judge Henry F. Greene); Bissell 1997.

This is an immoral system. No individual can, morally, promote unjust outcomes, regardless of whose interests they serve. The only thing a lawyer morally ought to do in his interactions with the legal system is to promote just outcomes and attempt to prevent injustices. Thus, it is wrong for a defense attorney to seek acquittal for a defendant whom the lawyer knows to be guilty of serious wrongs that merit the legal punishment attached thereto. It is even more wrong for a prosecuting attorney to seek excessive punishments, to seek convictions under unjust laws, or to seek convictions of factually innocent defendants. This is a more serious wrong, because it is in general worse to impose an unjust punishment than to fail to impose a just punishment.

In civil cases, it is morally wrong for a lawyer to represent a client pursuing a groundless or unfair lawsuit, or to pursue excessive compensation for a tort. It is equally wrong for a lawyer to attempt to defend a client who has wronged another party from having to pay just compensation for the wrong.

These actions that I have described as morally wrong are, admittedly, often part of the lawyer's professional responsibilities. The role the lawyer is meant to play in the system is that of a partisan advocate, blind to justice. This fact about the system does not conflict with any of my moral claims; it merely indicates that lawyers in the adversary system have been assigned an immoral role. The existence of this social role, I shall contend, does nothing to erase the moral duties individuals are generally under to avoid contributing to injustices.

To clarify, however, I do not argue that it is wrong for a defense lawyer to *represent guilty clients*, even clients whom he *knows* to be guilty. I argue that it is wrong for a lawyer to *promote injustice*—that is, to attempt to bring about an unjust outcome. It is entirely ethical to represent a guilty client for the purpose of preventing or minimizing injustices. For example, in the case of a client who is guilty of violating an unjust law, the ethical lawyer may attempt to secure an acquittal or, failing that, the minimum punishment obtainable. In the case of a client who is guilty of a genuine wrong, the ethical lawyer may attempt to prevent that client from suffering excessive punishment, as is common in the present system (see § 6.2).

An ethical lawyer may even verbally advance a position he believes to be false or unjust, *if* doing so is reasonably expected to increase the odds of an actually just result. For example, suppose A sues B for a wrong that B genuinely committed. Just compensation for the wrong would be about $10,000. A, however, is asking for $20,000. In the course of negotiations, B's lawyer advances the false claim that B only owes $5000, along with spurious arguments for this position. By doing so, B's lawyer successfully pressures A into accepting a compromise settlement of $10,000. In this case, B's lawyer acts ethically. What matters is not the justice of the position verbally advanced by the lawyer, but rather the justice of the *outcome* that the lawyer attempts to bring about.

Conventional legal ethics recognizes no such obligation to aim at justice. Lawyers are supposed to simply advance their client's position and leave it to the court to come to a fair decision. Lawyers are not, however, considered to be entirely ethically unconstrained in pursuing their clients' interests. In conventional legal ethics, a lawyer may not lie to the court about matters of fact. A lawyer may not falsify evidence, nor introduce evidence that he knows to have been falsified. A lawyer may not suborn perjury, that is, knowingly cause a witness to give false testimony.[3] These are serious ethical constraints on the pursuit of the client's interests. It is interesting, therefore, that these constraints are accepted in conventional legal doctrine, yet the constraint I advocate (prohibiting the intentional pursuit of injustice) is not. Why is this?

The reason for the accepted ethical constraints is obvious. To have a practice in which lawyers freely lie to the court, fabricate evidence, or deliberately solicit false testimony from witnesses would not contribute to the attainment of justice, which is the goal by reference to which the entire system is justified. It would instead cause courts to be regularly deceived about the facts that they need to know in order to render a just decision. Introducing falsified evidence into court, for example, undermines the function of a trial, that of determining the truth so that justice may be done. That is why it is unethical.

If this is correct, how can it nevertheless be ethical for a lawyer to intentionally pursue an unjust outcome? To pursue injustice is, by

---
[3] American Bar Association 1983, rules 3.3, 3.4.

definition, to directly undermine the goal of the legal system of attaining justice. It is to attempt to mislead the court, not simply about some of *the facts* that the court needs in order to render a just decision, but directly about what the just decision is. If it is wrong to intentionally deceive the court about particular matters of fact because doing so undermines the court's ability to make a just decision, then it must even more clearly be wrong to intentionally deceive the court about *what the just decision is*, since the latter deception even more clearly undermines the court's ability to make a just decision. There is, furthermore, no morally significant difference between lying and intentionally inducing people to draw false conclusions. These reflections support the following argument for a duty not to pursue unjust outcomes:

1. It is unethical for a lawyer to lie to the court about relevant matters of fact.
2. Lying to the court about relevant matters of fact is not superior to other ways of pursuing unjust outcomes, for:
    (a) Lying to the court about relevant facts is wrong *because* it misleads the court in a way likely to prevent it from arriving at a just outcome.
    (b) Pursuing unjust outcomes in general misleads the court in a way likely to prevent it from arriving at a just outcome.
3. Therefore, it is unethical for a lawyer to pursue unjust outcomes.

8.2.3 The Ethical Judge

Judges preside over court cases, determine sentences following criminal convictions, and interpret the law, including statutory, Constitutional, and case law. In carrying out these tasks, the primary consideration of the judge should be what justice requires for the individuals in the case at hand. Thus, following a criminal conviction, the trial judge should assign a sentence proportional to the moral seriousness of the defendant's crime. The judge should do this regardless of the sentencing guidelines. (In the

U.S., the guidelines written by the United States Sentencing Commission were intended as mandatory but have become only advisory due to a 2005 Supreme Court ruling.[4]) In the case where the law requires a grossly disproportionate sentence, or demands punishment for morally blameless behavior, the judge should attempt to manipulate the system so as to avoid inflicting the unjust punishment. This may include deliberately making false factual determinations about the case or lying about what the law says.

When a judge must interpret the law, the judge should generally "interpret" it in the manner that renders it the most just, provided his interpretation will be effective (i.e., it will not merely be immediately overruled by other judges or prompt the legislature to pass even worse laws). If, for example, there is a law that plainly says, "The President shall kill twelve innocent people each day", it would be ethically appropriate for a judge to rule that this law actually prohibits the President from murdering anyone, if the judge's making this ruling would prevent the President from carrying out such heinous acts.

In conventional legal theory, there are a number of competing views of the correct way of interpreting and applying laws. Most give a secondary role at best to considerations of what is morally right or wrong. Some theorists hold that judges should limit themselves to faithfully interpreting the original meaning of legal texts, as understood at the time they were written. Some hold that judges should consider the intentions of those who originally created a given law, and should then interpret the law so as to fulfil those intentions. Others think that judges should enforce the moral principles that provide the best justification for the written rules, including enforcing rules that were not actually enacted by the legislature but that follow from the same moral principles.[5] These are reasonable theories, if one's interest is in faithful interpretation of the law. In my view, however, faithful interpretation of the law has no intrinsic value. What matters is justice; hence, the morally correct way of inter-

---

[4] *United States v. Booker*, 543 U.S. 220 (2005). The problem with the mandatory guidelines was that the sentencing guidelines required judges, in assigning sentences, to take account of facts that might not have been proved to a jury.

[5] On textualism, see Scalia (1997); on legislative intent, see *Riggs v. Palmer*, 115 N.Y. 506 (1889) at 509; on the importance of moral principles, see Dworkin (1986, 2011, p. 402).

preting a law is whatever way results in the most justice, or the least injustice. For the purpose of determining this interpretation, it matters not at all what the authors of the law actually intended, nor what the written words mean in standard English, except insofar as these things bear on what effects a given interpretation can be expected to produce. Of course, interpreting a law in ways that conflict with its plain meaning or with the apparent intent of the law's original authors may cause one's decision to be overturned by other courts; judges must take this possibility into account in deciding what way of interpreting the law is most likely to produce the most just outcome. The proper task of legal interpretation is not one of figuring out what the law is; it is a task of figuring out (a) what one may get away with saying that the law is and (b) which, among the things one may get away with saying, is the most just.

The category of rulings that a judge can get away with is much broader than that of rulings that are legally defensible. A judge may often be in a position to make a ruling that will not be overturned, even though the ruling could not be plausibly defended based on the actual law and the facts of the case. This is obviously true of Supreme Court rulings, since there is no other court to overrule the Supreme Court. It is still possible for the legislature to alter the law so as to circumvent a Supreme Court decision or, in extreme cases, for political leaders to amend the Constitution; this, however, is rare. Thus, the Supreme Court can in fact create permanent or semi-permanent law. This power should be used freely to remedy injustices in the legal order.

In addition, most rulings of United States circuit courts (the appeals courts in the federal judicial system) will not be overruled even if legally erroneous. The only appeal from the circuit courts is to the U.S. Supreme Court, but the Supreme Court has discretion as to whether to hear any given appeal or not. Would-be appellants must petition the Court for a hearing, and only 1–2% of these petitions are granted. The rest are denied, meaning that the circuit court's ruling is allowed to stand.[6]

Even trial courts have substantial power to make law-defying rulings that will not be overturned. Trial judges have the power to acquit defendants, prior to the determination of a jury, and such acquittals cannot be

---

[6] Administrative Office of the U.S. Courts 2020.

appealed. (The judge cannot, however, decide unilaterally to *convict* a defendant who has opted for a jury trial, as this would violate the defendant's Constitutional right to trial by jury.) Short of acquittal, judges can also make false factual determinations about a case in order to affect the sentence. If the law requires a grossly disproportionate sentence to be assigned if the defendant satisfied some factual condition, the judge can and should declare that the defendant did not satisfy this condition. Such factual determinations are immune from appeal, except in extreme cases; appeals generally concern only alleged mistakes about the law, not mistakes about the facts of the case.

Again, when I speak here of what *can* or *cannot* be done in the legal system, I do not refer to what is or is not *legally permitted*. I refer rather to what one can or cannot *get away with* (which is affected by, but not identical with, what is legally permitted). Thus, for example, when I say that an acquittal "cannot" be appealed, I mean that if the prosecutor in a case tries to appeal an acquittal, the prosecutor's appeal will predictably be dismissed without accomplishing anything. When I say that a judge *can* unilaterally acquit but *cannot* unilaterally convict a defendant, I mean that if a judge declares a defendant not guilty, other courts will not overturn this decision, nor will they allow the defendant to be tried again for the same crime; if, however, a judge in a jury trial declares a defendant guilty, other courts will reject that declaration.

Acquittals of obviously guilty defendants may invite backlash. Conceivably, a judge who regularly defies the law might be removed from office. An alternative is to provide a jury with information likely to lead to jury nullification. If, for example, the law prescribes a draconian penalty in a particular case, the judge may inform the jury of this fact prior to their deliberations (or allow the defense attorney to do so), leaving it to the jury what to do with this information.[7] Juries may feel freer to pursue justice than judges do, since the juries have no fear of being removed from office.

---

[7] See *U.S. v. Datcher*, 830 F. Supp. 411 (M.D. Tenn. 1993), allowing defense counsel to argue the issue of excessive punishment to the jury and acknowledging the validity of jury nullification. Compare *U.S. v. Polizzi*, 549 F.Supp.2d 308 (E.D.N.Y. 2008), holding that the court erred in not informing the jury of the mandatory minimum sentence so that it could decide whether to nullify.

All of these techniques have been recommended by some legal theorists and practiced by some judges, though not, to my mind, often enough. There is a widespread recognition among both scholars and judges of the excessively severe sentencing practices in the U.S., which have led some to recommend various levels of defiance of the law on the part of judges.[8]

Some critics propose instead that judges who find the law unjust should resign, leaving the task of enforcement to others with fewer scruples.[9] This view wrongly assumes that the problem with enforcing unjust laws is not the actual injustice but merely the feelings of discomfort it may arouse in some judges. Resignation may assuage a judge's feelings of guilt, but it does nothing to combat injustice. On the contrary, the proposal for judges who object to the law to resign from office is merely a proposal to hand all power to those who support injustice. This makes sense if one assumes that all unjust laws should be enforced, or that those who consider the law unjust are always wrong. But if the law is often unjust, and if we regard injustice itself (and not merely judges' negative feelings about it) as a problem, then the best option for a conscientious judge is to stay and undermine the law. The most essential qualification for a judge is a strong sense of justice. It is therefore those who have *no* objections to enforcing unjust laws who ought to resign, since they fail the most basic qualification for their office.

All of the above is by way of clarifying the thesis of the Primacy of Justice—that is what I mean when I say that justice should come first in the legal system. I have not yet explained why I hold these radical views. That will be the main charge of the rest of this book.

---

[8] Greenblatt (2008) reviews a variety of techniques judges may use to circumvent harsh sentencing laws, along with evidence that these techniques are in widespread use. The editors of the *Harvard Law Review* in 2007 recommended "civil disobedience" on the part of judges in response to draconian sentencing laws. U.S. district court judge Jack Weinstein (2004) has recommended similar disobedience in the face of unjust laws.

[9] Cohn (1994); Rosenthal (1993).

8.3 The Role of Law in a System of Justice

It may seem that I leave no role for the law in the legal system, since each agent should always pursue justice irrespective of the law. This, however, would be an oversimplification. There is a legitimate place for the existing law to influence legal decision-making, for two reasons.

8.3.1 Law Affects Justice

The first reason is that, though the law does not necessarily determine what is just, the law often *affects* what is just in a particular case. The main reason for this is that the existing, publicly available legal doctrines affect the *expectations* that individuals have, or could reasonably have, about their interactions with each other. These expectations, in turn, affect what individuals can reasonably be understood to implicitly consent to in their dealings with others. To illustrate, consider a dispute that two individuals might have:

Oil Dispute: George and Ralph are neighbors. One day, the two discover that there is a deposit of oil lying underneath both of their properties. George wants to build an oil well on his land to extract the oil. If he does so, the well will extract oil from underneath both plots of land, as well as the surrounding, uninhabited area. Ralph claims that George has no right to any of the oil presently under Ralph's property, and accordingly he demands that George desist. George offers to split the profits with Ralph, but Ralph rejects this offer; as a committed environmentalist, Ralph does not want the oil to be drilled at all. Ralph thus takes George to court to stop construction of the oil well.

Assume that no one previously considered the possibility that there might be oil under this land, and thus the contracts under which Ralph and George purchased their respective plots of land do not anywhere mention oil rights. There is thus no way to decide on the basis of explicit agreements whether George has the right to drill the oil. How, therefore, can the case be justly resolved?

The answer is that when this case comes before a court, the court should resolve it in accordance with the applicable law, whatever (within reason) that law may be, assuming that the law addresses this. If the law says that George has the right to drill, the court should allow George to drill; if the law says that Ralph has the right to veto the drilling, the court should order George not to drill.

Why is this the just approach? The reason is that this is generally what Ralph and George would expect, or at least what they reasonably ought to expect, given the conventions of their society. Granted, neither party actually considered oil drilling rights at the time they purchased their properties. But if they had considered the question, they *would* have (or reasonably should have) expected that they each would have whatever oil rights are specified by law. George and Ralph would each have expected that, in the event there turned out to be oil underground, George would be able to extract it if and only if the law permitted this.

Note that they would both have expected this even if they did not know, or were mistaken about, the content of the law. Suppose, for instance, that George has always been under the impression that anyone may drill for oil on their own land, regardless of their neighbors' wishes. If, however, George had been asked, "*If* you are mistaken about the law, and the law actually says that you may not drill for oil on this land, *then* do you expect that, after purchasing this land, you will be able to drill for oil on it?", George reasonably ought to have answered, "No." In other words, George's expectation that the law, whatever it may be, will be followed by other members of society ought to be stronger than his expectation as to what the content of the law on this question is. (The "ought" here is the "ought" of epistemic rationality—George would be foolish to think that an exception to the law would be made for him.) Similar points apply to Ralph.

Because of this reasonable expectation, both parties can reasonably be understood as having implicitly consented, at the time they bought their respective properties, to pay the amount specified in the sale contract in exchange for *the package of rights legally associated with ownership of that land in their society*, whatever (within reason) that package may turn out to be. Neither party, therefore, will have a valid complaint if the court in fact enforces the law.

This explains how the law may determine the just resolution of a case. This explanation applies in certain kinds of cases, including all or most contract disputes and other property rights disputes. It does not, however, apply to the kinds of injustices discussed in earlier chapters. The above rationale cannot, for example, be used to justify enforcing drug prohibition, or applying draconian punishments for nonviolent crimes. It is worth taking a moment to clarify why this is the case.

The above account of how the law may affect justice applies to cases with the following features:

(i) *The relevant rights depend on consent:* By this, I mean that the rights claimed by each party in the dispute must be rights of a kind that the party would not have unless they acquired those rights with the consent (or at least lack of dissent) of other members of their society. In the Oil Dispute case, whatever property rights George and Ralph each have must have been acquired by them when they bought their land. Plausibly, these must have been acquired with the consent, or at least lack of dissent, of other members of their society, including the previous land owners and anyone else affected. George was not simply born with oil drilling rights, nor was Ralph born with rights to enjoin oil drilling. Matters are different with certain other rights, such as rights over one's own person. George *was* simply born with rights over his own body, rights against being physically harmed or used by others. Hence, if there were a dispute that turned solely on George's right to control his own body, there would be no need to consult the law; morality categorically requires respecting that right.

(ii) *The relevant parties did not refuse consent:* If the parties to a dispute have made an agreement contrary to the law, then this will generally render the law morally irrelevant. In the Oil Dispute case, if both Ralph and George had previously agreed, for example, that George may extract any resources found under either or both properties, then this agreement would render moot any appeal to the law. It is only because they did not make such an agreement that the law should be used to resolve their dispute. The reason is that the requirements of the law, on the account given above, only become relevant to justice as objects of *implicit or hypothetical agreement* in property transactions. If two parties have explicitly repudiated some condition that would otherwise be required by law, then it cannot be said that they have implicitly accepted or would have accepted that condition. (Fortunately, in most cases the actual law recognizes individuals' freedom to specify contract terms with one another.)

(iii) *Parties have a reasonable expectation of law enforcement:* Parties to property transactions can reasonably expect disputes concerning property rights to be resolved according to the law, given that this is in fact how such disputes are generally resolved in their society. If, however, there is a particular area in which the written law is rarely applied, and some informal conventions are generally followed instead, then cases should be resolved according to those informal conventions. In the Oil Dispute case, we assume that there are no such countervening conventions.

These conditions, particularly (i) and (ii), fail to apply to the examples of legal injustice cited earlier in this book. Consider, for example, the drug laws. If we view prosecutions for drug possession as disputes between the state and an individual drug user, the drug user is claiming the right to put substances of his choice into his own body. The state, by contrast, is claiming the right to control what other people do with their bodies. Condition (i) is violated: individuals do not require the consent of others, whether the state or anyone else, to acquire the right to control their own bodies; that is a natural human right. Therefore, there is no need to consult the law; the state's position is inherently wrong.

Condition (ii) is also violated: one cannot plausibly argue that individuals prosecuted for drug crimes have implicitly consented to this treatment of themselves. In a typical drug sale, both the buyer and the seller explicitly agree to the transaction, and hence obviously dissent from the government's rule prohibiting such transactions. Individual drug users obviously consent to their own use of drugs and could not be said to have agreed not to use drugs. The *state*, of course, does not consent to the sale or use of recreational drugs, but this is irrelevant, since the state is not a party to these transactions.

8.3.2 Resolving Unclear Cases

A second important reason why the law may affect the correct resolution of a dispute is that the dictates of justice are sometimes unknown or indeterminate. It may simply not be clear what the just resolution of a case is. It is often appropriate to resolve such cases in accordance with the law. This is not because the legally prescribed solution is thereby *more just* than alternative resolutions, but because values other than justice in the individual case may properly enter into consideration, when the dictates of justice are unknown or indeterminate. Some of these considerations will speak in favor of following the law.

Suppose, for example, that the penalty for armed robbery in one jurisdiction is 5 years in prison, and in another jurisdiction 10 years. (For simplicity, assume the law specifies a particular sentence, rather than a range of sentences, and assume that all relevant features of the crime are fixed, that is, that for crimes with exactly the same relevant features, the laws of the two jurisdictions differ on the prescribed sentence.) Which sentence, if either, is the more just?

This question is difficult to answer. It may be that neither is more just, because justice does not make such determinate demands. Undoubtedly, some sentences would be unjustly harsh and others unjustly lenient, but within a certain range sentences are merely acceptable—so one might reasonably argue. Be that as it may, even if there is a unique, optimally just sentence length, we do not *know* what that length is. A judge assigning a sentence for this crime, then, would not be in any position to declare that justice dictates a particular one of these sentence lengths. (Though the judge *could* say, for example, that justice rejects a sentence of probation, or a sentence of death by hanging.)

In this situation, it is appropriate to look to values other than justice. One such value is the predictability that results when courts follow definite, written laws. Predictability is not sufficiently important to justify imposing a definitely unjust sentence, but it may be important enough to justify imposing the sentence expected in one's jurisdiction, given that that sentence is not definitely unjust.

Another value is social harmony. In a society containing a variety of conflicting political, philosophical, and religious beliefs, social harmony is not to be taken for granted. There is a danger of cooperation breaking down, such that partisans of different factions strive to undermine each other at all turns. This can result in outcomes that are worse from everyone's point of view, relative to some attainable compromise. To attain a compromise that avoids destructive conflict, members of society need some willingness to *defer* to the rules that have been produced by the system (see § 11.4 for discussion). Thus, if there is no great reason to the contrary, it is generally better to follow the social rules that are in force in one's community.

Again, this value is typically not sufficient to justify imposing a clearly unjust outcome on an individual. But the value of social harmony *can* justify imposing an outcome that is neither clearly just nor clearly unjust, when that outcome is in accord with accepted practices.

One might wonder how far this reasoning extends. Suppose a judge, juror, or lawyer believes that a law is *probably* unjust, but she is uncertain of this. How likely must it be that the law is unjust before it becomes impermissible to enforce it? I have no general answer to this; I will not attempt to draw the precise boundary between permissible and impermissible law enforcement. However, I will defend one weak constraint on permissible law enforcement: in normal circumstances, it is permissible to enforce a law *only if* that law coheres with a *reasonable interpretation* of the law-independent requirements of justice.[10] That is, if one could not reasonably defend a particular rule as just (without appealing to the fact that this rule is encoded in the existing law), then one should not enforce that rule, even if it is required by the existing law.

This constraint, while perhaps not strong enough or precise enough to satisfy most philosophers, is nevertheless interesting and of practical import. Many actual legal requirements clearly violate the constraint. For instance, when Paul Hayes was sentenced to life imprisonment for an

---

[10] The "normal circumstances" clause is needed because philosophers can devise counterexamples to any claim that lacks some such clause. For instance, admittedly, if enforcing an obviously unjust rule were necessary to avoid a nuclear war, then of course one should enforce the unjust rule. But one should not enforce obviously unjust rules in the sort of circumstances judges, jurors, or lawyers are likely to actually encounter.

$88 forged check, or Larry Dayries was sent to prison for 70 years for stealing a tuna fish sandwich (see § 6.2.2), these sentences were definitely unjust. Setting aside the fact that they were required by the law, no reasonable person would have deemed them appropriate punishments. Yet the judges in these cases felt bound to hand down these sentences, merely because they were required by the law. It is that feeling that I want to argue against. The felt obligation to enforce unjust law is, I maintain, an illusion.

8.4 The Common Sense Case for Justice

The doctrine I have called "the Primacy of Justice" is very controversial in legal theory. Most legal practitioners (lawyers, judges, prosecutors) can immediately think of a few objections that will seem to them to be decisive. I will discuss these objections at some length in the following chapters.

In this section, however, I begin with the initial, intuitive case for a justice-based legal ethic. The Primacy of Justice contrasts most saliently with *the Primacy of Law*, the view that the chief duty of individuals operating within the legal system is to uphold the law, and *the Primacy of Role Obligations*, the view that one's chief duty is to faithfully carry out one's role in the system, as that role is conventionally understood. (Hereafter, I shall speak of the Primacy of Law, but what I say applies equally to the Primacy of Role Obligations.)

8.4.1 The General Duty of Justice

There are two intuitive arguments for the primacy of justice. The first relies on the premise that individuals have a *general obligation to respect justice*: as a general matter, it is wrong to knowingly bring about unjust outcomes. When given a choice between justice and injustice, one should choose justice. This premise is sufficiently intuitive as to scarcely require defense.

For example, it is morally wrong to steal your neighbor's car, because this is a violation of your neighbor's property rights. It is wrong to physically attack others without provocation, because this is a violation of their right against coercion. Injustice is a matter of violating the rights of others; hence, these actions are unjust. Intuitively, they are morally wrong even if they produce somewhat larger benefits than the harms they cause—for example, even if you have a better use for your neighbor's car than your neighbor does.

Notice that these are not mere *legal* wrongs. Even if it were somehow legal to attack your neighbor or steal his car, it would be wrong to do so. If, for example, the government passes a law authorizing all citizens to beat and rob any member of a particular disfavored race, it will be morally wrong for you to participate in this legally authorized oppression.

Notice also that the duty of justice applies not only to what one does *directly*, but also to what one does *indirectly*. In particular, if the way in which one brings about an unjust harm is through inducing *another agent* to inflict the harm, one is not thereby absolved of culpability. Thus, if the leader of a criminal organization pays an underling to assassinate an enemy, then the leader, in addition to the assassin, will be guilty of murder, despite that the leader does not pull the trigger herself.

The point applies even if one does not specifically *request* the other agent's unjust behavior, as long as one knowingly and needlessly *contributes* to that behavior. Thus, consider the following case:

Gaybashing Gang: A local gang of hoodlums has been roaming the streets, beating up individuals whom they take to be homosexual. One evening, as you are walking down the street with a gay acquaintance of yours, you run into the gang. The gang leader asks you if your companion is gay. "I cannot tell a lie", you answer, "my companion here is indeed a homosexual. However, I would ask that you please refrain from beating him up." The gang immediately proceeds to beat your companion senseless, as you knew they would.

In this case, you have obviously acted wrongly by causing your companion to suffer a serious injustice. The violent gang is more directly responsible for the wrong, but you are also culpable. You are hardly absolved merely because you did not directly beat your companion with your own fists.

Nor are you to be absolved simply because the alternative to contributing to the injustice would have required *lying*. Lying to the gang was obviously morally required in this situation. Perhaps if telling the gang the truth would have been required to prevent them from beating *you*, you would have an excuse. But if your motivation was merely to avoid lying to the gang, your decision was indefensible. (Homophobic hoodlums have no right to know who is or is not gay.) Nor, finally, was your error a minor or understandable one. While perhaps not as bad as participating in the beating directly, your callous contribution to your companion's oppression in this example is a very serious wrong.

I take all of these ethical judgments as obvious. Together, they show that we have a weighty, law-independent, moral obligation to avoid contributing to injustice, whether directly or indirectly.

On the face of it, then, it would seem wrong to knowingly contribute to injustices carried out *by the state*, including those imposed by the state's legal system. Punishments under unjust laws, disproportionate punishments, and punishments of factually innocent individuals are all examples of injustices that might be imposed by the legal system. It is therefore prima facie morally wrong to contribute to any of these outcomes.

Why do I say "prima facie"? Because all moral considerations, even considerations of justice, are subject to outweighing by competing considerations; there are no *absolute* rights. If punishing one innocent person were necessary to save a million innocent lives, then we would be justified in carrying out the unjust punishment. So we will later have to consider whether there are any competing considerations supporting deference to the law that are strong enough to outweigh the general obligation to respect justice. The objections to the thesis of the Primacy of Justice will consist of attempts to identify such considerations. For now, it is enough to have articulated the core, prima facie case for refusing to assist in the implementation of unjust laws and policies, and more generally refusing to carry out one's assigned role when doing so contributes to unjust outcomes.

This core case is almost trivial: *obviously* it is wrong to aid injustice, at least in the absence of some extremely good reason for doing so. Yet despite its obviousness, this point is worth drawing attention to, since agents in the legal system frequently appear simply to ignore, to not think about, justice to the individual. (See Chaps. 3, 4, 5, 6, and 7 above.) The immediate effect of the argument from the general duty of justice is to force those who would work injustice in the name of the law, or in the name of carrying out their assigned roles in the legal system, to identify a moral justification for their behavior strong enough to outweigh the value of justice.

8.4.2 The Argument from Instrumental Rationality

Instrumental rationality is rationality in the pursuit of one's goals. I assume that law and the legal system are justified by reference to some goal or goals; they are not simply *intrinsically* valuable. That is, when we establish and maintain a legal system, there is something that we as a society are trying to accomplish, and this goal would have to justify the expense and the coercion that are inherent in the system.

What might that goal be? The most natural answer is that the goal is *justice*. This view explains the main salient features of legal systems—it explains why they generally seek to punish the guilty and acquit the innocent, why they seek to assign greater punishments for more serious or more culpable wrongs, why they allow tort victims to recover damages from those who wronged them, and so on.

Given any device aimed at achieving some end, the rational design and use of that device must be constrained by the factual requirements for the device to promote its aim. It would be irrational to use a tool in a manner that conflicts with the goal that one is seeking to attain in using the tool. It would likewise be irrational to seek to preserve a tool at the cost of giving up the goal that the tool exists to attain.

For example, suppose you own an automobile solely for purposes of transportation. You notice that when you drive on the roads, the car suffers wear and tear and is at risk of being damaged in a traffic accident. You express your concern about these problems to a friend, whereupon your friend proposes to you that, the next time you want to use the car, you should simply use the car *in the garage*. If you never leave the garage, there should be minimal wear and tear and virtually no chance of an accident.

It is true that this proposal would preserve the car from harm, which is a reasonable goal. But this is an irrational way of pursuing that goal, since it would prevent you from actually reaching your destination in the car. *The car* cannot be more important than *transportation*, since transportation was the purpose for the sake of which you bought the car to begin with. Transportation must in general be more important than the car.

Similarly, then, if the purpose that justifies the legal system is the attainment of justice, then it would be irrational on its face to seek to uphold the law at the expense of justice. The law cannot be more important than the goal that justifies the very existence of the law to begin with. Thus, we have the following simple argument:

1. Law is justified by the goal of justice.
2. The means to a goal is less important than the goal that justifies that means.
3. Therefore, law is less important than justice.

There are two obvious objections to this argument. The first objection is that premise 1 may be false, since perhaps the law serves goals other than justice. Perhaps the purpose of the legal system is to promote *security* or general social *utility*. In reply, note that these alternatives are less explanatory than the justice theory. The goals of security and social utility fail to explain, for example, why we find it unacceptable to achieve deterrence against crime by punishing innocent individuals who are widely *believed* to be guilty (see § 6.1.2). That is best explained by the theory that the system's purpose is justice.

Moreover, morality imposes constraints on the pursuit of our goals. Even if we were to adopt the goal of promoting security without regard to justice, our adoption of this goal could not morally justify an institution that violates the requirements of justice. One cannot, for example, acquire a moral entitlement to violate others' rights merely by setting up a system aimed at some non-rights-related goal. The *strongest* justification of the legal system would be that it is both necessary and reasonably effective for the purpose of achieving justice. Any less morally important goal could only provide weaker justification for the system as a whole, and consequently weaker justifications for individuals to carry out their assigned roles in the system. Thus, if the goal of justice does not justify prioritizing law over justice, then neither, in general, will the goals of security or utility.

More precisely, as acknowledged earlier, the moral importance of acting justly makes it difficult, though not impossible, to justify intrinsically unjust actions by appeal to reasons of security or utility. In general, to justify bringing about an unjust harm requires benefits at least *many times* greater than the harm (see § 2.4). This demanding requirement for the justification of unjust harms is not overcome merely by citing the requirements of the law, since the value of the law is itself purely instrumental.

The second and more important objection to my argument is that permitting injustice in an individual case may in the long run promote greater justice overall. Thus, while one of course could not justify sacrificing justice *in general* in order to preserve the law, one could perhaps justify sacrificing justice *in an individual case* in order to preserve the law more generally.

Note, however, that the moral constraints imposed by justice are *agent-centered* (see § 2.4). This entails that one cannot justify imposing an unjust harm merely by the fact that doing so would prevent a larger but comparable amount of unjust harm by others. To justify an injustice to one individual by appeal to greater overall justice for others requires, again, a showing that the individual injustice at least prevents *many times* greater injustice from befalling others.

This cannot be universally ruled out. Nor, of course, have I confronted all the reasons why one might think it important to uphold the law. What is accomplished by the Argument from the General Duty of Justice and the Argument from Instrumental Rationality is essentially to make it clear that some substantive, weighty moral reasons are *required*. One cannot simply state that some action is required by law, or will help to uphold the law, and leave that as a justification for inflicting unjust harm on others. Since the central function of law is to *prevent* injustice, one must be able to state some good reason for upholding law in a case in which doing so *causes* injustice.

This should be an obvious point, but it is easy to forget. Many legal practitioners either overlook the need for a justification for upholding the law or simply assume that some very powerful justification is readily available. When we actually look for that justification, it proves more elusive than expected, as we shall see in the following chapters.

References

Administrative Office of the U.S. Courts. 2020. About the Supreme Court. https://www.uscourts.gov/about-federal-courts/educational-resources/about-educational-outreach/activity-resources/about. Accessed 28 June 2020.

American Bar Association. 1983. *Model Rules of Professional Conduct*. Text available at https://www.americanbar.org/groups/professional_responsibility/publications/model_rules_of_professional_conduct/model_rules_of_professional_conduct_table_of_contents/. Accessed 28 June 2020.

Biskupic, Joan. 1999. In Jury Rooms, Form of Civil Protest Grows. *Washington Post*, February 8, p. A1. Available at http://www.washingtonpost.com/wp-srv/national/jury080299.htm. Accessed 5 April 2012.

Bissell, John W. 1997. Comments on Jury Nullification. *Cornell Journal of Law and Public Policy* 7: 51–56.

Bork, Robert H. 1999, June/July. Thomas More for Our Season. *First Things: A Monthly Journal of Religion & Public Life* 94: 17–21.

Brooks, Thom. 2004. A Defence of Jury Nullification. *Res Publica* 10: 401–423.

Butler, Paul. 2004. In Defense of Jury Nullification. *Litigation* 46–9 (69): 31.

Cohn, Avern. 1994. Letter to the Editor: "A Questionable Exclusion". *Judicature* 78: 5.

Dworkin, Ronald. 1986. *Law's Empire*. Cambridge, MA: Harvard University Press.

———. 2011. *Justice for Hedgehogs*. Cambridge, MA: Harvard University Press.

Greenawalt, Kent. 1987. *Conflicts of Law and Morality*. New York: Oxford University Press.

Greenblatt, Nathan. 2008. How Mandatory Are Mandatory Minimums: How Judges Can Avoid Imposing Mandatory Minimum Sentences. *American Journal of Criminal Law* 36: 1–38.

Huemer, Michael. 2018. The Duty to Disregard the Law. *Criminal Law and Philosophy* 12: 1–18.

Pound, Roscoe. 1910. Law in Books and Law in Action. *American Law Review* 44: 12–34.

Rosenthal, A.M. 1993. On My Mind: Dismantling the War. *New York Times*, May 18, p. A21. Available at https://www.nytimes.com/1993/05/18/opinion/on-my-mind-dismantling-the-war.html. Accessed 30 July 2019.

Scalia, Antonin. 1997. *A Matter of Interpretation: Federal Courts and the Law*. Princeton: Princeton University Press.

Steigmann, Robert J. 1998. Concurring Opinion in *People v. Smith*, 296 Ill. Ap. 3d 435.

Weinstein, Jack B. 2004. Every Day Is a Good Day for a Judge to Lay Down His Professional Life for Justice. *Fordham Urban Law Journal* 32: 131–170. Available at https://ir.lawnet.fordham.edu/ulj/vol32/iss1/6. Accessed 13 July 2019.

9

The Authority of Law

9.1 The Need for a Theory of Authority

At the core of the state's perspective is the idea of *authority*. I have written at length elsewhere about the putative authority of the state.[1] In this chapter, therefore, I will only briefly summarize some of the most important issues and arguments on this subject.

The state is usually taken to have a special kind of *authority*, "political authority", which explains why the state is entitled to issue commands backed by force (laws), and why the rest of society is obliged to obey those commands. Of course the government, as a matter of descriptive fact, has the *power* to impose laws on the rest of society. But whether it also has the *authority* to do so is a *moral* question that is open to debate. The government needs authority, because it frequently engages in behavior that would be considered wrong if carried out by any other agent. Unless the government has some special authority, for example, taxation is simply a form of theft, conscription a form of slavery, and war a form of mass murder. The idea of authority is the idea that the government has a *special moral status* rendering its apparently immoral acts acceptable.

---

[1] Huemer (2013).

Importantly, political authority as standardly understood is held to be *content-independent*. What this means is that we normally have a moral reason for obeying any given law, and government officials have a moral reason for enforcing the law, *simply because it is the law*, independent of whether the particular content of the law is wise, beneficial, or even just.

This gives rise to a central problem of political philosophy: *why* does the government have authority? Where does this special moral status come from? This question is of fundamental import to legal theory. If the state lacks genuine authority, there will be no special reason to uphold the law in cases where its dictates appear unjust. If the state *has* authority, it will still be important to understand the basis of this authority, so that we may judge its proper limits and implications.

9.2 The Social Contract Theory

When confronted with the problem of political authority, most people appeal to one or more of a handful of theories. The first of these is the *social contract theory*, which claims that the state's authority results from an agreement between the state and the people, whereby the state agrees to provide protection, law, and order, and the people in turn agree to pay the state for its services and to obey the rules devised by the state.[2]

The main problem with this theory is well-known in political philosophy: it is factually false. That is, no one, as a matter of fact, ever wrote up such an agreement, no one presented it to the citizens across the country, and no one signed it.

In response, it is usually said that the social contract is an *implicit* agreement, not an explicit one. An implicit contract is one to which a person's assent is somehow implied in his behavior, rather than being actually stated in words.

What fact about our behavior might be thought to imply acceptance of a social contract with the state? The most popular suggestions are: (a) we accept the social contract by failing to explicitly object to it; (b) we

---

[2] Locke (1980), Rousseau (2012). Hobbes (1996) also defends a social contract theory, but in his view, the contract is an agreement of citizens *with each other*, rather than with the state.

accept the contract by using government services (for example, roads, schools, police protection); (c) we accept the contract by participating in the political system (for example, voting); and (d) we accept the contract by residing in the government's territory. Let us address these suggestions in turn.

(a) *Acceptance through failure to object:* The first suggestion fails because there is no available procedure for objecting whereby one would actually be released from the putative social contract. Individuals who explicitly state their rejection of government (anarchists) are not thereupon released from any legal obligations by the state. Since the state refuses to accept any form of objection, a given individual's failure to object cannot be taken to imply assent.

(b) *Acceptance through use of government services:* This suggestion faces two problems. The first problem is that failure to use government services does not release one from the putative social contract. If one refrains from using government services, the government will not return one's tax money or excuse one from obeying any of the laws. Since the same laws will be imposed upon one regardless of whether one uses government services, one's use of government services cannot be taken to imply consent to the imposition of those laws.

The second problem is that the services provided by the state are generally ones that the state has coercively prevented anyone else from providing. For instance, the government will not allow anyone to set up a competing police force or court system. Because the government has stopped us from obtaining these services from anyone else, the government would be obligated to provide these services to us whether or not we agree to obey its commands.

(c) *Acceptance through political participation:* The first problem with this theory is similar to the problem with the preceding two theories: if one never votes or otherwise participates in the political system, one will not be excused from paying taxes or obeying any of the laws. Therefore, one's participation cannot be taken to imply that one agrees to pay taxes and obey the laws.

The second problem is that a large portion of citizens do not in fact participate in the political system. Thus, on the present theory these individuals would have no obligation to obey the law, nor would the state have any right to coercively impose its laws on them.

(d) *Acceptance through residence:* The most popular theory is that we implicitly accept the state's authority as long as we continue to reside in the territory under the state's control. If we wish to reject the state's authority and be excused from its laws, we must vacate the country.

This theory rests on the assumption that the state *owns* all the land that its citizens occupy – in general, one may set terms on the use of one's property, but one may not set terms on the use of someone else's property. For example, I may demand that people pay me money if they want to stay in my house, but I cannot demand that people pay me money if they want to stay in *their own* houses. Now as a matter of fact, the state is not, and does not claim to be, the owner of all land. Most land is owned by private individuals. The state lacks the right to demand payment or obedience as a condition on individuals occupying their own land.

In a genuine, binding contract, as understood in contract law as well as common sense, it is necessary that all parties enter into the agreement voluntarily, which requires that they had some reasonable way of opting out. One reasonable way of opting out of an agreement, in general, is that of explicitly stating one's rejection of the agreement. But the social contract theory flouts these principles: explicit statements of dissent are not recognized as a way of not accepting the contract, nor is there any other way of avoiding subjection to government, short of giving up one's own home and relocating to Antarctica.

Another widely recognized condition on valid contracts is that in a genuine contract, both parties take on some obligation to do something for the other. If either party repudiates its side of the deal, then the other party is no longer bound to do their part either. In the standard social contract theory, the most central responsibility of the government under the contract is to protect us against violations of our rights. But the U.S. government has explicitly repudiated this responsibility. As discussed earlier (§4.4.2), official U.S. legal doctrine holds that "a government and its agents are under no general duty to provide public services, such as police protection, to any particular individual citizen."³ There cannot be a contract between the individual and the state if the state does not accept any obligation to the individual.

In sum, the social contract violates every major principle governing real contracts. The relationship between a government and its citizens bears no resemblance to a contractual arrangement.

9.3 The Hypothetical Contract Theory

Some thinkers, while conceding that we have never actually signed on to a social contract, maintain that the government has authority because we *would* have signed on to the social contract, in certain idealized conditions. More precisely, in a hypothetical situation in which all members of society were fully informed and reasonable and met to discuss how their society should be arranged, they *would* all agree to establish a government. This, it is said, explains why the actual government is legitimate and why we should obey it.

This conclusion is something of a logical leap. Why should anyone be bound by an agreement that they merely *would* have made in some imagined situation? Advocates of the "hypothetical social contract" theory say that the hypothetical contract matters because it demonstrates something about *fairness* or *reasonableness*: if a particular social arrangement would be agreed to by all reasonable people, under ideal conditions for deliberation, this proves that that arrangement is reasonable and fair to everyone.⁴

There are two major problems with the hypothetical contract theory. The first problem is that there is no reason to believe that all reasonable people would agree to establish a government. Some reasonable people are in fact opposed to government, and there is no reason to think that they would or should change their positions in the course of deliberating with others.⁵

---

³ *Warren v. District of Columbia*, 444 A.2d. 1 (D.C. Ct. of Ap. 1981), at p. 3.
⁴ Nagel (1991, pp. 33–40), Rawls (1999, pp. 10–15).
⁵ See, for example, Huemer (2013), Friedman (1989), Rothbard (2006), Barnett (1998), Sartwell (2008), Wolff (1998).

The second problem is that *even if* all reasonable people would agree to establish a state in ideal deliberative conditions, this does nothing to show that anyone actually has any obligations to follow that hypothetical agreement, nor any moral right to enforce it. The hypothetical agreement, again, is said to be important because it establishes what is *reasonable* or *fair*. But even if this is true, it does not suffice to generate any genuine authority. To see this, imagine the following scenario:

Reasonable Job Offer: Sam offers Mary a job programming computers. Mary loves computer programming and has long dreamed of a career in the field. Sam is offering a salary much higher than any salary she has any reasonable chance of obtaining from anyone else. The working conditions are pleasant, her future colleagues affable, with plenty of opportunities for advancement. Everything else about the job is wonderful. Sam's offer is, all things considered, utterly *fair* and *reasonable*. If Mary were reasonable, she would accept the offer. Nevertheless, in a fit of sheer pique, Mary rejects Sam's offer.

In this scenario, would it be ethically permissible for Sam to *force* Mary to work for him? And would Mary be morally *obligated* to work for Sam?

These questions are not difficult. Uncontroversially, the answer to both is "no". Mary may refuse the job, and Sam may not force her. This shows that, if an individual would normally have a right to refuse some arrangement, the fact that the arrangement is *fair* or *reasonable* does nothing to overcome that right. The fact that a reasonable person *would have* accepted some arrangement does not matter if the actual person actually rejected it.

Similarly, it does not matter whether the putative social contract is a fair deal. It does not matter whether a reasonable person would accept the deal. What matters is whether the actual people have actually accepted it.

9.4 The Democratic Theory

Recognizing the impossibility of convincing all individuals, or even all reasonable individuals, to support the government, many people instead appeal to the agreement of a mere *majority* of individuals. The democratic theory of authority holds that the democratic process, whereby a majority of the people have the opportunity to realize their preferences, creates a moral entitlement to enforce the laws that emerge from that process, as well as an obligation for citizens to obey those laws.

Despite the confidence with which this theory is often advanced, the moral reasoning is very sketchy. Compare the following case:

Dinner Party: You have gone out for dinner with some friends at a restaurant. During the meal, one of your friends proposes that you pay for everyone's meal. You demur. Your friend presses the issue, calling for a vote of all those present, whereupon it swiftly emerges that a majority of the diners want you to pay for everyone. Your friend declares that, since the group has spoken, you must pay. They are prepared to take your money by force if you do not hand it over.

In this scenario, would you be morally obligated to pay for everyone's meal? Would your friends be morally entitled to force you to pay, or to punish you with imprisonment if you refuse?

Again, these are not difficult questions. Uncontroversially, the answer to both is "no". This shows that the preferences of a majority of people do not suffice to overcome the rights of the individual. If an individual would normally have the right to refuse some arrangement, the individual does not lose that right merely because some larger group wishes to impose the arrangement. It is thus very unclear how the democratic process is supposed to do anything toward generating political authority.

Some thinkers appeal to the process of reasoned, public *deliberation* that determines, or at least might help to determine, public policy in a democratic state.[6] The problem with this appeal is twofold: first, rational,

---
[6] Cohen (2002), Habermas (2002).

public deliberation has very little to do with actual policymaking in actual democratic states. Policy is driven more by the unthinking emotional reactions of voters and the lobbying efforts of special interest groups.[7]

Second, rational deliberation makes no moral difference even if it occurs. To see this, imagine the following variant on the Dinner Party scenario:

Deliberative Dinner Party: As in Dinner Party, except that prior to the vote, your friends deliberate at length about whether you should be forced to pay for everyone's meal. Everyone, including you, has an equal opportunity to participate in the discussion. Many arguments are thoroughly examined, taking into account, for example, your unusually high income, the needless luxuries you sometimes consume, and what rational parties would choose from behind a Rawlsian Veil of Ignorance.[8] At the end, you still do not agree to pay for everyone's meal, but a majority of those present votes that you should.

This modification makes no relevant difference: you still obviously are not obligated to pay for everyone's meal, nor are they entitled to force you to pay.

Some democratic theorists point to the desirable way in which democracy treats everyone as equals and accords equal respect to each person's judgment.[9] These observations also go no distance toward establishing political authority. The procedure followed by your friends in Dinner Party treats everyone as equals and accords equal respect to each person's judgment, in the same sense that the democratic process in actual states does so. Each person is given an equal say in the decision-making process. This does not suffice to cancel your rights over your own money. It is therefore unclear

---

[7] On unqualified voters, see Achen and Bartels (2017), Huemer (2015), Caplan (2007), Somin (2013), Brennan (2016). On the influence of special interest groups, see Carney (2006).

[8] The Veil of Ignorance is a hypothetical situation in which people are ignorant of their positions in society and all other details about themselves. From this position, they are imagined to choose a set of rules to govern their society (Rawls 1999).

[9] Christiano (2004).

how the democratic process, however egalitarian it may be, would overcome the rights of individuals so as to establish an entitlement for the state to rule over them, or an obligation for individuals to obey the state.

You might think my Dinner Party example unfair, since it concerns an obviously unfair distribution of costs – one person pays for everything. Perhaps the state's actual policies are more reasonable.[10] But this example is in fact fair, since the problem of authority precisely concerns the state's entitlement to take actions *that would normally be wrong* – actions, that is, that would generally be agreed to violate the rights of individuals if performed by someone other than the state. There is no need for a theory of authority to account for why the state may undertake actions that would be perfectly *permissible* if done by anyone else. It is thus entirely fair that I imagine the friends at the dinner proposing to violate your property rights. (This imagined violation is in fact very mild in comparison to many actual government policies.)

At least one critic has suggested that my example illicitly depends on norms of friendship: the diners should not demand that you pay the entire bill, because this simply isn't the way friends treat each other.[11] But since the government is not a personal friend of yours, it does not have the same moral reason to refrain from treating you in similar ways. In reply, imagine the following modification of the case: assume that you and the other diners are not friends. You are a group of strangers who just met for the first time at a conference today and decided to go out to dinner to discuss philosophy. In this case, the other diners still may not force you to pay for everyone.

9.5 The Utilitarian Theory

Finally, it is often said that government is necessary to prevent a breakdown of social order. Without a powerful, central organization holding a monopoly over the use of force, we would all be subject to widespread

---

[10] I note in passing that the state's actual distribution of costs for its operations is in fact more lopsided than the distribution in my example. The actual distribution of tax burdens in the U.S. is closer to a case in which your friends demand that you pay 1.8 times the total restaurant bill, in order to provide rebates to three of the diners. See Huemer (2020).
[11] Verbeek (2020).

robbery and violence. None of the great achievements of modern civilization would be possible, because no one would bother creating things of great value when doing so would only invite others to rob them.[12]

It is worth noting that this sort of argument is not as compelling as it is usually taken to be. The argument is usually advanced with no effort to address any of the accounts given by anarchist theorists of how law and social order could be maintained without a state.[13] When Thomas Hobbes first wrote about the horrors of the "state of nature", sophisticated anarchist theories did not yet exist; hence, Hobbes could not be expected to address them. But such theories exist today. We cannot merely assume that none of them succeed.

For reasons of space, however, I will not address theories of non-governmental law and order here. I shall instead draw attention to a simpler problem for utilitarian "theories of authority": they are not genuine theories of authority.

Suppose it is true that only government can preserve social order, the breakdown of which would be disastrous for nearly everybody. What follows from this? It follows that we should continue to maintain some government, and that that government should undertake at least the minimal actions necessary to maintain social order. It does not follow, however, that the government has a special moral status placing it above other agents; that we are obligated to obey its commands even when those commands are unwise, harmful, or unjust; or that government officials are morally entitled to enforce commands that are unwise, harmful, or unjust. It does not follow that anyone has political authority.

To see the point, consider the following analogy:

Lifeboat, part 1: You and several other people are in a lifeboat far out in the ocean, awaiting rescue. You become aware that the boat is taking on water and needs to be bailed out; otherwise, it will sink and all will drown. You cannot

---

[12] Hobbes (1996). This theory is "utilitarian" only in the sense that it appeals to the usefulness of government and the negative effects on human welfare of anarchy. It is not a theory that actual utilitarians would be likely to endorse; utilitarians would deny that there is any such thing as "authority", as authority would generate moral reasons apart from the reason to maximize utility.

[13] See Huemer (2013, part II), Friedman (1989), Rothbard (2006), Barnett (1998).

bail sufficiently quickly on your own and thus need help from other passengers. For some reason, however, you are unable to persuade them to bail water voluntarily. Therefore, you pull out a gun and *order* the passengers to bail out the boat. They obey, and the boat is saved.

In this scenario, coercion on your part was necessary to save the boat from sinking, which would have been disastrous for everyone. Therefore, you were morally justified in coercing the other passengers. Similarly, one might argue, coercive imposition of laws by the government is necessary to save society from a breakdown of order, which would be disastrous for everyone. Therefore, the government is justified in making laws and coercively imposing them.

Now suppose the story continues:

Lifeboat, part 2: You have saved the lifeboat, as described in part 1. Believing that this establishes your authority over the boat, you proceed to order the other passengers to pray to Poseidon, the god of the ocean, to ensure his good will. Then you force the passengers to hand over to you a third of their valuables. Next, you see a passenger drinking from a bottle of gin, which you deem unhealthful; you point the gun at her and demand that she stop.

The appropriate evaluation of part 2 of the lifeboat story is, I take it, quite different from that of part 1. None of the coercion described in part 2 is justified. While you are justified in deploying the coercion that is *necessary to save the boat*, this does not give you the right to employ any further coercion. It does not, for example, enable you to claim the other passengers' property, nor to impose useless rules on them (praying to Poseidon), nor even to impose beneficial paternalistic rules (not drinking hard liquor).

What this shows is that, even when coercion by a given agent is justified to prevent some disastrous outcome, this fact does not establish any special *authority* for that agent. It does not grant the agent a general entitlement to impose his will on others. Rather, the agent may deploy the minimal coercion necessary to prevent the disaster in question. In other words, the moral entitlement to use force to avoid harmful outcomes is *content-dependent*, not content-independent as required by the notion of authority.

The utilitarian argument for government, then, does nothing to establish authority, properly speaking. It may explain why the government and its agents are justified in using the minimal force necessary to maintain social order. It does not explain how they could be justified in enforcing unjust, unwise, or harmful laws.

9.6 Conclusion

I cannot address all possible accounts of authority. I have, however, addressed the most influential theories. Each of them is, on reflection, very ill-considered. Other, less natural accounts exist, but none is drastically more plausible. If the state really has the authority that it claims, it is surprising that no one seems to be able to explain why that is so.

In my experience, most people appear to accept the authority of government officials. Many in the legal profession appear to be completely convinced of the doctrine of government authority. Judges are so unshakably certain of it that they will, for example, send people to prison for multiple decades for minor wrongs, or even actions that are not wrong at all, when the judges themselves know these sentences to be extremely unjust, all for no reason other than that the legislature *told* them to do it. One might assume, therefore, that there must be some well-known, extremely convincing proofs of the authority of the state.

But then one would be mistaken. Most people, despite unquestioning acceptance of government authority, do not have any account of its basis. Among those who do, their accounts tend to fall apart almost immediately under examination.

Why is it so hard to explain the basis of state authority? The most likely reason is that there *is no* explanation for political authority, because political authority is a fiction. Long ago, some human beings forcibly seized power over other humans for their own purposes. The dominant group then declared themselves entitled to rule over others and began devising rationalizations for this claim. This scenario played out many times in different societies. The social systems by which dominant groups control the rest of society developed over time, becoming much more sophisticated and, in most places, much less malign. Nevertheless, all such systems at least sometimes impose unjust harms on individuals living under them, and the dominant group typically demands that the rest of society cooperate with these injustices, because the dominant group is more interested in maintaining its own power than in serving justice, morality, or the good of others. After an organization has dominated a society for many generations, it becomes increasingly psychologically difficult for members of that society to question the dominant group's right to rule.[14]

In societies that practiced slavery, there were *some* individuals who challenged the practice on moral grounds. But the majority simply accepted the institution as normal. Most undoubtedly could not philosophically defend the justice of slavery, yet they were unconcerned by this fact, since they simply *assumed* the moral decency of the prominent institutions of their society.

In our present society, some individuals challenge the government's right to inflict severe injustices in the name of the law. But most simply accept the system as normal. Judges in particular are likely to assume that there is some special authority attached to the law, some compelling moral duty, especially for a judge, to uphold the law irrespective of its content, merely because it is the law. Most have no philosophical justification for this assumption. In reality, what makes us assume the authority of government and its laws is simply that the government in fact holds power, and has done so for many years.

Now, suppose I am right and political authority is a fiction. What follows from this? Must we abolish all law and dismantle the courts?

That would be absurd. For while *authority* may be a fiction, right and wrong are not; good and bad are not. The legal system is, as a matter of empirical fact, a useful tool for achieving justice in many cases. It can be used to punish those who have violated the moral rights of others, or to extract compensation from those who have negligently or intentionally

---

[14] For extended discussion of the psychological forces that make it difficult to question political authority, see Huemer (2013, ch. 6).

hurt others. We should continue to use the legal system in these ways. What we should not do is to use the legal system to inflict outcomes that we know to be unjust, merely in the name of *the law*. We should not do that, since the law has no intrinsic authority; whatever moral import is to be found in upholding the law must derive from the just and good outcomes that result from doing so.

References

Achen, Christopher H., and Larry M. Bartels. 2017. *Democracy for Realists: Why Elections Do Not Produce Responsive Government*. Princeton: Princeton University Press.

Barnett, Randy E. 1998. *The Structure of Liberty: Justice and the Rule of Law*. Oxford: Oxford University Press.

Brennan, Jason. 2016. *Against Democracy*. Princeton: Princeton University Press.

Caplan, Bryan. 2007. *The Myth of the Rational Voter*. Princeton: Princeton University Press.

Carney, Timothy. 2006. *The Big Ripoff: How Big Business and Big Government Steal Your Money*. Hoboken: Wiley.

Christiano, Thomas. 2004. The Authority of Democracy. *Journal of Political Philosophy* 12: 266–290.

Cohen, Joshua. 2002. Deliberation and Democratic Legitimacy. In *Democracy*, ed. David Estlund, 87–106. Malden: Blackwell.

Friedman, David. 1989. *The Machinery of Freedom*. 2nd ed. LaSalle: Open Court.

Habermas, Jürgen. 2002. Deliberative Politics. In *Democracy*, ed. David Estlund, 107–125. Malden: Blackwell.

Hobbes, Thomas. 1996. *Leviathan*, ed. Richard Tuck. Cambridge: Cambridge University Press.

Huemer, Michael. 2013. *The Problem of Political Authority*. New York: Palgrave Macmillan.

———. 2015. Why People Are Irrational About Politics. In *Philosophy, Politics, and Economics*, ed. Jonathan Anomaly, Geoffrey Brennan, Michael Munger, and Geoffrey Sayre-McCord, 456–467. Oxford: Oxford University Press.

———. 2020. Tax Breaks for the Rich. In *Ethics, Left and Right: The Moral Issues That Divide Us*, ed. Bob Fischer, 241–249. Oxford: Oxford University Press.

Locke, John. 1980. *Second Treatise of Government*, ed. C.B. Macpherson. Indianapolis: Hackett.

Nagel, Thomas. 1991. *Equality and Partiality*. New York: Oxford University Press.
Rawls, John. 1999. *A Theory of Justice*, revised edition. Cambridge, MA: Harvard University Press.
Rothbard, Murray. 2006. *For a New Liberty*. 2nd ed. Auburn: Ludwig von Mises Institute.
Rousseau, Jean-Jacques. 2012. *The Social Contract and Other Political Writings*, trans. Quintin Hoare, ed. Christopher Bertram. London: Penguin.
Sartwell, Crispin. 2008. *Against the State: An Introduction to Anarchist Political Theory*. Albany: State University of New York Press.
Somin, Ilya. 2013. *Democracy and Political Ignorance*. Stanford: Stanford University Press.
Verbeek, Bruno. 2020. Reply to Michael Huemer. In *Ethics, Left and Right: The Moral Issues That Divide Us*, ed. Bob Fischer, 251–252. Oxford: Oxford University Press.
Wolff, Robert Paul. 1998. *In Defense of Anarchism*. Berkeley: University of California Press.

10

Role Playing

10.1 Role Playing

A simple appeal to the authority of the state is not the only reason that may be given in support of upholding the law. In this chapter, I address some arguments in favor of faithfully executing one's assigned role in the legal system, which I refer to as "role playing".

It may be disputed what exactly the proper roles of participants in the legal system are. If we conceive the role of an agent in the legal system as one of pursuing justice, then I would insist that one *should* faithfully execute that role. In this chapter, when I speak of arguments in favor of carrying out one's assigned role, I mean carrying out one's assigned role on a conception wherein the role does *not* involve making judgments about justice and explicitly aiming at justice. Many believe that the role of a jury is merely to assess the non-normative facts of a case, that the role of a judge is merely to faithfully interpret and apply the law, and that the role of a lawyer is merely to serve a particular side in a dispute. That is the sort of role that, I argue, ought to take a back seat to the pursuit of justice in the individual case.

Notice that role playing, in the present sense, is not merely a matter of obeying the law. It requires, in the case of judges and juries, actively helping to *enforce the law against others*, though in the case of lawyers, oddly enough, it often involves trying to *prevent* enforcement of the law by getting criminals released. In most cases, faithful execution of one's role is not literally legally required. In particular, no law requires jurors to limit their judgments to the non-normative facts or prohibits them from nullifying the law on moral grounds. Jury decisions are legally binding and unreviewable, even if the jury explicitly states that they voted to nullify the law—nor can juries be sued, prosecuted, or punished in any way for such decisions.

Judge decisions, other than those of the Supreme Court, are at least reviewable and subject to reversal. Nevertheless, no law forbids judges from using their moral beliefs in deciding how to (mis)interpret or (mis)apply the law. If a judge misinterprets or misapplies a law for the purpose of preventing what he views as an unjust punishment, that judge can be *reversed* by another judge, but there is no law under which he can be prosecuted or sued. He will have failed to faithfully enforce the law, but he will not himself have violated any law.[1]

Lawyers are the agents in the system most subject to legal constraint, since serious failures to execute their role may be considered legal malpractice, which may expose lawyers to lawsuits in the event that the malpractice detrimentally affects legal outcomes for their clients. In extreme cases, a lawyer can be disbarred for malpractice, resulting in a legal prohibition on his future practice of the law. Lawyers may, however, refuse to take on clients in the first place if they consider the potential clients to be immoral or to be taking immoral positions.

Thus, to argue that agents in the legal system ought to set aside their beliefs about justice and morality in order to play their roles in the system requires going beyond the traditional thesis of political authority, which would only require us to refrain from literally breaking the law.

---

[1] Note, however, that if a judge intentionally misinterprets or misapplies the law to bring about a punishment that is legally unjustified, he may in theory be criminally prosecuted under 18 U.S.C., section 242, though this would be extremely rare. On criminal liability for judges, see *Ex Parte Virginia*, 100 U.S. 339 (1879).

10.2 The Knowledge Argument

10.2.1 Ignorance of Justice

Some object to the Primacy of Justice by citing the difficulty of knowing what justice really requires. For example, where I maintain that juries should refuse to convict a defendant under an unjust law, critics urge that a jury cannot *know* when a law is just or unjust. After all, there is widespread disagreement in society about which laws are just. By comparison, it is relatively easy for a jury to know what is or is not *illegal*. Therefore, a jury should make its decision based solely on whether the defendant violated the law. Compare Thomas More's lines in *A Man for All Seasons:* "I know what's legal not what's right. And I'll stick to what's legal. ... I'm not God."[2]

Similarly, where I maintain that a lawyer should not attempt to prevent criminals from receiving just punishment, some critics urge that a lawyer cannot know whether his client is guilty or innocent. Even if a client confesses to his lawyer, it is still *possible* that the client is really innocent (perhaps the client is insane, or is protecting someone else).[3] Therefore, it is said, the lawyer should not attempt to assess his client's guilt but should simply focus on carrying out his role of defending the client's interests.

A similar argument can be made regarding judges: that since they cannot know what is truly just or unjust, judges should stick to interpreting and applying the law as written.

10.2.2 Certainty Is Not Required

There are many problems with the preceding argument. Granted, it is not possible to know with 100% certainty in all cases what justice demands. It is, however, possible to be *reasonably* certain, certain enough for practical purposes, in *some* cases. This is all that is required for the thesis of the

---

[2] Bolt (1990, pp. 65–6). Bork (1999, p. 18) quotes the remark approvingly in his essay condemning jury nullification.
[3] D'Amato and Eberle (2010, pp. 14–15); Joy (2004, p. 1246n36).

Primacy of Justice to make sense: in those cases in which one is reasonably sure that a given outcome would be unjust, one should avoid promoting that outcome.

Why is certainty not needed? To rationally pursue a given value, it is not in general necessary that one have certainty, or anything close to certainty, about what promotes that value. One need only have reasonable assessments as to which courses of action are more and less likely to promote the value. Thus, suppose I value wealth. I may pursue wealth by investing in the stock market, despite having nothing approaching certainty that this will increase my wealth. My behavior is rational as long as I am able to make some reasonable judgments about which courses of action are more and less likely to promote wealth. Similarly, to rationally pursue *justice*, it is not necessary that one have certainty concerning what justice demands. One need only have some reasonable judgments about which courses of action are more and less likely to be just.

10.2.3 Uncertainty of Law

A second problem with the Knowledge Argument is that certainty about what will promote our goals is almost never to be had, regardless of whether one prioritizes justice, or the law, or the interests of one's client. Contrary to the implied premise of the knowledge argument, it is rarely if ever known with absolute certainty what the law requires. Often, indeed, the application of the law to a case is not even *reasonably* certain. Laws are often vague or ambiguous, they often require subjective judgment, they often conflict with one another, and the apparent intent of a law sometimes conflicts with a literal reading of the text. All of this introduces uncertainty and even indeterminacy (that is, there may in some cases be no fact of the matter as to what the law requires).

One might try to mitigate this problem, at least for jurors, by proposing that jurors should defer to judges about the interpretation of the law. There is no law that specifies that jurors should do this—this is merely a proposal devised by judges. However, even judges will often be uncertain as to what the law requires in a particular case. Yet no one argues that one therefore should not even attempt to apply the law in such cases.

Therefore, it is unclear why uncertainty about justice should prevent us from attempting to do justice.

Note that one of the sources of uncertainty about the law is the fact that the law often directly invokes morality. In the United States, the highest law of the land is the U.S. Constitution—a document so open to interpretation that bookcases can be filled with works dedicated to its interpretation. The Constitution explicitly employs normative terms in many places without specifying their extension. For instance, the Fifth Amendment prohibits the taking of private property for public use "without *just* compensation" (emphasis added); no further guidance is given regarding when compensation is just. The Fourth Amendment protects against "*unreasonable* searches and seizures" (emphasis added), without specifying when searches and seizures are reasonable. Perhaps the vaguest clause is the Ninth Amendment, which reads, in its entirety: "The enumeration in the Constitution, of certain rights, shall not be construed to deny or disparage others retained by the people." What other rights are retained by the people is, again, unspecified. Yet the Amendment was presumably written to protect those unenumerated rights (what other purpose could it serve?); thus, to prescind entirely from the question of what natural rights humans possess would be to refuse to faithfully implement this law according to its purpose.[4] Hence, it seems that one must employ substantive moral judgments *in order* to apply the written law.

The above are just three examples showing that moral judgments are often required in order to faithfully apply the law, including some of the most open-ended and subjective moral judgements to be found anywhere. Since the Constitution, by design, limits what other laws may be considered valid, the intrusion of morality into the application of the *Constitution* in effect introduces moral considerations into the application of *statutes*. Therefore, if one claims that agents in the legal system should not rely on their own moral judgments since they do not know the moral truth, one must also conclude that agents in the legal system cannot faithfully apply the law in a wide range of cases. The knowledge argument thus cuts against the Primacy of Law as well as the Primacy of Justice.

---

[4] On the proper application of the Ninth Amendment, see Barnett (1988).

In the case of lawyers, it is usually thought that their duty is not to uphold the law but to serve the interests of their clients (without themselves breaking the law of course). At least this duty, it seems, could be carried out without the use of fraught moral judgments. Nevertheless, the question of what serves the interests of one's client is often just as difficult as the question of what serves justice. Granted, a lawyer may know easily enough what his client's goals are—say, to stay out of prison, or to collect money from a lawsuit—but it is often extremely unclear what courses of action and what arguments will best promote those goals. And it is that knowledge that is needed to reliably pursue the goal. Yet no one claims that, because of this uncertainty, lawyers should not attempt to pursue their clients' interests. No more, then, should one claim that uncertainty about justice prevents one from pursuing justice.

10.2.4 Extreme Skepticism Is Unreasonable

Suppose one argues that individual jurors, lawyers, and judges are not merely *uncertain* about justice, but that they have *no reasonable basis* for judgments about justice. This really would preclude the rational pursuit of justice in legal contexts.

Yet this would be an extraordinarily implausible position. To cite a case mentioned earlier (§6.2.2), it is unjust to send a person to prison for sixty years for selling $40 worth of cocaine. I know that, and any person with a normal moral sense would know it. There is no reason not to accept that example of moral knowledge, if one accepts any moral knowledge at all. Yet that punishment was legally prescribed in an actual case. So there are cases in which one can know, beyond any reasonable doubt, that the law is unjust.

Some philosophers doubt that anyone can be justified in *any* moral belief, or even that there are any moral truths at all.[5] These philosophers would of course reject my claim to know that the 60-year sentence was unjust. But even if one holds this extreme view, there is no comfort to be had for the defender of the Primacy of Law. For if we have no justified or true moral beliefs, then the *legislature*, or whichever individual or

---

[5] Sinnott-Armstrong (1996); Mackie (1977); Joyce (2001).

organization created a given law, also had no justified or true moral beliefs. In particular, they could not have had a justified or true belief that the law they created was good or right. Nor could we have a justified or true belief that upholding the law would be good or right.

In general, any form of moral skepticism strong enough to rule out individuals' recognition of unjust laws would also rule out individuals' knowledge of an obligation to faithfully implement the law or to faithfully execute one's role in the legal system. So this version of the knowledge argument would deny our reasons for defying the law, at the cost of erasing any reason for playing one's role in the legal system.

10.2.5 The Streetlamp Fallacy

Finally, note that the difficulty of knowing a given type of truth does not show that that type of truth is not in fact what is relevant to our decision, or that some other, more easily ascertainable truth is relevant. The point is illustrated by a popular joke:

Streetlamp: You see a drunk searching the ground under a streetlamp. You approach and have the following exchange with him:
You: What are you looking for?
Drunk: My keys.
You: Where did you lose them?
Drunk Over there *[pointing to a dark alleyway]*.
You: Then why are you looking here?
Drunk: Because the light is better here.

The fact that it is very difficult to see in the alley does not show that one should instead look under the streetlamp. One must search the alley, however difficult it may be, if that is where the keys were lost.

Similarly, if we are operating a legal system, then we must do our best to ascertain justice, however difficult that may be. The difficulty of distinguishing the just and the unjust does not show that we should instead aim at some other goal, when the original purpose of the system was to achieve justice. We will not somehow achieve our purpose if we pick something other than justice that is easier to attain. Even if (contrary to fact) it were completely unproblematic to know what the law requires, that hardly shows that uncritically applying the law is more likely to achieve justice, or that it achieves some goal superior to justice, or that it is in any other way better than directly pursuing justice.

10.3 The Problem of Subjectivism

10.3.1 The Subjective Belief Objection

Some critics, on hearing the thesis that agents in the legal system should prioritize justice, interpret this as the thesis that agents in the legal system should do *whatever they believe* to be just. But individuals may have all manner of deplorable beliefs. For instance, white supremacists might regard racially-motivated hate crimes as acceptable, and thus consider it just to acquit those who commit such crimes. Therefore, my thesis might seem to imply that these white supremacists, if serving as jurors or judge in a hate crime trial, *should* try to prevent the defendant from being punished. But surely that is not correct—the jury and judge in such a trial should help to enforce the law so that a defendant guilty of hate crimes is punished.[6]

This argument may be summarized thus:

1. The Primacy of Justice entails that individuals should do what they believe to be just. (Premise.)
2. White supremacists believe that acquitting hate criminals is just, even when their crimes are proved beyond reasonable doubt. (Premise.)
3. Therefore, if the Primacy of Justice is correct, then white supremacist jurors should acquit hate criminals, even when their crimes are proved beyond reasonable doubt. (From 1, 2.)
4. Jurors should *not* acquit hate criminals whose crimes are proved beyond reasonable doubt. (Premise.)
5. Therefore, the Primacy of Justice is false. (From 3, 4.)

This argument is deductively valid and uses just three premises: steps 1, 2, and 4. Premise 4 is obvious on a common sense conception of justice.

---

[6] For something like this objection, see Leipold (1996, pp. 304–6).

In addition, there is no point in disputing 2, since there surely are *some* people who have the irrational belief mentioned in that premise, and that is all that a critic needs.

10.3.2 The Subjective Belief Objection Entails Absurdity

In reply, premise 1 is false. The Primacy of Justice does not recommend that one do whatever one believes to be just. It recommends that one do what is just (even when this conflicts with upholding the law or carrying out one's assigned role). Notice that "what is just" is not synonymous with "whatever one believes to be just". To substitute the latter for the former is to commit a confusion of the first order.

To make the error clearer, note first that the Subjective Belief Objection could also be used to "refute" the following view:

Trivial Thesis: Individuals should do what they should do.

Any objection that cuts against *that* claim must be confused. Now consider this objection:

1'. The Trivial Thesis entails that one should do what one believes one should do. (Premise.)
2'. Terrorists believe that they should murder random civilians. (Premise.)
3'. Therefore, if the Trivial Thesis is correct, then terrorists *should* murder random civilians.
4'. No one should murder random civilians.
5'. Therefore, the Trivial Thesis is wrong.

The argument consisting of steps 1'–5' is perfectly parallel to the argument consisting of steps 1–5 above. The logic is the same, and premises 2' and 4' are just as true as premises 2 and 4. But 5' is false. This is not a debatable philosophical opinion, nor does this issue have anything to do with any special features of morality, or the law, or human psychology. The Trivial Thesis is true as a matter of logical form; its denial is a contradiction. No further considerations are needed.

The false step is of course premise 1', which confuses "what one should do" with "whatever *one believes* one should do". If we then invoke the example of a person with a false belief about what that person should do, it is easy to derive contradictions.

Indeed, if the above arguments were cogent, a parallel objection could be used to refute the Primacy of Law as well; all that is needed is at least one person who holds an absurd view about the law. Suppose, for example, that Crazy Jack thinks he is legally required to murder ten innocent people. (Of course, Jack is radically mistaken.) Now consider the following "refutation" of the Primacy of Law:

1'. The Primacy of Law entails that individuals should do what they believe upholds the law.
2'. Crazy Jack believes that his murdering ten innocent people would uphold the law.
3'. Therefore, if the Primacy of Law is correct, then Crazy Jack *should* murder ten innocent people.
4'. No one should murder ten innocent people.
5'. Therefore, the Primacy of Law is false.

To avoid this objection, advocates of the Primacy of Law would have to distinguish what is legally required from what someone (perhaps irrationally) *believes* to be legally required—just as advocates of the Primacy of Justice distinguish what is just from what someone (perhaps irrationally) *believes* to be just.

10.3.3 Pursuing Real Versus Apparent Justice

One might object to my thesis that one should pursue only just outcomes—not the outcomes one *believes* to be just but those that *really are* just—on the grounds that it is impossible for an agent to separate what that agent believes to be just from what is really just. I know that what *is* just is not in general the same thing as what *I believe* to be just; nevertheless, if I try to follow the advice "Pursue what is just", I will behave in the same way as I do if I try to follow the advice "Pursue what you believe is just." Therefore, one might think, if the latter is bad advice, then so is the former. Granted, if individuals reliably had correct beliefs about justice, then there would be little problem. But if individuals are highly unreliable about justice, then advising them to pursue justice is foolish, even if justice is our ultimate aim.

In reply, note first that this objection is not genuinely an objection to my thesis. It is perhaps an argument against widely disseminating my thesis—for instance, giving juries copies of this book before their deliberations—but not an argument that the thesis is not true. The fact that people will make mistakes if told to do something does not show that that thing is not actually what they should do. It shows at most that we should not *tell* them that they should do it.

My thesis does not concern what the government should tell juries, judges, or anyone else. It is not a political thesis about what government policy or the institutional structure should be. It is a thesis of individual ethics, a thesis concerning what an individual acting within the legal system should do, taking the institutional structure and polices as they are. Thus, suppose that you are on the jury in a trial for the sale of drugs. The defendant is accused of selling a total of $40 worth of drugs to a police informant, during multiple sales. If the defendant is convicted, given his circumstances, he will face a sentence of 60 years in prison. (Actual judges rarely tell jurors of the sentence a defendant faces; in most cases, the juror would have to do outside research to learn this information. Assume, nevertheless, that you have learned it.) You consider this extremely unjust. Therefore, you are inclined to vote for acquittal.

Now suppose that another member of the jury tells you that there are white supremacists who might consider it just to acquit someone who was guilty of hate crimes. But it would obviously be wrong to do that. Therefore, this other juror concludes, it would also be wrong to acquit the drug seller. Does this other juror have a point?

If he does, it is extremely difficult to make out that point. Granted, one should not acquit people based on racial hatred. How does it follow from this that one should not acquit the drug seller who faces a 60-year sentence? Is the implicit premise, "It is unjust to imprison someone for 60 years for selling $40 worth of drugs *only if* it is also unjust to imprison people who commit hate crimes"? But that premise is absurd.

Is the premise, "If white supremacists are wrong about justice, then we can't ever know whether any legal outcome is just"? Or "All beliefs about justice are equally justified"? Those are also absurd.

Or perhaps the assumption is that, if you acquit this defendant, that will increase the odds that racist juries will acquit hate criminals? But that is extremely unrealistic. When the jury renders its verdict, no one will question the members on their reasons, and no account of their deliberations will ever be published. Other juries will never hear of this particular case, let alone know why it was decided as it was. Therefore, there is no need to worry about how racist juries in the future will react to this verdict.

Furthermore, the idea of imposing an extraordinary injustice on the individual presently before you, condemning him to spend the rest of his life in prison, because doing so might influence future juries full of extreme racists to follow the law, is immoral. It is on a par with knowingly convicting a factually innocent defendant, in the hopes that doing so will encourage future juries to convict more guilty defendants.

Finally, it is difficult to see how the advice to pursue justice could be bad advice, and yet the advice to enforce the law regardless of justice be good advice. Recall, again, that justice is the central purpose of the legal system. Now, admittedly, if agents acting within the system have seriously faulty beliefs about justice, then advising them to pursue justice will not reliably result in just outcomes. But it does not follow that advising agents to apply the existing law *will* reliably result in just outcomes. Nor is there any obvious reason for thinking that we will achieve greater justice if agents follow the latter advice. If most people have faulty beliefs about justice, then the *law* is probably similarly flawed, since the law, in a democratic society, tends to reflect the beliefs of most people.[7]

10.4 Faith in Democracy

10.4.1 The Problem of Undemocratic Decisions

Some critics object to the undemocratic nature of juries and judges. The law, in a democratic society, reflects the will of the people as a whole, or so one might argue. The decision of a particular judge does not. And

---

[7] There are exceptions to this, but these exceptions rarely inspire confidence—for instance, laws that reflect lobbying by special interest groups.

though juries are sometimes said to function as the conscience of the community, it is difficult for a group of twelve individuals to be representative of society as a whole.[8]

But what exactly is wrong with undemocratic decisions? One answer is that only the will of the people can generate political authority; hence, legal outcomes that are imposed as a result of democratically made laws have greater inherent legitimacy than outcomes imposed as a result of the moral judgments of a single person or small group of people.

While this may be the main thought that moves the advocates of democracy, it is difficult to fill in the reasoning beyond the first stage. *Why* does the will of the people generate authority? Inhabitants of democratic societies often *assume* that it does, but there is no satisfactory explanation for this (see §9.4). A group of people does not acquire the right to impose its will on another individual or group, to coerce or rob them, or to perform any other actions that would normally be unjust, merely because the former group is *larger* than the latter. The principle of majority rule may be appropriate for deciding among alternatives that are *already known to be ethically permissible* and not unjust. But a majority vote on whether to commit an *injustice* can do nothing to justify the injustice or convert it into justice.

There are many illustrations of this point. Perhaps the most pointed illustrations for Americans derive from the nation's history of racial prejudice, a history that saw the majority enslave and oppress a racial minority. This oppression was not rendered morally acceptable merely because it was supported by a majority. By the same token, an otherwise *just* action is not rendered morally wrong merely by *failing* to be supported by a majority.

10.4.2 The Reliability of Democracy

Perhaps the argument for trusting democracy is more pragmatic. Perhaps the democratic process is simply *more reliable*, in general, at producing morally correct results than the deliberations of a typical jury or judge;

---

[8] Leipold (1996, pp. 299, 307); Crispo et al. (1997, p. 3).

therefore, juries and judges in a democratic society should defer to the laws rather than relying on their own judgments about what is just.

Why might the democratic process have this superior reliability? Perhaps when a large number of judgments are aggregated, individual errors tend to cancel out, so that the judgment of the group is more reliable than that of any individual member.[9] Any given individual may be prone to random errors, but it is unlikely that many individuals will make the same random error; the probability of this occurring becomes vanishingly small with groups the size of an entire society.

The preceding logic is correct for certain situations. But it does not apply to the actual situations of democratic polities. One reason is that voters in democratic nations do not merely make random errors; they have systematic biases. For example, the reason that America's punishment regime has become shockingly draconian over the past few decades is not that many voters happened to make the same random error of overestimating the just sentences for crimes. The reason—at least, a large part of the reason—is that voters in general tend to have negative feelings about criminals, and thus a vague "tough on crime" message is emotionally appealing to voters, and thus politicians who promise to get tough on crime are more likely to be elected. The citizens who elect these leaders need not, and generally do not, have any non-negligible knowledge about actual sentences, nor need they have exerted any non-negligible effort to reflect on the demands of justice. They simply respond emotionally to the vague, superficial messages produced by politicians.

Unfortunately, in many cases, what justice requires differs systematically from what is emotionally appealing at the most superficial level. In many cases, identifying justice requires extended investigation, reflection, and reasoning. This is why it is not at all unlikely that the aggregated opinions of the electorate should be wrong.

Why do voters rely on emotional reactions to vague, superficial messages, rather than relying on diligent investigation and careful, impartial reasoning? The answer is that the democratic process gives voters *no*

---

[9] For a fascinating discussion of this phenomenon, see Surowiecki (2005).

incentive to be diligent, careful, or impartial.[10] In a society containing millions of voters, each individual knows that her odds of actually affecting the outcome of any election are minuscule. If one works to identify the objectively best policies, one may—with some extremely small probability—improve public policy, which would be a benefit to society as a whole. But the *costs* in terms of time and effort and the emotional strain of having to question one's own prejudices are virtually certain to occur, and must be borne by oneself individually, not by society. Most human beings will not take large, known costs on themselves, merely to have a minute chance of producing a benefit for society.

This explains why voters tend to be extremely ignorant of political issues and to be strongly, systematically biased.[11] For example, most Americans, when given the choices "direct democracy", "republic", "confederacy", and "oligarchy", *cannot name the form of government they live under*.[12] Only a third of Americans know what the three branches of their government are.[13] These are not minor details; these are the broadest, most basic facts about the political system. Can a group of people with this little intellectual engagement with politics be trusted to choose wise and beneficial policies?

Of course, voters rarely choose policy directly (the exception being the ballot initiatives that appear in many states). They usually only choose which politicians shall make policy. Faith in democracy therefore requires faith in the average voter's assessment of potential leaders, based on the information presented in political campaigns. But most voters do not even know their Congressional representative's name, which calls into question their ability to reliably judge that person's suitability for public office.[14] Can we really infer that a policy is just, merely on the grounds that it was created by a group of politicians who were chosen by average

---

[10] For discussion, see Surprenant and Brennan (2020, ch. 2). Surprenant and Brennan (pp. 32–3) also note that in the U.S., unlike most other nations, many prosecutors and judges are *elected*, which selects for more punitive, less justice-oriented candidates.

[11] See above, §3.2.5.

[12] Berry et al. 2009.

[13] Rozansky (2014).

[14] Caplan (2007, p. 8).

people, most of whom first learned the name of the person they were electing on the day they entered the voting booth?

Looking at actual democratic outcomes does not inspire great confidence in the reliability of democracy at identifying the just and the right. The laws enforcing slavery and racial segregation were made no less democratically than the laws against murder and theft. The abolition of slavery in the U.S. was achieved through civil war, rather than through the normal democratic process. In the present day, there appear to be many clear and serious injustices that have survived the democratic process (see Chaps. 3, 4, 5, 6 and 7).

One might object that this last observation begs the question, since perhaps, as the defender of democracy might say, the fact that these alleged injustices have been produced by a democratic government simply proves that they are not unjust after all.

But this retort, I suspect, is too implausible even for the acolytes of democracy. Imagine listening to a debate about whether it is just to sentence someone to sixty years in prison for selling $40 worth of drugs. The "affirmative" side claims that this is an appropriate sentence; the "negative" side that it is not.

The negative side begins by arguing that drug prohibition is unjust in the first place, since individuals have the right to control their own bodies (see §3.2). They supplement this with evidence about the extreme costs of the drug war and its meager results, arguing that *even if* we set aside the individual right to control one's own body, it would still be unjust to coercively impose a policy that has much greater costs than benefits. Finally, they argue that, *even if* drug prohibition is permissible, there must still be proportionality in sentencing—it is virtually universally recognized that the severity of sentences should be proportional to the seriousness of the crimes for which they are given. The negative team cites cases of thieves, rapists, and murderers who have received sentences much lighter than the 60-year prison term under discussion. And so on.

Now, in response to all this, the affirmative team presents the following argument: Democracy is reliable at producing just outcomes, and the 60-year prison sentence for drug dealing actually occurred in a democratic society. Therefore, that sentence is probably just after all.

The affirmative team's case in this hypothetical debate is extraordinarily weak. Perhaps the fact that an outcome was produced by a democratic government is *some* evidence in general for its being just. But it seems to be at best extremely weak evidence, easily outweighed by the arguments, in this particular case, that the 60-year sentence is unjust. One would need to have an amazingly strong faith in democracy to conclude that that sentence is morally correct merely because it was produced by a democracy. This faith would be particularly difficult to understand given that surely almost any voter, if confronted with the details of this case, would agree that the 60-year sentence was excessive.

Now, one may find it puzzling that the democratic process should sometimes produce outcomes that almost no voter would approve of. Part of the explanation for this phenomenon lies in the problem of voter ignorance mentioned above. Be that as it may, what matters for present purposes is simply the fact that that does indeed occur. In such cases, it is difficult to see what reason we have for deferring to the democratic outcome.

10.4.3 The Reliability of Juries and Judges

So far, I have only questioned the reliability of the democratic process as a means of producing justice. It remains possible that juries and judges are *even less* reliable, in which case it might still be rational for judges and juries, if aware of their own unreliability, to defer to the democratically-produced laws on questions of justice. In the case of juries, one might worry that the same ignorance and irrationality that renders ordinary citizens incompetent as *voters* would also mar their performance as *jurors* evaluating justice in individual court cases.

In reply, there are two key reasons why the moral judgments of juries and judges in individual court cases should be expected to be *more* reliable indicators of justice than a rote application of democratically made law to the cases. The first reason is that in an individual court case, the judge and each member of the jury know that they have a significant chance of affecting the outcome of the case. Most voters in modern democratic nations make no serious effort at voting wisely, because they understand that they are each only one among *millions* of voters, and thus that there is almost no chance that their efforts will make any difference. It is, indeed, perfectly rational for them to exert minimal effort in that situation.[15] By contrast, jurors and judges are more willing to make serious efforts to get things right in court cases, where they know that there is a realistic possibility of their altering the outcome.

Second, in individual court cases, the judge and jury typically *know the relevant facts*. At the beginning of the trial, they know nothing about the case, yet in the course of the trial, they will spend many hours listening to relatively full accounts of the evidence concerning what happened in the case at hand. Nothing like that happens to voters in an election—voters enter the polling booth almost completely ignorant of the facts relevant to their decision, and they leave the voting booth still almost completely ignorant of those facts. No one appears in the voting booth and presents a lengthy account of the policy-relevant details over the course of several hours before the citizens cast their votes.

Factual details matter to normative judgments. The truth about justice cannot be summed up in a simple, self-evident rule that can be applied algorithmically to all cases. What justice requires in a given case depends on details of the situation. Individual cases often have factual details not anticipated by the legislature. This is why individual judgment is required, and that judgment must be exercised by someone who knows the details of the case.

Consider, for example, the laws concerning child pornography. In order to protect children from psychological harm and exploitation, the distribution of child pornography has been outlawed. Few would question the justice of this law *in general*. But now consider the following application.

In 2017, an enterprising prosecutor in Minnesota decided to use this law to charge a 14-year-old girl with felony distribution of child pornography, for sending a sexually explicit image *of herself* to a boy at her school.[16] The prosecutor's decision was in fact consistent with a literal reading of the child pornography statute (Minn. Stat. 617.247.3)—the statute prohibits transmission of sexually explicit images of minors; it

---

[15] Caplan (2007).
[16] Nelson (2018).

does not specify that the perpetrator of the offense must be someone other than the person depicted in the images, nor does it state that the perpetrator must be an adult. Nevertheless, this application of the law is absurd. Surely when the legislature chose to prohibit distribution of child pornography, they did not have in mind teenagers sending photos of themselves via snapchat. They simply did not anticipate that a prosecutor would apply the law in that way.

This case illustrates a robust phenomenon in human experience: When a human being or group of human beings is called upon to enunciate some general, practical rule, they cannot be expected to anticipate every application of that rule. For this reason, a rote application of a set of pre-given rules, without the exercise of moral judgment, cannot be expected to achieve justice as reliably as an application informed by common sense moral judgment, together with the actual facts of individual cases.

Fortunately, in the Minnesota sexting case, the charges were dismissed by the judge, in accord with a brief filed on the girl's behalf by the ACLU. However, if the judge had opted to simply follow the law as written, with no exercise of his own sense of justice, the teenage girl would have faced up to ten years in prison and $20,000 in fines, in addition to being forced to register as a sex offender in Minnesota. It was only an exercise of *judicial nullification* that spared her from having her life pointlessly ruined.[17]

10.5 Promises and Role Obligations

10.5.1 The Obligation to Fill a Role

Sometimes, when we voluntarily take on a socially defined role, we acquire an obligation to satisfy the expectations conventionally associated with that role.[18] For example, when a physician takes on a patient, the physician acquires an obligation to care for the patient's health, to warn the patient about potential problems the doctor knows of that may threaten the patient's health, and to volunteer advice about how to remain

---

[17] Keyser (2019).
[18] Hardimon (1994).

healthy. These are not obligations that individuals generally have toward each other, or even that doctors have toward people who are not their own patients. These obligations are acquired when one accepts the role of doctor for a particular patient.

Similarly, lawyers, judges, and jurors each have a socially defined role with certain associated expectations. Lawyers are expected to serve their clients' interests, judges to uphold the law, and jurors to judge the facts of a case. Perhaps, then, individuals who take on these roles have an obligation to do what is generally expected of them.

10.5.2 Implicit Contracts

Why would there be such an obligation? One possible reason is a kind of implicit contract. When a doctor takes on a new patient, we might say that the doctor and patient make an implicit agreement with each other. The terms of that agreement are determined by the general understanding in their society of how the doctor-patient relationship works. The doctor and patient can of course voluntarily modify that agreement, but in the absence of any explicit statements to the contrary, each can be understood as accepting their role as generally understood in their society. If the doctor fails to faithfully carry out his role, he will be breaching an implied agreement with his patient.

Perhaps a similar point applies to agents in the legal system: perhaps, when one takes on the job of lawyer, judge, or jury member, one accepts a kind of implicit agreement to act according to the prevalent norms associated with the role in one's society. If one fails to perform the role, one will be violating one's duties to the other agents with whom that agreement was made—particularly, one's client (if one is a lawyer), or the state (if one is a judge or juror).

This argument overlooks the moral limitations of agreements. Granted, it is in general possible, by making an agreement, to expand one's moral obligations. However, it is not in general possible, merely by making an agreement, to *eliminate* one's pre-existing duties *to people not involved in the agreement*. If one contracts with another individual to violate the rights of a third party, that contract is morally invalid—that is, one does not thereby become morally obligated to violate the third party's rights. Thus, consider this case:

Mafia Employee: You have been hired by the leader of the local crime syndicate to perform various odd jobs. Your duties, which you have voluntarily accepted, include making coffee, picking up the boss' laundry, and beating up people who refuse to pay protection money.

In this example, you may genuinely be obligated to make coffee and pick up the laundry, since this is part of the role you have voluntarily agreed to play and for which you are accepting payment.

In addition, you are contractually required to beat people who refuse to pay protection money. If you do not administer said beatings, you will be violating the terms of your contract, taking the boss' money under false pretenses, and generally being a bad mafia employee. Nevertheless, it is obviously morally impermissible to carry out such beatings. This illustrates the general point that one cannot become obligated to commit acts that would otherwise be unjust, merely by *agreeing* to commit them or *accepting a role* that requires committing them. Such agreements are simply invalid, and such roles immoral. Of course, the victims who are to be beaten could, in theory, render the beatings permissible by agreeing to be beaten; but a third party, such as the mafia boss, cannot render the beatings permissible by hiring someone to perform them or extracting a promise to perform them. One may be morally required to return the boss' money, but, whether or not one returns the money, one simply is not morally permitted to beat people whose only crime is failing to pay protection money.

All of this is directly relevant to the duties of agents in the legal system. The Primacy of Justice enjoins agents specifically from bringing about *unjust* outcomes. Bringing about injustice is in general morally impermissible. It therefore does not become permissible merely by one's *agreeing* to do it. Therefore, it does not matter whether judges, jurors, or lawyers may be construed as having implicitly agreed to carry out certain socially defined roles—*if* those roles require them to commit injustice, then these agents simply cannot ethically perform those roles. The roles would be immoral and the agreement to perform them invalid.

In the Mafia Employee case, one might perhaps be guilty of an ethical breach even if one refuses to carry out the beatings desired by the boss, since one will have broken a promise and accepted payment under false pretenses. (Again, this does not justify carrying out the beatings, since doing so would be a much more serious ethical breach.) To avoid all moral blame, therefore, one must refuse to accept the role at the start.

Similarly, a lawyer who refuses to pursue unjust outcomes desired by his client may be guilty of violating an implicit promise to his client and taking the client's money under false pretenses. Therefore, to avoid all moral blame, a lawyer should refuse to make such promises in the first place. A lawyer should, for example, disclose from the start his intention to pursue only what he considers to be just outcomes, and let the client choose whether to accept representation under these terms. Granted, this would typically result in a much smaller clientele for a lawyer; perhaps an ethical lawyer would be unable to run a successful practice at all. This fact is unfortunate, but it does not render it permissible to pursue unjust legal outcomes, any more than the threat of being fired by the mafia boss renders it permissible for the mafia employee to beat innocent people. If one can only survive in a particular profession by agreeing to perform serious injustices, then one must renounce that profession.

10.5.3 The Juror's Oath

Jury members in the American court system are often required, by the judge in a particular case, to swear an oath to apply the law as given to them by the judge. This oath explicitly rules out jury nullification. If one has taken such an oath, is it nevertheless permissible to nullify unjust laws? Is it permissible to take such an oath in the first place?

The answer to both questions is "yes". Granted, breaking promises is *normally* impermissible. However, it is almost universally accepted, among both ethicists and ordinary people, that there are conditions under which breaking a promise is permissible. There are at least three intuitive principles governing permissible promise-breaking:

1. It is normally permissible to break a promise when doing so is necessary to prevent something *much worse* from happening. For instance,

you may break a promise to have lunch with a friend, if doing so is necessary to prevent a neighbor from being kidnapped and held hostage by terrorists.
2. A coerced promise is not morally binding. That is, if you are forced to make a promise by an unjust threat directed against yourself or others, it is permissible to make the promise with no intention of keeping it, and it is permissible to later break the promise. Thus, if a criminal threatens to kidnap your neighbor unless you promise to pay the criminal $1000 at a later date, it is permissible to make that promise while having no intention of keeping it. It is then permissible to break the promise as soon as your neighbor is safe.
3. It is permissible to break a promise to a specific person, if doing so is necessary to prevent *that very person* from committing an unjust act. The promisee (the person to whom you made the promise) has no valid complaint in such a case, since it is their own threat of wrongful behavior that makes the breaking of the promise necessary. For instance, if I have promised to lend you my rifle this week-end (even if this promise was freely made), and you then inform me that you plan to use the rifle to commit a murder, I must break my promise to you. You would then have no valid complaint against me, since it was your own unjust threat that forced me to break the promise.

All three of these conditions apply to the juror's oath to apply the law, in a case where the law is unjust. First, breaking that oath will in general be necessary to prevent the defendant from suffering a serious unjust harm, such as being imprisoned for an action that was not wrong or being imprisoned for many more years than the defendant deserves for a wrongful act. This unjust harm is much worse than the "harm" that the state would suffer as a result of the juror's breaking his oath—this putative harm being that the state would be unable to unjustly punish someone that it wanted to punish. This is comparable to the "harm" suffered by the terrorists in the example under principle (1) above, of being prevented from kidnapping someone they wanted to kidnap. This is not a genuine harm at all; indeed, the state might be *benefitted* by an acquittal, since it will not have to bear the expense of holding the defendant in prison.

Second, in the case of a trial under an unjust law, potential jurors must take the oath to apply the law in order to be seated on the jury. If one refuses to take the oath, one will be excluded from the jury. In the vast majority of cases, the defendant will then be convicted (conviction rates in trials in the U.S. are close to 90%).[19] That is to say that the state is threatening to unjustly, coercively harm the defendant *unless* you take this oath. If you wish to prevent unjust harm to the defendant, then, you are effectively coerced into taking the oath. This makes the juror's oath an invalid promise. It is entirely permissible to make this promise while having no intention of keeping it, and then to break it once one is seated on the jury. This is comparable to making a false promise in order to prevent a criminal from kidnapping your neighbor.

Third, when a jury nullifies an unjust law, the state, the party to whom the jurors made their promise, has no valid complaint about the jury's violating its oath, because it was the state's unjust threat that made it necessary both to make the promise and to break it. For the state to complain about the jury's behavior would be comparable to your friend in the above example complaining about being unable to murder people because you broke your promise to lend him your rifle.

10.6 Faith in the System

10.6.1 The Appeal to the System

Some lawyers, when confronted about the morality of defending heinous criminals, appeal to an idealistic faith in the system. Some believe the system is so well-designed that, as long as all agents involved play their roles faithfully, one should assume that justice will be done.[20] Granted, there are occasional miscarriages of justice, but that is inevitable in any system, and our adversarial legal system is the most reliable practicable system devised thus far. The best way of minimizing miscarriages of justice is simply for all parties to perform their assigned roles, so that the system can function as intended. If lawyers focus on pursuing their clients' inter-

---

[19] U.S. Department of Justice statistics show a 94% conviction rate in federal prosecutions in the U.S. (ABC News (2010)). Earlier data show a conviction rate of between 85 and 90% for state courts (Ramseyer et al. 2008, p. 17)

[20] Dershowitz (2013); Joy (2004, p. 1246n35).

ests, judges on interpreting and applying the law, and jurors on assessing the descriptive facts, then justice will emerge from all these agents' activities.

This defense turns crucially on the empirical assumption that the system is most reliable at achieving justice when all parties execute their roles, and that for a judge, juror, or lawyer to *directly* aim at justice will make it *less* likely for justice to be achieved. If true, this would indeed show that these agents should not directly aim at justice.

10.6.2 Increasing the Odds of Unjust Outcomes

That assumption, however, is extremely implausible on its face, and it is difficult to find any plausible reasons for believing it. To begin with, note that in most situations, a desired outcome is more likely to occur if someone tries to make it occur than if no one tries to make it occur. For instance, if I want to be wealthy, then I need to deliberately pursue money. If I want to be healthy, then I ought to learn about health and intentionally make health-promoting choices. If I want my students to learn in my classes, then I should think about how students learn and consciously aim at making that learning occur. And so on.

Admittedly, this is only an (extremely useful) rule of thumb. There *can* be cases in which expressly aiming at a particular goal is less effective in attaining it than aiming at something else. But we would need good reasons for believing that agents in the legal system are regularly in such unusual cases.

Take the case of a defense lawyer who is convinced that his client is guilty of serious crimes, which deserve the punishment prescribed by law. This could be because the client has confessed to the lawyer, or simply because the lawyer has reviewed the prosecution's evidence, which is extremely compelling. For simplicity, assume that there is to be a jury trial, and that the only issue is whether the defendant will be convicted or acquitted (leave aside sentencing issues). The client, despite his guilt, wishes to plead not guilty, in the hopes of bamboozling a jury and getting away with his crime. Now, if the lawyer tries his best to get the defendant acquitted, does this make it *more* likely or *less* likely that justice will be done?

The answer is "less likely". The reason is as follows:

1. Trying to get the client acquitted makes it more likely that the client will be acquitted.
2. Justice requires the client to be convicted.
3. Therefore, trying to get the client acquitted makes it less likely that justice will be done.

Step 3 logically follows from 1 and 2. Premise 2 is true by hypothesis, since the client is guilty of punishment-worthy crimes. And premise 1 must be true if there is any point to the client's hiring this lawyer. If the lawyer's efforts either have no effect on the client's chances or actually somehow *worsen* the client's chances, then the lawyer is merely wasting the client's money and should resign due to his own incompetence.

Notice that I am not claiming that most lawyers will in fact succeed if they try to get a guilty client acquitted. Of course, most will fail. What I am claiming is that most lawyers will *increase the probability* that such a client will be acquitted, if they try to get that client acquitted.

How do they do this? If the evidence of guilt is compelling, won't the jury inevitably be persuaded by the prosecution's expert presentation of that evidence, regardless of the defense lawyer's efforts?

Perhaps, but not necessarily. A defense lawyer has many options that have some non-negligible chance of misleading the jury. The Supreme Court has explicitly countenanced some methods of deception by defense lawyers:

> [D]efense counsel has no [...] obligation to ascertain or present the truth. [...] He must be and is interested in preventing the conviction of the innocent, but, absent a voluntary plea of guilty, we also insist that he defend his client whether he is innocent or guilty. The State has the obligation to present the evidence. Defense counsel need present nothing, even if he knows what the truth is. He need not furnish any witnesses to the police, or reveal any confidences of his client, or furnish any other information to help the prosecution's case. If he can confuse a witness, even a truthful one, or make him appear at a disadvantage, unsure or indecisive, that will be his normal course.[21]

---

[21] *United States v. Wade*, 388 U.S. 218 (1967), at pp. 256–7.

Beyond this, a defense attorney may attempt, during the jury selection process, to exclude jurors who are likely to understand the evidence, and to include jurors who are biased in favor of the defendant. During the course of the trial, she may make rhetorical appeals, attempt to play on jurors' emotions, sow confusion, and give fallacious arguments. She may even sow suspicion that someone else, whom she actually knows to be innocent, may have committed the crime, in order to deflect suspicion from her client.[22] All of these are common methods of "zealous advocacy", as legal theorists call it, on the part of defense attorneys.

Of course, a jury may see through all such subterfuges, and one hopes that most would do so. But some will not—which is why such methods would be tried in the first place. It is very difficult to see how such methods could be thought to increase the reliability of the system. Notice that all of these techniques can be used to defend the guilty as well as the innocent. It is thus difficult to see how a lawyer's playing her assigned role of zealous advocate, as currently understood in the legal profession, can be thought to result in a highly reliable system, compared to the possible situation in which lawyers refuse to make such efforts at deception.

10.6.3 Prosecutors Versus Defense Attorneys

The point I have just made is highly controversial in the legal profession. But the *analogous* point applied to *prosecuting* attorneys is an accepted part of conventional legal ethics: namely, that a prosecutor should aim at justice, not simply at winning. (Granted, most prosecutors *in fact* aim at winning, but the official norm is that prosecutors *should* aim at justice.) In particular, it is unethical for a prosecutor to attempt to secure a conviction for a defendant whom the prosecutor believes to be innocent.[23] That point is uncontroversial.

---

[22] As occurred in the 1840 murder trial of Benjamin Courvoisier. During the trial, the defendant confessed to his lawyer. The lawyer informed the judge's assistant of this; the assistant instructed the lawyer to do his best to defend his client nevertheless. The lawyer carried out this charge by painting a truthful witness as a liar and deflecting suspicion onto a woman he knew to be innocent (Asimow and Weisberg 2006).

[23] American Bar Association (1983, rule 3.8).

Why is this? Why do we not argue that the system is so reliable that if both sides simply play the role of zealous advocates—one for conviction and one for acquittal—then the truth will surely win out? And that if the defendant is convicted, then this will simply show that the defendant was almost certainly guilty after all?

The answer, I take it, is that when it comes to the behavior of prosecutors, we see the obvious: attempting to bring about injustice increases the chances that injustice will occur. It is utterly implausible to hold that the system is more reliable at securing justice when prosecutors ignore the truth, ignore justice, and focus solely on winning—as compared to a situation in which prosecutors only give arguments they believe to be correct and pursue outcomes they believe to be just.

Why the asymmetry between the conventional ethics for prosecuting attorneys and the conventional ethics for defense attorneys?

One might be tempted to claim that the asymmetry is due to the fact that wrongful convictions are *more unjust* than wrongful acquittals—that is, it is morally worse to punish an innocent person than to fail to punish a guilty person. But this does not explain what needs to be explained, because this point is already taken into account when we set the standard of proof for criminal cases. A criminal conviction requires a certain weight of evidence—conventionally known as "proof beyond a reasonable doubt"—which reflects the fact that it is better to allow several guilty people to go free than to convict one innocent person. So, taking that point into account, we can compare two situations:

The Obviously Guilty Client: A defense attorney believes that the evidence against his client adequately proves the client's guilt. (Assume also that the crime deserves the legally prescribed punishment.) The attorney thus believes, justifiedly and correctly, that the jury would convict as long as they understood the evidence and applied the correct standard of proof. Nevertheless, the attorney tries to secure an acquittal by confusing and misleading the jury.

The Plausibly Innocent Suspect: A prosecuting attorney believes that the evidence against a suspect does *not* adequately prove the suspect's guilt. The prosecutor thus believes, justifiedly and correctly, that the jury would acquit as long as they understood the evidence and applied the correct standard of proof. (The evidence in this case falls short of the correct evidentiary threshold by the same margin as it exceeds the threshold in the previous case.) Nevertheless, the prosecutor tries to secure a conviction by confusing and misleading the jury.

These cases are parallel. One cannot say that there is an asymmetry because convicting the innocent is worse than acquitting the guilty, because that point has already been fully taken into account when we set the standard of proof. In both cases, the lawyers are, by stipulation, making judgments using the correct standard of proof, the standard that correctly balances the risk of convicting the innocent against the harm of acquitting the guilty. There is the same degree of expected injustice in both cases. In the first case, the defense lawyer judges (correctly and justifiedly) that the correct standard is clearly *met*; in the latter, the prosecuting lawyer judges (correctly and justifiedly) that it is clearly *not* met.

I take it that most observers would find the prosecutor's behavior in The Plausibly Innocent Suspect case to be unethical, indeed, clearly and seriously so. By the same token, we should find the defense lawyer's behavior in The Obviously Guilty Client case to be seriously unethical. If the prosecutor cannot appeal to faith in the system to justify his efforts at misleading the jury, the defense attorney cannot similarly appeal to faith in the system. There is no reason why only prosecutorial efforts at deception should undermine the system's reliability, yet defense efforts be innocuous. If both undermine the system's reliability, then both should be deemed unethical; if neither do, then both should be deemed acceptable.

10.6.4 Judge and Jury

The argument for judges and juries is relatively straightforward. If a defendant is prosecuted under an unjust law, then, trivially, the odds of an unjust outcome occurring are increased if the jury votes for conviction. Indeed, this guarantees the unjust outcome. Similarly, if a judge assigns an unjust sentence to a defendant, this guarantees an unjust outcome. Neither the judge nor the jury can appeal to faith in the system, hoping that somehow the system will avoid the unjust outcome if only they play their assigned roles.

More precisely, the judge and jury could entertain this hope only by hoping that they themselves are mistaken about what justice requires—the jury might hope, for instance, that the apparently unjust law is really just, and the judge that the apparently unjust sentence is somehow really just. But, at least in many cases, the judge or jury would have no rational basis for any such hope. For example, there is no rational reason for thinking that it might be just to imprison someone for 60 years for selling $40 worth of cocaine. Thus, there is, at least in many cases, no reason to think that if one simply plays one's assigned role, then justice will be done.

10.6.5 Universalization

Perhaps the argument is not that, in the individual case, following one's assigned role increases the chances of a just outcome, but that if agents in the system *in general* follow their assigned roles, then just outcomes will in general occur more frequently than they will if agents directly aim at justice. Therefore, perhaps, each individual agent should follow their assigned role.

This argument has two main problems: it has a false moral premise and a false factual premise. The false moral premise is that one ought to make one's decisions based on the results that would occur if everyone followed some universal practice. This typically is not how one should make decisions. For instance, in choosing a career path, one should not make one's choice based upon what would occur if everyone chose the same career path. In choosing a restaurant at which to dine, one should not make one's choice based upon what would occur if everyone chose the same restaurant. One should not do these things because one knows that everyone will not in fact take the same career path or dine at the same restaurant, regardless of what one does. Similarly, when an individual agent in a legal case chooses to pursue justice, this does not in fact alter the behavior of all other agents across the system. The only significant effect that is likely to occur is that that particular case will have a more just outcome.

The false factual premise is that if agents *in general* follow their non-justice-pursuing roles, justice will be better achieved overall than if they pursue justice. There is no reason to believe this. The reasoning given above for the individual case can be generalized. On any given occasion, if a judge, juror, or lawyer attempts to bring about an unjust outcome, this will normally make it more likely that an unjust outcome will occur; therefore, if on many occasions judges, jurors, or lawyers try to bring about unjust outcomes, this will probably result in more unjust outcomes. If some behavior worsens expected outcomes in each case, then universalizing that behavior does not generally make the aggregate outcome better. If everyone in the legal system pursues justice in every case, then the most likely outcome is simply that much more justice will be done overall.

10.7 What Is the Role of a Jury?

Thus far, I have been granting for the sake of argument the conception of a jury's socially defined role as that of a morally neutral fact-finder, such that nullification of an unjust law would be a violation of the jury's role. I have argued that, even if this is the case, violation of the role is fully justified in the service of justice.

That conception of the jury's role is, however, incorrect. There is no good reason for claiming that a jury's role is limited to that of a morally neutral fact-finder. This claim has its basis in a false ideology, not in actual law, convention, or morality. In this section, I review the arguments that the jury's legally proper role includes the nullification of unjust laws and the prevention of unjust punishments. Accordingly, the thesis of the Primacy of Justice is fully consonant with the true role obligations of jurors. It is the opponents of nullification who are demanding that jurors abandon their role obligations.

10.7.1 Determining the Jury's Role

What do we mean when we ask "What is the role of a jury?" The question is not simply a request for a description of the actual behavior patterns of typical juries. I take it, rather, that the question of import is what is the *legally proper* role of a jury. And that amounts to something like this: what mode of behavior on the part of a jury is most consonant with the purposes for which jury trials were created or given a place of prominence in our legal system, and with the manner in which juries were intended and expected to operate?

In the U.S., the right to trial by jury is guaranteed both by the federal Constitution and by every state constitution. The U.S. Constitution grants this right three times: first in Article III, section 2 ("The Trial of all Crimes, except in Cases of Impeachment, shall be by Jury…"), then again in the Sixth Amendment ("In all criminal prosecutions, the accused shall enjoy the right to a speedy and public trial, by an impartial jury of the State and district wherein the crime shall have been committed …"), and finally in the Seventh Amendment ("In Suits at common law, where the value in controversy shall exceed twenty dollars, the right of trial by jury shall be preserved…"). What is the underlying rationale for guaranteeing such a right?

On this question, at least three sorts of evidence are of import. One sort of evidence consists of statements made by the nation's founders concerning jury trials. At the time of the founding, the right to trial by jury was widely and enthusiastically embraced as a crucial safeguard to liberty. We may best understand the prevailing attitudes by examining what was said by prominent figures at the time.

Second, we may examine the design of the system—especially what powers juries were as a matter of fact given and what powers other agents in the system were and were not given—and we may ask what interpretation of the jury's role makes sense of this design. All else being equal, we should assume that the system is designed in such a way as to facilitate the jury's performance of its proper role, and that it is not designed with pointless impediments to that role.

Finally, we may recruit reasonable judgments of morality and practicality. We should begin with the assumption that the legally proper role of the jury is one that generally makes sense as a way of serving some worthy aim. Other things being equal, we should not ascribe to the jury a role that it would be irrational or immoral to desire them to perform. Nor should we ascribe them a role for which juries are obviously ill-suited. Once we describe the jury's role, it should be clear why one might plausibly believe that a *jury* is needed, or at least is particularly useful, for the performance of that role, rather than a judge or other government official.

As we shall presently see, all of these forms of evidence converge on the conclusion that the legal role of a jury in a criminal trial is to serve as a check against oppressive government by evaluating the justice of the punishment that the state seeks to impose.

10.7.2 Framers' Intent

The historical record leaves no serious doubt that the right of trial by jury was understood at the time of the founding as serving to protect the individual from oppression by the government, and that jury nullification was part of the mechanism of this protection. Cases of jury nullification were well-known at the time and well-regarded by the former colonists.[24] This included the famous Zenger case discussed in §1.1 above, in which a jury, in open defiance of the instructions of the judge, refused to convict a journalist for publishing spirited attacks on the governor of New York.

Before the U.S. Constitution was ratified, three key founders—Alexander Hamilton, James Madison, and John Jay—wrote the *Federalist Papers* for the purpose of explaining and defending the proposed Constitution. This series of essays is one of the most important documents for understanding the meaning and purposes of the Constitution. In *Federalist* 83, Alexander Hamilton described prevailing attitudes toward the institution of trial by jury thus:

---

[24] Sauer (1995, pp. 1256–8).

The friends and adversaries of the plan of the convention, if they agree in nothing else, concur at least in the value they set upon the trial by jury; or if there is any difference between them it consists in this: the former regard it as a valuable safeguard to liberty; the latter represent it as the very palladium of free government. [...] [I]t would be altogether superfluous to examine [...] how much more merit it may be entitled to, as a defense against the oppressions of an hereditary monarch, than as a barrier to the tyranny of popular magistrates in a popular government.[25]

This leaves no doubt but that the purpose of trial by jury was understood as one of protecting citizens from tyranny, including the tyranny of judges in a democratic society ("popular magistrates"). It is difficult to see how jury trials could be understood to serve this function if the jury's role were one of deferring to the state and applying the law as given to them by the judge.

Another key American founder, John Adams (the nation's first Vice-President and second President), had this to say about the situation of a juror who disagrees with a judge about the principles of the Constitution:

> It is not only his right, but his duty ... to find the verdict according to his own best understanding, judgment, and conscience, though in direct opposition to the direction of the court.[26]

Thomas Jefferson, author of the Declaration of Independence and the third U.S. President, in explaining his reservations about the French Revolution, commented thus:

> Another apprehension is that a majority cannot be induced to adopt the trial by jury; and I consider that as the only anchor, ever yet imagined by man, by which a government can be held to the principles of its constitution.[27]

---

[25] Hamilton, Madison, and Jay (1952).
[26] Adams (1856, p. 255). Adams is discussing a case in which the judge gives instructions that conflict with the fundamental principles of the Constitution.
[27] Jefferson (1789, p. 496).

Again, it is very difficult to see how the trial by jury could possibly serve this function if jurors simply applied the law according to the dictates of a judge or other government official.

Perhaps the most striking indication of the jury's intended role comes from the case of *Georgia v. Brailsford*, decided in 1794.[28] That case was the only jury trial ever held by the U.S. Supreme Court. John Jay—the first Chief Justice of the Supreme Court and one of the three authors of the *Federalist Papers*—presided. If anyone should have understood the proper role of the jury under the Constitution, it would be Jay. Before the jury retired to deliberate, the Chief Justice instructed them as follows:

> It may not be amiss, here, Gentlemen, to remind you of the good old rule that on questions of fact, it is the province of the jury; on questions of law it is the province of the court to decide. But it must be observed that by the same law which recognizes this reasonable distribution of jurisdiction, *you have nevertheless a right* to take upon yourselves to judge of both, and *to determine the law* as well as the fact in controversy. On this and on every other occasion, however, we have no doubt you will pay that respect which is due to the opinion of the court: for, as on the one hand, it is presumed, that juries are the best judges of facts, it is, on the other hand, presumable that the court is the best judge of law. But still *both objects are lawfully, within your power of decision*. [...] Go then, Gentlemen, [...] and do on this as you ought to do on every occasion, equal and impartial justice.[29]

This makes explicit that the jury had the right to decide the law in the interests of justice.

10.7.3 Case Law

The subsequent case law concerning jury nullification is schizophrenic. On the one hand, trial judges often actively discourage jury nullification, going so far as to require jurors to promise not to exercise the

---

[28] 3 U.S. (3 Dall.) 1 (1794).
[29] 3 U.S. (3 Dall.) 1 (1794), at pp. 4–5; emphasis added.

power—and appellate courts have allowed this.[30] On the other hand, however, there is no question but that juries have the legal power to nullify the law. This has been affirmed many times in the history of American jurisprudence. The following quotations are all from judicial opinions in American court cases:

> If the jury feels that the law under which the defendant is accused is unjust, or that exigent circumstances justified the actions of the accused, or for any reason which appeals to their logic or passion, the jury has the power to acquit, and the courts must abide by that decision. (*U.S. v. Moylan*)[31]

> The judge cannot direct a verdict it is true, and the jury has the power to bring in a verdict in the teeth of both law and facts. (*Horning v. District of Columbia*)[32]

> By acquitting Zenger, the jury fulfilled its role as protector against unjust laws or their unfair application. In the century following the Zenger case, it was generally recognized in American jurisprudence that the jury, agent of the sovereign people, had a right to acquit those whom it felt it unjust to call criminal. (*Everett v. U.S.*)[33]

> In criminal cases, a jury is entitled to acquit the defendant because it has no sympathy for the government's position. (*U.S. v. Wilson*)[34]

> A right to jury trial is granted to criminal defendants in order to prevent oppression by the Government. Those who wrote our constitutions knew from history and experience that it was necessary to protect against unfounded criminal charges brought to eliminate enemies and against judges too responsive to the voice of higher authority. (*Duncan v. Louisiana*)[35]

---

[30] *United States v. Thomas*, 116 F.3d 606 (1997); *People v. Smith*, 694 N.E.2d 681 (1998).
[31] Judge Simon E. Sobeloff, *United States v. Moylan*, 417 F.2d 1002 (4th Cir. 1969), at 1006.
[32] Justice Oliver Wendell Holmes, *Horning v. District of Columbia*, 254 U.S. 135 (Supreme Court, 1920) at 138.
[33] Judge James Skelly Wright, dissenting in *Everett v. United States*, 336 F.2d 979 (D.C. Cir. 1964) at 986.
[34] Judge Gilbert Merritt, *United States v. Wilson*, 629 F.2d 439 (6th Cir. 1980) at 443.
[35] Justice Byron White, *Duncan v. Louisiana*, 391 U.S. 145 (Supreme Court, 1968) at 155–6.

The pages of history shine on instances of the jury's exercise of its prerogative to disregard uncontradicted evidence and instructions of the judge. (*U.S. v. Dougherty*)[36]

The American petit jury is not a mere factfinder. From the time the right to trial by jury was embedded in the Constitution [...], it has been expected to bring to court much of the wisdom and consensus of the local community. (*U.S. v. Polizzi*)[37]

[The right of jury trial] is no mere procedural formality, but a fundamental reservation of power in our constitutional structure. Just as suffrage ensures the people's ultimate control in the legislative and executive branches, jury trial is meant to ensure their control in the judiciary. (*Blakely v. Washington*)[38]

The continued prohibition on directed verdicts of guilt, on the set aside of not guilty verdicts, and on the use of special interrogatories in criminal cases, as well as the allowance of inconsistent verdicts, can only be understood as arising from respect for the jury's power to disregard the law and facts of a case in order to serve justice. [...] Indeed, to deny a defendant the possibility of jury nullification would be to defeat the central purpose of the jury system. (*United States v. Datcher*)[39]

The last quotation above cites several features of the legal system that cohere with the doctrine of jury nullification. All of the following are uncontroversial observations about American jurisprudence:

1. The judge in a jury trial has the legal power to unilaterally declare the defendant *not guilty*, if the judge finds the prosecution's case so weak that no reasonable jury could be persuaded. The judge does *not*,

---

[36] Judge Harold Leventhal, *United States v. Dougherty*, 473 F.2d 1113 (D.C. Cir., 1972), at 1130. Leventhal goes on to argue that it is permissible for a judge to verbally discourage jury nullification, because this has the desirable effect that the jury will only nullify when they feel very strongly about the issue.
[37] Judge Jack Weinstein, *United States v. Polizzi*, 549 F. Supp. 2d 308 (E.D.N.Y 2008) at 322 (finding that defendant Polizzi had the right to have the jury informed of the severe mandatory minimum sentence he would face upon conviction).
[38] Justice Antonin Scalia, *Blakely v. Washington*, 542 U.S. 296 (Supreme Court, 2004) at 305–6 (concerning the need for all sentencing factors to be proved to the jury).
[39] Judge Thomas A. Wiseman, *United States v. Datcher*, 830 F. Supp. 411 (M.D. Tenn. 1993) at 414–15 (granting defense permission to argue the issue of excessive punishment to the jury).

however, have the authority to declare the defendant *guilty*, regardless of how clear the prosecution's case may be.
2. Similarly, if a jury's verdict of *guilt* is unreasonable in light of the evidence presented in court, a judge may set the verdict aside; but judges may never set aside a jury's *acquittal*, however unreasonable it may be on the facts presented.
3. The jury may only be asked to give a general verdict of guilt or innocence; the judge may not require the jury to answer specific factual questions about the case from which the judge could then infer whether the defendant violated the law. Nor may the judge require the jury to explain the basis for their verdict.
4. The jury is permitted to give logically inconsistent verdicts, such as convicting a defendant of one crime but acquitting of a second crime, where commission of the first logically entails commission of the second. Such inconsistency does not enable the judge to set aside the jury's decision.

These procedural rules, as Judge Wiseman noted in *U.S. v. Datcher*, make no sense if the jury's only role is to serve as a morally neutral factfinder, applying the law as given to them by the judge. For example, if the jury is only a factfinder, why shouldn't the judge simply ask them a series of factual questions, and then decide himself whether the defendant is to be convicted based on the answers? The only rationale that makes sense of the above rules is that the jury is meant to be able to overrule the law in the interests of justice.

10.7.4 Moral and Practical Considerations

Finally, we should ask why a jury is needed in the system at all. Why not have decisions made entirely by judges, as in the inquisitorial systems of France and Germany?

The "neutral fact-finder" theory has no plausible answer to this. There is no obvious reason to think that a group of twelve ordinary individuals from the community would be the most reliable agent for weighing the evidence presented in a criminal trial and determining what in fact took place. The jurors will generally have no prior experience with making such judgments, no relevant training, and no background knowledge about the type of crime at issue. They may be prone to fallacies, confusions, and oversights. An experienced judge, having seen many cases and perhaps even received training in how to properly evaluate the types of evidence that arise in court cases, is much more likely to evaluate the evidence correctly. Judges are also, on average, significantly more intelligent and educated than the average person. How, then, could juries be the best judges of the facts?

It is, of course, no more plausible to think that juries would show superior performance in the task of understanding the content of the statutes written by the legislature. The superior education, intelligence, and experience of professional judges would make them better at that task as well.

What function is there, then, that (i) plausibly serves some worthy goal, (ii) may plausibly be carried out by a jury, and (iii) could *not* plausibly be carried out equally well or better by a judge or other government official?

There is one obvious answer. The jury's special province is not legal or factual judgment, but *moral* judgment. The jury is there to safeguard the values of the community, to ensure that political elites who may have become corrupt or lost touch with those values do not oppress the people through unjust laws and punishments. This function cannot be entrusted to judges, for reasons discussed earlier (§7.5). Judges belong to the same class of political elites against whom the framers of the Constitution sought to protect the people. Judges are either elected like politicians or appointed *by* politicians, and they identify with the state far more than with the hapless individuals who appear before the courts as defendants. In the event that the government becomes oppressive, government judges cannot be depended upon to stand against this oppression; they are far more likely to instinctively attempt to rationalize the perspective of the state (see §12.3). That is why the ultimate authority to decide who may be legally punished was rested in the hands of ordinary, private individuals.

References

ABC News. 2010, August 4. Feds' Conviction Rate Bad Sign for Blago. http://abclocal.go.com/wls/story?section=news/local&id=7593302. Accessed 3 Oct 2012.

Adams, John. [1856] 1971. *The Works of John Adams, Second President of the United States*. New York: AMS Press.

American Bar Association. 1983. *Model Rules of Professional Conduct*. Text available at https://www.americanbar.org/groups/professional_responsibility/publications/model_rules_of_professional_conduct/model_rules_of_professional_conduct_table_of_contents/. Accessed 28 June 2020.

Asimow, Michael R. and Richard H. Weisberg. 2006. When the Lawyer Knows the Client Is Guilty: David Mellinkoff's 'The Conscience of a Lawyer', Legal Ethics, Literature, and Popular Culture", UCLA School of Law Research Paper No. 06-44; Cardozo Legal Studies Research Paper No. 181. http://ssrn.com/abstract=948291. Accessed 30 June 2020.

Barnett, Randy E. 1988. Reconceiving the Ninth Amendment. *Cornell Law Review* 74: 1–42.

Berry, Mindy, ZeeAnn Mason, Scott Stephenson, and Annie Hsiao. 2009. *The American Revolution: Who Cares?* Philadelphia: American Revolution Center.

Bolt, Robert. 1990. *A Man for All Seasons*. New York: Random House.

Bork, Robert H. 1999, June/July. Thomas More for Our Season, *First Things: A Monthly Journal of Religion & Public Life* 94: 17–21.

Caplan, Bryan. 2007. *The Myth of the Rational Voter*. Princeton: Princeton University Press.

Crispo, Lawrence W., Jill M. Slansky, and Geanene M. Yriarte. 1997. Jury Nullification: Law Versus Anarchy. *Loyola of Los Angeles Law Review* 31: 1–61.

D'Amato, Anthony and Edward J. Eberle. 2010. Three Models of Legal Ethics. Faculty Working Papers, paper 73. Available at http://scholarlycommons.law.northwestern.edu/facultyworkingpapers/73/. Accessed 2 Feb 2014.

Hamilton, Alexander, James Madison, and John Jay. 1952. *The Federalist* in *Great Books of the Western World*, ed. Robert Maynard Hutchins, vol. 43. Chicago: Encyclopaedia Britannica. Originally Published 1787–1788.

Hardimon, Michael O. 1994. Role Obligations. *Journal of Philosophy* 91: 333–363.

Jefferson, Thomas. 1789. Letter to Thomas Paine Dated July 11, 1789. Reproduced on pp. 494–6 in *Memoirs, Correspondence, and Private Papers of Thomas Jefferson, Late President of the United States*, Vol. 2, Edited by Thomas

Jefferson Randolph. London: Henry Colburn and Richard Bentley, 1829. Available at https://archive.org/details/memoirscorrespon02jeff/ Accessed 30 June 2020.

Joy, Peter A. 2004. Teaching Ethics in the Criminal Law Course. *Saint Louis University Law Journal* 48: 1239–1248.

Joyce, Richard. 2001. *The Myth of Morality*. Cambridge: Cambridge University Press.

Keyser, Chris. 2019, January 11. What Minnesota Parents Need to Know About State Sexting Laws. Keyser Law Blog. https://www.keyserdefense.com/what-minnesota-parents-need-to-know-about-state-sexting-laws/. Accessed 8/10/2019.

Leipold, Andrew D. 1996. Rethinking Jury Nullification. *Virginia Law Review* 82: 253–324.

Mackie, John L. 1977. *Ethics: Inventing Right and Wrong*. New York: Penguin.

Nelson, Teresa. 2018, January 5. Minnesota Prosecutor Charges Sexting Teenage Girl with Child Pornography. ACLU Blog. https://www.aclu.org/blog/juvenile-justice/minnesota-prosecutor-charges-sexting-teenage-girl-child-pornography. Accessed 10 Oct 2019.

Ramseyer, J. Mark, Eric B. Rasmusen, and Manu Raghav. 2008. Convictions Versus Conviction Rates: The Prosecutor's Choice. Harvard Law and Economics Discussion Paper No. 611, http://papers.ssrn.com/sol3/papers.cfm?abstract_id=1108813. Accessed 3 Oct 2012.

Rozansky, Michael. 2014, September 17. Americans Know Surprisingly Little About Their Government, Survey Finds. Annenberg Public Policy Center. http://www.annenbergpublicpolicycenter.org/americans-know-surprisingly-little-about-their-government-survey-finds/. Accessed 15 Nov 2018.

Sauer, Kristen. 1995. Informed Conviction: Instructing the Jury About Mandatory Sentencing Consequences. *Columbia Law Review* 95: 1232–1272.

Sinnott-Armstrong, Walter. 1996. Moral Skepticism and Justification. In *Moral Knowledge? New Readings in Moral Epistemology*, ed. Walter Sinnott-Armstrong and Mark Timmons, 3–48. Oxford: Oxford University Press.

Surowiecki, James. 2005. *The Wisdom of Crowds*. New York: Doubleday.

Surprenant, Chris W., and Jason Brennan. 2020. *Injustice for All: How Financial Incentives Corrupted and Can Fix the US Criminal Justice System*. New York: Routledge.

11

The Rule of Law

11.1 The Appeal to the Rule of Law

Many of those involved in the legal system, particularly those employed by the state, believe that one must in general uphold the law, even in particular cases where the law appears to one to be unjust, or one even *knows* that the law is unjust. In support of this, one often hears grand appeals to the principle of "the Rule of Law".[1] This sonorous phrase gives the impression of invoking a value of great import, perhaps important enough to outweigh the occasional serious injustice. But what exactly is the principle of the Rule of Law, and why is it important?

Perhaps the principle is simply that one ought in general to obey the law. This principle, however, would generate no objection to my thesis of the Primacy of Justice. For individuals in the legal system can typically prioritize justice, in precisely the manner that I have advocated, without themselves violating any laws (see §10.1). For instance, juries may vote their conscience, judges may interpret laws in accordance with moral principles, and lawyers may refuse clients who take immoral positions, all

---

[1] *People v. Williams*, 106 Cal.Rptr.2d 295 at p. 311; Bissell (1997).

without any of these individuals violating any laws. The Principle of the Rule of Law, therefore, must be something stronger than the principle that one ought not to violate the law.

What proponents of "the Rule of Law" seem to have in mind is something more like this: legal outcomes should be determined solely by the pre-existing, written law, and should not be dependent on judgments that might vary from one person to another. The problem with jury nullification is that it makes the outcome of a trial dependent on the moral judgments of the jury, which are not predictable based on any written principles and may vary from one jury to another. One jury may consider drug possession a punishment-worthy offense, while another considers it a blameless exercise of liberty; hence, two defendants guilty of violating the same law may receive drastically different treatments, depending upon which jury they happen to draw.

By the same token, judicial decisions that are based on the judge's own sense of morality or justice suffer the problem of not being predictable based on the written law, and of potentially differing from the judgments that would be made by other judges.

Why is this important? Some writers warn that abandoning the Rule of Law may set a dangerous precedent, leading to "anarchy". Some simply value predictability and uniformity in a legal system. Finally, one might worry that competing factions in our society with differing values can only peacefully cooperate if everyone can agree upon a norm of following the written rules. We shall examine these concerns in turn.

11.2 Anarchic Precedents

11.2.1 Warnings of Anarchy

In his essay on jury nullification, the famous conservative judge Robert Bork openly worried about our society's allegedly excessive regard for individual conscience, warning in the end that liberty of conscience may bring "religious, moral, and legal anarchy".[2] Many others have similarly

---

[2] Bork (1999, p. 21).

drawn associations between jury nullification and anarchy.[3] Similar concerns could presumably be raised, with comparable plausibility, about the prospect of *judicial* nullification, that is, of judges disregarding the law in the interests of justice.

Those who invoke "anarchy" generally do so vaguely and without elaboration, leaving their objection open to interpretation. The most literal reading of the concern is that the government will collapse as a result of judge and jury nullification. Because this seems hyperbolic, it may be that these authors have something less drastic in mind, perhaps a general state of social unrest and disrespect for the law. My most charitable interpretation is that these authors are concerned that jury nullification may lead to a more general disregard for the law, as members of society imitate the attitudes of judges and jurors, and that this disregard for law will spread from the unjust laws to affect even the just laws. Thus, there may in the end be more rights violations in society as a whole.

This concern rests on two plausible, broad generalizations about human nature: first, that human beings have a strong tendency to imitate one another, and thus ideas and behavior patterns can sometimes spread across a society once they have been initiated by a few individuals. Second, that human beings often rely upon simplistic conceptions of one another's ideas and behaviors, such that they may fail to distinguish the principle "disregard unjust laws" from the principle "disregard all laws".

Both of those observations have considerable truth to them. Nevertheless, I shall presently explain why I find this argument on the whole unpersuasive.

11.2.2 Existing Precedents

Recall that our primary question is a question of *individual ethics*, a question of what an individual judge or jury member ought to do in a case in which that individual finds the law he is asked to uphold unjust. Our question is not a social policy question—for instance, whether there ought to be some general policy whereby all judges instruct juries about nullification—as interesting as such questions may be. Bearing this in

---
[3] Sobeloff (1969, p. 1009); Leventhal (1972, pp. 1133, 1137); Crispo et al. (1997, pp. 39, 41); Biskupic (1999), quoting Colorado circuit Judge Frederic B. Rodgers.

mind, the argument for the Primacy of Law must be that, if an individual decides to prioritize justice over the law, then *that individual's* behavior carries a risk of setting a precedent that would undermine obedience to the law more generally.

But this concern is extremely implausible in view of the existing precedents. Many individuals have disregarded the law on many occasions throughout the nation's history. This includes many juries, in addition, of course, to millions of criminals. If the concern is about *setting a precedent* for disregard of law, that precedent has already been set. In addition to the famous Zenger trial, it is widely reputed that juries often nullified the law in trials under the Fugitive Slave Laws prior to the Civil War, and in trials for alcohol crimes during the Prohibition era. During the 1990's, three juries apparently nullified in three separate trials in which Dr. Jack Kevorkian was charged with assisting terminally ill patients in ending their lives. And drug trials today often end in hung juries, most likely due to widespread opposition to the nation's drug laws.[4] Some of these cases, particularly the Kevorkian cases, were widely reported in the media; thus, whatever negative effects might be expected to result from public awareness of jury nullification ought to have occurred already. It is unlikely that an acquittal in an ordinary, unremarkable trial would cause widespread disregard of the law if none of the above cases did so.

Judges, too, have often disregarded the law in the interests of justice. Above, we discussed a case in which a 14-year-old girl was charged with distribution of child pornography, for sending naked pictures of herself to a boy at her school (see §10.4.3). Though the text of the child pornography statute clearly, literally applied to the girl's action, the judge dismissed the case, thus averting a serious injustice. In recent decades, since the advent of draconian minimum sentencing laws, judges often manipulate trials in a variety of ways to avoid applying mandatory minimum sentences—for instance, inventing spurious reasons to exclude evidence, making false factual findings, providing juries with information that might invite jury nullification, and intentionally misinterpreting the law.[5]

---

[4] On cases that have incurred jury nullification, see Leipold (1996, pp. 297–8); Biskupic (1999); Bork (1999, p. 20).
[5] These methods and the evidence of their use are discussed in detail by Greenblatt (2008).

Besides these cases motivated by justice, courts have also disregarded the law for the sake of convenience or fiscal savings for the state. Some of these cases have been discussed earlier. Thus, the Supreme Court has authorized plea bargaining, in contravention of the Constitution and its own then-recent precedent, for the sake of avoiding a flood of court cases that would strain the system's resources. This requires interpreting decisions motivated by threats of imprisonment or even death as "voluntary" and uncoerced (see §5.5). The courts have created a legal doctrine protecting prosecutors and judges from lawsuits; maintaining the doctrine requires interpreting "every person" in the text of a particular statute to exclude prosecutors and judges (see §7.3.3). The courts have also created a doctrine excusing government officials in general from any obligation to provide government services to individuals (see §4.4.2). That doctrine was explicitly justified by the concern that, if government officials were held civilly liable for failures to do their jobs, then "[a]n enormous amount of public time and money would be consumed in litigation of private claims."[6] None of those judicial outcomes could have reasonably been predicted based solely upon the written laws; all were motivated by the public policy views of the judges involved. These therefore should be taken as violations of the Rule of Law, if anything is.

None of this has generated the anarchic consequences of which conservative legal theorists warn us. When John Peter Zenger's jury disregarded the law, the government did not collapse, nor were there riots or looting in the streets. The only known result was that a blameless man avoided unjust punishment, and the governor was unable to use the power of the state to silence his critics. When the Minnesota judge dismissed child pornography charges against the 14-year-old girl, the government again gave no signs of collapsing. No riots or other social unrest occurred. All that occurred is that an innocent girl's life was not pointlessly ruined. Even the cases where judges disregard the law for the convenience of the state do not seem to have occasioned either anarchy or civil unrest, and no one seems to be concerned that they will. Of course, one could simply hypothesize that there would be fewer crimes of all kinds if nullification by judges and juries did not exist, but there is no empirical evidence supporting this.

---

[6] *Warren v. District of Columbia*, 444 A.2d 1 (1981), at p. 9.

11.2.3 The Influence of Juries

In a typical case—not a high-profile case reported in the news media, but just an ordinary case—a jury's decision can reasonably be expected to have no impact on other cases or on the culture more generally. (I focus here on juries; judges are in a different situation, since they write explanations of their decisions, which are often consulted by other judges.) It is worth pointing out why this is so.

First, note that juries in general only give an overall verdict, "guilty" or "not guilty". They do not normally provide any further information to the court, the media, or anyone else. In particular, they are not expected to explain the reasons for their decision, and they almost never do so. Thus, if a jury decides to acquit based on the injustice of the law, outside observers will usually not know that the jury acquitted for this reason, rather than because they simply were not convinced by the prosecution's evidence. Granted, there are some cases in which observers could reasonably infer a nullification motive, if the evidence in the case is particularly compelling and the law particularly morally questionable. But if the defense makes a reasonable effort at disputing the evidence, then it will usually be impossible for observers to tell why the jury acquitted.

Second, the overwhelming majority of cases are simply not significant enough or entertaining enough for anyone other than the people involved in that particular case to pay any attention at all to them. State courts in the U.S. conduct approximately 150,000 jury trials per year.[7] Only a minute fraction of those cases are covered in the media or followed widely by people not involved in the case. This must be so, since the public does not have time to attend to hundreds of court cases every day. Because of this, in the overwhelming majority of cases, if a jury chooses to nullify the law, however clear their motive may be, almost no one will even notice that this occurred.

For these reasons, juries need not be concerned, in normal cases, about the effects that their decisions will have on the rest of society. They will have no such effects.

---

[7] Barkan and Bryjak (2011, p. 366).

11.2.4 Lawyers' Duties

In conventional legal ethics, defense lawyers are considered to be not only permitted but professionally *obligated* to assist criminals in attempting to get away with their crimes—or, failing that, to assist criminals in obtaining the least punishment for breaking the law that the lawyer can secure. This behavior is widely accepted in the legal system, even by those who condemn jury and judge nullification. Few if any express concerns that this behavior on the part of a lawyer will engender widespread disregard for the law in society.

Yet this behavior by lawyers would seem on its face *more* likely to promote social disorder than jury or judge nullification. The reason is that the standard lawyerly behavior is *indiscriminate* in a way that judge and jury nullification are not: no matter what law a criminal has broken, regardless of whether the law is just or unjust and regardless of whether the legally prescribed punishment is just or unjust, a defense attorney helps his client to minimize or avoid punishment for breaking the law. It is widely known that this is how lawyers generally operate. On its face, this would seem more likely to encourage an attitude of *general* disrespect for the law than the relatively discriminating behavior of judges and juries who only try to prevent enforcement of certain particularly morally problematic laws. Therefore, if the active efforts of lawyers to prevent the law from being enforced have not created anarchic conditions in our society, it seems unlikely that occasional cases of jury or judge nullification will do so.

Perhaps the objection would be that, whereas lawyers are following their prescribed role in the system when they try to prevent enforcement of the law, judges and juries are violating their prescribed roles when they act to prevent enforcement of the law. Furthermore, perhaps outside observers make this distinction and are only encouraged to disregard the law when they see someone trying to prevent enforcement of the law *outside their legally prescribed role*.

There are two problems with this argument. First, observers with the sophistication to distinguish between *undermining law enforcement while following one's social role* and *undermining law enforcement in general*, are probably also sophisticated enough to distinguish the refusal to enforce *unjust* laws from the refusal to enforce *just* laws. Therefore, it is not likely that observers would be prompted to disregard laws in general by their awareness of the phenomena of jury and judge nullification, if they are not so prompted by the awareness of the phenomenon of lawyers helping their clients get away with crimes.

Second, as noted earlier (§10.7), juries who nullify the law *are not* violating their legally prescribed role in the system; they are precisely fulfilling that role. It is the judges attempting to prevent jury nullification who are violating their role obligations.

Perhaps, however, it might be objected that the public (mistakenly) *perceives* the jury's role as that of merely applying the law, and it is the public *perception* of a jury's violating its role obligations that encourages anarchy. If this is the case, however, then the underlying problem is not that juries have been nullifying the law; the underlying problem is the public's incorrect perception about the jury's role—a perception that is encouraged by judges who instruct juries to merely apply the law, as well as by authors and public figures who attack the doctrine of jury nullification. These authors would in fact be encouraging the very descent into anarchy that they warn us of, by creating the mistaken impression that juries often violate their role obligations.

It may seem implausible that such figures are creating a serious risk of society's degenerating into chaos. After all, few potential criminals are likely to be studying the issue of jury nullification. And few are likely in any case to decide whether to commit a crime based upon their opinions about whether juries often violate their role obligations. Still less likely is it that—taking the concern about "anarchy" literally—the government will be overthrown due to public perception that juries often violate their role obligations. But all this simply illustrates the deep implausibility of the original warnings of jury nullification leading to anarchy.

11.2.5 The Importance of Justice

The first concern in a trial should be to do justice in that particular case. We should insist upon a very high bar to justify knowingly imposing an unjust outcome. Those who raise the "anarchy" objection may accept this point; they simply believe that the risks to society when individual agents disregard the law are so serious that it is morally correct to allow some serious injustices in individual cases rather than to create the risk of a breakdown of social order. I believe, on the contrary, that the risks are not close to being serious enough to justify imposing a serious injustice on an individual.

To test our ethical intuitions, consider a hypothetical scenario discussed earlier (§2.4.1), the Framing example:

Framing: A crime has been committed that has caused great public outrage in a certain town. The sheriff knows that unless someone is punished for the crime, there will be riots, during which multiple innocent people will be unjustly injured and possibly killed. The sheriff cannot find the actual perpetrator; he can, however, frame an innocent person, which will cause that person to be seriously and unjustly punished but will forestall the riots. Should the sheriff frame the innocent?

In this case, it is stipulated that there will be social unrest if the sheriff does not bring about the unjust punishment. Nevertheless, nearly everyone agrees that it would be wrong for the sheriff to do so.

Now compare the Framing case with an ordinary case in which a jury would vote to convict a person for violating an unjust law, for example, to convict a defendant for drug possession. The argument for framing the innocent person in the Framing case is *much stronger* than the argument, based on fears of "anarchy", for convicting the drug offender. In both cases, the action would result in an individual suffering serious, unjust punishment at the hands of the state. We may stipulate (realistically) that the punishment in the two cases would be comparably severe. In the Framing case, it is, by stipulation, *known* that social unrest will result from a failure to punish. In the drug possession case, it is vaguely speculated by, for example, conservative judges that perhaps social unrest might someday result if many juries refuse to punish in such cases.

One might additionally hypothesize that the social unrest resulting from jury nullification might eventually result in collapse of the government. This is no more plausible than the speculation, which we might entertain in the Framing case, that the riots resulting from failure to frame the innocent person might lead to government collapse. Neither speculation is particularly plausible, but it is, if anything, more plausible to suppose that riots might lead to a collapse of government than to suppose that a case of jury nullification in an otherwise unremarkable drug possession case might lead to a collapse of government.

Thus, the danger that the sheriff would avert in the Framing case is, on its face, much more serious than the alleged danger that the jury in the drug possession case would avert by convicting the drug user. Since the unjust harms are of comparable magnitude in the two cases, and the harm to be imposed on the defendant is unjustified in the Framing case, the harm must also be unjustified in the drug possession case. That is, in neither case can the harm be justified by citing the risk of social unrest.

11.3 The Value of Uniformity

11.3.1 Advantages of Uniformity: Fairness, Planning, and Deterrence

Some would argue that similar legal cases ought to be treated similarly, and that the only way this can be accomplished is for the outcome of a legal case to be determined by written rules, rather than by the moral judgment of particular individuals.

One reason to desire uniformity in the legal system is fairness. If two defendants come before the courts, having committed the same crime in relevantly similar circumstances, and one of them receives a much harsher treatment than the other, this would seem intrinsically unfair.

Another reason to desire uniformity is that individuals must be able to predict the behavior of the legal system in order to plan their own actions. A business owner, for example, must know in advance what health and safety requirements will be applied to his business, in order to arrange matters so as to comply with the law. If the requirements change frequently according to the whim of various bureaucrats, law enforcement officers, or other officials, then it may become impossible for the owner to know how to maintain compliance. In such an environment, entrepreneurship may be squelched.

Finally, note that social order relies on effective deterrence: individuals are deterred from harmful and rights-violating behavior by the threat of legal sanctions. This deterrence is strongly dependent on the probability of legal sanctions being applied if one transgresses the law. But if juries and judges nullify the law whenever they consider it to be unjust, then legal punishment will become less certain in general. Thus, the general deterrent to crime may be reduced.

So, at any rate, the advocates of the Rule of Law would argue. I shall presently explain why I do not find these considerations persuasive.

11.3.2 Factual and Moral Innocence

Punishment is unjust when it is undeserved. There are three basic ways in which a punishment may be undeserved:

(i) *Factual innocence:* The defendant did not commit the act for which he is punished.
(ii) *Moral innocence:* The act for which the defendant is punished is not wrong.
(iii) *Unfitting punishment:* The punishment attached to the given action is too harsh, too lenient, or otherwise not appropriate to the crime.

For simplicity, I focus here on the first two kinds of cases. Other things being equal, cases of factual innocence and cases of moral innocence are equally unjust. In both, someone is punished who does not deserve to be punished.

Now, the argument from the value of uniformity (§11.4.1) can, with a little imagination, be applied to cases of factual innocence just as well as to cases of moral innocence. Thus, consider two cases:

Innocent Alan: Alan is truthfully accused of being a homosexual. There is nothing wrong with homosexuality; however, Alan lives in 1950's England, where homosexuality has, irrationally, been outlawed.[8] If convicted, he faces a few years in prison

---

[8] This actually happened to the founder of computer science, Alan Turing. He accepted chemical castration as an alternative to imprisonment. Two years later, he committed suicide.

for his blameless behavior. Sitting on the jury, you find that Alan's homosexuality is proved beyond reasonable doubt in court. Should you vote to convict Alan?

Innocent Jane: Jane is accused of burglarizing a store. If convicted, she faces a few years in prison for this wrongful action. Sitting on the jury, you find the evidence in the case insufficient; in fact, you are convinced that Jane did *not* burglarize the store. Unfortunately, however, you also know that, due to biases and other cognitive failings, most members of the public who know about the case mistakenly believe that Jane is guilty. You also know that most juries would vote to convict Jane. You know this because there have been many previous cases that were similar to this one, and the juries usually voted to convict. Should you vote to convict Jane?

Jane is factually innocent, while Alan is morally innocent. Neither has done anything wrong, and neither deserves punishment.

In the case of Innocent Alan, the proponents of the Rule of Law would argue that you should vote to convict, due to the value of establishing uniformity in the outcomes of trials under the unjust law. If Alan is acquitted due to the jury's moral objections to the law, this will render trial outcomes less predictable, making it more difficult for individuals to plan their behavior. Considering that many *other* defendants have been convicted under this same law, there will also be an unfairness if Alan is let free. Finally, the decrease in the general probability of being convicted after one violates the law may undermine the general deterrent to crime in your society. These are precisely the arguments cited above (§11.4.1) for upholding the Rule of Law.

Notice that all of these arguments can be applied with equal force to Jane. Since most juries convict in cases similar to this one, if your jury votes to acquit, this will reduce the predictability of trial outcomes. Since other defendants (most of whom were also factually innocent) have been convicted in similar circumstances, there will also be an unfairness if Jane is let free while others are punished. Finally, since Jane is widely *believed* to be guilty, if she is acquitted, other members of society will conclude that a criminal was set free and may thereupon slightly diminish their estimate of how likely criminals are in general to be punished. This may reduce the general deterrent to crime in your society.

Yet no one thinks that Innocent Jane should be convicted. The alleged benefits are far too dubious to justify imposing a serious, known, undeserved harm on an innocent person. Though conviction would indeed be the more *predictable* outcome, this hardly outweighs the obligation to do justice to the individual.

Concerning the problem of unfairness, notice that the unfairness involved in unequal treatment is unfairness *to* the individuals who are *mistreated*. If A is unjustly punished for some action while B is not unjustly punished despite performing the same action, this situation is unfair *to A* and only to A. The only remedy for this would be for A not to be punished. It is no remedy to mistreat B as well. Compare the case of the Gaybashing Gang (§8.4.1), wherein a gang of hoodlums aims to physically attack homosexuals. If the gang beats some but not all gay people, one might say there is an unfairness involved in such unequal treatment. But obviously it would not be preferable for the gang to beat *all* gays; the only acceptable remedy for the unfairness is for the gang to beat no one.

Concerning the value of deterrence, it may be true that deterrence to crime is very slightly increased whenever individuals who are widely believed to be guilty are convicted. But this tiny increment of deterrence is not enough to justify unjustly punishing someone who has done nothing wrong. As a rule, we may not treat individuals as mere tools of social engineering in this way. Only when punishment is *deserved* is it an acceptable means of deterring future criminals (see §6.1).

I expect the preceding points to be readily accepted since, again, the case of Innocent Jane is not controversial. Yet essentially the same arguments apply to Innocent Alan. The value of predictability hardly justifies imprisoning someone unjustly, merely because the state has unjustly imprisoned others in similar circumstances. It is true that this would render the state's behavior predictable, but that is either no advantage or at best a trivial advantage. It would be better for trial outcomes under the unjust law to be uncertain, rather than for them to be uniformly bad. If Alan is acquitted, there might indeed be an unfairness in the non-uniform treatment of gays charged under this law, but this would only be unfairness to the gay people who were punished. This situation would not be improved by punishing more gays; the unfairness could only be reduced by punishing *fewer* people. Finally, since Alan has done nothing wrong, it is morally impermissible to use him as a tool for increasing deterrence. In addition, of course, in this case the deterrence provided would be entirely or almost entirely deterrence against other homosexual acts, something that we have no reason to try to deter—thus, the case here for convicting Alan is *weaker* than the case for convicting Jane.

11.3.3 Negative Versus Positive Rule of Law

Part of the appeal of the argument from the Rule of Law rests on a failure to distinguish between *unexpected punishments* and *unexpected acquittals*. The main threats from which the Rule of Law would protect us are threats of unexpected punishments. If citizens are often unexpectedly punished, at the discretion of government officials, for alleged wrongs not announced in the written laws, then this can indeed be extremely harmful. It can introduce a climate of fear, squelch economic activity and individual liberty, and give free reign to corruption. Such punishments are also generally unfair, since it is in general unfair to punish an individual for failing to conform to demands that the individual had no reasonable way of anticipating.

But none of these problems apply to the case of unexpected *acquittals*. If, that is, the state periodically shows unexpected leniency (or unexpected decency) by failing to punish some of those whom it had threatened to punish, *this* sort of unpredictability does not create the negative effects listed above. It does not create any greater fear, relative to the possible situation in which the state punishes *all* of those whom it threatened to punish, nor does it prevent individuals or businesses from planning their actions, since individuals and businesses still know that they will not be punished *unless* they violate the written laws. For example, individuals who do not wish to use drugs are not prevented from planning any of their activities by uncertainty about whether they would be punished in the event that they took up recreational drug use. Individual who *do* wish to use drugs, on the other hand, can only welcome a reduction in the probability that they would be punished for doing so.

Notice that the case of possible unexpected leniency differs markedly from the case of possible unexpected punishment: if government officials have the power to punish one for unwritten and unanticipated crimes, this creates a threat to the plans of nearly anyone. No one should welcome this situation, compared to a situation in which officials may only punish one for crimes recorded in the statutes.

Admittedly, the possibility of unexpected leniency may open the door to a certain kind of corruption, but a less worrisome kind than the corruption invited by unexpected punishments. The power to give punishments for unwritten crimes creates a possibility of government officials using their power for purposes of extortion, to settle personal vendettas, to retaliate for political criticism, and otherwise to oppress the people. The power to exercise unexpected leniency, on the other hand, creates a possibility of government officials using their power to reward criminal friends, to extract bribes from criminals, or simply to fail to protect the public from criminals. These latter threats are less troubling than the threat of oppression created by the power to give unexpected punishments.

Thus, we should distinguish two principles of the Rule of Law, a negative principle and a positive principle. The Negative Principle of the Rule of Law is a *constraint* on government action designed to protect the individual from the state: legal punishments should *not* be imposed *unless* an individual has violated a written law. The Positive Principle of the Rule of Law, on the other hand, is a positive demand for government action: legal punishments should be imposed *whenever* an individual has violated a written law.

For the reasons discussed, the Negative Principle is far more plausible than the Positive Principle. Most arguments for the Rule of Law are arguments only for the Negative Principle.

11.3.4 Sources of Uncertainty

A final note concerning the value of uniformity: Even if one considers uncertainty about whether lawbreakers will be punished to be a serious problem, the practices of judge and jury nullification would have little effect on this problem. When an individual violates a written law, it is in general extremely uncertain whether that individual will ever receive legal punishment for the violation. This is not primarily because trial outcomes are uncertain, but because it is in most cases uncertain whether the government will ever detect the crime to begin with, and if they do, extremely uncertain whether government agents will ever arrest anyone for that crime. Government statistics show that only about 46% of violent crimes and 18% of property crimes known to the police result in an arrest.[9] There undoubtedly are many additional crimes not known to the police. It is unknown how many drug crimes go undetected every year (for example, individuals who use a recreational drug in their own homes), but it must surely be much larger than the number of drug crimes for which individuals are arrested. Even among those who are arrested for a crime, only a tiny fraction go to trial (see §5.1). Thus, if juries and judges never used their powers to nullify the law, there would still be almost exactly as much uncertainty as there presently is about whether one will actually be punished for violating the law. If judges and juries used the power twice as often as they presently do, there would again remain about as much uncertainty as there presently is. Thus, the fear of increasing the uncertainty is not a strong reason for a judge or jury in an individual case not to engage in nullification.

11.4 The Virtue of Social Deference

11.4.1 The Problem of Normative Disagreement

Before addressing the next objection to the Primacy of Justice, we need to discuss some theoretical background concerning a widespread problem faced by human social groups, and a common solution to that problem. Any human organization or group that needs to cooperate will inevitably face the problem of *normative disagreement*: when individuals consider normative questions, especially questions about what the group ought to do, they very often arrive at incompatible conclusions. The problem affects businesses, private clubs, university departments, and, of course, whole societies.

---

[9] Federal Bureau of Investigation 2019, table 25.

Very often, this disagreement is intractable. Extended discussion and debate do not produce agreement. Statistics, scientific studies, expert testimony, and logical argumentation prove impotent. This occurs often enough to pose a threat to social cooperation. There is a danger that competing factions within the group will undermine collective action, so that *no one's* favored policy is faithfully adopted. The factional struggle may waste resources and cause direct harm to the struggling partisans. The result may be worse, from everyone's point of view, than what would have occurred if the group had agreed upon *any* of the proposed courses of action, even a relatively bad one. In other words, in some cases, it is more important for a group to unite behind a single plan of action, whichever it might be (from among the reasonable contenders), than it is for the group to identify the *best* plan of action.

11.4.2 The Process-Based Solution

There is one particularly common and effective solution to the problem of normative disagreement. It is that the individuals who disagree substantively about what is the best course of action may nevertheless agree upon a *process* for making the relevant decisions. They might, for example, agree that certain individuals are responsible for making certain kinds of decisions. Or that certain issues are to be resolved by majority vote. Or that certain decisions should be made by lottery.

For this kind of solution to succeed, two conditions are necessary: (i) there must be much greater agreement about what the results of the process actually are than there is about the original normative issue; (ii) group members must have a strong disposition to *defer* to the process, even when it settles on what they initially consider a bad result.

For example, when an academic department needs to hire a new professor, the members usually disagree about who is the best candidate. Nevertheless, they can generally agree that the way to select a candidate is through a majority vote of all department members. When a vote is taken, there will typically be no disagreement about what the outcome of the vote in fact was. Department members are then generally disposed to accept that outcome, perhaps even actively helping to recruit the candidate, even if they believe the person selected by the vote was not the best person for the job.

The process used to resolve a normative disagreement need not involve voting. Sometimes, random selection is more appropriate. For instance, employees of a restaurant might agree to draw straws to decide who has to clean the grease trap (an unpleasant task that must be performed periodically in restaurants). In society more broadly, disagreements about how resources ought to be used, or simply conflicting *desires* about the disposition of resources, are generally resolved by assigning specific items of value to specific individuals (their "property"), where each individual decides the use of those items assigned to himself. This of course creates the possibility of disagreements about who owns a given piece of property, in which case a further process (generally involving the courts) must be agreed upon to resolve *those* disagreements.

Normative disagreement is extremely pervasive in social life, as is the process-based solution to the problem. For this reason, the disposition to *defer to accepted processes* is a crucial social virtue. Without it, social cooperation is nearly impossible. If an individual refuses to defer once the outcome of the accepted process is known, other members of that person's social group typically will rightly strive to punish that person or force the person to accept the result of the process. They generally should not give in to the recalcitrant individual, even if the particular issue presently in dispute is a minor one, because the broader principle of resolving disputes by appeal to process is at stake. If individuals are permitted to reject the outcome of the process once it is known, this defeats the purpose of having a decision-making process and leaves the group with the original problem of disagreement.

Thus, consider the following hypothetical example:

Hiring Dispute: A philosophy department is trying to decide between two candidates for a job, candidate C and candidate D. One department member, Alice, favors C and argues strenuously for that view. When the vote is taken, however, D emerges as the department's most preferred candidate. The department prepares to extend a job offer to D, pending approval of the university administration. Alice then attempts to sabotage the hire by looking for negative information about candidate D, and impugning the motives of department members who favored D over C, in order to persuade the administration to reject the hire.

In this example, Alice's behavior is unacceptable, regardless of whether candidate D is really better than C. Alice is of course permitted to argue strenuously for her preferred candidate prior to the vote. But after the vote is taken, the refusal to accept the outcome is a refusal to accept the process-based solution to the problem of disagreement. That, in turn, amounts to a rejection of orderly cooperation among department members—a value far more important than securing the best candidate in this particular case. If a social group is to maintain cohesion and order, it must strongly reject such behavior.

11.4.3 Deference to the Law

Applying these ideas to the broader society, the accepted process for resolving disagreements about the rules governing our behavior is (in the countries that have this institution) the process of representative democracy: individuals vote for representatives, who in turn vote on what the laws should be. To have peaceful cooperation in society, it is necessary that citizens be disposed to accept the outcomes of that process, even when they appear sub-optimal.

This brings us to an important objection to the principle of the Primacy of Justice. Justice to the individual, it might be argued, is not the highest value at stake in the courtroom. The most important value at stake is that of peaceful, orderly social cooperation. The existing laws in a democratic society, however misguided they may at times appear, are the outcomes of the accepted process for resolving disagreement about the rules of social interaction. It is possible for peaceful social cooperation to continue even while some few members of society refuse to accept those outcomes; however, the great majority of individuals must defer to the accepted process the great majority of the time. Those few individuals who refuse to defer are, one might argue, acting as free riders: they are depending on the virtuous willingness of *others* to defer, even while these individuals themselves refuse to defer. This seems like morally objectionable behavior, similar to that described in the Hiring Dispute example above.

Now, the idea of the Primacy of Justice might seem to entail precisely such a refusal to defer to process. When a jury or judge refuses to enforce the law on the grounds that the law is unjust, or that its application to a particular case would be unjust, that jury or judge is refusing to defer to the accepted process for resolving disputes about what justice requires—for that process is precisely what generated the law in question. In view of what we have said above, how can this refusal be justified?

11.4.4 The Limits of Social Deference

For the reasons discussed above, the willingness to defer is indeed an important social virtue. Nevertheless, this virtue has limits. Consider the following variation on the Hiring Dispute case discussed above:

Kidnapping Dispute: A philosophy department is trying to decide how to respond to a grade complaint from an undergraduate student. Some professors think the complaint should be ignored, while others believe the student should be kidnaped at gunpoint and locked in the basement of the department building for three months. One professor, Mike, argues strenuously against the kidnapping plan. When the vote is taken, however, the kidnapping plan emerges as the department's top preference. The faculty dispatch a posse of grad students to take the undergraduate complainer hostage. Meanwhile, Mike attempts to sabotage the kidnapping plan by calling the undergraduate on the phone to warn her.

The Kidnapping Dispute is parallel to the Hiring Dispute in obvious ways. In both cases, the department members disagree about what course of action should be taken. In both cases, a vote is taken to resolve the dispute. And in both cases, one department member on the losing side of the vote refuses to cooperate with the group decision. Yet opposite moral judgments apply in the two cases: Alice acts wrongly, but Mike acts rightly.

What explains the differing moral verdicts? A tempting explanation is that the virtue of social deference is constrained by justice: one should defer only to decisions that are not seriously unjust. In the case of the Hiring Dispute, whichever candidate the department hires, the department will be acting within its rights. Hiring the worse candidate, one might argue, may be foolish but not *unjust*. By contrast, in the Kidnapping Dispute, the department's decision is seriously unjust. The department has no right to kidnap students, so no vote on whether to kidnap students should have been taken in the first place, and the results of such a vote cannot legitimize the kidnapping.

But while this explanation is tempting, it has the implication that a process-based solution could not be applied to disagreements about justice. The explanation implies that we are morally barred from deferring when the accepted process for resolving a dispute results in an *unjust* decision. But in the case of a dispute about justice itself, an incorrect decision will *ipso facto* be an unjust decision. So in the case of a dispute about justice, we could only morally defer if the process gives *the correct* result. Of course, a disposition to accept a result if and only if it is the correct result is not deference at all. Furthermore, this would be a major problem, since disagreement about the demands of justice is common in the political sphere. The inability to refer such disputes to an agreed-upon process would pose a major threat to social cooperation. We should be reluctant to accept an ethical principle that, if regularly followed, would pose such a threat.

Still, surely some sort of constraint on social deference is needed to prevent complicity in major injustices. Surely a philosophy department—or any other social group—cannot create a moral obligation for its members to aid in carrying out an obvious, severe injustice, merely by adopting a democratic norm and then voting in favor of the injustice.

What I think the preceding considerations show is that the injustice of the outcome in Kidnapping Dispute is a part, but not the whole, of the explanation for why social deference is impermissible in that case. A fuller explanation would cite at least two conditions:

(i) The outcome of the process is seriously unjust; and
(ii) That outcome is not plausibly seen as the product of a reasonable, good faith effort to identify the requirements of justice in the particular case.

These two conditions are jointly *sufficient* for canceling the obligation one would otherwise have to defer to the outcome of an accepted dispute-resolution mechanism. Note that there are two parts to condition (ii): The "good faith" condition requires that those who adopted a given resolution sincerely aimed at justice (or whatever moral values are relevant in the case) in so doing. The "reasonableness" condition, as I intend it, requires at least a moderate degree of competence on their part in reasoning about what justice (or other relevant moral values) demands.

Why should we recognize such a restriction on social deference? The proper function of the virtue of social deference is to enable social groups to resolve reasonable disputes about what is just, right, or otherwise desirable in difficult cases—not to enable unscrupulous agents to disregard justice and morality in perfectly clear cases. The effort to use dispute resolution mechanisms to *override* morality or justice is an abuse of process. Virtue cannot require us to play into the hands of such abuse. That is why some such restriction as I have described is required before we can endorse social deference.

In the Kidnapping Dispute, kidnapping the student is seriously unjust, and a reasonable person sincerely trying to identify the just resolution of a grade complaint could not plausibly conclude that kidnapping the student was the correct resolution. There is thus no obligation to defer to such a conclusion, even though it is arrived at using an accepted method of dispute resolution. When the faculty vote to kidnap the complaining student, they are abusing the process, rather than making a good faith use of the dispute-resolution mechanism.

11.4.5 The Abuse of Democracy

How does the preceding reasoning apply to political disputes about the appropriate laws in the larger society? In some cases, there are sincere, reasonable disagreements about what justice requires, and it may in some such cases be morally appropriate to defer to the outcome of the democratic process. However, this is at most a small class of cases. In the typical case in a modern democracy, condition (ii) is violated: most unjust laws, or unjust applications of the law, are not plausibly viewed as products of a reasonable, good faith effort to identify what justice demands. It is these cases that concern me, both because they are of great practical significance and because we can determine with high confidence the correct way of treating such cases: one should refuse to defer to the unreasonable or bad faith positions.

That is how I would classify drug prohibition policies in the U.S. and other nations. As argued earlier (§3.2.5), these policies are not the product of a sincere and competent effort to pursue justice. They are most likely the product of vague emotional associations on the part of uninformed voters and cynical political calculations on the part of politicians, with neither group deigning to consider the rights or interests of those imprisoned under the drug laws. Again, my complaint about prohibitionist positions is not that voters and legislators *disagree with* the notion of individual rights that I claim renders drug prohibition unjust. My point is that voters and legislators are *indifferent* to the relevant questions about individual rights.

This kind of situation is common in a modern democracy. Voters and politicians routinely fail to devote even modest effort to reasoning about what justice or morality requires, and routinely lack basic competence for such reasoning (see §§3.4 and 10.4.2). Voter opinions often disregard basic rationality constraints, as in the case of voters who wish government spending in general to be cut, but do not want any particular actual program to be cut.[10] Some political scientists argue that typical political opinions do not even strive to conform to reality but simply function as devices for expressing group affiliation.[11] All of this prevents the outcome of the democratic process from being plausibly viewed as a competent, good faith assessment of the demands of justice. In other words, voters and politicians routinely abuse the power given them under the democratic system. This obviates any obligation that conscientious individuals

---

[10] Sears and Citrin (1985, p. 217); Bernstein (2010).
[11] Achen and Bartels (2017).

would otherwise have to defer to democratically chosen policies, in cases where those policies are substantively unjust.

What should we say of the case where the justice of a given law *in general* is not at issue, but the law's application to some particular, unusual case seems to generate an injustice? For example, recall the case discussed in §10.4.3, in which a girl was charged with distribution of child pornography for sending a picture of herself to a boy at her school. The law prohibiting child pornography is in general just and reasonable. The legislators who made the law, however, did not consider this possible application of it; thus, they neither endorsed nor rejected this application (though one imagines that they surely *would* have rejected it if it had occurred to them). In such a case, since the law is the product of a reasonable, good faith effort to achieve justice, would there be an obligation on the part of a judge or jury to implement the law as written?

Surely not. In the case where a generally reasonable legal rule has unanticipated consequences, there are at least two sufficient conditions for setting aside the rule. First, the implications of a rule should be disregarded in a given case if those who made the rule would not clearly have intended those implications, and thus, the implications for the present case may plausibly be a mere product of oversight. Thus, if it is *unclear* what the legislators would have intended, then one should follow the dictates of justice, rather than the text of the law. Second, the implications of a rule for a given case should be disregarded if, had they been explicitly chosen, this would not have been a reasonable, good faith effort at pursuing justice.

In the child pornography case, both conditions apply: (i) the legislature almost surely would not have intended a 14-year-old girl to be prosecuted for sending a picture of herself; (ii) regardless, *had* the legislature explicitly written that a girl should be imprisoned for sending naked photos of herself to a classmate, then the legislature would not have been engaged in a reasonable, good faith pursuit of justice. Their law would thus have been appropriately disregarded. Since, in the actual case, they didn't even say that, the proposed application of the law is even more clearly unjustified.

On my account, in other words, agents in the legal system should disregard the requirements of the law in any given case in favor of whatever justice requires, *unless* (i) it is clear that the lawmakers would have intended the law to be applied in the way it is being applied in the given case, *and* (ii) that application would be a reasonable, good faith interpretation of the requirements of justice in the given case.

One strong indicator that condition (ii) is violated and that a given law is *not* a reasonable, good faith interpretation of justice is that the chief argument offered in support of what the law requires is merely that it is the law. If a given requirement cannot be defended on moral grounds without appealing to the fact that it is the actual law, then that requirement is not a reasonable, good faith interpretation of the demands of justice.

11.4.6 Jury Nullification as Part of the Process

There is one final point to be made in response to the argument from the virtue of social deference. This virtue, in general, requires deferring to the results of accepted procedures, even when those results do not independently strike one as correct. The objection to jury nullification would then be that jury nullification involves a jury's refusing to defer to the democratic process.

Even if we overlook the problems with the democratic process, particularly its frequent failure to make a reasonable, good faith effort at pursuing justice, it still is not clear that the virtue of social deference would rule out jury nullification. This is because the jury's own exercise of moral judgment, including their sense of justice, is itself a part of the relevant dispute-resolution process to which deference is due. Granted, the democratic, legislative process is the established process for resolving disputes about what laws should exist in our society. Yet there is also a process for resolving disputes about what should be done with individual defendants who are accused of legal violations. That process is the jury trial. As argued earlier, the jury's exercise of its own conscience in deciding whether to enforce the law in a given case is part of the normal functioning of the jury trial (§10.7). Jury nullification is not a malfunction of the system; it is the system working as designed.

Those who believe in the virtue of social deference should thus be prepared to defer to the decisions of juries in individual cases. Judges who attempt to interfere with jury nullification are thus guilty of refusing to defer to the accepted process of dispute resolution.

11.5 The Virtue of Defiance

Advocates for the Rule of Law tend to regard social conformity and obedience to authority figures as pro-social behavior, and they view a strong reliance on individual conscience as selfish and dangerous to society.[12] The actual situation, however, is the reverse. It is the exercise of conscience in defiance of authority that is truly pro-social, and unquestioning obedience to authority that is selfish and socially harmful.

11.5.1 The Difficulty of Defiance

Most human beings find it extremely psychologically difficult to defy authority figures. This has been demonstrated by the famous Milgram experiment in social psychology. Briefly, subjects in this experiment were instructed by an experimenter in a white lab coat to administer a verbal test to another person (the "learner"), who was strapped into a chair located in the adjoining room. When the learner made repeated mistakes, the subject was to administer increasingly severe electric shocks to the learner. As the shocks increased in intensity, the learner would make increasingly strenuous protests, ranging from grunts of pain to screams, to demands to be released, to refusal to answer any further questions. Ultimately, the learner would go completely silent, suggesting that he had been either rendered unconscious or possibly killed. Each time the subject tried to discontinue the shocks, the experimenter in the lab coat would order the subject to continue. Milgram found that about two thirds of ordinary human beings can be induced to comply fully with the

---

[12] Bork (1999).

commands of the experimenter, even to the point of administering repeated 450-volt shocks to an apparently unconscious or dead victim.[13,14]

It is important to understand why most subjects complied with the experimenter. Subjects were not sadists who enjoyed tormenting the learner, nor did they have bizarre moral views that would justify electrocuting hapless volunteers in the name of scientific research. Milgram's subjects in fact showed signs of extreme discomfort with what they were being ordered to do, repeatedly protested to the experimenter, and at the end of the experiment showed great relief when they discovered that the learner had not actually been electrocuted. The reason most complied was that they felt very strong psychological pressure to *obey the authority figure* in the room—the scientist in the white lab coat. Most of us are unaware of just how strong this pressure can be; when given a verbal description of the experiment, virtually everyone predicts that they themselves would refuse to electrocute the learner. Psychologists, too, were stunned by Milgram's results.

This experiment demonstrates that human beings do not have an excessive tendency to defy authority. The natural tendency is just the opposite: most human beings have a shockingly powerful drive to obey even the most outrageous commands of authority figures. Two thirds of the experiment's subjects would literally rather commit murder than defy an authority figure. As Milgram himself argues, this drive to obey plays a

---

[13] Milgram (2009). Of course, the learner in the experiment was an actor pretending to be shocked—Stanley Milgram did not actually have hapless volunteers electrocuted for his experiment. Burger (2009) offers a replication with similar results.

[14] Unfortunately, it has recently become popular, when the Milgram study is mentioned, for lay people to claim that the study has been debunked, referring to Perry et al. (2020). Perry et al.'s paper is sometimes misreported as showing that the obedient subjects "did not believe" that they were really electrocuting the learner. In fact, what Perry et al. report is that most subjects, after the fact, claimed to have been less than fully *certain* that they were really electrocuting the learner, and that the people who had fully complied reported lower certainty on average than the people who had disobeyed the experimenter. Nevertheless, 74% of the fully obedient subjects reported that they had either fully believed that the shocks were real or had some doubts but still thought the shocks were probably real. Only 4% claimed to have fully disbelieved in the reality of the shocks (Perry et al. 2020, table 3). Note also that the obedient subjects may have lied after the fact about their earlier belief state, with the aim of making their behavior appear less reprehensible. If one genuinely thought that the shocks were not real, then one would have no reason for continuing the charade of pretending to shock the learner.

key role in explaining how ordinary human beings could have participated in such atrocities as the Holocaust.

This point is important to bear in mind when we come to assess the morality of defying the law, or other government commands, in the name of justice. It is absurd to describe such defiance (as Robert Bork does) as "selfish". Often, defiance of the government requires heroic levels of courage and commitment to principle, when it would be much easier to simply go along with what the powerful authority figure wants.

Milgram's results also show that there is no need to fear excessive disobedience by ordinary citizens. The natural bias of ordinary human beings is toward obedience, even in the most extreme cases, not defiance. Thus, for example, even if the doctrine of jury nullification were to become widely accepted in our society, we should still anticipate that the power of nullification would be drastically *underused*. (It is true that jury nullification would not technically be a defiance of the law or any other authoritative command, but average jury members are still likely to feel as though they are in some sense defying the state by refusing to enforce its laws.)

11.5.2 The Harm of Obedience

The doctrines of political authority and of the Primacy of Law are extremely dangerous to society. The chief problem is that these doctrines invite those with power to abuse their power for private gain or other personal inclinations, at the expense of the rest of society.

Positions of authority must be filled by human beings, with the standard frailties and flaws to which human beings in general are subject. We do not, for example, have angels or perfect robots to fill government positions. And human beings are often incompetent, lazy, ideological, uninformed, unreasonable, or (almost always) selfish. To accord special privileges and immunities to a position—be it judge, police officer, prosecutor, or legislator—means giving special privileges or immunities to some of these flawed human beings. Any observer familiar with human beings should expect those privileges and immunities to swiftly be turned to the private benefit of the individuals who wield them. Merely telling these human beings that their powers are meant to be used to serve the public does not convert them into altruists who henceforth serve only the public.

This does not show that there should never be positions of authority. But it shows that there is a need, at least, for society to be on guard against the abuse of such positions. If such positions exist, the rest of society must be prepared to monitor the justice and appropriateness of the decisions made by those in positions of authority, and to act on the basis of that assessment.

The doctrine of the Primacy of Law is an invitation to the government to make unjust laws. When lawmakers know that whatever laws they make will be faithfully implemented regardless of whether they be just or unjust, then many lawmakers will disregard justice. When we declare that we will follow the will even of leaders who abuse their power, we are inviting leaders to abuse their power. If, on the other hand, lawmakers anticipate that juries will vote to convict or acquit in individual cases based on the juries' own sense of justice, then lawmakers will have to take into account the perceived justice or injustice of the laws they propose to make. This might make them more wary of creating obviously unjust rules. In any case, individuals should not facilitate and become complicit in abuse of power by agreeing to help implement unjust laws without question.

Recall the case of the Kidnapping Dispute (§11.4.4), in which a philosophy department votes to kidnap a complaining student and hold her prisoner. When Mike acts to sabotage this plan, he is not being antisocial. It is the department that is behaving in an anti-social manner, and Mike who is acting conscientiously and altruistically. One of the reasons why it is morally right for Mike to sabotage the department's plan, as discussed earlier, is simply the injustice about to be visited upon the hapless student. But there is another important reason as well: to avoid inviting future abuse. If all department members go along with the kidnapping plan—perhaps with some verbally expressing their opposition during the meeting but nonetheless faithfully helping to implement the plan after the meeting—then it will become easier for the department to entertain other outrageous plans in the future. If, by contrast, the department's unscrupulous members learn that they cannot count on cooperation from the rest of the department when they vote for outrageous violations of students' rights, they will be less likely to cast such votes in the future. Even if they do vote for other outrageous plans, the conscientious faculty members who refuse to cooperate would still have acted in the morally decent manner.

References

Achen, Christopher H., and Larry M. Bartels. 2017. *Democracy for Realists: Why Elections Do Not Produce Responsive Government*. Princeton: Princeton University Press.

Barkan, Steven, and George Bryjak. 2011. *Fundamentals of Criminal Justice: A Sociological View*. Sudbury: Jones & Bartlett Learning.

Bernstein, Jonathan. 2010, April 9. Voters Want to Cut Spending, But Only If We Keep It Vague. *Salon*. https://www.salon.com/2010/04/08/budget_opinion_open2010/. Accessed 30 June 2020.

Biskupic, Joan. 1999. In Jury Rooms, Form of Civil Protest Grows. *Washington Post*, February 8, p. A1. Available at http://www.washingtonpost.com/wp-srv/national/jury080299.htm. Accessed 5 Apr 2012.

Bissell, John W. 1997. Comments on Jury Nullification. *Cornell Journal of Law and Public Policy* 7: 51–56.

Bork, Robert H. 1999, June/July. Thomas More for Our Season, *First Things: A Monthly Journal of Religion & Public Life* 94: 17–21.

Burger, Jerry. 2009. Replicating Milgram: Would People Still Obey Today? *American Psychologist* 64: 1–11.

Crispo, Lawrence W., Jill M. Slansky, and Geanene M. Yriarte. 1997. Jury Nullification: Law Versus Anarchy. *Loyola of Los Angeles Law Review* 31: 1–61.

Federal Bureau of Investigation. 2019. Crime in the United States, 2018. https://ucr.fbi.gov/crime-in-the-u.s/2018/crime-in-the-u.s.-2018. Accessed 27 June 2020.

Greenblatt, Nathan. 2008. How Mandatory Are Mandatory Minimums: How Judges Can Avoid Imposing Mandatory Minimum Sentences. *American Journal of Criminal Law* 36: 1–38.

Leipold, Andrew D. 1996. Rethinking Jury Nullification. *Virginia Law Review* 82: 253–324.
Leventhal, Harold. 1972. Majority Opinion in *United States v. Dougherty*, 473 F.2d 1113.
Milgram, Stanley. 2009. *Obedience to Authority: An Experimental View.* New York: Harper.
Perry, Gina, Augustine Brannigan, Richard A. Wanner, and Henderikus Stam. 2020. Credibility and Incredulity in Milgram's Obedience Experiments: A Reanalysis of an Unpublished Test. *Social Psychology Quarterly* 83: 88–106.
Sears, David O., and Jack Citrin. 1985. *Tax Revolt: Something for Nothing in California.* Enlarged ed. Cambridge: Harvard University Press.
Sobeloff, Simon E. 1969. Opinion in *United States v. Moylan*, 417 F.2d 1002.

12

Conclusion

In this final chapter, I summarize what I have argued up to this point, followed by some remarks on why conventional legal philosophy has often gone wrong and what the U.S. legal system has gotten right.

12.1 Flaws in the U.S. Legal System

No single book could detail all the flaws in any real-world legal system. I have tried to focus in this book on flaws in the American legal system that are clear, serious, and pervasive. In other words, these are features of the legal system that (i) can be known to be unjust with a high degree of confidence, (ii) are extremely unjust, not just slightly unjust, and (iii) affect a large range of what the legal system does. There will, however, inevitably be controversy about some of the alleged injustices I have listed, particularly those of the first category below.

12.1.1 Unjust Laws

The first charge against the legal system is the charge of overcriminalization. The government has designated too many activities as crimes. The reason this constitutes an injustice derives from the coercive nature of law. Any criminal law will be enforced through harmful coercion against those who violate that law. But individuals in general have a prima facie right against being harmfully coerced. This prima facie right means that an act of harmful coercion is unjust, *unless* there exist sufficiently weighty moral reasons to justify it. Self-defense and defense of innocent third parties generally qualify as sufficiently weighty reasons to justify harmful coercion against those who threaten to violate the rights of others. However, there are a number of laws for which no justification of that kind is available, since those who violate these laws do not thereby violate or threaten to violate the rights of others. This plausibly includes, for example, the laws against recreational drug use, prostitution, and gambling, as well as immigration restrictions and many economic regulations.

Each of these laws has defenders who offer arguments in their support. The reasons offered, however, are insufficient to justify harmful coercion. This can be seen by imagining non-political contexts in which an individual deploys harmful coercion against another, based upon similar sorts of reasons. For example, it is said that the state must prohibit most recreational drug use because the proscribed drugs harm users' health. But if an individual were to deploy a similar kind of harmful coercion against another individual for similar reasons, nearly everyone would see this as seriously wrong. For example, if you were to take a neighbor prisoner at gunpoint and confine the neighbor for a period of months or years because of his unhealthy habits, this would be an extremely serious, unjustified violation of the neighbor's rights. Similar observations apply to all of the common arguments in defense of drug prohibition, as well as each of the other kinds of unjust laws I have mentioned.

12.1.2 Unjust Prices

The extraordinary expense of accessing the legal system is an underdiscussed form of injustice in the system. Most criminal defendants are unable to afford high-quality defense and receive limited services from overworked and underpaid public defenders. Citizens who have disputes with one another are commonly unable to access the state's court system to resolve these disputes, due to prohibitive prices of legal services. Even simply consulting an expert for advice about a legal question is frequently beyond reasonable reach for ordinary citizens. This situation is not merely a misfortune for citizens who need legal services, but an injustice these citizens suffer at the hands of the state. There are three reasons for this.

First, the high prices of legal services are a predictable consequence of features of the system that are intentionally imposed by the state, which the state did not need to impose. For example, government licensing requirements in this area are extremely onerous, leading predictably (and by design) to drastically inflated prices for legal services. Economic research does not indicate that licensing laws improve quality. Rather, they serve to reduce supply and raise prices, preventing a large number of individuals from obtaining the relevant good or service. The state also predictably inflates legal service prices by creating excessively complex and opaquely-written laws, by creating too many laws, and by operating a dangerous system that has a high risk of imposing large, unjust costs on those who do not obtain third-party legal representation.

Second, the state has a positive obligation to provide justice for citizens. This is in part because the state has coercively monopolized large parts of this industry, and the state coercively collects revenues from citizens with the stated justification that this collection is necessary for the state to provide justice. In addition, in many cases, the state's failure to provide a just resolution of a case will in fact involve the state in imposing an *unjust* resolution. For example, if a criminal defendant is wrongly convicted, the state will not merely fail to do justice; it will actively impose an unjust punishment. If a civil court wrongly finds for the plaintiff in a lawsuit, the state will not merely fail to do justice; it will unjustly rob the defendant of his money. For these reasons, the government has an obligation to provide justice for each individual, even if the individual cannot or will not expend large sums of money on a private attorney.

Third, the extraordinary prices of legal services turn the state into a tool of injustice in the hands of unscrupulous agents. In some cases, individuals or organizations can threaten to financially ruin innocent persons merely by involving them in legal action. In other cases, an individual or organization can get away with cheating or otherwise mistreating others by relying on the inability of their victims to afford the legal services needed to pursue a remedy. Since the state has an obligation to avoid contributing to these sorts of injustices, it is obligated to remedy the excessive costs of legal services.

12.1.3 Plea Bargaining

Individuals accused of a crime have a natural right to have their cases adjudicated in a reasonably reliable, impartial manner. In the U.S. justice system, they also have a legal right, more specifically, to have their guilt adjudicated by a jury trial.

These rights, however, are violated in nearly every criminal case in the United States. Nearly every criminal defendant (about 97%) is coerced by the prosecutor into surrendering the right to a trial. Defendants who insist on a trial regularly face more charges, more serious charges, and longer sentences—on average, more than three times longer—than those who agree to plead guilty. The actual process by which almost all criminal charges are adjudicated in the U.S. is a negotiation between lawyers, wherein no impartial third party ever weighs the evidence. Courts have been sidelined and most of their power handed over to prosecutors.

The U.S. Supreme Court has upheld the practice of plea bargaining, claiming that guilty pleas obtained by threats of harsher sentences are nevertheless voluntary, as long as the defendant is fully informed and able to make a rational decision in the face of the prosecutor's threat. The problem with this notion of voluntariness is that it ignores the central reason why coerced confessions are prohibited. Coerced confessions in general are unacceptable because they are not a reliable way of ascertaining guilt, since innocent individuals can be coerced to confess. For example, nearly anyone will confess to nearly any crime under torture. Similarly, innocent individuals can be induced to confess to crimes they never committed by the pressures of America's plea bargaining system. There are hundreds of known cases in which criminal defendants pled guilty and were sentenced to prison, only to be later proved innocent. We must assume, however, that the majority of individuals who are coerced to falsely condemn themselves are never exonerated.

12.1.4 Unjust Punishments

Most crimes in the U.S. that are more serious than traffic offenses are punished with imprisonment.[1] The U.S. uses prison far more often, and gives far longer terms of imprisonment, than otherwise similar nations such as France, Germany, Finland, England, and Canada. Often, American sentences are several times longer than those that would be given for similar crimes in other nations. As a result, the U.S. has in recent decades become the world leader in incarcerating people, with 700 prisoners per 100,000 population, over four times the world average of 145 prisoners per 100,000 population.[2]

There are two main problems with this situation. The first is that most prison sentences given in the U.S., particularly for non-violent offences, are drastically disproportionate as punishments. They inflict a harm on the prisoner that is many times worse, sometimes hundreds of times worse, than the harm caused by the crime for which the sentence is given. The Code of Hammurabi famously prescribed "an eye for an eye", but many American punishments are closer to "200 eyes for an eye".

The second problem is that inmates in American prisons are often subjected to physical and sexual abuse by both guards and other prisoners. This problem is widely recognized, but there is little concern about it on the part of government officials or the public, due to general lack of

---

[1] 66.9% of cases, according to Petteruti and Fenster (2011, p. 21).
[2] Walmsley (2018, p. 2).

sympathy for convicted criminals. It is unlikely that prison abuse will drastically decline in the foreseeable future. Since it would be wrong to intentionally sentence defendants to receive such abuse, it is also highly questionable to assign prison sentences to defendants in the knowledge that many of them will in fact suffer such abuse. For this reason, incarceration should be seen as something closer to a last resort, rather than a first resort as in the present system. Incarceration should be reserved for serious violent crimes, where the criminal poses an ongoing threat to the community.

12.1.5 Abuse of Power

Individuals in positions of power commonly abuse that power. This is not an occasional fluke, but an extremely common, robust feature of social institutions that give some people power over others, a feature that has been observed for all of recorded human history. The problem is rooted in human nature and is therefore not likely to end soon. There is thus a critical need for social institutions to provide for the enforcement of the law against the powerful.

Police, for example, sometimes brutalize or kill suspects unnecessarily. This is particularly common in the U.S., which has a much higher rate of police homicides than otherwise similar nations. Prosecutors, as well, sometimes pursue charges against innocent individuals, pursue grossly disproportionate sentences, or illegally suppress exculpatory evidence. Anecdotal evidence suggests that most prosecutors are more concerned about winning than about doing justice. Finally, other government officials often violate the law under the guise of public policy, as in the case of the U.S. President ordering terrorism suspects to be tortured or assassinated. *Pace* Richard Nixon, U.S. laws against murder, torture, burglary, kidnapping, and so on do not contain special exceptions for the President or other government officials, nor should they.

Defenders of the American legal system often speak about the importance of "the Rule of Law". One of the things this phrase is generally taken to imply is that all individuals—the rich and the poor, the meek and the powerful—should be subject to the same laws. But the rule of law in this sense is a fiction which the government has no evident interest in making a reality. The same system that sentences one man to life in prison for forging an $88 check, and another to 60 years for a non-violent drug offense, becomes extraordinarily lenient when members of the government are found to have committed crimes. Police, for example, are almost never prosecuted when they kill citizens, even unarmed citizens. When prosecuted, they are almost never convicted. And when convicted, they receive sentences a fraction as harsh as those given to private criminals for the same crime.

Prosecutors are even more protected. It is virtually unheard of for a prosecutor to be charged with a crime, no matter how egregious the prosecutor's conduct may be. No prosecutor wants to turn against one of their own. Furthermore, the legal system grants prosecutors and judges absolute immunity from lawsuits for any wrongs committed while performing their duties, however clear and malicious they may be.

Other executive branch officials, including the President, can in theory be prosecuted or sued for using the powers of their office to commit crimes. Yet even in the clearest cases of such criminal behavior, the President is never held accountable. The next President can be counted on to either pardon his predecessor or simply ignore his predecessor's crimes. The legal system is lacking in needed safeguards against the abuse of power.

12.2 Toward a Justice-Oriented Legal Philosophy

12.2.1 Placing Justice Before the Law

The primary purpose of a legal system is to achieve justice. The innocent should be acquitted, the blameworthy should receive proportionate punishment, debts should be enforced, and culpable harms should be compensated. All who come before the legal system should have their rights respected and their cases fairly and impartially resolved. Those who operate within the system, including judges, prosecutors, lawyers, and juries, should carry out their functions with these goals in mind. Thus, prosecutors should not seek unjust punishments, judges should not assign such punishments, lawyers should not seek unjust trial outcomes, and juries should not convict defendants for morally blameless behavior.

From a certain point of view, all this seems obvious (who could be in favor of injustice?). Yet this philosophy is highly controversial among legal professionals. The orthodox view today is that the primary function of the legal system is to enforce the law, regardless of whether the law and its enforcement are just or unjust. Furthermore, individuals operating within the legal system, it is said, not only have no obligation to consider the requirements of justice, but actually *should not* entertain such considerations. They should simply carry out the role that the system has assigned to them, blind to the moral implications of their actions in the individual case. Thus, on this view, lawyers should pursue whatever legal outcomes best serve the interests of their clients; judges and prosecutors should strive to faithfully enforce the laws given to them by the legislature; and juries should weigh the factual evidence in a case and report on whether that evidence establishes a violation of the law.

What is wrong with this conventional legal philosophy? The primary problem is that while *justice* has intrinsic normative force, *law* does not. All persons have a natural moral obligation to act justly and to avoid knowingly contributing to injustice. No ulterior justification is needed for the pursuit of justice. A justification *is* needed, however, for the social institution of law—that is, some reason is needed for forcibly imposing certain rules on everyone, through the mechanism of the legal system. That reason is not far to find: the central purpose of the law is to establish justice. The law, when functioning properly, does this by publicly identifying the natural rights of individuals, as well as specifying society's expectations for certain interactions where the general principles of morality leave indeterminate what should be expected of individuals. If this is the case, then the value of justice in general must come before that of fidelity to the law, since in general the means to an end cannot be more important than the end itself.

This does not prove that justice to the individual must be an overriding consideration in all cases. There may be cases in which doing justice to the individuals involved in the particular case stands in tension with promoting justice in the wider society. There may also be cases in which some other important value stands in tension with justice, such as the value of peaceful social cooperation. What the above considerations establish, therefore, is only a *presumption* in favor of individual justice: by default, we should assume that participants in the legal system should render justice to the individuals involved in a particular case, unless there are compelling reasons to the contrary.

12.2.2 Against Authority

Political philosophers have developed several theories to account for the presumed authority of the state. These theories seek to explain, in brief, why the government is entitled to forcibly impose rules on the rest of society, and why individuals have an obligation to obey those rules. If some theory of political authority were to succeed, it might explain why participants in the legal system should strive to faithfully uphold the law.

The leading accounts of political authority, however, all fail. One account claims that the authority of the state derives from a contract between citizens and the state, whereby citizens agree to obey the government in return for the government's providing law and order. This theory faces the problem that the contract in question is purely fictitious; no such contract has ever in fact been offered or signed. The claim that individuals "implicitly agree" to the social contract merely by living within the country is analogous to my claim that my neighbors "agree" to pay me protection money by living in their own houses.

Another account claims that the authority of the state is established by a *hypothetical* contract—that is, by the fact that individuals in certain idealized conditions *would* agree to establish a government with certain powers, in order to provide law and order. Advocates of the hypothetical social contract theory claim that such hypothetical agreement is morally relevant because it demonstrates the *fairness* and *reasonableness* of the would-be contract. The problem with this theory is that such fairness and reasonableness do not suffice to generate obligations of obedience, nor do they suspend the rights of individuals. For example, if I make an offer of employment to another individual, the other party acquires obligations under the offered employment contract only if they *actually* sign the contract. If they do not sign, I may not forcibly impose the terms of the contract on them, regardless of how fair and reasonable my offer may have been.

The social contract theory requires unanimous consent to establish political authority. A third theory, the democratic theory of authority, claims that a government may acquire authority through the consent of a *majority* of citizens, obtained through the popular election of leaders. This theory runs into the difficulty that a vote of a majority of individuals in a group does not morally suspend the rights of the minority. If, for example, a group of three people decide to rob a fourth of his money, the theft cannot be made just merely by its being supported by a larger number of people than the one who opposes it. Nor does a person acquire an obligation to obey a command simply because it is supported by a majority. In view of this, there is no reason to think that the democratic process generates political authority.

Finally, the utilitarian account holds that authority is generated by the large benefits of government. Government, it is said, is needed to avoid a breakdown of social order which would be extremely detrimental to human well-being. In order for the government to provide social order, it is necessary that the government make and enforce laws, and that most people obey the government's laws voluntarily. Therefore, the government is entitled to enforce its laws, and citizens ought to obey those laws. The principle is illustrated by the example of a lifeboat that needs to be bailed out in order to stay afloat. If the passengers do not voluntarily bail the water, one would be justified in coercing them to do so, in order to save all from drowning. Furthermore, passengers on the boat would have an obligation to help bail water.

The shortcoming of this argument is that it fails to account for a key defining feature of the notion of authority, that of *content-independence*. This is the idea that the government is not only entitled to enforce objectively correct laws, e.g., laws that codify pre-existing moral obligations, but that the government is entitled to enforce the laws that it has actually made, including the laws that are useless, harmful, or unjust. To return to the lifeboat analogy, the individual who saves the boat from sinking by forcing the passengers to bail water would not thereby acquire a moral entitlement, in addition, to demand that the passengers hand over their jewelry, say, or that they pray to the God of the Ocean. Similarly, the presumed benefits of law and order do not explain what entitles the state, in addition to enforcing just and beneficial laws, to also enforce useless, harmful, or unjust laws.

12.2.3 Role Obligations

Many believe that, when one is assigned a particular role within a social institution, one typically has a moral obligation to faithfully execute that role, according to the norms in place within that institution. Perhaps this suffices to explain the obligation of individuals to faithfully carry out their assigned roles in the legal system. Those roles, it is said, do not include making moral judgments about the justice of legally prescribed outcomes; therefore, judges, juries, and lawyers should not allow such judgments to affect the way they carry out their roles.

But it is not always desirable or even permissible to carry out one's assigned role within an institution. In particular, if a social role requires one to violate the rights of other persons, it is not ethically permissible to faithfully execute that role—a social group cannot suspend individual rights merely by creating a *role* for people who violate rights. For example, an assassin working for a criminal organization cannot justify murder by appealing (truthfully) to the requirements of his position within the organization. In that case, of course, the organization as a whole is undesirable. But a similar lesson applies to organizations that are overall beneficial. If, for example, my university were to invent a special position within the school that calls for unjustly persecuting a random student each year, it would remain wrong to persecute that student, even if I had been assigned that role, and even if my university were overall beneficial to society. Similarly, if one's assigned role within the legal system requires one to inflict unjust harms on other people, it is ethically impermissible to carry out one's role in that respect.

Some argue that it is permissible to carry out one's role, even when doing so seems to generate injustice in the individual case, because the legal system operates most reliably to achieve justice when all participants faithfully execute their assigned roles. Unfortunately, there is no obvious reason to believe this. In human experience, desirable outcomes usually do not occur spontaneously if no one aims at bringing them about. It is of course *possible* for this to occur, but one needs a reason for thinking that it would occur in the case of the legal system. If judges, juries, and lawyers all disregard judgments about the morality of legal outcomes, why would we expect that morally justifiable outcomes will transpire? Indeed, we have seen above that the system regularly generates injustice.

Perhaps if the democratic process were extremely reliable at generating precise, just, and beneficial laws, it might be more reasonable for the individuals operating the legal system to defer to the laws passed by the democratically elected legislature. But there is, again, no reason to believe that this is the case. Research in political psychology regularly confirms the very low degree of sophistication to be found among typical voters, due in part to the incentive structure created by a large democratic society: each voter knows that there is a negligible chance of her vote affecting the outcome of any election, and therefore the voter has little incentive to exert effort to vote wisely. Accordingly, the democratic process is often driven by superficial emotional appeals, insensitive to central justice-related concerns. Thus, an individual who finds a seemingly persuasive argument that a particular law is unjust has little or no reason to reconsider that conclusion merely because the law was produced democratically.

Finally, when considering the argument from role obligations as applied to the case of jury nullification, it is important to ask what the proper role of a jury is. Opponents of jury nullification commonly assume that the jury's role is that of a morally neutral fact-finder. There is, however, no reason to believe this. The historical record leaves little doubt that, at the time the right to trial by jury was enshrined in the U.S. Constitution, the role of the jury was understood in an expansive way: the jury was intended to represent the conscience of the community, to protect the individual against unjust, tyrannical, or unconstitutional laws, through the jury's absolute power to acquit defendants whom the jury finds undeserving of punishment. This is, indeed, the only plausible explanation for why juries are needed, since the functions of weighing factual evidence and interpreting legal texts would be better carried out by legal professionals. It is only distrust of the state that justifies the right to trial by jury.

12.2.4 The Need for Uniformity

Some thinkers argue that the importance of the Rule of Law outweighs that of doing justice to the individual, and thus that judges, juries, and prosecutors should enforce the existing law even when the law has unjust implications in the individual case.

On one natural interpretation, this argument begs the question: it assumes the unconditional desirability of enforcing the law, when this is precisely what is in dispute. Fortunately, appeals to the Rule of Law are often supplemented by accounts of why the Rule of Law is important. It is said that consistent enforcement of the written, publicly accessible laws is necessary for individuals to be able to predict what will be expected of them, and what sorts of behavior will and will not be punished. This predictability is needed for individuals to plan their lives. By contrast, if legal outcomes are dependent on the moral judgment of individual judges and juries, the results will be unpredictable, since different judges and juries may differ in their moral beliefs.

This argument, however, paints with too broad a brush, failing to distinguish unexpected *punishments* from unexpected *leniency*. The possibility of unexpected punishments—as in the case where an individual is punished for behavior that violates no written law—does indeed make it difficult for individuals to plan their behavior. Business owners, for example, need to know, before they invest a large amount of time and money in starting a business, that their business will not be shut down by the government six months into its operation. They therefore require an assurance that they will not be prosecuted if they do not violate the law.

But unexpected *leniency*—the possibility that one *may not* be punished even if one violates a written law—does not create the same problem. It is not the case, for example, that one cannot plan one's behavior if one is unsure whether one would be punished for using recreational drugs or whether instead a jury would vote to acquit due to moral qualms about the drug laws. If one wishes to be assured of not being punished, one still has the option of refraining from drug use, even if juries sometimes vote to nullify the drug laws. If, on the other hand, one is willing to risk being punished, one can only welcome the reduction in that risk resulting from the occasional case of jury nullification.

It is not even clear, in fact, that jury nullification renders the consequences of lawbreaking more uncertain in any interesting sense. The great majority of law violations are never prosecuted because the government either does not discover the crime, cannot identify the perpetrator, or cannot gather sufficient evidence to convict the perpetrator. Thus, it is already uncertain, in general, whether one will be punished for violating the law, and yet no one raises alarms that this situation violates the Rule of Law and makes planning impossible. It is not clear that the existence of jury nullification makes things more uncertain in any interesting sense.

One may object that there is an inherent injustice in the *non-uniformity* of treatment that results from individual judges and juries exercising their own judgments: individuals who violate the same law in relevantly similar circumstances may be treated very differently, depending upon which judge or jury they happen to draw. While this is true, the injustice involved in the non-uniform treatment can only be an injustice *to* the person who is mistreated. Thus, suppose that the drug laws are unjust, and suppose that because of this, some but not all juries in drug trials vote to acquit regardless of the evidence. As a result, of two defendants guilty of similar illegal drug use, one is unjustly punished while the other is set free. This non-uniformity of treatment is unfair, but it is only unfair to the one who is punished. The only acceptable remedy, therefore, would be to persuade more juries to acquit in such cases. To convince more juries to *convict* would only be to expand the injustice.

12.2.5 Social Deference

In human social groups, including whole societies as well as smaller groups, it is common for people to have intractable differences of opinion regarding how the group should act. In such cases, it is important that the group nevertheless be able to engage in coordinated action, without members continually striving to undermine each other. For this to occur, individual group members must possess the virtue of social deference: the disposition to defer to the results of an accepted decision-making procedure, even in those cases where one believes the decision to be unwise.

This observation gives rise to another argument in favor of enforcing unjust laws. It can be reasonably argued that, in the case of an organization whose function includes enforcing the requirements of justice (as is the case with the state), there must be a place for deference to collective decisions concerning what the demands of justice should be taken to be. Since one cannot expect perfect agreement on what justice requires, members of such an organization, or non-members who are asked to assist the organization in enforcing the demands of justice, must be disposed to defer to some decision-making procedure, even when they disagree with its outcome; otherwise, collective action is undermined, and justice itself will suffer.

Even in this case, however, there must be constraints on what a conscientious person will defer to—one cannot be morally required to defer to *any* collective decision, however egregious. Two important constraints are particularly plausible. First, one should defer to a collective decision regarding what putative demands of justice should be accepted, only when the decision appears to be sincerely aimed at justice. If other members of the organization have used the decision-making procedure to disregard justice—for example, to cynically pursue their own interests without regard to what is right or wrong—then one is no longer obligated to respect such decisions.

Second, one should defer to collective decisions regarding the accepted principles of justice only if one finds those decisions to be at least somewhat competent and reasonable. That is, one is not morally obligated to defer to decisions that are irrational or extremely ill-informed, even if the decision-makers believe their chosen policy to be just.

The reason for these constraints lies in the original justification for social deference: the function of social deference is to facilitate coordinated action in pursuit of a legitimate goal—in this case, the enforcement of the demands of justice. The function of social deference is not to enable a group to cynically pursue self-interest while ignoring morality. If social deference becomes a tool for undermining morality, it ceases to be a virtue.

In the case of the injustices in the legal system that we have reviewed in this book, the above two constraints are violated. The drug laws, for example, do not represent a reasonable, good faith interpretation of the requirements of justice. Nor does the practice of coercing defendants into giving up their right to a trial. Nor do many draconian punishments handed out in the criminal justice system. And nor do the legal doctrines that insulate government officials from being held accountable for abuse of power. The explanation for these laws and practices is not that reasonable, competent evaluators on reflection have found them just. The explanation is that government decision-makers are largely indifferent to justice, and average voters are largely both indifferent and incompetent.

Granted, reasonable disagreement about justice is possible. But lack of reasonable disagreement is also possible. There is no reasonable disagreement, for example, about whether it is just to sentence a person to 60 years in prison for a non-violent drug offense. The existence of reasonable disagreements cannot be taken to justify knowingly imposing unjust resolutions in cases in which there is no reasonable disagreement.

12.3 An Error Theory: The Cognitive Handicap of Jurisprudence

Most of the widely-accepted ideas in legal theory are reasonable and show sensitivity to relevant moral considerations. Indeed, common law doctrines often display a subtlety and sophistication hardly to be found in the writings of mere philosophers. Yet there are some orthodox legal doctrines—and not just ones devised by cynical politicians but ones originating in the opinions of experienced and sophisticated judges—that appear obviously unreasonable and for which the standard, accepted reasoning is of strikingly poor quality. In this connection, I would cite the legal arguments in defense of plea bargaining (see §§5.2 and 5.3), for prosecutorial immunity (see §7.3.3), and against jury nullification (see Chaps. 10 and 11). Assuming I am right about this, what accounts for these peculiar jurisprudential lapses of reason?

The pattern becomes more understandable once we take into account the distinctive intellectual handicap under which legal professionals labor. Standard moral reasoning is, or at least strives to be, conducted from an objective point of view. But reasoning in professional legal contexts is not conducted from an objective point of view. Professional legal reasoning is constrained by the need to cohere with *the point of view of the state*. This prevents legal reasoners from following arguments where they lead and drives them, in certain cases, to adopt what third parties can see to be thin rationalizations.

The reason for this constraint is that legal reasoning is reasoning conducted within or about the legal system, a system created and operated by the state for its own purposes. This reasoning is designed to be presented *to* or *by government officials*, namely, judges presiding over government courts. In most cases, this poses no major problem, since most legal cases do not turn on challenges to the state's point of view. In disputes between two private parties, the state may well serve as an impartial referee. It is when the state or its employees are parties to a dispute—or more generally, when the viewpoint of the state is under challenge—that the state becomes unqualified to judge. But judge those cases it does, because there is no alternative, non-state court system available.[3] And it is in those cases that we see the clearest motivated reasoning on display, because the courts are concerned to vindicate the viewpoint of their own organization.

What is the state's point of view? The viewpoint of the state involves, above all, an assumption of the state's own unquestionable authority. It assumes that the state is exclusively entitled to rule over the rest of society—to issue commands, backed by threats of violence, that would be illegitimate for any other person or organization to make. It assumes a remarkable power to create or suspend moral obligations simply by the government's own say-so. It assumes that the state is trustworthy and good, and that its own plans, judgments, and interests are paramount over those of anyone else. These assumptions, from an external point of view, may appear as self-interested and self-aggrandizing biases, yet it is also part of the state's ideology to *deny* that these assumptions are the self-centered biases of the organization in power. Thus, a pretense of

---

[3] A non-state legal system is, however, possible; see Barnett (1998); Huemer (2013, ch. 11).

objectivity must be maintained, even while indulging the most obvious biases. This is why, when courts issue rulings designed to protect the interests of the state's own members, they do not frankly declare their motivation to protect the interests of the powerful. They devise rationalizations based on nominally impartial values, such as "the public interest" or "the rule of law". See, for example, the arguments for prosecutorial immunity discussed in §7.3.3.

At the same time, there is a fiction of legal absolutism—that court decisions are always driven by and consistent with the existing law as of the time of the decision, and that the importance of fidelity to the law is never outweighed.[4] In reality, the courts often find the implications of a law so inconvenient that they simply decide to change the law. When they do this, they do not frankly declare that they are creating a new law or rejecting an existing law due to the social benefits they foresee from doing so; they devise rationalizations to maintain the fiction of interpreting the law. See, for example, the arguments for the Constitutionality of plea bargaining (§§5.2 and 5.3). With respect to that issue, a previous Supreme Court decision (*U.S. v. Jackson*) obviously entailed a rejection of plea bargaining; yet when directly confronted with the issue (*Brady v. U.S.*), the Court shied away from the implication that over three fourths of all criminal convictions in the nation at the time were legally invalid. Rather than frankly confess that they were abridging Constitutional rights for pragmatic reasons, the Court pretended to be interpreting the notion of voluntariness. They never explained how their decisions in *Jackson* and *Brady* could be consistent with each other.

When judges produce opinions that flatter the point of view of the state, it need not be through dishonesty. In all probability, many judges sincerely subscribe to the viewpoint of the state. They may instinctively revere and trust government. This explains, in part, how they came to be judges to begin with. A U.S. President, for example, is unlikely to appoint to the bench anyone who distrusts the power of the executive branch. The U.S. Senate is unlikely to confirm anyone who distrusts the power of the legislature. And anyone who distrusts the power of the judiciary is unlikely to choose to become a judge. Thus, federal judges tend to be

---

[4] Or as Martin Shapiro (1994, p. 156) tactfully puts it, "Courts and judges always lie."

12 Conclusion

people who, at a fundamental level, trust government power. At the state level, some judges are elected by popular vote, while others are appointed. There may thus be a lesser degree of bias among state judges; nevertheless, those who become judges, in general, tend to identify with the state.

Legal arguments are aimed at this group of people. Lawyers will not bother making arguments that they do not expect to receive a sympathetic hearing from a judge. The legal arguments given by judges themselves are designed to fit with the ideas and arguments that *other* judges have advanced. Thus, lawyers and judges have internalized the norm that legal reasoning must cohere with the self-conception of the state.

It is worth noting that academic opinion often diverges markedly from judicial opinion in legal matters. Thus, while the Supreme Court unanimously upheld the constitutionality of plea bargaining in *Brady v. United States*, opinion among academic researchers tends to be sharply against plea bargaining. The most likely explanation for this divergence is a lesser degree of bias among academics, who tend to have much less identification with the state, as compared to judges. Plea bargaining, despite its injustice, is of course an enormous convenience for the state.

Yet even academic scholars are influenced by the government perspective. Law professors, after all, exist to train lawyers. A good lawyer is not one who makes *correct* moral or legal judgments; a good lawyer is one who can accurately anticipate what *a judge would accept*. And therefore a good law professor is not one who teaches students the most accurate or reasonable views; a good law professor must teach students *the views of judges*. If judges have taken an objectively untenable view, one must still learn to reason under the pretense that that view is correct and reasonable. While academic researchers are at least *more* independent of the state than judges, there is nevertheless a kind of anchoring effect, whereby the natural default view on legal issues is taken to be the view that would be adopted by judges.

All of this would be unproblematic, if the point of view of the state were on all matters objectively correct. But that is too much to expect. The perspective of the state may be flawed. The state may not, after all, have a right to command the rest of society. Its agencies may not be trustworthy. Its laws may be immoral or irrational. Its policies may be driven more by the interests of the powerful than by the good of society. If any of these things were the case, the field of legal theory, influenced as it is by the perspective of the state, would most likely be afflicted with serious and widespread error. That, I believe, is the best explanation for the main errors of conventional legal philosophy.

12.4 Virtues of American Justice

This book is apt to give the impression that the American legal system is irredeemably deficient and entirely unconcerned with justice. That is the natural consequence of focusing attention on the system's greatest flaws. Yet when we think about reforming the system, it is important to appreciate the system's virtues so that those virtues may be preserved. For this reason, I want to conclude this book by mentioning some of the most important aspects of the system that are genuinely aimed at justice. Indeed, despite the flaws mentioned above, the U.S. legal system remains superior to the great majority of legal systems that human beings have employed throughout history.

The first thing to appreciate about the system is the presumption of innocence, which requires a prosecutor to prove the defendant's guilt beyond reasonable doubt; the defense need not prove anything. One reason for this presumption is that it is morally worse to unjustly punish a person than it is to merely fail to justly punish; it is therefore appropriate, when there is no strong evidence for either guilt or innocence, to take no action, rather than to risk imposing unjust punishment. In addition, there will typically be a very large number of individuals for whom little to no evidence can be brought to bear, either for or against the hypothesis that they committed a given crime. Of these individuals, the overwhelming majority will be innocent. If we employed a mere preponderance-of-evidence standard, enormous numbers of innocent people would be susceptible to criminal punishment, when some shred of evidence suggested that they may have committed a crime and no evidence of their innocence could be found.

The standard of evidence also affects the behavior of investigators, since police will stop investigating a crime when they believe the evidentiary threshold for a conviction is met. Thus, if we had a lower standard of evidence, then police would perform less careful investigations, and many revealing pieces of evidence would never surface. If we used a preponderance-of-evidence standard, for example, then police might stop investigating as soon as a suspect was implicated by a single witness; they might forego collecting forensic evidence, interviewing other witnesses, and so on.

The second great virtue of the American system is the institution of trial by jury. Though jury trials have unfortunately been drastically curtailed due to the practice of plea bargaining, they remain an option that is at least occasionally exercised. The possibility of insisting on a jury trial exerts some pressure toward preventing prosecutors from filing frivolous charges not supported by the evidence. It also provides an opportunity (albeit one too rarely exercised) for ordinary citizens to veto the enforcement of egregiously unjust laws, or the imposition of egregiously unjust sentences. In this connection, it is important that the jury is protected against retaliation for its verdict, whether it be one of guilt or innocence. Of course, if the state could punish jurors for voting to acquit (as occurred before the modern traditions regarding the independence of the jury were fully established[5]), then the purpose of the jury would be undermined.

The third important feature is the right to counsel. Though this right is greatly weakened by the extremely high prices of legal services, it is nevertheless important that individuals who are prosecuted or sued have a legal right to retain professional counsel to represent their case. Without this right, inexperienced defendants would too often be unjustly convicted or receive unjust judgments against them due to their failure to effectively articulate their case. Government prosecutors, being far more familiar with the system and far more practiced in argumentation, would find it too easy to manipulate trials to the disadvantage of defendants, both the guilty and the innocent alike.

Fourth, the justice system has a collection of rules requiring transparency. Defendants have the right to be informed of the charges against them, to access all the evidence that the prosecution has, and to cross

---

[5] Chisholm (1911). The practice of punishing juries became obsolete after the famous trial of William Penn (the same man who later founded Pennsylvania), in which the judge unsuccessfully tried to coerce the jury into convicting Penn of speaking to an unlawful assembly.

examine the witnesses against them. This is important because a defendant may be able to rebut the case against him *if* he knows exactly what the case is, but will generally be unable—even if innocent—to rebut a case that he is not adequately informed of. Even the most innocent person cannot prove himself innocent of a crime if he does not know what crime he is supposed to have committed, nor can he rebut seemingly incriminating evidence if he does not know what that evidence is. Thus, without the process of discovery and the right to cross examine witnesses, innocent people would be too easily convicted.

Fifth, the justice system separates the roles of police (who investigate crimes), prosecutors (who present the case against the defendant), jurors (who evaluate that case), and judges (who preside over the trial and assign sentences upon conviction). It is particularly important that those who arrest or file charges against a defendant are distinct people from those who *evaluate* the case. If those functions were combined—if, for example, the police who investigated a given crime were also given the authority to make final determinations of guilt or innocence, then conviction would be all but guaranteed. Since police want to close cases and take credit for solving crimes, they would arrest and convict people even on the flimsiest of evidence. Unfortunately, the plea bargaining system has, again, greatly attenuated this virtue of the American justice system by cutting out the impartial evaluator from the vast majority of cases.

Each of these norms is crucial to protecting against unjust punishments. Each of them embodies a non-trivial insight, one that could easily be overlooked by someone designing a justice system. To illustrate this point, note that American universities during the last several years have created their own quasi-judicial systems, dedicated to investigating allegations of sexual harassment or assault at the university.[6] University offices conduct investigations and hearings, issue findings regarding such

---

[6] This was mandated by the "Dear Colleague letter" sent by the U.S. Department of Education to all colleges and universities in the U.S. in 2011 (Ali 2011). For a window into how universities have handled these cases, see Kipnis (2017). Though the Department of Education's requirements for sexual harassment investigations were later softened in 2017, few universities have changed their practices.

accusations, and specify punishments or other remedies in the event that the accused is found to have committed misconduct. In these quasi-judicial systems, all five of the features of the U.S. justice system mentioned above are commonly absent—there is usually no presumption of innocence, no right to a jury trial, no right to counsel, no right to be informed of the accusations or the evidence against one, and no right to confront witnesses. The investigator, prosecutor, jury, and judge functions are all performed by the same office. That office is also potentially subject to lawsuits filed in the court system of the larger society, in the event that the university fails to convict or sufficiently punish alleged sexual harassers.

All of which illustrates that, flawed as the American legal system is, it is far from the worst that a legal system could be. Many of our traditions reflect deep insights and are well-tuned to the pursuit of justice. Some of the worst flaws in the legal system (overcriminalization, the rise of plea bargaining, the rise of mass incarceration, the active discouragement of jury nullification) are in fact departures from earlier and wiser traditions. It is to be hoped, therefore, that recent trends can be reversed so that America's legal system can live up to its promise of "equal justice under law".

References

Ali, Russlynn. 2011, April 4. Dear Colleague Letter. https://www2.ed.gov/about/offices/list/ocr/letters/colleague-201104.pdf. Accessed 5 July 2020.

Barnett, Randy E. 1998. *The Structure of Liberty: Justice and the Rule of Law*. Oxford: Oxford University Press.

Chisholm, Hugh. 1911. Attaint, Writ of. In *Encyclopædia Britannica*, 11th ed, vol. 2, 879. New York: Encyclopedia Britannica, Inc. Available at https://archive.org/stream/EB1911WMF/VOL02_ANDROS-AUSTRIA. Accessed 5 July 2020.

Huemer, Michael. 2013. *The Problem of Political Authority*. New York: Palgrave Macmillan.

Kipnis, Laura. 2017. *Unwanted Advances: Sexual Paranoia Comes to Campus*. New York: HarperCollins.

Petteruti, Amanda, and Jason Fenster. 2011. *Finding Direction: Expanding Criminal Justice Options by Considering Policies of Other Nations*. Washington, DC: Justice Policy Institute. http://www.justicepolicy.org/uploads/justice-policy/documents/finding_direction-full_report.pdf. Accessed 27 June 2020.

Shapiro, Martin. 1994. Judges as Liars. *Harvard Journal of Law and Public Policy* 17: 155–156.

Walmsley, Roy. 2018. *World Prison Population List*. 12th ed. Institute for Criminal Policy Research. https://prisonstudies.org/sites/default/files/resources/downloads/wppl_12.pdf. Accessed 4 July 2020.

Index[1]

A

Absolutism, 50, 362
Abuse of power, 7, 169–223, 341, 350–351, 360
Adams, John, 304, 304n26
Adversarial system, 94, 97, 105, 125
al-Awlaki, Anwar, 200–206, 207n71
Anarchy, 264n12, 314–315, 317, 320, 321
Arbitration, 105, 106, 106n47, 139, 140, 222
Augustine, Saint, 14, 14n2, 15, 17
Authority, political, 255, 256, 261, 262, 264, 266, 267, 267n14, 272, 283, 340, 353, 354
Autonomy of ethics, 13–14

B

Barbaric punishment, 148, 232
Bentham, Jeremy, 17n7, 20
Bordenkircher v. Hayes, 118, 145
Bork, Robert, 273, 314, 338, 340
Brady v. United States, 112, 115, 116, 123, 133, 362, 363
Bush, George W., 197–200, 206, 208, 214, 217

C

Charge stacking, 117
Coase, Ronald, 86, 87
Coerced confessions, 113–116, 348
Confirmation bias, 212–214, 222
Consequentialism, 28–29

---

[1] Note: Page numbers followed by 'n' refer to notes.

D

Deference, virtue of, 328–338
Defiance, virtue of, 338–342
Deliberative Dinner Party example, 262
Deterrence, 69, 144–147, 162, 251, 322–323, 325, 326
Deterrence Framing example, 144, 145
Dinner Party example, 261–263
Disproportionate punishment, 118, 120–121, 125, 136, 148–153, 161, 232, 237, 249, 349
Doctrine of Double Effect, 30
Drug prohibition, 53–63, 69, 70, 160, 230, 243, 286, 335, 346
Duke lacrosse case, 185, 186, 211, 218
Duty of justice, 91, 247–250, 252

E

Error theory, 360–364
Ethical intuition, 21, 24, 24n18, 26, 28, 35–39, 37n29, 71, 72, 321
Exclusionary rule, 137
Executive abuse, 195–210

F

Factual innocence, 323–326
False convictions, 7, 119
Fifth Amendment, 122, 123, 205, 206, 275
Forged Check example, 127, 145, 151, 152, 247
Framing example, 21–23, 26, 27, 39, 47, 67, 145n3, 321
Freedom of the press, 4, 130–131
Frivolous lawsuits, 102–104, 194

G

Gaybashing Gang example, 248, 325
Georgia v. Brailsford, 305
Gideon v. Wainwright, 94

H

Hamilton, Alexander, 303
Hayes, Paul Lewis, 118, 120, 121, 127, 145, 146, 151, 152, 246
Hiring Dispute example, 330, 332, 333
Hobbes, Thomas, 17n7, 19n8, 256n2, 264, 264n12
Holder, Eric, 198–204, 206, 207n71
Hume's Law, 19

I

Imbler v. Pachtman, 190, 191, 191n50
Immigration restrictions, 64–66, 70, 346
Imminence condition, 206–208
Immunity
  absolute, 190–194, 190n47, 220, 351
  qualified, 190, 220
Incapacitation, 144–146, 153, 163–165
Incapacitative Framing example, 146
Incarceration, v, 6, 55n11, 128, 143–145, 148–150, 153, 157, 160, 161, 163–165, 350, 367
Indigent defense, 94–98, 95n38
Ingroup bias, 216–218
Innocent Alan example, 323–325
Innocent Jane example, 324, 325
Inquisitorial system, 97, 105, 308

Instrumental rationality, 250–253
Island Hermit example, 18, 19, 71

J

Jay, John, 303, 305
Jefferson, Thomas, 304
Judicial nullification, 289, 315
Jury nullification, 314–316,
 319–322, 327, 337–338, 340
Jury selection, 187, 233, 297
Jury trial/trial by jury
 function of, v, 304, 337
 right to, 123, 139, 140, 208,
  239, 302, 306, 307, 356,
  357, 367
Justice
 duty of, 91–98, 135,
  247–250, 252
 primacy of, 8–12, 229–253,
  273–275, 278–280, 291, 301,
  313, 328, 331, 332
 requirements of, 68, 88, 246, 251,
  332, 334, 337, 352, 359, 360

K

Kevorkian, Jack, 316
Kidnapping Dispute example,
 332–334, 341
King, Martin Luther, 15, 204
Knowledge argument, 273–278

L

Legalese, 78
Legal relativism, 14, 17–20
Legal services
 prices of, 77, 79, 90, 98, 347,
  348, 365
 total revenues, 89
Libertarianism, 71, 72
Licensing laws, 77n5, 82, 104, 347
Lifeboat, part 1 example, 264
Lifeboat, part 2 example, 265

M

Mafia employee example, 291, 292
Market competition example, 49
Mass incarceration, 148–150, 367
McMahon, Jack, 187–189, 187n41
Milgram, Stanley, 338–340,
 339n13, 339n14
Moore, G.E., 20
Moral innocence, 323–326
Moral realism, 39–40
More, Thomas, 34, 273
Morton, Michael, 183–186,
 212–214, 218

N

Natural law, 14–17
Nifong, Mike, 186, 211
Nixon, Richard, 131, 169–172,
 196–197, 208, 210, 350
Normative disagreement, 328–330

O

Obama, Barack, 77n5, 83, 198–206,
 208, 210, 214, 217
Obviously Guilty Client example,
 298, 299
Oil Dispute example, 241, 243, 244

Organ Harvesting example, 21–23, 26–33, 28–29n21, 35–37, 39, 47
Overcriminalization, 60n19, 79, 84, 346, 367

P

Plausibly Innocent Suspect example, 299
Plea bargaining
  coerciveness of, 129
  constitutionality of, 362, 363
Police brutality/police violence, 7, 173–175, 177, 178, 181, 328
Powell, Lewis, 191, 194, 195
Power
  deference to, 218–220
  love of, 214–216
Presumption against law, 45–54, 46n2
Presumption of innocence, 46, 46n2, 364, 367
Primacy of Authority, 8–11
Primacy of Justice, 8–12, 229–253, 273–275, 278–280, 291, 301, 313, 328, 331, 332
Primacy of Law, 247, 275, 276, 280, 316, 340, 341
Prison abolitionism, 163
Prison abuse, 153–161, 164, 350
Proportionality, 120, 121, 137, 146–149, 161, 286
Prosecutorial misconduct, 138, 185, 186, 192, 193

R

Race/racism, 181–182, 188, 189, 248
Reasonable Job Offer example, 260
Regulation, 60, 78, 79, 85–87, 105, 138, 190, 346
Restitution, 160–162, 165
Retributivism/retributive justice, 144–146, 149, 153, 161
Rights
  against harmful coercion, 46–54, 56, 62, 65, 67, 69, 71, 72
  definition of, 24, 25
  enforceability of, 25, 58, 70
  law-independent, 20
  motivation for, 21–34
  prima facie, 46, 50–54, 61, 64, 65, 346
Role obligations, 171, 289–294, 301, 320, 355–357
Rule of law, 9, 171, 197, 201, 210, 313–342, 350–351, 357, 358, 362

S

Self-incrimination, 130, 134, 136
Sixth Amendment, 121–123, 134, 139, 302
Social contract, 19, 19n8, 37, 256–260, 353, 354
Starving Marvin example, 64, 71
Stockholm Syndrome, 219, 219n80
Streetlamp example, 277–278
Suicide Prevention example, 48, 49, 54, 55

T
Thomson, Judith Jarvis, 29, 31
Torture, 114, 114n10, 116, 155, 198–200, 210, 214, 218, 349, 350
Trial penalty, 112, 120, 135–137, 153
Trivial Thesis, 279
Trolley example, 26–34, 28n21, 68, 69
Trolley exception, 32–34, 68–69
Trump, Donald, 98n40, 206, 206n70

U
Unconscionable punishment, 7, 148, 153–160, 163, 164
Uniformity, advantages of, 322–323
United States v. Datcher, 307, 308
United States v. Jackson, 122, 123, 362
Unjust laws, 5, 6, 9, 14–15, 14n2, 17, 45–72, 79, 81, 232, 234, 240, 240n8, 247, 249, 273, 277, 292–294, 300, 301, 306, 309, 315, 320, 321, 324, 325, 335, 341, 346, 355, 359, 365
Unjust punishments, 6, 118, 143–165, 234, 237, 249, 272, 301, 317, 321, 347, 349–350, 352, 364, 366
Utilitarianism, 23, 23n16, 24, 39

V
Voluntariness
 as lack of undue pressure, 116
 rational choice interpretation, 114–116

W
War, interpretation of, 214
Warren v. District of Columbia, 317n6
Wiseman, Thomas A., 308

Z
Zenger, John Peter, 4, 5, 8, 303, 306, 316, 317

The manufacturer's authorised representative in the EU is Springer Nature Customer Service Centre GmbH, Europaplatz 3, 69115 Heidelberg, Germany. If you have any concerns regarding our products, please contact ProductSafety@springernature.com

Printed and bound by CPI Group (UK) Ltd, Croydon, CR0 4YY

23/03/2026

02076746-0002